The Cognitive Structures and Processes of Human Motivation and Personality

The Cognitive Structures and Processes of Human Motivation and Personality

Vernon Hamilton

University of Reading
UK

JOHN WILEY & SONS

Chichester · New York· Brisbane · Toronto · Singapore

Library of Congress Cataloging in Publication Data:

Hamilton, Vernon.
  The cognitive structures and processes of human
  motivation and personality.

  Includes indexes.
  1. Motivation (Psychology)   2. Personality.
  3. Cognition.   I. Title.   [DNLM: 1. Cognition.
  2. Motivation.   3. Personality.   BF 683 H221c]
  BF503.H35   1983   153.8   82-13649

ISBN 0 471 10526 0

British Library Cataloguing in Publication Data:

Hamilton, Vernon
  The cognitive structures and process of human
  motivation and personality.
  1. Motivation (Psychology)   2. Cognition
  I. Title
  153.8   BF503

ISBN 0 471 10526 0

Typeset by Input Typesetting Ltd., London.
Printed by Pitman Press Ltd., Bath.

For My Children And Grandchildren . . .

'And you shall teach them diligently . . .'
Deut.vi.7

'If we cannot see things clearly, we will at least see clearly what the obscurities are.'
S. Freud

Contents

PART III. RETROSPECTIVE AND PROSPECTIVE
APPLICATIONS

Acknowledgements

Acknowledgements for permission to reproduce figures are made to the following:

Academic Press: Figure 5.10;

American Psychological Association and G. H. Bower: Part of Figure 6.13;

Automobile Association: Figure 5.3;

Holt, Rinehart and Winston: Figure 9.4;

John Wiley & Sons: Figures 5.11, 8.3, 8.6.

Preface

There is no shortage of academic textbooks on the topics of human motivation and personality, and the present offering is not intended to compete with what is already available. Apart from satisfying a subjective urge to impose a more genotypic structure on existing theories and models which would provide me with a personal cognitive framework, I have had two other major goals. These were firstly to state that distinctions between motivation and personality traits are artifacts of the constructs we use for the purpose of achieving tentative explanations, whereas different constructs would make categorical differentiations redundant. Secondly, I intended to try to show that the selection of goals and preferred methods of obtaining them are the result of problem-solving operations in which physiological and biochemical events play a necessary and facilitating but *secondary* role. As a consequence of this orientation, I have reinterpreted motivation and personality in cognitive processing theory terms. One of the major implications of this exercise was assigning dominant roles to the semantic labelling and identification of goals, to the choice processes apparent in the evidence of goal hierarchies, and to the decision-making processes involved in the selection of preferred, characteristic ways of achieving preferred goal-outcomes. A further implication of this approach was a more radical cognitive analysis of emotion, mood, or affect than had been found acceptable to date.

Although the book has been conceived as being in the nature of an ongoing discussion with fellow theorists, I have used much of the material in the teaching of senior students. Attempting to explain the new model to them sharpened my own thinking, though clearly the last words remain to be spoken.

Without research fundings over the last 15 years the experiments reported in the various chapters could not have been carried out, and the book would have remained unwritten. I am particularly indebted to the Canada Council for supporting many years ago some highly idiosyncratic studies, and to the (British) Social Science Research Council for subsequent research grants. It is a pleasure to acknowledge the support and critical comments received from Magdalen D. Vernon over a number of years. Her careful reading of the manuscript considerably improved its readability and rationality. I am also grateful to Philip Smith for his separate comments on some crucial chapters, and I am happy to acknowledge the facilities made available to me by Emory University, Atlanta, and the Chairman of its Psychology Department, Jay Knopf, during my term as Visiting Professor in 1981.

Without the assistance of my secretarial and technical colleagues at Reading, the book would not have been completed. I am very grateful to Sandra Stonard, Audrey Conner, Yvonne Robinson, Ted Miller, and Dave Martin and Joe Gibbs and their staff.

Vernon Hamilton

University of Reading
May 1982

PART I

INTRODUCTION

CHAPTER 1

Aims and justifications

It is common knowledge that authors frequently write the introduction to their book after they have completed the main task. This strategy has some merit and has been adopted here. It prevents the author from undertaking an unmanageable task, and allows him or her to match the result of the effort with its original, enthusiastic conception. Inevitable *post hoc* rationalization, contrary to some opinions, is actually minimized by having already structured a set of chapter headings and chapter contet. Hypotheses cannot be phrased without focusing in the first instance on a section of a theoretical framework, and a contract to write is not offered unless at least two assessors find the match between project and executor acceptable. The major advantage, perhaps, of writing an introductory chapter last, is that it provides the opportunity for a rectifying operation on propositions that may have been overstated in the text, and to allow objectivity to temper any possible evidence of omniscience. Of course, undertaking to write about new conceptions of motivation and personality must mean that one feels that one knows something that others do not know, or know less well. What matters, however, is how new and how well. In retrospect, and on the basis of publications that have appeared since undertaking my task, for example, Dixon (1981), the novelty aspect is likely to apply primarily to certain elaborations of current concepts, and their integration in a particular form. I cannot comment on task quality beyond expressing my belief that it could have been improved given a number of different antecedents.

I have had three general aims for this project: to offer a belated attack on what I have regarded always as a 'faculty' approach to human motivation and personality; to diminish if not discard the categorical distinction between motivation and personality; and to offer a possible synthesis between so-called non-cognitive processes and behaviour and cognitive processing theory. When Bruner wrote his complimentary review of Kelly's (1955) personal construct theory, he termed it '. . . a theory of cognition extrapolated into a theory of personality . . .' (Bruner, 1956, p. 357). I cannot predict what a reviewer may, or may not say about the model I am offering. There is just a possibility, however, that I am inverting Bruner's assessment by aiming for

3

a theory of motivation and personality extrapolated into a theory of cognition. The reason for this may be sought in my agreement with Hebb's view (1949, 1980) that motivation and emotion are expressions of organismic intelligence. I have discussed this proposition in the last chapter, without agreeing, however, with Hebb (1980, p. 64) that arousal from some 28 separate pairs of nuclei provides sufficient cues to distinguish one type of emotional arousal from another (see Chapter 6).

It has been my impression, and that of others, that the study and concepts of motivation and personality reflect a field of behavioural science in a state of disarray. I have elaborated the reason for this impression in Chapter 2, and have offered there, and elsewhere, the conclusion that even recent developments in cognitive social psychology, and in cognitive social learning theory, important though they are, have not closed the conceptual gap between cognitive and non-cognitive 'faculties'. A conceptual reorientation in this area of behavioural science seems to be essential for several reasons. Firstly, to overcome historical and continuing controversies over whether motivation and personality can be adequately defined by traits with their implications of behavioural consistency. Secondly, to account more adequately than before for the large number of research findings demonstrating interactions between cognitive and so-called non-cognitive variables. Thirdly, to provide a definition of behaviour strategies which reflect the role of memory, selective attention, and decision-making operations in trait-defining activity. This last task, particularly, can be undertaken now because developments in cognitive processing theory have been successfully applied to account for the adverse effect of one important personality and motivational dimension – anxiety – on the capacity to handle increasing amounts of information (see Chapter 8), and because recent evidence provides for direct cognitive-semantic links between mood and/or emotion, and the encoding of associated information (see Chapter 6).

By regarding personality as a system of preferred methods or strategies of responding, and motivation as action towards a hierarchy of preferred goals, methods and goals become susceptible to reinterpretation as cognitive data because preference requires pre-knowledge of the outcome of response alternatives, and of alternative goals. On this basis, preferred behaviour results from decision-making operations and problem-solving processes availing themselves of memory data which encode stimulus demand characteristics and their meaning, and the meaning of response alternatives. The presence of these data defines outcome anticipation and expectancy. A dominant human technique, however, for registering meaning, that is, fine-grained conceptual information, and especially complex meaning in permanent memory, is by semantic labelling.

If goal expectancies, preferred behaviour strategies, and preferred goals show any element of internal consistency and predictability, then they are likely to be parts of interrelated conceptual structures. Like other conceptual organizations differentially available for retrieval and response selection, they are likely to be associated with class- and attribute-defining semantic markers. Functional relatedness, variable experience, and interpretations of the importance to the person of stimuli determine the range and content of cognitive-semantic behaviour categories. Together with non-verbal images (including abstract propositional networks) they form the cognitive schemata of personality and motivation. In this context they cease to be separate behaviour systems. Moreover, the definition of personality traits and motivation as preferred methods of achieving preferred goals identifies their actions as problem-solving. In this event the cognitive processes and operations involved are intrinsically not different from other problem-solving situations requiring fine-grained analysis of stimulus meaning, and implicit testing of response adequacy before executing a response. These propositions are comprehensively elaborated in Chapter 6.

Since it is likely that some readers are only superficially acquainted with modern theories of cognition and information processing, and since the concepts of these theories provide the basis for the new approach in this book, Chapters 3 and 4 present an introductory outline of that approach. It is more than likely that I shall have used concepts in an idiosyncratic way which will not always be accepted by those who make major contributions to that theoretical framework. In Chapter 5 I have tried to apply what I see as the implications of dynamic cognitive information processing theories to the acquisition of socially mediated knowledge. I have tried to show there how it is possible to view the acquisition of a social behaviour repertoire as the outcome of four primarily cognitive factors. First, the principal caretakers' own cognitive structures representing social reality; second, their capacity to communicate it in the process of socialization; third, the child's capacity to conceptualize this information and to integrate it with functionally related representations in permanent memory; fourth, the attenuation or elaboration of transmitted objective, socially-relevant information by cognitive structures encoding a child's self-concepts, preferred goals, and the capacity to achieve preferred goal-outcomes by preferred ways of responding. For these events I have assigned a necessary, but secondary role to peripheral and electro-cortical physiological arousal for reasons supported by experiments reported in Chapter 8. In a major departure from current views I have assigned cognitive interpretations and structure to affective, emotional, or mood-related events and experiences, and have argued that affect-specifying information is conveyed by semantic labels (see Chapter 6).

The content of Chapter 8 largely accounts for the term 'retrospective' in the title given to Part III. That chapter contains an account of experiments carried out with my students and assistants on a cognitive interpretation of anxiety as a motivational and personality variable. These studies were originally concerned to show whether a peripheral arousal explanation of performance deficits in high anxious subjects is valid, or whether an inability to handle increasing amounts of environmental complexity was directly related to the simultaneous cognitive processing demands of the objects of anxiety.

Propositions of the possible role of informational overload on performance in the presence of high anxiety were the results of extrapolations from studies with schizophrenics which I had carried out a number of years before. These had lent themselves to an interpretation of size constancy and conservation impairments involving self-restrictions in information processing (Hamilton, 1963a, b, 1966, 1972). Self-restriction was regarded as the result of subjective preoccupation with task-irrelevant cognitive data.

Chapter 7 contains my attempts to relate the new cognitive-semantic model of personality and motivation to some other theoretical positions. The intention was to reinterpret rather than to reject. This exercise had to be limited in scope since a full set of analyses applied, for instance, to existing definitions of goal-directed characteristic behaviour would have required more space than was available. Although I had already on previous occasions presented a cognitive reconceptualization of 'stress', and of vulnerability to stressors, my propositions about the role of semantic signifiers in the interpretation of what is stressful required incorporation into the earlier statements. This task was undertaken in Chapter 9. It includes a consideration of the cognitive nature of coping and denial processes, and illustrations of hypothetical semantic network structures operating in depression induced by bereavement, and in paranoid psychosis.

Author's licence is pre-eminently applied in Chapter 10 in that I undertook there to develop Hebb's views of the relationship between intelligence, motivation, and emotion. It is uncertain that Hebb would approve the direction I have taken. I present no paradigms from animal studies and make enormous assumptions, unsupported as yet by experimental detail, about the inevitable role of genetically determined physiological structure-forming capacities in the development of behavioural differentiation. Apart from applying a cognitive-semantic approach to the role of Hebb's 'intelligence B' in motivation and personality development, Chapter 10 contains an analysis of group conflict based on semantic network structures with a bias towards hostility, rejection, or incongruity. I am arguing there that social attitudes are basically semantically coded concepts which may aid or prevent the problem-solving processes required for conflict resolution. My cognitive analysis of types of leadership is novel only to the extent that I have set the development of leadership characteristics into a general cognitive-affective framework of semantically coded self-concepts which may become dominant in interaction with others. I have not regarded it as academically disreputable to select examples of conflict, and characterizations of their protagonists, existing in an everyday socio-political context.

References to the required physiological and neurochemical underpinning of the new model will be found to be sparse. I regard myself insufficiently qualified for this difficult integrative task. Where I have drawn on pertinent theories, I have argued in favour of stimulus analysis preceding the innervation of all arousal systems, whether at the level of the limbic system, or at the cerebral cortex. Little consideration has been given to philosophical contributions to the analysis of personality and motivation. While there is full agreement that careful and logical phrasing of questions is a prerequisite for logically adequate answers, many philosophical assumptions and interpretations of psychological concepts are incomplete or misleading in view of their obvious lack of technical sophistication (see also Chapter 2). In many respects I would wish that Peters' (1958) much applauded analysis of the concept of motivation had been written more recently so that his statements could have benefited from the demise of orthodox behaviourism, and the growth of cognitive processing theory. If it were written in these days, it is possible that he might have revised his view that hedonistic dispositions are logically unrelated to behaviour serving it. It will be clear that like Dixon (1981) I have given a dominant role to hedonistic principles in behaviour by specifically referring to the cognitive structures of behaviour anticipation and of goal-outcomes as determinants in preferring one type of goal, and manner of reaching it, to others. Peters (1958, p. 144) wrote that '. . . hedonism is not an explanatory theory, it is only a way of distinguishing some sorts of sensations and activities from others'. This, I would regard as a conveniently incomplete argument. It would need to be followed by asking why such distinctions are made, and which events facilitate them. If this were done, common sense as well as behaviour acquisition data will direct us towards *preference* for one type of sensation or activity rather than another. Preference does not only involve decision-making of a problem-solving kind, it distinguishes between what is acceptable, and what is less acceptable to the current goals and contexts of an individual. Distinguishing on the basis of differential acceptability, however, must involve a distinction between 'I like' and 'I don't like'. Masochism is actuarially rare, and humans are not lemmings, despite some ostensibly powerful signs to the contrary.

Let me leave issues for a moment, to refer to more mundane matters in order to anticipate certain types of critical comment. There is a tendency in all specialist areas of work to coin specialist terminology in order to present with greater accuracy fine-grained concepts and conceptual distinctions. It is in fact the same process by which I have respecified the topics under discussion here by using the terminology of cognitive processing theory. I have good evidence, however, from journal referees, and anecdotally, that a specialist lexicon can be regarded as the preserve of workers within that field, and that if others use it, it can be labelled as meaningless 'jargon', or as a 'trendy' attempt to appear theoretically respectable. Such comments, of course, are disingeneous. They forget that the consideration of cognitive structures and the differential retrieval of their content in solving the problems of human adaptation requires the use of the most definitive lexicon available so as to specify the processes involved. This strategy can only reflect credit on specialists in cognition, and simultaneously demonstrate that criticisms of the unscientific nature of so-called non-cognitive psychology are now redundant.

Objection may be raised against my use of box diagrams and the symbolic implications of lines and arrows linking them. These conventionally represent components of an information processing system, their functions, relationships, or the hypothetical content of a component. No one reading this book will be unfamiliar with the limitations of this notation. What I have tried to do in several chapters, however, is to break up 'boxes' previously just labelled 'personality', 'motive', or 'affect' to allow for a representation of processes and their interactions. Remonstrations that I have not devoted space and time to all issues or determinants are acknowledged. The volume of theoretical and experimental work in the areas under discussion is clearly too large to be adequately reconsidered in a single volume. If my new conceptualizations arouse interest they may well be extrapolated to the omissions.

It may appear almost presumptuous to suggest that changes in existing theories are required. However, the modification of theoretical explanations in science has been an ongoing and accelerating process for at least 200 years, and there are no good reasons why psychological theory should be immune. On the contrary, it would be surprising *and indeed* presumptuous if the nature of psychological explanations were considered immutable. Nor is it necessary that theoretical developments should adversely affect the "brand image" of a science of human behaviour. There is general agreement that 'schools' of psychology have given way to distinctive approaches, distinctive levels of analysis of human thought and action, and to limitations in generalism as a result of the massive gain in knowledge from brain physiology, psychopharmacology, and molecular neurochemistry.

The proposition of a new model of behaviour regulation does not necessarily diminish the enormously influential and insightful contributions of earlier theories. All theories are built on existing concepts none of which are inevitably false, unless perhaps they have been presented and reiterated with an unwarranted degree of exclusiveness and dogmatism. On the other hand, theory building, as the result of the theorist's cognitive processes and operations, is necessarily constrained by the conceptual knowledge of its era, and even the act of creation – the act of conceptualizing a previously unavailable relationship – is heavily influenced by existing phenomenological data. As these data accumulate new relational thinking becomes possible, hopefully accompanied by more powerful generalizations.

It is possible to accuse experimentally oriented psychology of being excessively – and perhaps defensively – preoccupied with deductive rather than inductive methodology. Good reasons can be cited, however, for the flood of mini-studies directed at hypothesized mini-processes, especially perhaps in the areas of attention, memory, and concept formation. These have correctly attracted some self-searching criticisms which were perhaps unnecessarily severe at the time on the absence of theory building. If inductive power has been somewhat restricted in any area of investigation, it usually means that the discrete data bases have been achieved without an agreed hypothesized unifying principle, and/or by sampling data at *different levels* of a behavioural chain, at *different times*, with *different tools*, and with *different conceptions* of the possibilities of controlling multiple and/or biasing variables.

If this assessment is correct, it underlines the special difficulties of behavioural science which have been with us from the start: how to handle simultaneously the large number of process variables which are activated by any single response requirement, and how to achieve the most reductive level of explanation. The first difficulty is methodological and economic. There is a limit to the number of criterion variables which can be assessed for any research sample without introducing bias from concurrent life events, or life-event changes. Even if estimates of such effects can be obtained in separate and preceding studies which could supply normative range values, the costing would be unsupported by present levels of research funding. The answer may well lie in being able to estimate the contribution of individually dominant characteristics to the cognitive selecting and integrating operations required of a person in situations *not primarily directed* at these dominant characteristics.

The second major difficulty of behavioural science in my view – the level of reductive explanation – is perhaps the core feature of this book. My discussion concerning the nature of our present concepts of personality, motivation, cognitive skill and power, and the development of these characteristic response dispositions and capacities as well as their interactions, will indicate my belief that we need to attempt the redescription and redefinition of complex processes, which textbooks and theories so far have not undertaken. In this reorientation I subscribe with others to the biological 'final cause' of behaviour and to its genetically limited modification by external events. In contrast, however, I propose that the acquired modifications are not only the proper professional sphere of psychology, but that the limited range of modification *causes* what is individually distinctive, socially adaptive, goal-achievement oriented, and what is emotively consistent with demonstrated response characteristics.

CHAPTER 2

Explanatory and integrative status of current theories

1 CONCEPTS OF PERSONALITY AND MOTIVATION

In planning this book I had initially regarded it as desirable, if not essential, to review systematically the major body of existing theory. This analysis was to be undertaken by reference to the following criteria: the genotypical level of explanation presented; the role played by mediating processes; the specified relationship between the two core concepts; the parsimoniousness of the explanations given; the role assigned to cognition; and the integrative capacity of the model favoured with respect to other behavioural domains. I came to the conclusion that this plan was overambitious and that my goal could be equally well achieved via two routes: by presenting a more loosely structured appraisal of what has been before us for a number of years, and by stating an alternative conception at greater length than would otherwise be possible. By this approach I have probably offered the reader greater freedom for a comparative and inferential exercise based on large-scale, classical accounts (e.g. Cofer and Appley, 1964; Hall and Lindzey, 1970). Although my appraisal has led me personally to be dissatisfied with all existing theoretical statements, it is self-evident that all of them have contributed in various ways to the development of behavioural science.

Several general points can be made at once about the current status of the concepts of personality and motivation. For example, there are good grounds for regarding them as superficial, as simultaneously narrow, loosely generalized, and as incapable of being integrated with more objectively defined capabilities of the human adaptive and productive systems. Furthermore, the specification and demonstration of general individual characteristics and their goal-seeking strategies still depends in the largest number of cases on self-report evidence from questionnaires which sample response dispositions in private or social settings, on introspective judgements of types of emotions, feelings, moods, and their intensity, or on the interpretation of projective test materials. On the other hand all theories hold to some extent that behaviour types and traits develop on the basis of genetic predispositions

10

mediated either by physiological structures and their functions, or by the hormonal influence of the autonomic nervous system which affects peripheral physiological arousal, or by patterns of corticosteroid neurotransmitters which affect cortical arousal, or by a combination of all of these biological systems. All theories also accept the importance of developmental factors which reflect the interaction between genetic disposition, environmental influences, and the mechanisms and processes of learning.

Apart from biological structures and processes mediating emotion and mood, and their facilitation of the mechanisms of learning, a viable theory requires not only information-mediating structures, but an information processing system which encodes the cognitive specifications and content of hierarchies of behavioural strategies and goals. Except possibly in Sullivan's (1953) cognitive classification of experience in the prototaxic, parataxic, and syntaxic modes, these requirements appear to be absent from existing theories. Biological arousal and temperament theory has structure and mechanisms, but no cognitive content – characteristics shared by early classical and operant S-R theories. Neo-S-R theories of imitation, or of modelling by anticipation of behaviour outcome (Bandura, 1977), or of learning expectancies (Bolles, 1974), have gained some content by virtue of the recognition of mediation processes, but have lost precision in postulating mechanisms and structure, and hence some theoretical status. Trait theory with or without factor-analytic structure has no clear-cut mechanisms, possesses only superficial cognitive conceptualizations, and where it gains structure it loses content. Classical psycho-dynamic theories are presented without physiological mechanisms, and their cognitive content and structures depend on the theorist's criteria of subjective plausibility frequently lost in speculative elaborations. All the theories are silent on the *nature of the representational memory data* conveyed by cognitive processes and mechanisms, which must be embodied in structures and which constitute the cognitive content. It is evident that no single existing model has sufficient definitive power.

It follows that there can be no adequate theories of personality and motivational development. What we do have are maturation theories of emotional development (e.g. Bridges, 1932; Chess *et al.*, 1968), socialization theories (e.g. Feffer, 1970; Bowlby, 1971; Schaffer, 1971), and quasi-cognitive theories of moral development (Kohlberg, 1969). What is lacking once again is any reference to the nature of the representational memory data of environmental and situational factors by which gradually more mature, socially sensitive response dispositions become established which can be expressed in behaviour. During the bygone heydays of behaviourism it was sufficient to argue that the experience of reinforcing agents purveying positive or negative reinforcement led to the establishment of rewarding habits and habit systems. Neo-behaviourism applied to animal learning now postulates the presence of cognitive mediating processes to account for the development of response-selecting mnemonic processes required for the perception of stimulus distinctiveness and response expectancies (e.g. Bolles, 1972, 1974;

Estes, 1973, 1978; Mackintosh, 1974; Wagner, 1976). So far, however, the animal-learning theorists have failed to specify the nature of these mediating processes.

If these assessments have only some validity, it will be necessary to enquire whether existing definitions of personality and motivation are still adequate. Because this could be a somewhat tedious exercise for the reader as well as the author, I shall proceed from a tabulation of a cross-section of stated, accessible, or inferable definitions beginning with personality. The order in which they are shown in Table 2.1 is not intended to be correlated with any

Table 2.1 Sample Definitions of Personality

'The dynamic organization of interlocking behaviour systems that each of us possesses as he grows from a biological newborn to a biosocial adult in an environment of other individuals and cultural products.' (Cameron, 1947)

'The sum total of one's behaviour.' (Watson, 1930)

'The learned pattern of individually important modes of adjustment to tension which uniquely characterises the individual.' (Krech and Crutchfield, 1948)

'Personality consists concretely of a set of values or descriptive terms reflecting the theoretical preferences of the theorist.' (Hall and Lindzey, 1970)

'Personality is all the behaviour of the individual, both overt and under the skin, which permits a prediction of what a person will do in a given situation.' (Cattell, 1950)

'Personality is the dynamic organization within the individual of those psychophysical systems that determine his unique adjustment to this environment.' (Allport, 1937)

'Personality is defined by the attributes of ability, motives, knowledge, beliefs and conceptions which give a lawful account of action.' (Atkinson, 1977)

Personality can be defined by the causal stability of outcome and expectancy.' (Weiner, 1978)

'The pattern of conditioned habitual responses facilitated by physiological arousal and activation processes identifying the individual's position in a 3-dimensional factorial space of introversion-extraversion, stability-neuroticism and psychoticism.' (Eysenck, various (*my condensation*)

'Individually characteristic ranges of operant responses established by reinforcement contingencies in specific situations.' (Skinner, various, (*my condensation*)

'Personality is definable by the competencies, constructs, expectancies, subjective values, rules, or self-regulatory plans and other person variables that mediate the effects of conditions upon behaviour.' (Mischel, 1973, 1978 (*my condensation*)

'A person's processes are psychologically channelized by the ways in which he anticipates events' (elaborated by 11 corollaries). (Kelly, 1955)

judgement of their utility and explanatory power. Some theorists successfully evaded the opportunity to summarize their views in a single economic statement so that I had to construct a definition from my interpretation of their position from various sources. This may not please them, nor anyone else who believes that 'personality' reflects a pre-scientific terminology, and that it is preferable to avoid the required 'omnibus' definitions. Condensations of psycho-dynamic and Murray's positions were omitted because these mega-theories are incapable of representation in a single sentence without distortion.

With notable exceptions, the collection of defining statements in Table 2.1 indicates that it is far easier to delineate the topics of the study of personality than to specify what the dispositional and causal attributes of personality actually are (see also Sanford, 1970). It is equally significant that to date little progress has been achieved in improving on Allport's (1937) comprehensive defining statement. It is possible to make this claim, not only because of Allport's search for distinctive dispositional elements or traits and his emphasis on individual uniqueness, but also because of his sophisticated insight that this individuality must be a reflection of multivariate behaviour systems which contain complex organizations which in turn are dynamically related to each other in responding to situational demands. This global conception, however, had the counter-productive effect of separating the study of individuality from the study of other general behaviour processes. More significantly, it left the questions of *what personality is*, and *why* it produces characteristic behaviour basically unanswered. This must be so whether semantic trait labels are drawn from a non-specialist lay vocabulary, or whether their grammatical roots lie in antiquity. As Fiske (1974) has argued, semantic sophistication is no safeguard against idiosyncratic meaning or interpretative contamination.

In retrospect it may be wondered why so much time and effort was devoted to the prediction of regularities of characteristic behaviour when it must have been clear that unsolved problems of specification and definition would not yield fundamental clarity. In these circumstances, evidence of intra-individual trait consistency by low but significant correlations must be considered important evidence (e.g. Block, 1977, 1981), rather than overpowering grounds for critical comment (Mischel, 1968, 1973). On the other hand, there must be some doubts about the general utility of so-called behavioural equations for the prediction of performance (e.g. Cattell, 1965), even if, as in this case, there is full recognition of the importance of situational variables. What is absent, of course, from a multifactor equation representing the contributions of source traits, temperament traits, drives, sentiments, role traits, and mood or other modulating states, is a specification of *the nature of these components*. In its absence, any assumptions (which were rarely stated) about how these diverse processes interact with each other remain untested and uncertain. The gaps in knowledge left by the correlational approach are reflected in the general absence of attempts at definition even in some of the most voluminous recent surveys of personality theory (e.g. Cattell and Dreger, 1977).

Eysenck's initial two-factor structure of personality (Eysenck, 1957, 1960) may be regarded justifiably as an oversimplification of behavioural reality, but it had merit in that it led to attempts to isolate physiological processes which covary with personality type and which might account for typological differences in learning and memory relevant to the development of traits (e.g. Eysenck, 1973). The resulting specification of personality by different patterns of arousal and activation provided a temporarily useful link with drive theories of learning. Simultaneously, however, it undermined attention to specifiers which would reflect the involvement of higher-order symbolic operations by assigning these functions to processes and mechanisms which can do no more than facilitate such operations.

The definition of personality by reference to traits has permeated theory building for centuries. Moreover, with the possible exception of the study of the achieving person, recent progress in the analysis of dominant behavioural characteristics was left, almost by default, largely in the hands of taxonomists. With increasing statistical sophistication, they consolidated theories of trait psychology, in direct succession to, and as an amplification of the typologies of antiquity (e.g. Cattell, 1957, 1965; Eysenck, 1967; Eysenck and Eysenck, 1969). This development had two profound and inhibiting effects. First and foremost it distracted attention from fine-grained definitions and explanations of 'causes' and 'mediators' in favour of factor-analytic structures. Secondly, and as a consequence, it limited experimentation to the search for trait and type covariants, or to systematic second- and third-order structures which continued to beg the question of the nature of traits. The search for systematization was basically an important and worthwhile effort of seeking regularities of responding to controlled stimulation, but despite plausible arguments that factorial analysis represents a valid application of the hypothetico-deductive method (Eysenck, 1950), it is now possible to view the method primarily as sophisticated induction. Nevertheless, since there is no deduction without induction, there are no *a priori* grounds for rejecting the work done during the last 30 years.

Apart from avoiding some of the fundamental questions, trait psychology invited merited objections for its more extreme assumptions about behavioural consistency. An important series of articles by Mischel (e.g. 1973, 1977) was significant not only for its critical reassessment of the role of environmental variability in trait consistency, but also for its reasoned introduction of some cognitive concepts relevant to the '*what*' and '*why*' questions. It is significant, however, that even in a more recent article (Mischel, 1979) distinctions between personality and cognition are retained by conceptualizing an *interface* relationship rather than *conceptually integrated* systems.

Motivational variables were never systematically included by the taxonomists while setting up generalizations. The exception was a possibly premature attempt to confirm deductions involving some broad drive and arousal concepts applied to individual differences in conditioning and in higher-order learning and memory (e.g. Eysenck, 1973), which, generally, have been considered inconclusive (e.g. Hamilton, 1979a). On the other hand, workers in the area of achievement motivation realized early on that motivational variables needed to be considered an integral part of the concept of personality. I will return to the relationship issue below because it has not been expressed with a great deal of clarity. As shown in Table 2.1, however, the study of the achieving person has made a notable advance by introducing necessary cognitive parameters into response dispositions reflecting type of goal-seeking and expectation of behaviour outcome. This is possibly the most significant aspect, too, of Kelly's clinically oriented personal construct theory, in that 'man the scientist' must adapt his needs to external stimuli by testing the anticipated results of expressing them in action, and thus construing sets of hierarchically structured concepts of the self and of the external world. Inevitably, however, Kelly's notions are difficult to integrate with the mainstream of cognitive behaviour, and can be said to have greater affinity with Allport's multidimensional proposition.

Let us turn to an assessment of the concept of motivation. In Table 2.2 I have collected a set of defining statements available in the literature. As

Table 2.2 Sample Definitions of Motivation

'Motivation is defined by the regulatory and directive determinants which arouse and sustain patterns of activities.' (Young, 1961)

'Motivation is a specific state of endogenous activity in the brain which, under the modifying influence of internal conditions and sensory input, leads to behaviour resulting in sensory feedback, which then causes a change . . . in the initial endogenous activity.' (Dethier, 1964, p. 1139)

'Motivational functions depend on rule-governed relationships defined by the contingencies between occasions, behaviour and consequences such that action and behaviour are determined by the reinforcing effects of an action.' (Skinner, 1969 (*my condensation*)

'Motivation is a constant, never ending, fluctuating, complex and universal characteristic of practically every organismic state of affairs.' (Maslow, 1954)

'Motivation is emotional conditioning to specific as well as complex stimuli directed by the source of reinforcement.' (Staats, 1975)

'Goal-directed behaviour is expressed by intention, striving and expectation in the context of a balance of environmental field forces.' (Lewin, various (*my condensation*)

'Motives are cognitive representations of desired goals which are hierarchically organised and resemble the representation of concepts generally.' (Kagan, 1972)

'Motivation is the effect of two sensory events – a cue or cognitive function guiding behaviour, and an arousal or vigilance function which provides the energy of movement.' (Hebb, 1955, p. 249)

Table 2.2 *Continued*

'A motive is the redintegration by a cue of a change in an affective situation.' (McClelland *et al.*, 1953, p. 27)

'Motive is a relatively stable personality disposition which may have an innate basis but is more likely the product of early learning of approaching or avoiding stimuli.' (Feather, 1963, p. 501)

'A motivational variable is one that facilitates or energises several different responses, whose termination or removal following a new response leads to the learning of that response, whose sudden increase leads to the abandonment of responses, and whose effect on behaviour cannot be attributed to learning, sensation, innate capacities and sets.' (Brown, 1961, p. 55)

'Motivation has three aspects: to attend spontaneously to some things rather than others; to exhibit a characteristic emotion specific to the drive and its action; and an impulse to a course of action which has a particular goal as its end.' (Cattell and Kline, 1977, pp. 164–5)

---

noted before, theorists have found it either easier or more congenial to state the antecedents and consequences of manipulated motivational variables, than to commit themselves to an economic defining statement. My tabulation, therefore, had to include assigned definitions which are the result of extraction, construction, and condensation, and which are not verbatim. I have tried to be true, however, to the theoretical orientation of each author, and any misinterpretations are quite inadvertent. Again, order of tabulation is unrelated to evaluated status. Although the term motivation occurs rather later in the literature than the term personality, its specification does not appear to be an advance on the definition of the earlier term. Apart from operational definitions based largely on the similar constructs of drive and arousal (see also Ferguson, 1976), relatively little progress appears to have been made since Young's economical statement that it refers to the processes by which behaviour is activated and directed, and Cofer and Appley's (1964) amplification that these processes vary in direction, intensity, and duration at different points in time for different individuals. The introduction of operationalism is generally regarded as a necessary and forward-looking departure from the historical concepts of instincts or propensities. Such an assessment, however, has required attenuation because operational definitions of behavioural characteristics were generally confined to simple and externally observable responses. This has been the case in the orthodox application of the drive concept which supplanted the earlier concepts. To re-enter the controversy between simple and more complex conceptions of human motivation is not particularly elevating, and would be going over well-trodden ground. I will confine my comments, therefore, to a minimum.

Although one must agree with Hall and Lindzey (1970, p. 419) that a theory should not be judged on the species of experimental subjects from which it was developed, it would be futile to believe that the resulting concepts were uninfluenced by it. It can be argued that as a result learning theorists have bequeathed us two fundamental confusions: equating general arousal with general drive potential (D), and designating a habit by the strength of a unitary stimulus and a similarly unitary response link ($_sH_R$). We have begun now to unravel these problems by defining arousal reductively in terms of ANS and CNS events showing the effects of hormonal, electro-physiological, and electrochemical activity. This has allowed us to regard peripheral and electrocortical arousal as the basis of all behavioural activity. Consequently, drives have become specific behaviour, energized by arousal, directed towards an equally specific goal and goal outcome. The obvious complexity of human acquired or secondary drives has led us to reconsider so-called habit strength, the implications of the (S) and (R) terms, and of the reaction or excitatory potential ($_sE_R$), or its inhibitory variant ($_sI_R$). It is significant that Hull (1943) himself realized that the drive and habit concepts required elaboration in order to represent human goal-directed behaviour as formally as he had done for rat behaviour and that he had not formulated definitions suitable for all learning situations. His actual expression for mo-tivation (reaction or excitatory potential) included from an early stage indices representing the intensity of external stimuli associated with a response (V), and the value or desirability of the goal stimulus (K). The latter, in particular, provided every opportunity for the next generation of learning theorists to incorporate into subsequent formulizations the most significant individual differences in acquired motives, goal hierarchies, and goal elaboration; that is, supplying the hypothetical drive and conditioned habit constructs with a more fine-grained analysis of their intervening variables. Attempts to deal with these deficiencies were indeed made particularly by Spence. By sug-gesting that drive (D) is a function of the magnitudes of a hypothetical mechanism yielding persistent emotional responses (r_e) which provide a re-sponder with drive stimuli (S_D), he usefully expanded not only the construct but also the intervening evaluative variable (K) (e.g. Spence and Spence, 1966). By employing the Manifest Anxiety Scale as a criterion of anxiety drive potential, however, the authors not only manipulated the conditioned emotional response and thereby the drive variables – they actually varied the motivational component (K). Although they make no reference to this in their complex paper, they are aware that their theorizing about the relation-ship between an anxiety drive and complex learning is at a primitive stage of development (Spence and Spence, 1966, p. 303). The disservice to theory development, however, has not been generally recognized. This rests on the tacitly assumed identity between emotionality or anxiety arousal on the one hand, and drive or motivation on the other, an assumption which is main-tained in Staat's definition included in Table 2.2. Inevitably one concludes that mechanistically conceived S–R theories lack the most important com-ponents of human need and outcome-directed behaviours. These are their content in terms of type of goals to be attained, their predictive capacity associated with a choice between means to achieve them, and particularly as implied by the term content, a cognitive representation of learned goals, outcomes, and goal-achieving strategies.

With the exception of the definition assigned to Lewin, and the near verbatim quotations from Hebb, McClelland *et al.*, and Kagan, cognitive specifiers are absent from the list in Table 2.2. My earlier comment was to the effect that it was difficult to assemble a group of 12 definitions. It is unlikely, therefore, that I deliberately excluded cognitively oriented statements specifically about motivation. Two unmentioned theoretical systems do, however, lend themselves to a cognitive construction. Although the instinctual drives of the Freudian framework are commonly conceived in biological arousal terms, the integrative directive function of ego and super-ego processes more than implies the participation of stored, cognitively represented knowledge. This includes conflict-free, or conflicting goal-outcomes associated with actual behaviour, fantasied wish fulfilment, and their antecedent derivation from unreportable internal selection processes. It has been frequently pointed out that translating the German word *Trieb* as drive is somewhat inaccurate since it omits the directiveness component of the linguistic root. It would not be misleading, therefore, to suggest that there is a greater affinity between psycho-analytic instinct theory and Tolman's concept of purposiveness, than between the former and the sign-releaser instinct theories of Tinbergen and Lorenz.

The other theoretical system for which a cognitive orientation can be constructed is Murray's, even though it defies attempts at condensation. Murray's (1938) motivational theory is organized around a minimal list of 20 'needs' which are descriptively conceived rather than as being statistically univocal and independent. This is less important, however, than the conceptualizations which he offered for their expression in behaviour. There can be little doubt but that processes arising from 'press' data representing the experience of socialization and social interaction are cognitive processes operating on cognitive data. Moreover, the concept of the 'thema' is an integrative concept of cognitive structures and their connotative content, with direct or inferred contributions to samples of behaviour in 'vectors' (broad directions) guided by a series of 'value' systems incorporated in the thema.

Mischel's (1973, 1979) reassessment of personality variables will prove to be of considerable importance for social psychology. These papers, however, as well as the latest available contribution from a cognitive orientation to social learning and personality (Cantor and Kihlstrom, 1981), appear to be unable or unwilling to extend a cognitive reconceptualization to motivation. On the other hand the definition offered by Kagan (1972) in an infrequently quoted paper specifically treats motives in cognitive terms. Because, however, he appears unable or unwilling to attach cognitive labels to the affective components of goal-directed behaviour, he can be regarded as retaining an interface rather than an integrative concept of the relationship between motivated behaviour and cognition.

There is an aspect of motivation, or a motive as I would prefer to call it, that is ignored by the theories and definitions considered so far. This is variously termed stimulus or information drive, exploratory drive, the need for sensory or perceptual stimulation, or information seeking. Several lines of research have converged to support Hebb's (1955) statement that cognitive processes without any intermediaries have immediate drive value. Studies employing a habituation paradigm with monkeys by Montgomery (1953) and with infants by Fantz (e.g. 1963) have been able to demonstrate the incentive value of stimulation which was not considered to be intrinsically rewarding. Exploration declined almost linearly with exposure, and increased almost monotonically with increasing intervals of non-exposure, particularly when a change in stimulus characteristics was introduced. Similarly, Butler and Harlow (1954) were able to demonstrate that the probability of visual exploration of novel stimuli by monkeys increased as the interval between opportunities for such exploration increased. These results are supported by and consistent with the evidence of self-administered cognitive stimulation found by Bexton *et al.* (1954) in the McGill 'sensory deprivation' studies, and multiple evidence produced by Berlyne (e g. Berlyne, 1957; Berlyne and McDonnell, 1965) of the relationship between stimulus novelty or complexity and subjects' viewing time of displays varying on these dimensions. Austin Jones (1966), in a more rigorously controlled replication of the McGill studies, was able to demonstrate not only that information deprivation shows almost all the characteristics predicted and obtained for the deprivation of the more commonly studied drives, but that a 50 per cent uncertainty level of stimulus availability generates the greatest amount of information-seeking activity. I shall return to this important issue in Chapters 8 and 9. For the present it is sufficient to be aware that there is motivation for cognitive activity *per se* and that the reasons for this particular goal-directed behaviour are probably more relevantly sought in the role of this activity for a person's level and direction of expectancy and preparedness, than in its possible role of maintaining an optimal level of electrocortical arousal. This body of data alone, I am inclined to suggest, is sufficient to stamp non-cognitively conceived notions of motivation as defective, and consequently as in need of revision.

2 CONCEPTS OF INTERACTION

In this brief assessment I propose to limit myself to two issues; (i) the degree to which a systematic relationship between personality and motivation has been formulated in presently available theories; (ii) the nature of the processes by which the consistently obtained interaction between cognitive and so-called non-cognitive (personality and motivational) variables has been thought to be mediated.

Although the achievement of 'end states' and 'purpose' has been regularly implied by descriptions and definitions of personality and motivation, the relationship or distinction between these behaviour systems seems not to have been systematically considered anywhere. This raises the question of why there should have been dual concepts in the first place. The answer seems to be that in some contexts one needs to discriminate between *pattern of behaviour which generally characterize* the individual or a group of people, while in others one focuses on the *variability in the directionality of behaviour* to be observed in the same or different individuals at different points of time with differential intensity and duration (Cofer and Appley, 1964). In other words goals may define motivation. To the extent that at least some dimensions of goal-achievement appear directly in observed behaviour, that is, frequency, singularity, perseveration, or duration, motivational variables can provide components for a more comprehensive analysis of personality. In a four-page reference to this issue, however, Cofer and Appley are unable or unwilling to offer an explanation of *how* these components interact, for example, in the relationship between traits, values, attitudes and their expression in behaviour said to exhibit cognitive control.

A component-interaction type of analysis, however, does not necessarily resolve conceptual problems arising from alternative 'push' or 'pull' models of motivation, nor the intransigent controversy concerning the psycho-analytic propositions of unconscious motivation and the variable externalization of one particular motive. These problems do not appear insoluble now, partly because the habit systems which previously defined motivation in radical behaviourism (Bandura and Walters, 1963) have been conceptually enlarged to include the *effects* of social reinforcers and stimuli (Staats, 1971; Bandura, 1977). As shown in Table 2.2 social behaviourism as interpreted by Staats (1975, 1977), regards motivation as emotional conditioning to specific as well as complex stimuli which is *directed* by the source of reinforcement. The acceptance by behaviourists of the contribution of complex events *in* the person to the development of environment-guided behaviour (Rosenthal and Zimmerman, 1978), removes the major obstacle towards more general agreement on a higher-order conceptualization of personality and motivation. Apart from granting external stimuli an internal symbolic role in goal-directed behaviour, the revised social behaviourism is able to address itself to a definition of personality which had to be avoided by its radical forerunner. This definition, in terms of emotional-motivational systems, does not require two separate concepts for motivation and personality.

'Push' models of motivation, especially those based on self-perception of need and hierarchies of goals, require reference to knowledge of the differential directing stimuli received and inferred from goal objects in order to account for the most efficient, most rewarding and least painful control of behaviour. Bandura's (1977) revision of social learning theory now makes it clear that where there is evidence of self-direction in behaviour (as for example in modelling), cognitive control factors must operate as mediators. This expansion of theory is important because it provides a bridge between the mediational theories of animal learning, and human need-related behaviour, and because it adds a learning dimension to the concepts of achievement motivation theory.

My recent survey of the literature has shown that many texts on personality do not even list the term motivation in their index (e.g. Mischel, 1968; Hall and Lindzey, 1970; Wiggins *et al.*, 1976; London and Exner, 1978; London, 1978; Pervin, 1978). The same lack of cross-reference appears to occur in texts on motivation: there is no reference to personality in the index of Vernon (1969), Madsen (1974), Ferguson (1976), Wong (1976), Buck (1976), or McClelland (1976). It is possible, of course, that my survey was incomplete and biased. The most cautious interpretation of this state of affairs can only infer that the relationship between these huge fields of research and theory has not been seriously attacked, or has been considered too self-explanatory to merit mention. Sarason (1972a), however, does include a discussion on motivation in his comprehensive student text. Cattell and Kline's (1977) book is actually entitled *The Scientific Study of Personality and Motivation* (my emphasis), but the reader will not find a systematic treatment of their relationship, as distinct from their measurement. Although Cattell has actually used the term 'motivational trait' (Cattell in Royce (ed.) 1973, p. 466), it would be unsafe to conclude that he regards motivational variables as determinants rather than as expressions of personality. Although Madsen (1974) does not list personality in his index, his erudite comparison of motivational theories actually includes a short section on 'motivation in personality theory' (pp. 84–91), but a relational analysis is omitted.

The relationship issue, however, has not been entirely avoided by various theorists. Motivational variables were to some extent regarded as having the properties of personality traits by Allport (1937), expressing nuclear aspects of personality. A similar conception seems to have arisen as a result of renewed interest in the structures and processes of person $\times$ environment interaction (e.g. Endler and Magnusson, 1976a, b; Magnusson and Endler, 1977), which has developed as a result of dissatisfactions with trait concepts of personality. In a recent brief analysis Endler (1981) correctly points out that consistency at the behavioural level need not be related to consistency at the behaviour-mediating level, and that identical mediational events need not result in behavioural consistency. In a discussion of the relationship between levels of response selection, Endler could be said to limit the implications of the interactional concept to an interaction between 'faculties', or at least to an interface relationship, because motivational variables are considered as distinct from structural cognitive competence and from the stored content of previous stimulation. Thus, like Allport's, this analysis provides the possibility of defining personality by subsumed motivational variables. A similar type of hierarchical relationship seems to be acceptable to some fields of social psychology. Fiedler (1977), for example, regards personality aspects of leadership, defined by a 'Least Preferred Co-worker' score, as a reflection of different motivational goal structures.

The most thoroughly studied area of human motivation is probably achievement motivation, and we could have expected that nearly 40 years of research might have contributed some clarity to the relationship between personality and motivation. It is my impression that this has not occurred. Atkinson (1977, p. 54) himself admits that it is very easy to shift from a process (motivational) orientation to a personality orientation. Although he first seems to suggest a linear relationship: personality–motivation–action, at the end of the same article he identifies abilities, knowledge, beliefs, conceptions, and *motives as attributes* of personality. Thus, the motivation to achieve success (M_s) identifies simultaneously a motive for achieving and a personality disposition. While the relationship and sequential order of the two constructs has remained unclear, it will be argued in subsequent chapters that work in this area has helped to produce an explanatory principle. Weiner (1972, 1978) in particular has offered a cognitive interpretation of achievement striving and failure avoidance by referring to the role of the perceived causes of success and failure, and thus expectancy of behaviour outcome. Since this activity involves an awareness of environmental and intra-personal facilitations and constraints, and behaviourial adjustments that match these factors, it provides one avenue for a more full-scale cognitive conception of goal-directed behaviour as well as for the role of motivation in behavioural strategies. Weiner's elaboration of the motivational process is supported by a study by Winter (1978) discussed by McClelland (1978). The object was to design an optimal methodology for Navy Officer selection techniques which would benefit from a more careful analysis of the interaction of situational and personal (trait) determinants. It was less concerned with a cognitive reinterpretation of motivation. This interest must have been implicitly present, however, because leadership role-playing characteristics which would reflect a potential leader's capacity to evaluate the demands of the post and to generate the most suitable strategies to achieve results were added to a more traditional test battery. McClelland's Table 2 (1978, p. 107) refers to this set of characteristics as schemas – clearly implying a set of cognitive structures required to achieve a desired goal-outcome. The results of this study showed that leadership schema ratings made the biggest contribution to performance prediction. The manner in which these cognitive variables were able to interact with behaviour dimensions not directly conceived as cognitively determined remains to be specified. Since Mischel, however, has already argued persuasively that trait characteristics require cognitive specification, and since one type of motivation – achievement-orientation – has virtually acquired cognitive labels, the route towards a more comprehensive cognitive reinterpretation of personality and motivation and their relationship seems to be marked out.

As pointed out already by Baldwin (1969), the advantage of a cognitive approach to motivation and personality resides in the capacity of general cognitive mechanisms to simplify the relationship between external stimulation and resultant behaviour. This relationship is thought to be mediated by the perceptual system according to Forgus and Shulman (1979). In their view personality differentiation depends on the differentiation and integration of perceptual structures which affect equally the organization and differentiation of motives. The individual self is defined as '. . . a cognitive mediator which consists of operational instructions for the pursuit of motive satisfaction' (p. 196). The characteristics of the perceptual mediating system, however, are not defined with the degree of specificity expected by cognitive processing theorists, a deficiency which also applies to the proposition of a regulatory, discriminative self-monitoring process. On the other hand, Forgus and Shulman offer some clarification of the relationship between motivation and personality. They suggest, for example, that changes in motives and incentives lead to corresponding changes in personality because of changes in expectancy. Furthermore, motives which are directed and organized by the most differentiated cognitive structures will give rise to the most dominant goal when motivation is activated (Forgus and Shulman, 1979, pp. 221, 241). Their notion of the role played by self-instruction in the direction and manner of action is similar to suggestions by Hilgard (1949), but is more specific in that self-instruction is seen as the transmission of information about external and internal events. The focus of these theoretical concepts is clearly cognitive. As a cognitive redescription it remains superficial, however, in the absence of specifications of the postulated perceptual mediating system. It can be argued that this is the main reason why Forgus and Shulman's concept of interation between motivation, personality, and cognition seems to have remained at the level of an interfacing rather than being considered as an integrated relationship. This, of course, takes us back to non-cognitive concepts of personality and motivation, that is, separate systems capable of interaction, but conceived without the content-mediating mechanisms and operations required for integrated, feedback sensitive goal-directed action.

Let me now turn to the second issue that requires examination for the adequacy of its explanation of interaction processes: cognitive styles and controls. With the acceptance of a concept of cognitive self-direction, many of the problems attending the perceptual defence research of the 1940s and 1950s become amenable to updated explanations. As Bruner (1951) stated, the notion of perceptual defence requires a specification which clarifies the role of the perceiver in perception. The first specification, developed jointly by Bruner and Postman, was provided by the concepts of cognitive predisposition, set, hypotheses, or expectancies. Selection and direction of responses, according to this proposition, are guided by basic and enduring needs and values required by the individual to maintain or advance his personal adjustment (Bruner, 1974, pp. 108–10), where the processes involved are *cycles of informational analysis*. This last conception correctly anticipated present theoretical developments, but was ignored at the time by most learning and personality theorists. The terms needs, values, and adjustment, of course, require additional specification of a kind which would enable a visual or auditory perceptual system to be responsive to information from a motivational system concerned with a hierarchy of goals serving personal adjustment. Adjustment itself refers to preferred states of goal achievement which identify needs and values, as well as expectancies of behaviour outcome.

There were two related aspects of the now historical approach to the effects of personality and motivational determinants on cognitive character-istics. On the one hand we had a search for evidence of intra-individual consistency in perceptual behaviour. The most substantial contribution to this area initially came from Thurstone (1944) and his large-scale factorial study of perception. He showed that individual differences in widely varying perceptual tasks could be substantially accounted for by two factors – speed of closure and flexibility in manipulating percepts – a result which required the presence of considerable internally consistent individual styles of respond-ing. Substantial evidence towards a concept of cognitive typologies was pro-vided by the productive group of personality theorists at the Menninger Foundation (e.g. Klein, 1951, 1954; Klein and Holzman, 1950; Klein and Schlesinger, 1951; Gardner, 1953; Holzman and Klein, 1954; Klein and Smith, 1953; Gardner et al., 1959). A detailed examination of these experi-ments after an interval of nearly 30 years would be very illuminating, but need not be undertaken here because substantive recent reviews are available (Vernon, 1973; Hamilton, 1976). The following are some of the dichotomized 'perceptual attitudes' or cognitive styles inferred from the studies: assimilat-ing new to old experience vs. accentuating differences; levelling vs. sharp-ening; coarse categories vs. fine categories; form-boundedness vs. form-lability; intolerance of instability vs. tolerance of instability; interference proneness vs. resistance to interference; intolerance of overlap vs. tolerance of overlap; constriction vs. flexibility; need dominance vs. reality dominance; wide scanning vs. narrow scanning; field articulation vs. non-articulation.

The last dichotomy is, of course, primarily identified with the work of Witkin (Witkin et al., 1954, 1962). Cognitive styles which were not inferred from perceptual characteristics appeared at a later stage in the concrete vs. abstract belief systems postulated by Harvey et al. (1961), and Kagan's (e.g. 1966) impulsivity vs. reflectivity dimension. My own early studies (Hamilton, 1957, 1960) with a largely perceptual orientation lent themselves to a confir-mation of a number of dichotomies proposed by the Menninger team with results suggesting two inter-related dimensions: broad vs. narrow categoriz-ing, and avoidance vs. non-avoidance of perceptual ambiguity. Many aspects of the search for generalized cognitive response strategies should be regarded as methodologically fairly sound because of their operationalism and fairly close match between prediction and results. The interactional evidence was accepted, moreover, by Neisser (1967) as evidence of one of the organizing functions of a superordinate executive control system.

More controversial and deservedly subject to critical appraisal (e.g. Ver-non, 1970; Erdelyi, 1974) was the second aspect of this theoretical framework – to link cognitive control with emotional need and motivational goals. Considering the period – pre-cognitive processing theory – and the gross tools which were (and still are) available for the assessment of motivational and personality dispositions, some of the criticism was possibly excessive. It is also probably true that the rejection of the Menninger approach was not unrelated to a pervasive discomfort with psycho-analytic concepts. It could be argued that the obtained experimental support for the relationship between so-called primary and secondary processes and perceptual events was slight and capable of interpretation by less complex and objectifiable events. Klein's (1954) proposal postulated an ego control system with a threefold function: regulating, modulating, and delaying need-satisfaction; reality appraisal; and reconciling the claims of reality with those of drive and inner values. These functions were conceived as organizing processes with dominance assigned to the motivational function. Thus, extreme latencies in tachistoscopic response times (when controlling for response bias, expectancy, or puzzlement) could be regarded as either the effects of sensitization to social anxiety, or as being due to attempts to inhibit a potentially anxiety-arousing recognition. The same explanation could be applied to the production of associates in response to a word stimulus assumed to trigger sensitizing or repressor processes. For the Menninger team's concepts, the implication of mediating ego control processes extends beyond this interaction statement which is descriptive rather than explanatory. For them it was a system of unconscious, deterministic need regulating general principles which selected mnemonic, perceptual, and cognitive labelling strategies which expressed the generalized functional requirements of the responder.

Erdelyi's (1974) cogent reanalysis of the perceptual defence area was both timely and useful in its focus on what was and what ought to be implied by the term 'perceptual'. It is a pity, perhaps, that he did not extend his evaluations to Klein, Gardner and their collaborators whose concept of dynamic control implied most, if not all, the selective events preceding a response which form the core of Erdelyi's evaluation. It would have had the advantage of filling in the cognitive reassessment of psycho-analytic theory which Klein (1977) completed shortly before his early death. I would regard a distinction necessary, therefore, between the type of notions developed by Bruner, Postman, McGinnies and others, and those originating in the Menninger Clinic at Topeka. Neither approach was able to offer a satisfactory explanatory framework for the interaction between cognition, personality, and motivation. It is likely that I am going against the mainstream of opinion by saying that Erdelyi's effort has its own shortcomings. My reason for this assessment lies in the absence in Erdelyi's own experimental reports (Erdelyi and Applebaum, 1973; Erdelyi and Blumenthal, 1973) of any reference to the processes, that is the operating mediators, by which an *emotionally* toned stimulus can affect stimulus labelling and thus affect recognition behaviour.[1] In other words, and in my view, even this attempt to account for defensive personal strategies with an information processing paradigm omits to present

[1] This deficiency has been minimized recently by Dixon's (1981) analysis of pre-conscious, meaning-directed cognitive processes.

us with the necessary mediators for an emotion (i.e. personality and motivation)–cognition interaction. This, of course, is one of the reasons for offering the present book. Erdelyi's omission would not have been made good by assigning a cognitive-directive role to peripheral and/or electrocortical arousal processes. I have argued already in the preceding section that arousal *per se* does not contain information, it can only transmit it to the analysing and labelling components of an information processing system. Whereas arousal does not appear to feature in Erdelyi (1974), there ought to be general agreement that it must function as a necessary if not as a sufficient process in any model of personality–motivation–cognition interaction, even though, as will appear in successive chapters, I am intent on minimizing their classical categorical distinctiveness.

3 A METATHEORETICAL COMMENT

All theories have tried hard to reflect and to systematize as adequately as possible the observed variations in peoples' interaction with their environment in the light of their own conception of existing knowledge. It is, however, in the nature of science to produce new knowledge which requires to be related to existing bodies of explanation. What Kuhn (1974) calls the shift of explanations under the influence of new paradigms is simply a statement of fact. It refers to the application of new explanatory concepts resulting from the availability of research findings obtained with new technologies and methods on issues which themselves reflect paradigm shifts in other areas of scientific work. It does not imply a rejection of the experimental method, quite the contrary. A change in explanatory analogues or metaphors most commonly requires a change in scientific method and the level of cause and effect events at which it is applied. That is, scientific endeavour has reductionist objectives because of the degree of generalization such explanations offer. In behavioural science reductionism has been rejected frequently because it has been thought to imply that all behavioural events and their interactions are sufficiently explained by neurophysiological or neurochemical structures and processes. In the ultimate sense this conclusion is probably correct, at least given the present state of knowledge. The fear of reductionism may have been affected, however, by fears of academic loss of status and by fears of professional redundancy. There is, of course, not the slightest shred of evidence that theories of nerve cell metabolism or corticotrophic hormone distribution in the association areas can have any direct relevance to the *type* of information and its elaboration of thought content which is transmitted. This has been and will remain the major focus of psychology rather than of any other discipline.

All the concepts and definitions of personality and motivation, as well as the concepts of interaction, which I have discussed, are in fact reductionist. Confusion has arisen because the term disposition has been rather superficially applied to goal-directed behaviour as well as to the methods, manners, or actions defining the behavioural characteristics themselves. This has been confounded by a careless application of the modelling concepts of hypothetical constructs and intervening variables, and the lack of clarity apparent in conceptualizations which fail to distinguish between organized structures and the processes to which they give rise and by which they are maintained. Historically this distinction has always been difficult but no longer need be so with recent developments in cognitive processing theories. In the absence of paradigms derived from them, it is not surprising that the concepts that were evaluated above have shown themselves to be defective. Although Mischel deserves credit for pointing to some of the deficiencies, it is clear that he has not been able to go far enough. We will require far more fundamental definitions of what we mean by reinforcement, goals, wishes, intentions, reality orientation, affect, emotion, expectancy, and particularly 'broad dispositions'. Of course, our conceptions of personality and motivation as dispositions, determinants, or 'causes' of behaviour have not remained unchallenged on purely logical grounds by philosophers (e.g. Anscombe, 1957; Peters, 1958; Alston, 1976). While it is important to be reminded that precision in formulating questions is a prerequisite of the types of answers that can actually be obtained, philosophical criticisms have tended to be based on definitions of psychological variables which then and now would be considered inadequate.

Many of the theories and concepts to which reference has been made have claimed predictive validity as the criterion of utility. While it has been both fashionable and scientifically reassuring to model ourselves on the criteria of the physical and chemical sciences, it could be said that we have frequently sacrificed complexity for the sake of predictive power. In some contexts with some antecedents the probability of behaviour direction and outcome is so high that a predictive test is virtually redundant. Conversely, experimental data from complex multivariate contexts and antecedents with lower predictive power have been rejected on many occasions by reviewers of submitted papers because they do not measure up to simplistic notions of verification. Plausible explanations for what might be called a misapplied purism lie in the historical antithesis between so-called experimental and correlational methodologies, in suspicion of the procedures and implications of multivariate designs and data treatments, and foremost perhaps in a misguided and idealistic search for that logical fallacy: a univariate explanatory process.

It was a source of bafflement to me that in my rereading of the basic literature I found no more than vague and implied assumptions that behaviour strategies and their goals require memory and its stored content. It can only be a truism, of course, that the recognition of a particular need, deficiency, or goal requires its identification through a process of comparison with and differentiation from others, that is, retrieving its stored signifiers. Similarly, the choice and preference for one particular behavioural method of satisfying a need state requires a process of selection, however simple, habitual, or fast it may be, to facilitate most economically a state of goal-achievement. The occurrence of these events should have provided long ago a more comprehensive reductionist definition of personality and motivational dispositions, and of the means by which they are inter-related. Moreover, evidence from children on the expanding, generalizing, and conceptualizing capacity of their memory during the long years of exposure to knowledge, social conventions, and environmental constraints and facilitations, should have provided long ago a new explanatory strategy for a fuzzy terminology. It is a relatively small step to proceed from a consideration of the role of memory in characteristic preferred behaviour toward preferred goals and goal-outcomes, to the role of memory content and its deterministic function in the choice process *preceding* the selection of what is preferred. One cogent analysis of pre-conscious processing events has been presented recently (Dixon, 1981) and will be referred to later on. For these, and other reasons to be elaborated, the bulk of my discussion will centre on the cognitive components of what we have called non-cognitive variables.

PART II

TOWARDS A NEW MODEL

CHAPTER 3

An outline of cognitive structure and process concepts

This chapter and the next are intended to introduce the non-specialist in cognitive processing theories to concepts which form the basis of the reanalysis I am attempting in this book. My comments are no substitute for the large number of textbooks and monographs in the field of cognitive processing theory now available from those workers who have made, and continue to make, significant contributions in this area. My task is to synthesize what I regard as dominant themes in still separately conceived research areas, but my use of cognitive concepts may lack the incisiveness and precision of the specialist. I have, however, attempted to represent current approaches as faithfully as I was able. It will be apparent that for some issues I have applied interpretations which have struck me as plausible in the context of my general aim, but which may not be received with approval by those concerned with fine-grained analytic cognitive operations. To those readers I offer apologies for my presumptiveness, of, if they prefer, pretentiousness.

1 STRUCTURES AND PROCESSES

Modern interpretations of the term cognitive follow in the footsteps of Kant and interpret cognition as knowledge. Cognitive processes are those internal, so-called, 'mental' activities from which knowledge is derived and by which responses are generated, whereas cognitive structures are the assemblies and organizations of elements or components of knowledge. Structures represent the content of knowledge domains, processes utilize selected items of content when we are required or wish to make a response to a specific stimulus. The major processes are orientation, selective attention, short-term storage of sensory events, rehearsal, retrieval of stimulus-identifying memories, and committing to permanent memory by encoding and storage stimulus and response characteristics.

Operations and functions are the vehicles of each process which is regarded as having a limited working capacity (e.g. Miller, 1956; Broadbent, 1958, 1971). To anticipate subsequent more detailed discussion, we can say, for example, that selective attention and retrieval require a limited focus for full efficiency, an operating restriction which is achieved by techniques of inhibition and filtering. Rehearsal operations are required to maintain stimuli in a temporary holding memory to permit other operations to be carried out, and the retrieval process may require a series of converging matching operations with progressively more fine-grain tests of their appropriateness.

Diversity, elaboration, and cross-referencing of the structures and their elements, determine the power of the processes preceding a response. That is, the greater the store of knowledge, and the greater the extent of cross-referencing between organized knowledge structures, the greater the potential of the processes to generate responses required for an optimal adaptation to difficult and changeable environments. Reference to a knowledge store implies that cognitive structures constitute memory, and to the extent that knowledge continues to be available after it has been acquired, we refer here to long-term or permanent memory (LTM).

Memory requires antecedent perceptual events. A pattern of stimulation, transmitted via the sensory pathways, comes to be discriminated as having systematic implications for action, need satisfaction or any other consequences, and as being different from stimulus patterns with different implications. This capacity requires several functional processes: attending to the stimulus pattern without interference from other patterns, maintaining an orientation towards the dominant sensory features in a temporary or short-term working memory system (STM), while attempting to match it with the best fitting element or elements retrieved from the long-term memory store. This is the process of identification, or of the application of existing knowledge, without which an appropriate or rewarding response cannot be made.

It is quite true, of course, that perception occurs without immediate implications for behaviour. For example, when identifying a friend farther down a road, at a distance estimated at 50 yards, the environmental cues available between the observer and the friend have contributed to that estimated distance judgement. Houses, trees, motor cars, and other people have been perceived correctly on a size–distance continuum, but these objects in themselves have no implication for the observer's response of lengthening his stride in order to catch up with his friend. It is obvious, however, that without a memory system that has in the past successfully computed size–distance relationships, a correct inferential perceptual act could not have occurred. In other words, the relationship between perceiving and remembering operates in both directions. Orienting towards a distinctive cue and its perceptual recognition is a relatively simple problem for the attentional and memory systems. Recognizing and hastening to meet a *friend*, however, will stimulate a large number of cognitive structures representing this type of social stimulus setting. And knowing that one knows the social implications of a stimulus cannot be achieved without applying special attentional energy to working memory content. Many of the difficulties in defining the term consciousness (e.g. Underwood *et al.*, 1979, 1981), can be avoided, as I shall argue in a later chapter, by regarding it as a working memory process, in parallel with those processes by which other content is currently being processed in that system.

2 COGNITIVE DATA CONSIDERED AS INFORMATION

So far the general discussion has referred to cognitive structures as an organization of related elements of knowledge and to cognitive processes as activity systems required for integrating current events and elements with elements of knowledge existing in long-term memory. Thus structures contain data, and processes establish them and generate operations on them. We must now turn to definitions of knowledge elements and data, in order to conceptualize what goes on in the cognitive system prior to and during behaviour.

When we cannot objectively observe and identify the nature and characteristics of forces in a system and how they may be related, we consider the unknown by reference to analogies, 'constructs', models, or metaphors. We say, 'let us suppose it works as X does', or 'if this is the way it works, then such and such follows'. We then derive testable hypotheses from our deductions, and attempt to falsify them (Popper, 1959). We retain our hypotheses either until they are falsified, or until developments occur in science which suggest a more plausible, economic, or valid model, metaphor, etc. Substantial changes in scientific methodology are usually responsible for shifts in paradigms (Kuhn, 1974). For cognitive psychology, such a shift occurred some 30 years ago with the development of computer technology and science, and of communication theory, both of which benefited from the rather older discipline of cybernetics. As a result of these scientific achievements the terms information, information encoding structures or networks, and information processing systems and operations, have come to be applied to cognition as reflected in human behaviour. The history of the effects of this paradigm shift is long and interesting, and there is every indication that the man–machine analogue is as important a step forward in behavioural science as the earlier human–infra-human organism metaphors. This is not the place, however, to do full justice to the fascinating story. A brief reconsideration of its basic concepts may well be profitable for the non-specialist.

Cybernetics developed from the existence of feedback devices in machines operating according to the laws of physics. Two well-known examples may be cited: (i) the safety-valves in steamboilers which open to emit steam pressure in excess of a pre-determined pressure safety limit, and which close again when pressure has fallen below this limit; (ii) the thermostat which when a pre-set temperature limit has been reached shuts down the heating device, and conversely reactivates the heater when the ambient temperature falls below the pre-set level. Wiener (1948) first systematized the underlying concepts of error-activated devices or servo-mechanisms, and noted their valid application to non-machine systems in which the presence of homeostatic, adaptive processes and events can be demonstrated. In the simplest self-controlling system signals of a given frequency or intensity are transmitted to a signal receiver with a pre-determined reception sensivity, and there is an additional signal transmission channel to an energy source.

Clearly, even the simple control systems so far considered appear to operate as receivers of communications as well as communicators. And, we may add, the communication contains information, and also transmits it. In the steam valve this information is some appropriate value of pounds/sq. in. to which the control unit operating the opening or shutting of the valve is adapted, whereas the control unit of the thermostat responds to air temperatures on the Centigrade or Fahrenheit scale. Fluctuations of pressure or temperature are fed back as information which is discrepant with respect to a desired standard in the energy source.

Homeostatic mechanisms of adaptation in organisms appear to be fundamentally similar to the kind of error-activated subsystems just described. Optimal biological states constitute the standards of the species. When signals from the external or internal environment indicate to state-monitoring receptors deviations from the pre-set standards or safety levels, this information is transmitted to centres which are concerned with the maintenance of overall balance of the system. Heat- or oxygen-preserving reflexes may be activated, or at a more complex behavioural level an active search for food or liquid will be triggered off. There are at least two major differences between mechanical and biological control systems. The latter responds to patterns of signals which are often only indirectly triggered. More fundamentally, perhaps, biological control systems are capable not only of self-modification in response to a wider range of integrated signals, but also on the basis of self-generated signals representing a wide range of future requirements. The obvious differences between homeostatic machines and human organisms can be reduced in a number of ways. Firstly, by considering only rudimentary adaptive skills such as simple colour or feature detection or discrimination which implies approach or avoidance learning (e.g. Grey-Walter, 1953; Ashby, 1952). Secondly, by building into the machine a network of binary decision-making processes which are capable of differentiating, for instance, between the printed labels of words. Thirdly, by programming a computer to play a high-powered game of chess or of 'Cannibals and Missionaries' (e.g. Selfridge, 1959; Newell and Simon, 1972; Simon and Reed, 1976). The actual power of the analogue is evident, however, when comparing the correct perception of a spatial or graphic feature or the implications of a chess move, with such considerations as the *implications* of a perceived word in the *context* of a written or spoken passage, or the *implications* of a lost chess game for the self-esteem *needs* of the player. This kind of comparative exercise raises questions of categorical relationships. These have tended to terminate in logical decisions about the inadmissability of truth statements incorporating qualitative dissimilarity, and thus a rejection of the analogue or metaphor. In the present context it must be sufficient to say that there is enough evidence from the physical and biological sciences that qualitatively differing entities or concepts can be quantitatively defined within as well as between classes for all present practical purposes.

All the examples considered so far operate with a number of common systems: an information source, a transmission sensor, an information receiver, a source of irrelevant information, a comparator which matches incoming information with a standard or standards by which the information is interpreted, and an activator transmitting information to the original source. A simple relationship between these systems is shown in Figure 3.1, with the systems designated by the now conventional box units, and arrowed links between them indicating the flow and direction of information transmission. These systems represent the components of communication theory (Shannon and Weaver, 1949), though not as yet the method of defining and quantifying information. The model serves us simultaneously as a metaphor for the human processing system so that as indicated in Figure 3.1 we are able to duplicate communication theory terms with the terms of systems which we assume to be operating in human cognition. Since both systems are subject to interference either from an insensitive or oversensitive trans mission channel, or from irrelevant information, the significant points or stages in the system at which the interference may operate have been included in the display.

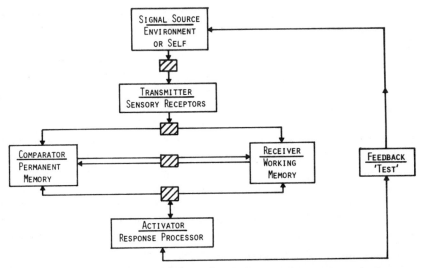

Figure 3.1 Self-rectifying communication system as analogue of cognitive processing system. Shaded sections represent 'noise' or 'irrelevant information'

There is no need to dwell on the capacity of computer design to model some of the capacities of our biological cognitive processing system. The similarity of the general purpose information processor is particularly well illustrated in two capacities: (i) to translate the language of the programmer's instructions into appropriate machine language; (ii) its ability to modify basic programme instructions as a result of achieving pre-programmed subgoal outputs, that is making up its own procedural rules in problem-saving situations for which only general rules or strategies have been programmed (Newell and Simon, 1972). While the metaphor for cognition is valid for at least those areas where it achieves a predicted outcome, considerable problems have emerged in the simulation of problem-solving behaviour requiring analysis of human natural language. Simulation programmes attempt to programme the representation of knowledge and its appropriate use by associative or propositional networks (Anderson and Bower, 1973; Anderson, 1976, 1980). The inadequacies of existing computer program simulations are now thought to lie in the absence of semantic information and its relational intricacies (Waterman and Hayes-Roth, 1978; Findler, 1979). These admissions fairly represent the present power of the mechanical analogues of cognitive structures and the processes in which they can be involved. The shortcomings underline the special role played by language in complex human behaviour, and maintain a valid distinction between simulated and actual behaviour.

Information theory is derived from probability theory and is often used as an alternative term for communication theory. The central measure of information theory is the 'bit': that amount of information that distinguishes between two equally likely alternative outcomes or implications of a stimulus. The probability of whether spinning a coin gives heads or tails can be expressed, therefore, in amounts of information involved in the outcome. The number of possible outcomes (N) is here two. The appearance of a suit card in a sequence of suits in a well-shuffled pack of playing cards has four alternatives ($N = 4$), and the probability of any given letter of the alphabet appearing in a randomly operating teleprinter is 26. Thus informational load increases with the number of discrete alternative identifications and decisions. This is expressed by $I = \log_2 N$, where the logarithmic transformation to the base two expresses the fundamental operation of distinguishing two equally probable events which may be nested in a longer series of also equally probable events. Where the events or outcomes are equally probable, and a decision or response has been made, the information determining the decision becomes redundant and need neither be repeated nor re-examined in subsequent operations. The measure I of information, therefore, is simultaneously a measure of information redundancy, and in extended information-analysing and decision-making operations this is stored as a subgoal in computer memory, or in the short-term working memory system of human cognition.

Two predictions of this mathematical model have been confirmed repeatedly in experiments: (i) the greater the amount of information the longer the time required for a response and the greater the number of errors; and (ii) the less well-established the concepts which the information represents, as in children, the longer the response time and the greater the number of errors.

Figure 3.2 shows on a composite graph the results of just two experiments confirming the speed aspect of these predictions. Two groups of children previously tested for their conserving capacity carried out a playing-card

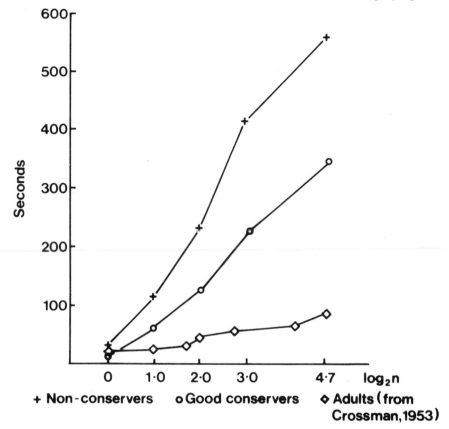

Figure 3.2 Mean decision times for sorting 52 playing cards

sorting task differing in binary choice demands (Hamilton and Launay, 1976). That is, the card-sorting categories increased from Red/Black ($\log_2 n = 0$) to Ace to King in sequence subclassified by colour ($\log_2 n = 4.700$). It was predicted that children not yet capable of the Piagetian conserving operation – interpreted as an information processing task – would be substantially slower than children of the same age who possessed good conserving competence. Figure 3.2 shows that this prediction was confirmed (controlling for motor slowness), and also demonstrates the near-monotonic relationship between binary choice level of difficulty and response times. Data from Crossman (1953) have been adapted and included in the graph to make the same point for adults, and to demonstrate the predicted difference for adults and children. As a paradigm of human cognitive processing, however, many difficulties have emerged which have severely limited the applicability of the communication theory model. Signals reaching the human receiver and processor are only infrequently of the kind of simple alternatives described previously, and where such stimulus situations exist, for example, where a figure is to be identified as either female or male, it is quite unlikely that a simple category response is the only cognitive operation.

Whereas the model processor is inoperative until it receives externally generated signals, the living processor is continuously and actively operating on information from internal physiological sources, postural signals, or preoccupations with goals to be reached at some later point in time, or consolidating and schematizing cognitive data received and responded to earlier. Moreover, the human operator receives a large number of ambiguous signals. This is so (i) because the context or background against which signals are transmitted is itself capable of several interpretations; (ii) because the criteria or sensitivity applied to stimulus recognition may vary according to time of day or stimulus category; (iii) because of the subjective uncertainty of an event; or (iv) because a particular class of events is involved. As a result, non-events may be recognized as having occurred, and events that have occurred may not be registered. These considerations have led to the development of signal-detection methodology and of mathematical decision theory which have been applied with some success in reaction time and recognition experiments in the laboratory (e.g. Sperling, 1960; Sternberg, 1966; Broadbent, 1971). There is little evidence as yet, however, that these sophisticated approaches to relatively simple cognitive skills provide a suitable methodology for the prediction of socially, culturally, and subjectively complex behaviours (Neisser, 1976; Anderson, 1980).

Somewhat greater promise attaches to the development of *information processing theories* in which the units of information handled by the processing systems are larger and decision-making occurs either as a result of evaluating a sequence of *broad* mutually exclusive steps, or as the result of analysing the *relationships* between a number of stimuli, or because both processes operate. The former is illustrated by flow charts, the latter by semantic or propositional networks. Both of these modifications of the unit of information derive from Miller's (1956) proposal that meaningful response dispositions are organized in permanent memory in the form of chunks. Because of the functional unity of chunked information, the analysis of discrete stimulus units such as individual printed letters, individual spoken words, or step-wise scanning of a pictorial display, are often redundant. If feedback from a response indicates, however, that the anticipated well-known meaning of a stimulus input was changed by one particular item in the stimulus field, a more analytic and slower stimulus-identifying process has to be employed. Whereas the validation of the first response depended on an external test against the stimulus source, the second procedure will engage in step-wise internal testing of the output of processes before the overt response is made. This procedure was conceptualized as the *TOTE* sequence by Miller *et al.* (1960). Test-feedback is an essential feature of a processing system whose output has to match a particular goal or subgoal by utilizing one of a number of available plans or strategies which control the flow of information through the response-generating system. Let us now consider this system in somewhat greater detail.

3 THE INFORMATION PROCESSING SYSTEM

It has become a convention to regard the processing system as an assembly of functional units. The influence of communication theory and computer science modelling is very apparent as we have seen in Figure 3.1 with its advantages of pictorial structuring, and its disadvantages of oversimplifying the whole system and fudging some important distinctions between structures and functions. It may be helpful, therefore, to scrutinize the representative diagram of Figure 3.3 in order to be more aware of the complexities hidden away in such models. What we have here represents a *functionally integrated system* of repositories of information, information transmitting and filtering units, and a response-integrating or general process control unit. The functions of the system are: orienting towards and perceiving and storing information or knowledge; retrieving it as required, encoding relationships between events which have been experienced as important for satisfying needs and attaining goals (learned associations); attending to stimuli transmitted from outside the system and to those internally generated stimuli which appear as responses to the external information; searching or scanning for the optimally relevant identifiers of external stimuli in permanent memory, and for functionally relevant associations among the internally generated responses; maintaining and focusing attention on those stimuli which the response-integrating subsystem identifies as the most relevant in a given situation and filtering out those that are not, and those that exceed the processing capacity limit; checking or testing the output of the integrating subsystem prior to emitting signals to the response-executing system.

(i) Attention

The distinction between processing units and processing functions are to some degree artifical and primarily utilitarian since an intact and mature brain operates as if it were a single unit. On the other hand, the distinction is very real when contrasting memory stores as units, some of which are not only very specific but are also localized, with what is implied by the term attention. The latter cannot be considered so much as a specialized working unit as an energized directional activity which participates in and facilitates the work of all system units and their functional capacities. Two conclusions follow if this conception is valid – that attention is the indispensable functional mediator of all the cognitive processes, and that *attention itself does not contain information*. Its actual function can be compared to that of a searchlight beam (Wachtel, 1968) which can vary on several dimensions: intensity of illumination, width of the illuminating beam, degrees of arc swept by the beam, number of halts or foci in a sweep, duration of focal illumi-

40

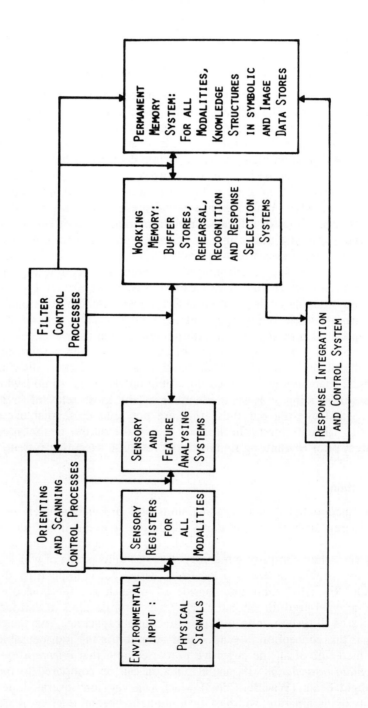

Figure 3.3 The hypothetical components of the cognitive processing system (freely adapted from a number of prototypes)

nation, number of oscillations across an information-bearing field, or any combination of these dimensions. The beam of attention is under the control of an operator and transmits information according to operator needs and instructions. The source of control is most likely in short-term working memory, although dominant theories are silent on such issues.

Attention is frequently presented as a unitary concept or function although it is accepted that a neurophysiological orienting response (Sokolov, 1963; Pribram, 1971) does not necessarily involve cognitive as distinct from autonomic/reticular system activity. Since the hippocampus is fully equipped to generate general alerting or 'pointing' responses to certain changes in stimulation from the external stimulus field it is considered to play a dominant role in orientation. Once again a communication theory paradigm is useful if a stimulus *field* is conceived as undifferentiated noise in a system and the *stimulus* as a signal. Suddenness, intensity, duration, or intermittency of signals will stimulate a biologically programmed orienting response. This, then, supplies the trigger for the involvement of *stimulus-identifying* processes, because the person may have to execute an adaptive response, that is, a response that fits best his current state as well as his next planned goal.

A further distinction appeals, however, because of its intrinsic meaningfulness. Orienting and cognitive attending must further differ according to whether the source of stimulation is external to the system or whether stimulation is internally and possibly volitionally generated. Orienting to signals generated by the person himself, such as the sudden signals of pain or panic, requires internally directed processes as to location, source and implication. Focusing attention on stimuli arising from day-dreaming phantasies or self-generated imagery similarly is confined to internal signals for the purpose of retrieving relevant implications for the person, or to direct the elaboration of the self-stimulated experiences. The major difference between external and internal orienting and attending resides in the locus of verification of information sources and their further implications. Pain, panic, or phantasy do *not necessarily* lead to search-and-scan operations applied to the external environment.

Attention is frequently discussed as if it were a processing unit, at least, this is one valid interpretation of the term selective attention. If attention, however, is seen as the transmitter of information rather than its interpreter, as is implied by a selective function, it does not seem appropriate to retain the term. Selection implies identification of meaning which can only be carried out by system units which are capable of this complex activity. None of this distracts from the dominant function of attention in the cognitive processes because it *facilitates* all the crucial functions of the total system: perceiving, storing, retrieving, focusing, sequencing, and testing. It is an energy-demanding function on whose effort and limited capacity (Kahneman, 1973) the adequacy of a response, that is, of cognitive performance, depends. This effort is mediated by electrocortical arousal which interacts with changes in sensory evoked potentials. Because of the neural pathways connecting the cortex, the hippocampus, and the autonomic nervous system, the stress steroids cortisone and corticosterone contribute in complex ways to the arousal process (Warburton, 1979). Because the evidence from vigilance studies shows that sustained attention is optimal for only limited periods of time, it is assumed that a sustained allocation of effort is fatiguing and reflects the limited capacity of the information seeking and processing system (e.g. Hockey, 1979; Rohmert and Luczak, 1979). Instead of saying, therefore, that processing capacity is limited because of the inevitable bottlenecks of a 'single-channel' process control unit, it is probably more plausible to assign processing limitations to more than one component of the system, and certainly to attention required for similar tasks.

(ii) Memory

An indispensable component in any information processing system is a unit which stores information that has been transmitted from other components which have already processed and utilized it. While a computer analogue is quite apposite for this function, its topographical characteristics are not, at least not without many amendments and elaborations. The memory unit of the cognitive processing system is best conceived as a flexibly active functional subsystem, or as systems serving as repositories of information. The nature of the tasks performed by and with memory may be illustrated by the goals which researchers in 'artificial intelligence' have set themselves in order to model the flexible heuristics so characteristic of the human problem-solver. A particularly good, recent example of these goals is shown in Table 3.1. Each of these nine processing goals requires the search of task-related memory data banks for entries which are directly or indirectly associated with, or matching, the representation of a goal which is held in another functional unit of the system. If the same task has been presented before, the search process will be short, if the task is novel, or requires a sequence of searches, it will take longer. If task-relevant data are not stored, or are for various reasons inaccessible, or if irrelevant entries are retrieved, a behavioural response may be impossible within the time available for it. Since the mature

Table 3.1 Goals of a search strategy

Assimilating new information
Responding to demands to categorize, sort, assess, revalue, identify, and/or discard elements of information at a variety of levels
Recognizing and ignoring irrelevant and faulty data
Finding sensible compromises in situations of conflict
Distinguishing between more and less useful information
Making global, inductive judgements on the basis of disjoint sample values
Applying general principles and techniques to specific cases
Discovering and utilizing partial similarities and analogies
Constructing, adhering to and, when necessary, modifying plans

---

Source: From N. V. Findler (ed.) (1979), p. 309.

processing system constantly receives information by which we are able to monitor from moment to moment our positions in space, the current point of time and a daily occupational plan, most tasks begin with pre-knowledge of the area of functioning needed, and thus an approximate pre-attentive process (Broadbent, 1977). This basis of responding has long been referred to as perceptual or conceptual 'set', but task-specific attentional effort is not generated until the specifications of a particular goal or subgoal have been registered. Since the goals can change from moment to moment and since there is either clear self-knowledge or consciousness of these goals, or this knowledge is available to a process control stage without self-awareness, there is logical support, in addition to the experimental evidence, for either several memory components, or functionally distinct components of the same processing unit.

This chapter is not intended to replicate the many excellent publications available on memory systems and their functions (see for instance Bower, 1972; Baddeley, 1976; Estes, 1976a; Klatzky, 1980). Nor is it appropriate for me to take sides in the ongoing controversies between memory theorists. Figure 3.4 may help, however, to conceptualize certain agreed aspects along the durability dimension of memory and the known specialization of its two major stages and/or components. There is consensus agreement on a number of issues. For instance, there is no dispute that there is memory for verbal as well as for non-verbal stimuli, that there is specialization in the memory system by which modality-specific stimuli are recognized, that there are stages in the memory process, that some of these stages can retain or hold information for only a short time, and that a large amount of information on a particular topic, some of it less frequently verified, some of it true only in certain conditions, lengthens a response time considerably.

The most basic requirement of memory is its capacity to retain new information (see Table 3.1). This process is agreed to involve three memory stages: sensory, short-term-working buffer, and permanent. Sensory memory, whether iconic or echoic is of very short duration. Sperling (1960) and Darwin et al. (1972), for instance, have shown that it fades rapidly after initially outlasting the stimulus event, and that no more than 4–5 items of a display can be reported after about 2 seconds. The 'partial report' technique introduced by Sperling has shown, however, that virtually the whole display has been perceived, but that if immediate recall is required of only part of the display, the rest of the information is lost. The pre-attentive recall requirement has here strengthened a memory process by pre-direction to the meaning of selected symbols (letters or numbers).

Particularly important are the effects of backward masking, one of the most frequently studied interference conditions: following one brief display by another equally brief one with also brief intervals between them. In these conditions there is either some summation between stimuli or erasure of the first stimulus input (Averbach and Coriell, 1961). Intervals and stimulus durations in tens of milliseconds are critical in investigating the capacity of

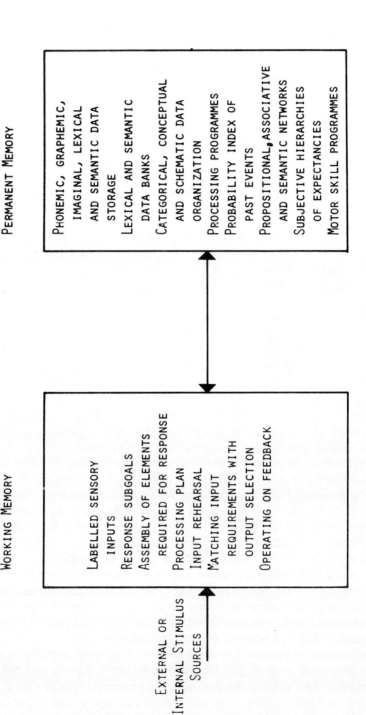

Figure 3.4 The memory systems and their hypothetical specializations

this memory system because of the evidence that attentional scanning can handle one item in 8–10 milliseconds, and even a comparison process as to whether one particular item was present in a prior display takes less than 40 milliseconds (Sternberg, 1966). Unless an event has received immediate attention, it seems to be lost to the cognitive processing system. It seems plausible to suggest that the combination of focused attentional scanning and of labelling represents the essentials of the perceptual process. This can occur, of course, outside self-awareness.

The experimental analysis of very short-duration events so far has not been extended to internally and self-generated stimuli. Introspective reports, self-evident and available from almost every person, indicate that a very rapid succession of thoughts is also only partially retrievable and reportable, and only if effort is made to use selected items for the next stage of a cognitive sequence. Fading or decay, and the effects of backward masking, seem to apply, therefore, to what occurs internally. It seems plausible to assume that the locus of registration for these events resides in short-term working memory, rather than at a sensory receptor site.

The capacity to report an event, to label or identify it, and to use this knowledge for subsequent stages in a procedure, defines the characteristics of the working memory system. Because this system is able to clear its registers for work on newly arriving and different information, and because information stored in it also decays in the presence of interpolated tasks, the designation 'short-term' has been and still is useful. From Ebbinghaus's work in the last century on nonsense syllables, to Craik and Lockhart's (1972) explanations of memory decay for meaningful verbal material, the evidence is overwhelmingly that of a negative relationship between per cent of new material remembered and recall interval. Interpolated tasks interfere with the consolidation of the new material in physiological structures because they prevent rehearsal operations on what is to be remembered. Rehearsal requires attention, but since this is also required for the interference tasks, the available attentional energy needs to be divided. Although spare resources can be generated to sustain a higher demand on the information processing system (Kahneman, 1973), we have conclusive evidence that the total capacity of the system and certainly individual components or functional systems are limited at any given time (e.g. Broadbent, 1958, 1971; Treisman, 1969; Norman and Bobrow, 1976). As a consequence the working memory system itself has finite capacity even with requests for immediate recall of a string of digits. With the division of attention in the presence of more than one task, therefore, only a fraction of working memory content can be easily encoded in a more durable form.

There are ongoing controversies on at least two working memory issues: (i) how to define an item of information and thereby measure the capacity of the system; and (ii) whether working memory load is adequately defined by the stimulus items presented in a laboratory task (Anderson, 1980). The problems with (i) are, firstly, that information may be chunked and we do not know the person's chunking strategy and capacity, and, secondly, that preliminary chunking operations will produce a mnemonic symbol representing many items of information from task-relevant data in permanent memory. That this transformation of stimulus items received by the system may actually occur more frequently than is granted is supported by the many studies on levels of information processing or so-called depth of encoding (Craik and Tulving, 1975; Moscovitch and Craik, 1976; Craik and Jacoby, 1980). Summarizing grossly, this approach argues that if meaning can be attached to discrete stimuli by which they are assigned to existing conceptual categories for which semantic labels exist in permanent memory, then these stimuli can be remembered better and for longer. While this is another way of saying that meaningful material is easier to remember, there are implications which go well beyond this truism. It means, for example, that the working memory system is an active information processing unit which mobilizes and holds alternative representations of information input, and that it can decide whether a particular transformation or reorganization is valid and useful.

Another way of looking at this issue is to consider the importance of inferred context in the ability to remember a list of words representative of one or two meaning categories. To discover the context requires a conceptual organizing principle which allows the related individual items to be grouped. While this conceptual process is intuitively and intrinsically more difficult, it is tempting to compare it to the Gestalt principles of perceptual organization. After many years in oblivion, 'proximity', 'similarity', 'closure', and 'good continuation' have reappeared as important factors in analysing complex stimuli by imposing segmental generalized structures prior to more detailed perceptual processes (Anderson, 1980). The original theory was severely shaken by Hebb's (1949) criticisms and his physiological approach to perceptual learning. Because of the confirmed role of learning in the development of the principal strategies of perceptual analysis, it is plausible to regard these strategies themselves as conceptual units in permanent memory which transform, in this case, spatial discreteness and multiplicity into a more generalized information entry into working memory.

From the point of view of this book the controversy over what the information content of the working memory unit actually consists of during a prescribed task is more important as well as more interesting. The additive load of the external environment and of task-peripheral information on working memory during an experiment is, of course, recognized. Thus, we employ soundproof rooms, transmission of a visual task by a computer-driven display screen, separate rooms for experimenter and subject, and electronic recording of responses. But it seems to be true that, in the behaviourist tradition, internal stimuli are excluded from methodological controls except for the phrasing of instructions. It seems inevitable, however, that the pre-attentive processes do not restrict themselves only to literal and intended interpretations of the instructions. Even the interpretation of the meaning of the instruction will require selection from a group of seemingly appropriate strategies, while the task itself is likely to trigger associated memory data which facilitate the strategy. If this is correct, as suggested by EEG desynchronization data (e.g. Buchsbaum, 1976), then this constitutes an active process in working and permanent memory rather than a passive one, as suggested by Broadbent (1977). This conclusion seems inevitable if the content of the instructions is meant to be a 'primer' of one type of response rather than another. There are very few good reasons to assume that the experimental task will be interpreted as being without consequences or implications for the self-evaluation of the subject. Arguments that this effect will appear in a standard deviation, and that small standard deviations by definition rule out individual difference factors, would carry greater weight if studies employed wider socio-occupational ranges in their subject samples. Suffice it to say at this stage that affectively and emotionally loaded identifiers of stimulus input are more rather than less likely to be elicited in settings inevitably 'priming' the response system for *adequacy* of performance. I shall consider this effect in some detail at various later stages.

The information processing system cannot operate without the store of durable memories which encode knowledge and experience, strategies for applying them, as well as long-term plans. If we consider the last item in Table 3.1 of the goals of a search strategy it is obvious that no matter how efficient and effective working memory, or how flexible attention, to construct, adhere to, or modify behaviour plans requires knowledge of similar plans in the past, knowledge of past constraints and facilitations, and knowledge of the outcome – success or failure – of previous, functionally related responses. In the present context it is less important to know how long-term memory behaves in a variety of conditions requiring recall, recognition or their inhibition, than to evaluate theories of its development, its organizational characteristics, and its methods of representing knowledge. These aspects will be examined in the next chapter. For the moment we need to turn our attention to that part of the information processing system which has control over the integration, selection and execution of a response decision.

(iii) Response process control

Koffka (1935) asked 'How does a problem find its solution?'[1] He thereby seems to have anticipated the instructional procedures written into a computer program, a succession of theories of a detector operating at the analytic level of wood recognition or stimulus identification, Neisser's (1967) concept of the 'executor' in perception, and the varieties of cognitive control theories discussed in Chapter 2. There seem to be many reasons why the concept of process control is essential in cognitive processing theory, even though regarding it as a unit of a system may be too concrete and misleading.

[1] I am indebted to Blumenthal (1977) for reminding me of this aphorism.

Perhaps the simplest way of exemplifying process control, and of defending the concept itself, is to ask how the system *knows* that it has generated the best possible answer to a request to respond. This process requires a series of operational steps and intermediate and subordinate decisions. To imagine that only a narrow range of identifying and relevant responses will be elicited by a memory or problem-solving task is, as I argued before, oversimplifying as well as simplistic. Each person comes to any situation with a set of priorities and response biases which describe his current behavioural plans as well as his past strategies of responding in particular situations. Therefore, we are justified in arguing that response selection must fit, and be integrated with, an overall plan. It is generally accepted that incoming stimulation is subject to filtering, scanning, attenuating, and categorizing operations which are applied at more than one stage of the information transmission process (see Figure 3.3). There seem to be no good reasons why these operations should not be applied at a superordinate level to an existing body of plans, procedural rules, and strategies. This, of course, is what is basically meant by set, predisposition, or bias. Priming of a response system, therefore, is internally as well as externally controlled, and the priming of one particular direction for the handling of stimulus input will effect the direction of the allocation of available processing capacity (Kahneman, 1973). This in turn energizes orienting and attentional functions in pre-selected directions.

If these assumptions are approximately correct, then they demonstrate so-called 'top-down' processes (Norman and Bobrow, 1975; Bobrow and Norman, 1975; Rabbitt, 1979; Norman, 1980). 'Top-down' processes are identifying, recognizing, or labelling events stimulated by knowledge of the context of a task so that even 'noisy' or degraded stimuli can be identified. They require a deductive approach and the application of existing conceptual structures. 'Bottom-up' processes operate in the absence of context cues, the flow of processing is inductive, and may be considered passive. In an ambiguous situation context itself has to be discovered, or cued, so that 'top-down' processes reflect the general interpretative bias of the system.

The term central processor has frequently been used to identify the locus of general principle application, and of response integration and decision-making. One of those decisions may be to restructure the organization of incoming stimuli, to articulate some features, to attenuate others, and to test, verify or reappraise the results of each intermediate step until an output requirement appears to the system to have been matched. The earlier discussion has indicated that the intermediate steps depend on finely tuned interplay between attentional effort and capacity, working memory, and the retrieval of discrete data from permanent memory. It is now plausible to suggest that the derived outcome of a general plan as well as its sequences of selected strategies must operate through the working memory system. Let us illustrate with an example suggested by Mandler *et al.* (1974). Supposing I am asked to remember the following long list of numbers: 5 5 4 9 5 3 5 2 3 2 2 7 1. This task is well beyond the digit span of people who are not mnemonic specialists in the entertainment world. Provided, however, I am allowed to read the numbers at normal speed, I am able to reproduce them because they are the birthdays of members of my family in back-to-front order. A 'top-down' grouping strategy has discovered regularities, discarded phone numbers, shoe sizes and vehicle registration numbers, probably because of a cue from the first two numbers: 5 5 may mean 1955. The rest is simple since birthday presents and greeting cards have had to be regularly remembered. But some people are more sensitive than others to the implications of *forgetting* a birthday, and this contributes another and perhaps more important bias for a central processing control unit. The bias is not only towards birthday dates, but towards the *implications* of forgetting them. We are dealing here with an organized system of representational knowledge, its attributes and personal relevance rather than discrete items of information. In the above example, a central processor sensitizes other components of the system to apply chunking and grouping strategies, and also to examine further implications of the results of these procedures. Some of the long-term memory structures must facilitate this task by having previously encoded birthdates and the implications of forgetting, *as well as* other functionally relevant material, in some interrelated organization.

A memory structure of this type has some similarity with what was termed a schema many years ago (Bartlett, 1932). It is of some interest, that despite the difficulties experienced in defining the schema, or schemata, adequately, the concept has acquired new relevance and importance in the production system paradigms of artificial intelligence methodology. Furthermore, it is now recognized that adaptive production systems working with associative networks of objects, and relationships between them in simulated problem-solving, may require a higher level of encyclopaedic knowledge (Findler, 1979). Thus, problem-solving requires the organized memory structures of schemata as well as the semantic representation of the knowledge they contain (Simon, 1980a). Allport (1980) is probably correct in concluding that cognitive psychology lacks a theoretical notation of mental processes, that is, of mechanisms capable of realizing a given psychological function, a deficiency which he relates to the chaos engendered by testing out experimental preliminaries. Allport is also probably correct to question the validity of a single processing channel of limited capacity (Allport *et al.*, 1972), and to reject it in favour of processing and memory capacities that are widely distributed throughout the brain (see also Rollins and Hendricks, 1980). I am not certain that these strictures help to supply what artificial intelligence production systems require for the representation and utilization of goals and subgoals of its pattern recognition processes. What seems to be required ultimately is a conceptualization of how the semantic signifiers of pattern meaning and implication achieve a neurochemical notation which subsequently can be transformed into a mathematical language. Since these are not psychological systems of notation, it seems more realistic to seek concepts of notation which fit considerations of cognitive naturalness such as propositions and schemata (Anderson, 1981), provided that the language of the knowledge which they have organized by internal structuring of relationship can convey fine-grained meaning and its implications.

CHAPTER 4

Memory and the representation of knowledge

If the purpose of this book is to search for and identify the critical functional components of idiosyncratic and characteristic goal-directed behaviour, special emphasis needs to be given to the storehouse of past behaviours from which the general and specific directions of present behaviour will be selected. Although the previous chapter has already described briefly the role of memory in a general cognitive processing sequence, a more detailed analysis is required.

Cognitive psychology is primarily concerned with two issues: (i) with the identification of the organizing principles people employ in storing information which is subsequently required for retrieval; and (ii) with models of how information encoded in permanent memory is made representational of external events and of internal thought processes. The first concern is with the structure of memory, that organization of information-carrying brain cell assemblies which contain the memory trace, the engram, as it used to be called (Lashley, 1950). The second object of current memory research is to produce a workable notion of how knowledge is represented in memory structures. In the tradition of experimental methodology, the bulk of the huge volume of recent work has been carried out in the laboratory, employing relatively simple verbal or non-verbal material to test for recall or recognition characteristics.

This short chapter is not intended to be a substitute for the many distiguished specialist accounts available, and cannot hope to do more than to select some of those current findings and models which seem to fit my general purpose: the redefinition of personality traits and goal-directed, motivational behaviour in terms of cognitive structures and their content. I am much more concerned, therefore, with the organization and data language of gross chunks of memory than with memory for words, sentences, pictorial features, or holistic visual or auditory displays. Without the findings from the more analytic work, however, macroscopic inferences would lack validity. At the same time, we must be aware that the present fine-grained models may be inadequate when attempting to identify the acquisition and retrieval processes required for general strategies of behaviour. And this may be particularly so because of the hierarchical approach that is presently favoured in modelling any particular concept encoded and available in memory. It is true that a succession or combination of sensory events may be built up by the cognitive processing system to represent a *meaningful* stimulus, and there are ample grounds for arguing that this 'bottom-up' strategy is most likely in the early developmental years. 'Top-down' anticipatory matching processes which facilitate perceptual and conceptual identification occur more frequently, however, after the early years of childhood (Norman and Bobrow, 1975; Bobrow and Norman, 1975).

Apart from considering the structures of types of long-term memory, some space will have to be devoted to the relationship between memory and perception. Our main emphasis here, however, will have to be on the organization and representation of conceptual structures.

1 MEMORY AND PERCEPTION

Whereas the close connection between memory and learning is fully accepted and is clearly demonstrated either in designated studies in learning or in studies in memory, very little is written specifically about the relationship between memory and perception. There is, of course, a two-way relationship. Stimulation with lists of words or displays or spatial or figurative material by which memory capacity of strategies are to be assessed, requires perceptual activity. Conversely, the perceptual act requires a search of appropriate long-term memory data in order to retrieve the best-fitting match for the stimulus material that has entered a sensory, or very short-term memory stage. To know what a stimulus is, means to identify it. In order to identify stimuli we require past knowledge which is available only in memory. If the object, event, or situation to be identified is novel, we identify it either by an approximation to what we know, or we search the repositories of other people's memory, or we refer to reference books, dictionaries, or encyclopaedias.

Perceptual capacity or skill, as well as memory for what has been perceived, grow with biological maturation and experience of environmental events. For example, if it can be demonstrated that a stimulus attracts more than cursory attention from an infant, that is if the stimulus is fixated, and is preferred to another, we feel justified to infer that perceptual discrimination has occurred. This means that the infant's response system is able to distinguish between one visual pattern and another. Whatever the reasons for the preference, and there are many (e.g. Vernon, 1976; Vurpillot, 1976), preference implies a process of selection between in this case primitive alternatives which have been experienced before. The experienced alternatives must be available for a choice process prior to a response, however, no matter how immediate or unpremeditated this appears to be. For a choice process to take place, the different visual patterns must have been preserved or conserved within the response-generating system and some rules of differentiating must have become available at the same time (Bruner, 1974). The availability of representations to which rules of identification are applied pre-supposes the presence and essential participation of memory.

There are good reasons why it is necessary to restrict the discussion of the interplay between perception and memory to those stimulus events which convey *meaning* to the perceiver, that is to restrict ourselves to the events which are concerned with *knowledge* of events, with *predictions* of event meaning, with response requirements and with response outcomes. Such events can range, however, from identifying tachistoscopically presented letters, or a young child's recognition of a desirable toy and reaching for it in an efficient manner, to a complex verbal request to produce an answer to a difficult symbolic problem. Events to which knowledge and prediction do not seem to contribute in the perceptual process, are purely sensory neurological transformations of stimuli by which the information-analysing system extracts basic details about stimulus colour, orientation, contours, amount and direction of movement of visual stimuli, characteristics concerning loudness and pitch of acoustic stimuli, and spatial and temporal relationships between visual and acoustic events. These transformations of externally arising signals reduce and simplify stimulus events, and occur before perceptual and conceptual data encoded in memory can be applied for the identification of meaning (Norman, 1976; Anderson, 1980). Useful examples of one aspect of the separation between perception and memory come from neurophysiological studies (e.g. Hubel and Wiesel, 1962; Blakemore *et al.*, 1970; Sekuler and Levinson, 1974; Moulden, 1980). They demonstrate that the neuro-visual system is pre-programmed with stimulus-specific neurons whose patterns of activity can lead directly to sensory events which equally directly are perceived, for example, as changes in stimulus orientation, or movement.

Similar, neurophysiologically oriented approaches are applied to the capacity limitations of the sensory information reception system to which reference has been made already in the previous chapter. The term sensory memory or sensory store is often used for the first stage of the perceptual and remembering process. This stage has very short durability, although it is thought to be able to receive *all* of the information transmitted to the sensory surfaces at any given time. In a series of prototypical experiments Sperling (1960, 1967) was able to demonstrate that the sensory store stage can retain for up to 5 seconds (with a dark post-exposure mask) nearly all 12 random letters of the alphabet arranged in 3 rows of 4 letters each, with only 50 milliseconds exposure, provided that subjects were required to reproduce only the letters of one row. This row was signalled only after exposure of the material. Since subjects do not know in advance which letters they must reproduce, the total memory is the number correctly reproduced multiplied by the number of rows. If this 'partial report' method is compared with a 'whole report' procedure in which reproduction from the whole display is required, the number of letters correctly reproduced by the latter method is usually only slightly larger. Sperling's experiments established that the short duration capacity of this memory system is due to physiological factors either of *decay* of a trace which takes usually about 1 second, or of masking by a new visual input which overlays the previous input.

For our present purpose it is important to note that sensory registration in and by itself does not facilitate memory. The ability to recall any letters in this type of experiment depends on a perceptual process. This has two components here, and in almost all other memory experiments. Firstly, a cognitive and volitional readiness to identify stimuli of a particular class in a párticular place and at a particular time. Thus, the experimental instructions produce an external attentional focus as well as an internal one in terms of the long-term memory categories that are being sensitized. It is in fact highly likely that an instruction that letters of the alphabet will have to be reproduced will lead to the retrieval of alphabetic information from long-term memory prior to the stimulus exposure and its transfer to the short-term working memory stage of the processing system. Unless this were the case it would be difficult to account for the speed and accuracy with which this task can be carried out. Neither would it be possible to make sense of experiments in which it is shown conclusively that 'priming' or 'setting' leads to faster response times than responding to variable material presented randomly with respect to content.

The second perceptual component is the act of recognition of visuo-spatial features fleetingly available on a sensory surface, or in a first durable buffer store. This requires the matching of the sensory information against a selection of items in the working memory system. To reproduce vocally for the experimenter the name of a letter requires reference primarily to a working memory stage rather than to a sensory memory, so that memory of the visual icon (or iconic memory) requires perception, and the perceptual identification of the stimulus requires reference to previous knowledge of the distinct alphabetic features in memory. It seems appropriate to suggest, therefore, that when we refer to 'recognition memory' we are substantially referring to perceptual activity.

In the present context, the really important question is how some rapidly decaying sensory information remains available for further perceptual analysis and therefore, for memory reproduction. Coltheart (1976, p. 37) has argued that this is achieved by an active mode of transfer from an iconic store (or in the case of auditory information echoic) to durable storage. The question is, however, what does the activity consist of? According to Seymour's (1976) review of retrieval and comparison operations in permanent memory, visuo-spatial features require analysis by graphemic registers and memory stores. From these two points of view it can be argued that it is perceptual activity that transfers information from a sensory to a more durable memory store, and that without an appropriate memory bank perceptual activity could not occur, and the information would be lost. Clearly a 'first cause' position has to be adopted, and the one preferred here is that perception precedes memory.

2 THE ORGANIZATION OF KNOWLEDGE STRUCTURES

(i) Developmental aspects

The comments in this section are intended to be neither a summary of the recent literature on the development of perception and memory, nor even a complete statement of the development of cognitive structures. Apart from considerable gaps in our knowledge which are substantially related to our inability or unwillingness to engage in analytical longitudinal studies, there are available several recent substantial surveys of various aspects of the development of cognitive structures and processes (e.g. Cohen and Salapatek, 1975; Hamilton and Vernon, 1976; Kail and Hagan, 1977).

If perception precedes memory, and if memory is the store of knowledge, then perception is the process by which knowledge is acquired. There are at least three levels of knowledge. To know that we know is most probably not only the level which best defines consciousness, it also represents the most integrated level of stimulus and of response-outcome analysis. The second level is probably best represented by the intermediate steps of stimulus identification and response selection during which permanent memory is searching for matching identifiers that fit the stimulus demands and their response implications temporarily held in short-term working memory. Knowledge operations at these first two levels have to be established through maturation and learning. The most primitive as well as the most fundamental level of knowledge is represented by the pre-programmed and unlearned capacity of mid-brain centres to respond to gross sensory inputs such as brightness, loudness, stimulus suddenness or intermittency, gravitational changes, tactile stimulation or metabolic deficiencies. It is accepted that responses to these classes of stimuli do not reflect the utilization of knowledge in the usual cognitive sense of the word. At the same time, homeostatic events of this kind, which are mediated by primitive, reflexive activity, require the matching of a current state of the response system with its pre-programmed optimum state. This is a feedback-driven interaction which ought to be regarded as a precursor of later cognitive memory and knowledge.

Clearly, the feeling tones, or temperamental responses mediated by the interaction of autonomic nervous system and mid-brain centres are the acknowledged antecedents of behaviours that are subsequently regarded as an integral part of personality and motivational characteristics. Although we lack all direct evidence that the emotional experiences of earliest infancy or even late sensory experiences of pre-natal events participate in the subsequent development of the individual's cognitive structures, conditioning of internal to external events is likely to occur as soon as integrated neuronal networks become established in the cortex. These sensitize the response system to classes of stimuli and determine the speed and permanence of habituation processes. In this manner they would be likely to contribute to the organization of knowledge structures and the content of permanent memory.

It is safe to assume that the first objective signs of knowledge acquisition are to be found in infants' *attention* to sensory stimuli. Two of the more usual experimental parameters considered here are length of time of visual fixation or head-turning, and evidence of reduction of fixation time after repeated exposure during one experimental session, or across a developmental span of a number of weeks. The first is thought to be a response to novelty, the second is evidence of habituation. Habituation to one stimulus, as well as preference for one of two novel stimuli presented simultaneously, is considered evidence not only of perceptual discrimination but also we are assuming that the infant has started to construct internal representational models of the environment. For older children, or where it has been possible to monitor physiological arousal, additional objective evidence of attention to novel stimuli has been obtained from heart-beat records showing deceleration.

With increasing age complex configurations attract more attention than simple ones probably because they contain more novelty and more information. At roughly the same time it appears that more than one dimension of a (visual) display will become the focus of attention thus increasing the categories of object variation. Once objects are perceived as discrete entities, they soon assume another characteristic – that of permanence. The emergence of object permanence in children is perhaps the first truly objective sign that conceptual structures have formed in memory. If a child reaches for a toy that has been moved across his field of vision to disappear behind a cushion or under a cloth, and he reaches for it in the new position, then he has acquired an internal representational model of an object and its movement that requires only minimal sensory cues for a decision that absence does not mean non-existence, but only displacement. Children only gradually acquire attentional skills of focusing on detail which will provide adequate information about complex visual patterns. It takes longer still for the emergence of voluntary central control of attention, to ignore unimportant or irrelevant detail, and to move generally from attentional behaviour that is stimulus-bound to goal-directed attentional strategies (Vurpillot, 1976). In the latter case, of course, we have a concept and memory-driven perceptual search process rather than merely perceptual learning.

While object permanence is an early and primitive example of goal-directed and conceptually driven attention, it is only the beginning of a long process in the development of knowledge structures. There is a great deal of evidence, for example, of the developmental sequence of pattern and form perception from visual preference and memory for simple design to preference for more complex displays with a smaller amount of informational redundancy (Vernon, 1976). We have no direct evidence, however, as to what aspects of the cognitive structure of an object that can be discriminated by the child, or how a structure representative of, say, a circle with an internal cross, of more complex geometrical figures, of a house, or of a motor car develop. There is in fact continuing controversy over whether the analysis of separate component features is a necessary preliminary step in the acquisition of a holistic percept, or whether perception of the whole precedes perception of constituent parts. It seems, however, that children adopt both strategies. Where physiological feature analysers are available it is inevitable that discrete feature detection should contribute to the perception of overall form or pattern. For example, the brightness of the eyes in the human face may account for infants' early fixation on the face of the mother (Vernon, 1976). Kagan *et al.* (1978), in a well-controlled dishabituation study, demonstrated that transforming stimuli on dimensions of 'largeness' and 'vertical rearrangement' of circles in a circular frame elicited the greatest increase in attention, compared with altering the shape of stimuli within the frame. The authors believe that these results suggest that infants have special sensitivity to spatial pattern and relative size, and that complexity defined by number of elements and amount of contour in a display may be less salient for attention, at least at the age of 10 months (pp. 66–8). Findings such as these suggest that feature analysers are capable not only of extracting information about extension, orientation, or brightness from sensory receptor sites, but that they appear to be able to extract information about relationships between features at some very basic level. If this is a plausible deduction, then neonatal perceptual development starts with an existing physiological basis for differentiating one simple visual display from another and for subsequently recognizing, for example, the mother's face as distinct from the face of a stranger.

While there is no question of the biological significance of an infant's capacity to attend to and orient towards the mother's face, this does not apply to other objects in early development. In the course of the acquisition of form and pattern perception it has been found, however, that there is a growing tendency to attend to and fixate the most striking, most salient, or most information-yielding aspects of a visual display, such as the corners of triangles, or sudden changes in contours. Once again, therefore, the perception of feature detail and holistic pattern perception are complementary.

Although fine-grained documentation is still lacking, what seem most likely are the following approximate time sequences of fixation preceding full perception:

Objects	Age	Sequence
FACE	1 mon.	– features (eyes) → whole
	6 mon.	– whole → feature → whole
OTHER	1 mon.	– whole → feature (say, corner) → whole
VISUAL	6 mon.	– feature → whole → feature → whole
STIMULI		reappraisal reappraisal
ANY	1 mon.	– whole → feature (say, contrast) → whole
STIMULUS	6 yrs.	– feature → whole → feature → whole
		reappraisal reappraisal

Perceptual development – in relation to stimuli which have little or no biological significance requires learning on the basis of maturational progress. There cannot be any memory structures representing the activity of feature detector neurones if these have not been previously stimulated. It seems likely, therefore, that the nativism of Gestalt psychology was wrongly conceived in this principal statement except possibly for figure-ground differentiation. At the same time it is plausible to account for the developing preference for complex visual patterns not only as preference for a greater amount of visual information. What seems likely is that complex patterns, by virtue of being complex, stimulate the operation of configurational organization initially on the basis of proximity and similarity, and subsequently, when object memory structures have been developed, employing the principles of good continuation and closure. Similarity and proximity permit the isolation of items into sets to which conventional meaning can be applied eventually, and represent primarily a sensory-perceptual activity. Evidence of good continuation and closure, however, pre-supposes prior knowledge, that is, memory, of what may be *plausibly* 'continued' or 'closed', as well as the capacity to identify contextual characteristics. At this stage of development perception by feature analysis is supplemented by or superseded by template matching (Neisser, 1967). In template-matching perception, incoming stimuli search for an existing match in memory with the participation of selective attention directed by short-term working memory requirements. In this and in the case of closure, however, it seems appropriate to assume that a process akin to 'chunking' of information has occurred. This must mean that the available memory structures have employed an inductive strategy and have started to achieve conceptual status.

Although it is conceptually necessary to employ models of the development of organized memory and knowledge structures, we are a long way from objective insight. As a result of the evidence of visual perceptual impairments in the congenitally blind, and those resulting from traumatic brain injury, we know that neurological competence is necessary for visual perception and for the correct recognition of previously learnt forms and objects. While we are not entitled to hold notions of structural isomorphy, such limitations do not necessarily apply to models of *functional isomorphy*. In other words, spatial

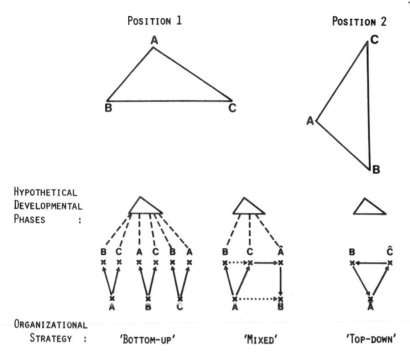

Figure 4.1 Possible stages in the development of the memory structures of a triangle

relationships in the external world may be modelled as the functional relationships between features detected by a sensory analysing system and the perceptual or conceptual whole which they define. Developmentally, this approach is shown in Figure 4.1 in relation to phases in the perception and mnemonic structuring of the representation of the same triangle in two orientations. Several theoretical positions are combined here. Those of Phase 1 assume that the percept has to be constructed from an analysis of three vertex points and the lines extending from them. This assumption takes account of the possibility that angular points or points of intersection dominate in the distribution of attention, and that a triangle can be differentiated from a cube at this developmental stage. However, an obtuse-angled triangle in two different positions cannot yet be identified as the same triangle by this strategy. The assumption is consistent with Zaphorozhets' (1965) experimental data which show that eye movements tracing around the external edges of a figure are still only partial at ages 5–6 years, but complete tracing occurs with 6–7-year-old children. This analytic approach is also consistent with neuropsychological theorizing on, respectively, the establishment of cell assemblies (Hebb, 1949) and cross-modality, cross-referenced connection forming in holographic space (Pribram, 1971) in perceptual learning. Concurrently, it demonstrates what Norman and Bobrow have termed 'bottom-up' data-driven processes in early cognitive development.

Hypothetical Phase 2 is intended to illustrate the emergence of informational redundancy and the encoding of the sensory features of an angle. The relationship between a line A–C and an angle at A permits the deduction that C must meet B – a 'top-down' process. At Phase 3 the top-down process as well as redundancy are complete since the registration of two angle stimuli and the perimeter lines joining them result in a high probability deduction that the triangles in Positions 1 and 2 are identical. The probability judgement will then be tested by attempts at mental rotation.

I have focused the discussion so far entirely on the role of the visual input system in the development of perceptual and memory structures. This system facilitates the most direct representation of knowledge and, therefore, is the most preferred sensory channel. Moreover, a great deal more is known about visual than about auditory information processing. We shall have to be concerned with audition, however, when we turn presently to the role of language in the development of cognitive structures. Furthermore the search for tactile information and its role in perceptual and conceptual learning is of the greatest importance. The Piagetian approach to the development of knowledge of objects and the relationship of objects to each other does not require restatement here. Piaget's accounts of the development of sensori-motor schemes provide much evidence of the importance of haptic stimulation and of the experienced effects of actions for object and cause-and-effect knowledge. At the same time, the Piagetian phasic concepts of cognitive development have been attracting criticism (Farnham-Diggory, 1976), and various researchers have been seeking redescriptions of early skills which would better fit the existing evidence of changes in information processing capacity (e.g. Pascual-Leone, 1970; Hamilton and Moss, 1974). To some extent it would be true to say, however, that we have not yet discovered the rules and organizational procedures by which information from more than one sensory channel yields a concept or percept. Cross-modality integration clearly starts developing at an early stage where visual, touch, and sound stimuli from objects precede the subsequent addition of verbal information. And although we have some evidence from correlational studies that pre-conceptual capacity can predict later intelligence, these correlations are low, so that pre-verbal capacity in the acquisition of sensori-motor skills provides insufficient predictive evidence for the subsequent acquisition and utilization of knowledge. Nevertheless sensori-motor schemes are a prerequisite for later skills as shown, for example, by their absence in severely subnormal children (Woodward, 1959). The later skills, however, and particularly those for optimal adult development, require natural and induced motivation in a social context, in which verbal information can be integrated with sensory information to yield more complex and elaborated cognitive structures.

(ii) Schemata as cognitive structures

The term schema was first used by Bartlett (1932) in relation to changes that occur in memory in recall and in recognition following stimulation with complex material. The recall of such material produced evidence that subjects tended to *simplify* that which had been complex, to abbreviate what had been lengthy and elaborate, and to distort content. The terms *normalizing* or *levelling*, and *accentuating* or *sharpening* have been used to describe, respectively, simplification and the retention of dominant detail. Bartlett argued that remembering was a dynamic activity involving primarily an '*effort after meaning*' which required '*turning round upon schemata*'. The schema was defined as a dynamically flexible organization of past events, their characteristics, contexts, and implications, with a large capacity for further modification by new events. Bartlett regarded remembering as an active process of reconstruction. Complex stimulation with a long and involved story containing unfamiliar concepts and words, or with pictorial material containing much detail, is *assimilated* to existing knowledge, concepts, and schemata. This process comes to reflect an individual's knowledge, attitude, and subjective interpretation of the external environment and its stimuli, rather than the veridical, objective stimulus event or events. The greater the complexity or ambiguity of stimuli, the greater the probability of subjective distortion.

Although Bartlett was clearly concerned with what we now call the encoding and retrieval operations respectively creating and depending on cognitive structures, it has been very difficult to derive precise deductions for experimental testing from his framework. Baddeley (1976), for example, seems to regard the notion of the schema as an untestable concept. But an untestable concept is not necessarily an unfruitful one in subsequent modelling of what in the nature of things are unobservable processes. Considerable evidence is in fact scattered throughout the literature to support the general idea that 'effort after meaning' is one of the most fundamental and general cognitive processes.

Quite early experimental work showed that an ambiguous visual stimulus, that is a stimulus that is capable of representing more than one object, will be recalled according to the alternative cue words that accompanied the stimulus. For example, when subjects were asked to reproduce **O—O**, those who had been 'primed' with the word 'eye-glasses' drew **O~O**, those that were primed with 'dumb-bells' drew **O—O** (Carmichael *et al.*, 1932). To prime a response means, of course, to create a response set or bias. This in turn means creating a focus of expectancy in the cognitive processing system to the effect that schematic structures serving one class of objects or events are given a low retrieval threshold prior to being stimulated by an external demand.

Again, an early experiment in social psychology was concerned to show the effect of pre-existing political attitudes on the recall of, respectively, pro- and anti-Communist prose passages (Levine and Murphy, 1943). The results showed that the stimulus material and existing political belief structures interacted, affecting both the quantity and the content at recall. Studies by Allport and Postman (1948) demonstrated the striking effects of prejudiced ethnic beliefs on visual memory. None of these results, as far as reproduced content or meaning is concerned, could have occurred without the interaction between new events and existing cognitive structures in memory which had encoded the classificatory elements of previous experience to which the experimental stimuli logically belonged.

There is abundant evidence from much more recent experiments, largely in the area of verbal learning and memory, to support the notion of an organizational schematic system of memory. Just as visual stimuli are interpreted partly by reference to categories of visual memory, so is verbal material by reference to categories of verbal representations in memory to which the verbal material refers. For that reason one finds that if subjects are asked to learn lists of unrelated words, there occurs a clustering in recall of words that are functionally and conceptually related (e.g. Bousfield, 1953). Moreover, clusters or word groups so formed tend to possess some permanence (e.g. Tulving, 1964). The important question is, of course, why does clustering occur and why is it maintained? The question can be answered from at least two angles.

In the first instance we must refer back to the development of concepts. Despite all attempts to reject an association theory of perception and memory, there seems to be no doubt that items of experience that have occurred together, which form part of the same event, or which describe the same or similar functions or characteristics, have a tendency to be more frequently recalled together, or to participate jointly in perception, than items, events, or functions that are not so related. Associative operations and structuring would be minimal if we were simply asked to say whether an event had or had not occurred. If, however, an event requires a constructive response, such as answering a verbal or written question, or if an analysis of a visual display needs to precede a response, identifying search processes guided by the interpretation of the question or task set need to be performed. These search processes are directed towards those cognitive structures which are appropriate for the analysis of the stimulus and its implications. Theoretically, and certainly developmentally speaking, this is a step-wise process. Figure 4.2 gives a hypothetical example of how a *question* about an event or object would need to be processed in general terms. Of primary interest in the present discussion, is the achievement of matching processes and their conceptual integration. Suppose the question sentence was 'Is a "House" a "Street", a "Building", or a "City"?' (Tasks of this kind are frequently found in verbal memory experiments and preferably should not be interpreted as a lack of logical sophistication of the researcher!) After the semantic and pictorial recoding stages the task of answering the question is directed by short-term working memory because the terms, 'Building', 'Street', 'House', and 'City' require interpretation and definition, both singly and as to their relationship. Clearly each term here is a separate concept but with verbal and pictorial identifiers which in the present example form an integrated cognitive structure. The information-matching search process ideally enters a conceptual organization which is mainly hierarchical, with 'City' as the concept that contains the subsidiary concepts 'Streets', 'Houses', and 'Buil-

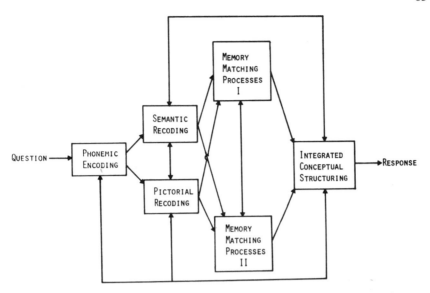

Figure 4.2 Hypothetical stages for processing a question

dings'. (Separate hierarchies can be constructed, of course, for 'Buildings' and 'Houses' as shown in Figure 4.4, since these terms describe classes of concepts.) The comparison between the concepts requires 'bottom-up' operations to check the sensory characteristics of the semantic terms. 'Top-down' operations are required to check that the principal defining features of 'House' and 'Building' match, for the inference that people may live or work in a 'House' as well as a 'Building', and for the necessary deduction that a 'House' is a 'Building'. The hypothetical example just described may clarify various aspects of what we term the classifying or categorizing of information. It also illustrates one particular type of memory schema, and the utility of information redundancy. For example, constructions which have walls, a roof, windows, and a door are the minimally required features of a house, or of buildings generally. Therefore, to know that a house is a building rather than a street or a city, one does not need to consider types of houses or streets, nor do we need to search through types of buildings or the defining characteristics of streets such as type of lampstandards, whether tree-lined or not, or the material used for surfacing and paving. This kind of knowledge is encoded in subsidiary schemata provided we have had earlier needs for fine-grain discriminating informational data which will make it available for some future decision-making operation.

The schematic structures discussed so far are those which are available to most of us because they contain organized knowledge of our basic environment. The simple examples, however, are capable of being substantially extended through subjective and idiosyncratic elaborations – as initially discussed by Bartlett. Occupational or general experiential history and, therefore, the varieties of meanings and implications which we attach to our classes of objects, events, or human characteristics, become embedded in our schematic cognitive structures. Conceptual structures, therefore, are a direct reflection of behaviour in the context of experience, and encode the meaning and implications of behaviour and experience. (This assumption is discussed in greater detail in subsequent chapters.) Any task which engages memory codes of meaning is not concerned with isolated instances or features of a stimulus situation but with a higher-order abstracted definition. It was because of such considerations that the concept of depths or levels of processing entered into memory research (e.g. Craik and Lockhart, 1972; Craik and Tulving, 1975). This model of memory holds that generally speaking events will be better remembered if they stimulate perception of meaning, that is superordinate class concepts rather than perception of isolated instances or features of classes. Although there has been some criticism of a simplified model of depth of processing (e.g. M. W. Eysenck, 1977; Baddeley, 1978), the majority of experimental findings seem to be consistent with it. In fact, it is possible to argue that deep-level conceptual processing increases the level of informational redundancy, and by reducing the need to remember a larger number of individual items increases information processing capacity. For many purposes we do not require a detailed memory, but either only the gist of it, or knowledge of the memory category to which it belongs.

A rather neat experiment by Hyde and Jenkins (1973) serves as an illustration. Two groups of subjects were shown a list of 24 words at the rate of 3 seconds per word. One group was asked to check whether a word had an *e* or a *g* while the other group was asked to rate the words on a *pleasantness* dimension. On recall trials the words which had been rated for pleasantness were nearly twice as frequently reproduced. There were no effects from prior knowledge that this was a memory experiment, or from a manipulation of incidental learning. It is reasonable to assume that subjects required to analyse the differential degree of pleasantness of words had to process word meaning and conceptual implication, whereas this cannot be assumed to have entered into the instructions and task performance for the detection of letters. Quite the contrary, any preoccupation with the conceptual aspects of the words would have interfered with the detection task.

It is necessary to remind ourselves that when we refer to the structures and hierarchical organization of memory schemata, we do not refer to actual physiological structures with fixed locations and inter-connections. Our attempt to model what we think is implied by structure and organization has to be interpreted in a functional as well as in a temporal sense. Temporal, because a different stimulus situation must by definition change the information-bearing structural organization, and functional because memory and its activation during a task do not behave like a system of cables and terminals. Any connection-forming during the process of interpreting stimuli-in-a-context, while generating a best-fitting response from available classes of responses, may need to be seen as an information processing activity employing *logical structures* and *logical connection-forming* according to the *logical* rules of the memory system (Estes, 1976a).

Estes has been working on a modified association theory of memory that could overcome the implications of a concretely conceived theory of memory structures. In this modification a 'control element' is encoded together with other stimuli, so that if two similar stimuli are presented, it is their control elements which convey the message that the stimuli are similar. Therefore, it is not the stimuli themselves but the control elements which facilitate higher-order classification of functional similarity or, I am inclined to add, identity of meaning. His approach has let Estes (1972, 1976a) to propose a model that can account for the actual process of association *as well as* the development of hierarchical conceptual memory structures. Previously, the difficulty in learning theory had been in identifying *that* aspect of associative connection-forming that is required for the development of cognitive organizations which have their origin in *diverse instances of an experience*, and in *different experiences*. A question mark remains with this model, however, in that it provides no suggestions as to how logical associational structures are used by a processing system that receives and operates on sensory, pictorial, and verbal stimulus inputs whose logical implications cannot be identified until they have been identified themselves by some symbolic 'language' which can convey meaning and outcome implications. Some of these issues will be examined in the next section.

The preceding discussion has really been concerned with the role of abstraction in category formation. Studies of abstraction and concept learning with social stimuli of different degrees of complexity have produced evidence that further supports the concept of schematic memory structures. A study by Reed (1972) investigated subjects' ability to classify simple line drawings of faces after having first learnt to classify to criterion a set of face drawings. The drawings were Brunswik faces differing in height of forehead, distance between eyes, length of nose and height of mouth from chin level. The results showed that subjects were able to extract a central tendency from the set of studied instances and to use this central tendency to help judge whether the new face drawings belonged to one or the other of two face categories. The operative strategy seemed to be to abstract a *prototype* representing each category and to compare the *distance* of novel patterns from each prototype, emphasizing those features which discriminated best between the categories of facial characteristics (Reed, 1972, p. 382). Here the schema is a prototypical combination of instances which can be applied to the identification of new instances of that type of object.

A study by B. and F. Hayes-Roth (1977) employed a more complex social stimulus setting to investigate the role played by prototypical instances, or exemplars as they call them, in conceptual schematic learning and structuring. The material here consisted of two hypothetical 'Clubs' where the relevant categorical instances defining dominant membership characteristics were marital status, age, and education. The experimental subjects were shown details of 51 hypothetical members of each 'Club'. One list showed that a majority were 30-year-old, married, and had not received higher education; the other list contained mainly people aged 50 years, unmarried and with some form of college education. No individual member of either 'Club' met all three defining characteristics of his or her 'Club'. The 'Club' prototype was defined, therefore, by any combination of two attributes. In the test trials subjects had to say whether a list of given sets of attributes was characteristic or prototypical of 'Club 1' or of 'Club 2'. As in Reed's study above, subjects were able to extract or abstract the central features of differential 'Club' membership, and employ these in the classification of previously unknown combinations of features. B. and F. Hayes-Roth (1977) posit that the demonstrated ability is an increasing function of the memory strengths of its component sets of properties, and that exemplars or component properties are classified on the basis of their most diagnostic attributes. In a further paper B. Hayes-Roth (1977a) argues that component properties become associatively linked, and that a component configuration strengthened by learning processes may become associatively structured in such a manner, that a single element may subsequently be sufficient to represent the more detailed component assembly. This developmental outcome is referred to as 'unitization'. 'Ultimately an entire knowledge structure may have a single, unitized, all-or-none activatable memory organization' (B. Hayes-Roth, 1977a, p. 260).

Like other attempts to specify the acquisition of stimulus and response meaning, this conceptualization owes much to the seminal work of Osgood (Osgood *et al.*, 1957). The acquisition of semantic labels is perhaps the crux of both the development and the utility of the cognitive schema. The schema contains abstractions of experienced events as well as the individual features and instances subsumed by the conceptional or symbolic level of the most general as well as the most characteristic unitary transformation. We may also call the unitary abstraction a *principal referent* in our knowledge structure which, to the extent that some kinds of knowledge are permanent, is likewise permanent. A principal referent will have *principal attributes*, and referents and attributes will have constellations of instance as well as feature representation. Exposure to an instance or a feature will lead in most cases to the retrieval of a high-level referent or abstraction so that the area of responding can be quickly identified by the information processing system (the 'bottom-up' process). Subsequently, and depending on the degree of precision required from a responder, the high-level prototype will stimulate the lower-level instances and features which are required for matching more precisely the details of the demand situation held in short-term working memory.

I have confined the discussion so far to knowledge structures which represent aspects of the objective and veridical physical environment. It should be apparent, however, and not only by reference to Bartlett's germinal concept, that world knowledge does not remain uninfluenced by the personal and idiosyncratic evaluations that we apply to external events. Also the degree of satisfaction and utility which we derive from the external objects of experience become important components in the representational organized cognitive structures. Satisfaction and utility, however, largely define the characteristic directions of goal-seeking behaviour. Among the dominant prototypical abstractions or dominant schematic referents, therefore, we expect to find classes of dominant goal dispositions, social attitudes, self-evaluations and response outcome expectancies which are themselves organized in schematic structures. It follows that it is not only that schemata in themselves have hierarchical structure, but that hierarchical structuring occurs *between* schemata. Moreover, the evidence of between-schemata hierarchies (some of it reviewed or implied above) makes it necessary for schemata to be able to communicate so that an orderly process of stimulus evaluation and a subjectively most acceptable response-generating decision process can be carried out. In this context, McDougall's (1923) dated concept of the 'self-regarding sentiment', and Neisser's (1967) concept of 'the executor' seem to be useful if we were to be searching for an ultimate process-controlling super schema. I shall return to the discussion of complex self-expression schemata elsewhere.

My comments regarding a hierarchical between-schemata structural organization of knowledge is in some respects a restatement of the depths and levels of processing hypothesis. As Norman and Bobrow (1976, p. 129) state: '. . . memory units use different types of descriptions at different levels of processing. Shallow depth of processing often produces descriptions of the limited physical context in which the material . . . was presented. Slightly deeper analysis yields descriptions based on the initial encoding of the information. Still deeper analyses yield descriptions based on the *semantics* of the items' (my italics). We might add that the really important factors in memory generally, as well as in schema structuring, are (i) the degree of elaboration imposed on encoded incoming stimuli as suggested by Craik and Tulving (1975), and (ii) the implications for between-schemata activation and reorganization created by elaborated coding. Elaboration, after all, can only mean that additional conceptual classes, not necessarily and directly given as stimulus features, are employed in the identification of stimulus input.

In concluding the discussion on schematic cognitive structures in the overall context of the human information processing system, I feel that I can do no better than to offer the following quotation from Norman and Bobrow (1976, pp. 124–5):

> There is a single, limited pool of resources from which processes must draw. Memory is constructed of active units – schemata – that use the data available in a common pool, perform computations upon these data, and then both send new results back (into the common pool or to other schemata) and/or request specific information from other schemata. Schemata communicate with one an-

other either directly or through the data pool. A schema consists of a framework for tying together the information about any given concept or event with specifications about the types of interrelations and restrictions upon the way things fit together. Schemata can activate procedures capable of operating upon local information and the common pool of data. Schemata can be invoked by the occurrence of data in the common data base relevant to their operations, or by requests from either other schemata or the central communication mechanism. A schema can request information of other schemata. There are no fixed memory locations in the head; therefore, memory structures must refer to one another by means of descriptions of the information that they seek. We call such references context-dependent descriptions.

I might add that it would be difficult to find a more deserved posthumous appreciation of Bartlett's much neglected original insight.

3 THE 'LANGUAGES' OF COGNITIVE STRUCTURES

This section addresses itself to issues some of which probably have no clear-cut answers. Moreover, if there were answers it is unlikely that they could be validated in any direct manner. The question is *how* and *in which form* information is stored in the cognitive structures that are composed of memory schemata. Subsidiary questions are whether all knowledge is stored in a similar form, and *how* items of knowledge stored in different forms or languages can communicate with one another.

Fortunately we have some peripheral answers to the first subsidiary question. For example we are able to demonstrate the existence of distinct memories for motor activities or skills, and there is evidence that we have pictorial, spatial, auditory, and even tactile and olfactory memories. We also know that information from different sense modalities *can* interact, that cross-modality connection-forming improves memory and also increases the amount of elaboration of the characteristics of objects and events encoded. As a result, concepts become more powerful, and fewer cues may be required to carry out successful recognition and recall tasks. And, of course, we have a verbal memory towards which the most substantial amount of experimental effort has been directed. Irrespective of the form of the encoded information and knowledge, there is general agreement that information from different sources and in different data codes combines associatively to form an internally related conceptual structure or network. One of the most recent developments in the conceptualization of the nature of the internal representation of information that has *meaning* for the person is the propositional code theory (e.g. Anderson and Bower, 1973; Norman and Rummelhart, 1975; Anderson, 1980).

In this rather brief section I am not concerned with making a case for a particular theory of memory. I am also not concerned to reaffirm that imagery, or the representation of pictorial and spatial memories involve different types of cognitive activities and are subject to different constraints, interesting though this exercise may be. Not only am I not fully competent to contribute fruitfully to this now highly specialized area of work, but it is peripheral to the major question of *how we know* that one image differs from another, and whether one particular spatial memory is a correct memory of, say, the layout of a particular building, or of a city neighbourhood. When, for example, a distinction is drawn between a visual task and a spatial task, that is, *what* something is, or *where* it is, which is a usual distinction in memory research, the *what* may be determined by the *where* and vice versa. We may only know what it is that is visually imaged by having an accurate image representation of its location. Conversely, imagery may be entirely determined by a preceding set of verbal processes which supply the relevant associational context. Clearly, information-encoding systems must have a capacity for communicating with each other. And to do that the language of communication *ultimately* must be the same.

There is a great deal of experimental evidence to show, for example, that visual and verbal memories interact. Some of the early evidence that ambiguous visual stimuli were differently recalled when different cue names had been attached to them has been mentioned before. More recent work by Bower *et al.* (1975) with ambiguous line drawings ('droodles'), presented with and without explanation of their meaning, led to better pictorial reproductions on a recall test for subjects who had verbal labels available. Rather different approaches employed an interference technique. In a frequently cited study by Brooks (1968) subjects had mentally to trace around a self-generated visual image of a three-dimensional letter *F* and either to say 'Yes' when they came to a bottom or to a top corner, and to say 'No' when it was another corner, or to point to a series of 'Ys' or 'Ns' printed irregularly on a piece of paper in front of them. The verbal response task was done more than twice as fast as the pointing response. Conversely, when subjects were asked to identify mentally the nouns of a sentence which they had previously studied by either saying 'Yes' or 'No' or pointing to a 'Y' or an 'N', pointing was substantially faster. This experiment is usually cited in support of the special interference effect resulting from two separate activities in the same modality using the same encoding language. It is also cited in support of different types of encoding for, respectively, verbal and visuo-spatial tasks. Of greater interest for the present purpose, however, is the demonstrated capacity that verbal processes can direct visuo-spatial imaging, and that a spatial activity such as pointing to a location on a piece of paper can facilitate a semantic response. If the coding languages of verbal, spatial, and visual processes are respectively indeed different, how is it possible that they can interact? It clearly requires a single data coding system to understand the specialized codes of different systems, because for associative links to become meaningful, different codes must be transformed into comparable codes.

This interpretation appears to be supported by a series of experiments carried out by Paivio (1975, 1978). In one of these, subjects were asked to make a size comparison between two objects presented as pictures. Sometimes the pictorial representation exhibited a correct size relationship between the objects, sometimes the relationship was incongruent. Subjects were able to respond more quickly when the pictorial representations were size-congruent. To say, as in one of Paivio's examples, that a zebra is bigger than the picture of a very much larger table-lamp, means that the visual and verbal-meaning processing systems must interact, even though dual-encoding memory systems may initially be required to distinguish between the visual size stimuli from objects, and between the verbal labels of objects. To overcome discrepant perceptual cues, cue meaning needs to be established. An experiment carried out by Mandler and Ritchey (1977) makes this point too. After allowing children to study a target picture of a schoolroom scene, they were later tested on recall with the target picture as well as two types of distractor pictures. One of these distractors varied in some unimportant detail, but the other altered the meaning of the original (changing a geographical map into a nature scene). This last change was detected by children more than 90 per cent of the time, illustrating once again the interacting capacity of different information coding systems in the service of analysing meaning correctly. Although there are now many studies involving verbal, visual, as well as verbal plus visual material which demonstrate conclusively that stimulus meaning is that which is best remembered (e.g. Klatzky, 1980), this still amounts to relatively little more than a restatement of Bartlett's (1932) 'effort-after meaning' concept. The question still remains: how is meaning stored and mediated in the cognitive processing system, and what is the nature of the memory code?

There may well be some general agreement that these issues are probably the most difficult and most intractable in behavioural science. Certain conceptualizations, however, are relatively unexceptional and can be stated clearly. Thus, knowledge resides in concepts; concepts are abstractions from facts and states; abstractions are propositions about relationships; and propositions are units of meaning. We are able to add that meaning in propositions is denoted by semantic labels, and that the sense of a word is the concept it denotes (e.g. Clark and Clark, 1977). Semantic labels are derived from a verbal lexicon and form themselves into associative networks which describe and define the conceptual components of objects, persons, situations, events, and issues. This is what we usually mean by encyclopaedic knowledge. Conceptual structures, therefore, consist substantially of associative semantic networks (whichever theory is preferred) which contain propositional statements about the relationships between subject, object, predicate, agent, and context. Here (though not necessarily elsewhere), context defines location and time, and must be capable, therefore, of being affected by episodic events. Anderson (1980) defines a proposition as the smallest unit of knowledge that can stand as a separate association about which it is possible to make a true or false judgement. Units of knowledge then form themselves into propositional networks – connections between abstract representations of relationship structures. The structures contain nodes or concepts by which associations are linked, and associations between nodes lead to higher-order propositions, that is, combinations of propositions. Figure 4.3 shows some examples of the propositional network approach to the representation of knowledge. These are usually in some such form as shown.

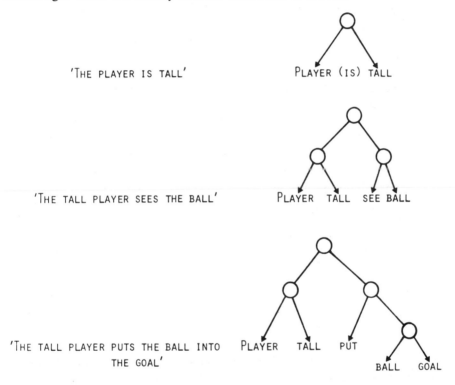

'THE PLAYER IS TALL'   PLAYER (IS) TALL

'THE TALL PLAYER SEES THE BALL'   PLAYER TALL SEE BALL

'THE TALL PLAYER PUTS THE BALL INTO   PLAYER TALL PUT
THE GOAL'   BALL GOAL

Figure 4.3 Examples of propositional networks

Although a common language for communication between modality-specific memory events would be available by applying propositional network theory to pictorial or auditory images, Anderson (1978) has also argued against this. In fact, the dual-code representation of a hypothetical chess game position which he cites there leads to a possible quite different conclusion. The positions of the pieces on the chessboard are, of course, visually imaged. But the context of the game and the identification of the implication of the positions of the pieces require semantic elaborations (Anderson, 1978, p. 253). Propositional networks have been an important feature in the development of artificial intelligence work and have contributed to the writing of computer programs which can model human comprehension and problem-solving. More recently doubts have been expressed, however, over the adequacy of the analogue in view of the limitations of their natural language encyclopaedia (Waterman and Hayes-Roth, 1978; Findler, 1979).

To integrate the different implications of a dual-code and a propositional memory model, what seems to be required initially is to confirm what is actually known.

(1) People do have sensory imagery data available for retrieval as well as propositional associations.
(2) Sensory and perceptual features are organized early in life into sensori-motor schemes of the Piagetian kind so that visual, auditory, and tactile attributes combine to form primitive denotative and connotative concepts.
(3) The lexical terms of objects, events, and situations are presented by parents together with the concrete stimuli as soon as reciprocal social interaction between parents and child is possible and appears to be enjoyable for the child.
(4) Similarly, the attributes of objects, events and situations are progressively taught by presenting together lexical terms and physical characteristics, both with and without action words. As a result associative structures develop which are simultaneously complementary and the beginnings of informational redundancy. Without lexical information our children would remain fixated at the sensori-motor stage of development and implicit action would remain the major component of thought. (See also Bates, 1979) for a biological approach to this issue.)

It is otherwise, however, and no amount of sensory imagery, or capacity to manipulate these images, is a substitute for conveying to self or others the *conceptual meaning and implications* of images. Let us assume for argument's sake, that a child of between, say, 18–24 months appears to want to obtain a piece of chocolate from a table with the help of a chair. We see him moving the chair, attempting to climb it, but then he stops, looks around, and runs into the garden from which the voices of other children can be heard. Are we to analyse this behaviour by saying that auditory cues have changed a visual image involving the eating of chocolate to another image of children playing with him in the garden, or is it more appropriate to say that his *evaluation* of a new stimulus makes him give priority over the original physically and socially risky plan? And what does the new evaluation consist of? Other visual images, images of outcomes, or the *meaning of images and outcomes*, on the basis of knowing what the words 'ball', 'garden', 'spade' and 'other children' convey to him?

We have similar problems of understanding the processes operating at an earlier stage of the pre-verbal child. The manipulation of a toy which the child has himself selected from a box of other toys, and which forms part of a sequence of actions with known results (because he has done it all before), require us to think of communication between visual, tactile, and outcome memory images. The correct behaviour logic shown by the child indicates the presence of cognitive structures which may contain some kind of propositions and relational associations. Some form of abstraction must have occurred if there is evidence of learning and planning in the activity and, therefore, of communication between visual, tactile, and motor memories. In the days of simple conditioning theory we might have been content to refer to contingency learning. Today, the evidence of developing conceptual structures requires more. What we might say in the present example is that what has been learnt and what guides the behaviour sequence is a representation of the goal, probably in the form of motor schemata. The goal maybe putting one hollow cube into another in such a way that it matches an existing memory structure of past visual and tactile representations and its associated motor movements. That leaves us to account for the ability of visuo-perceptual ability to select the correct objects to achieve the representational goal. And this raises the question of how that is possible without verbal knowledge, unless we are prepared to consider the possibility that eye movements and other ocular events produce motor data in addition to visual representations. In this case a common motor language is available for the child to help him obtain his goal. Clearly, his level of speculation is basically unhelpful. Fortunately, we have a better approach available to explain the development of knowledge and conceptual structures *once the memory systems are able to utilize verbal cues and labels.* This must occur much earlier than has been accepted so far, and is clearly a function of parental verbalization during early play with the child.

I want to argue, therefore, that the language of perception, memory, and thought for all practical purposes is lexical, semantic, and verbal-relational. Without words there would be no higher-order concepts, no economic encoding of diversity of meaning, of fine-grain differentiation between stimuli and their most appropriate response demands, and no capacity to communicate to others concepts, shades of meaning, or fine-grained implications of objects and events. We can argue *with* Aristotle that categories of thinking require words, *with* Whorf (1956) that specificity of a lexicon determines the differentiation of thought, and can accept anthropological findings that levels of complexities of organized societies are matched by the vocabulary and semantic differentiation of the societies' languages. In other words, there are mutually supportive interactions between language, thought, and response demands from the external environment.

I have previously discussed at some length the possibility that the combination of sensory features, the combination of instances of feature extraction and the experienced utility of a response, lead to organized conceptual structures. These are hierarchically arranged, no matter which model of the process we are considering. We assume that the apex of the structure represents the higher-order conceptual abstraction. Let us return to our example of the child above who joins other children for play in the garden. If his mother had intervened and had said to him: 'The chocolate *is for you after your lunch. Go* and *play with* the *others* in *the garden now*', the child's action would be called verbally mediated. This short-hand definition, however, hides what I would regard as the core of concept formation and of abstraction. Each italicized word has acquired the power of conveying knowledge, understanding, and meaning, each of them stands for and is a symbol of implicit assumptions and actions, and of outcome expectancies.

Miller (1978), in concluding a symposium on language organized by the Society for Research in Child Development looks at linguistic, philosophical, and psychological perspectives in language acquisition. He comes to the conclusion that at present we have no method of following the process of lexical acquisition, and that we have no theory of how it occurs. What we do have is empirical evidence that words can assume the role of actions, images, intentions, and plans, and knowledge of their results, implications, or outcomes. From this it must follow that language plays a dominant role in the development of concepts, that verbally oriented processes participate in perception, and that the schemata of long-term memory, their referents and constellations of attributes and their causal and relational implications have attracted verbal labels and signifiers. It is a truism to say that a single word can open a treasure trove of experience or a manual of instructions.

Although cognitive theorists favouring a propositional network of memory agree that an abstract modelling of the representations of knowledge cannot yet specify the *method* by which we become aware of verbally or image-driven stimulus meaning, they nevertheless believe that propositional networks encode meaning (e.g. Anderson, 1976; Schank, 1975; Bower *et al.* 1979). If we cannot conceive of non-semantic propositions this can only mean that relational associations without verbal denotation cannot exist. Since higher-order propositions encode higher-order meaning, this must also mean that lexical labels give way to semantic labels and their connotations at the higher conceptual level.

A lucid paper by B. Hayes-Roth (1977b) makes a very strong case against a non-lexical representation of concepts in memory. In three separate experiments she showed that when subjects in a recognition test were asked to discriminate between 'studied' and synonymous words and sentences, they verified the 'studied' material faster and with greater confidence than the synonymous, and were less distracted by synonymous words. She concluded that lexical information is present and persists in memory. Lexical representation is regarded as more economical than the many components required to specify propositions, its direct input is more efficient, it provides ease of access, minimizes interference, and facilitates direct inferential operations. Since propositional networks in any case require lexical specification, the direct lexical encoding of conceptual information reduces the number of encoding levels. The assumption actually receives considerable unintended support from the work of Rosch (1973, 1975; Rosch and Mervis, 1975; Rosch *et al.*, 1976) on the role of family resemblance, or category prototypes. Rosch was able to demonstrate that even in societies which do not possess colour names, typicality or centrality of an instance of a particular colour could be easily acquired. Like Hayes-Roth (1977a), therefore, she regards a process of unitization essential for the representation of a concept category. Moreover, where verbal labels are available, applying a name or attribute to a prototypical abstraction produces a semantically defined category allowing direct access to a core meaning. Criticisms that no single prototypical unit can define a whole category are probably misplaced because the identification of meaning requires access to associated or subsidiary conceptual classes, and to contexts in a given relationship. This more complex function, however, belongs to a schema and not to isolated semantically labelled prototypes.

The advantages of the propositional model of supplying a generally applicable model of inference rules need not be lost if inferences are expressed in terms of category words. It is worth noting in this context that it is not propositional relationships and associations that are actually recalled when we try to remember, but verbalized specifications and relationships, and/or constructed images conforming to rules of meaningfulness (Anderson, 1980). For practical purposes I will assume, therefore, that concept specifications, knowledge, and the abstraction of meaning in the verbally competent person are encoded lexically, that lexical units provide our encyclopaedia of the referents and attributes of our external and internal experiential environment, and that concept-specifying relationships between lexical units symbolize semantic knowledge – the meaning of words, of concepts, and of the classes of concepts. Theoretical views of this type have led to the development of semantic network models as a paradigm of the content of the memory schema.

There are at least three variants of semantic memory and knowledge theories, but I will refer briefly to only two of them because they are particularly central to my overall aim. The first gives prominence to the hierarchical semantic organization of concepts and is associated with the work of Collins and Quillian (1969, 1972). In this model superordinate and subordinate concepts are so structured that the necessary defining features of subordinate class concepts are stored only at the superordinate level. Figure 4.4 shows a hypothetical and idiosyncratic semantic network of this kind around the superordinate concept of 'Building'. Some of the arrows stand for *is* or *has*. They show the relationship links between super- and subordinates, or between referents and attributes, and link the concepts to the features and attributes which are characteristic of each concept. In this example subordinate referents have been defined by attributes which are either conceptually necessary and sufficient, or subjectively elaborative. The meaning of the concept 'Building' can be obtained directly by entering the network at the superordinate level. To answer the question 'Is a castle a building?' would hypothetically require an additional search and verification process to a subordinate conceptual structure because the attributes 'Rooms', 'Door' and 'Roof' may be insufficient to define a castle ruin. The model was proposed not only to make a case for semantic conceptual codes, but to suggest a

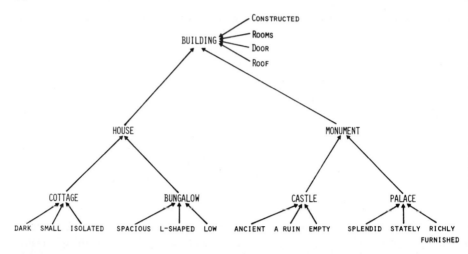

Figure 4.4 A fragment of a hypothetical network defining the concept 'building'

method of information storage economy which appears to be so characteristic of memory as well as of the concept of the schema itself. The basic form of this model, however, and its predictions about differences in speed of verifying verbal statements involving exemplars, features, and attributes combined within a network, have been difficult to confirm in a number of experiments.

The second variant of semantic network theory involves a modification of Collins and Quillian's original model and is usually referred to as a spreading-activation theory of semantic processing (Collins and Loftus, 1975). This variant maintains the basic idea of a hierarchical structure involving super- and subordinate semantically coded concepts, but also provides for a lexical network so that a large number of inter-connected concepts can be directly activated by a stimulus, even before their attributes are activated.

Complex networks of a single concept develop as a consequence of a multiple specification of the concept. For example, 'Domesticated Farm Animals' requires links between the properties of 'Animals', 'Domesticated', and 'Farm'. Closeness of concepts is defined by the number of direct and indirect links between them, where the links are determined by the degree of semantic association. Because of the larger number of cross-referenced and associated conceptual links, any stimulus to which a response is required may progressively activate greater proportions of a semantic network until a decision in working memory terminates the process. In other words, the greater the number of links between concepts or referents, or between different exemplars of a category or between referents, exemplars, and attributes or characteristics, the larger the network, and the more elaborate the schematic structure. The more complex a stimulus, and particularly a stimulus in a complex context, the more widespread the activation of the linked structures will be (Collins and Loftus, 1975). This version of semantic network theory is more generally accepted because it accounts for a larger number of experimental results. Furthermore, the notion of spread of activation describes a cognitive process that must be fundamental not only in memory search but also in the act of perception. Spread of activation is certainly also central to the propositional network model discussed earlier (e.g. Anderson, 1980). This more complex approach to the semantic encoding of experiences and knowledge will provide the basis for the reinterpretation of characteristic goal-directed behaviour in subsequent chapters.

We have seen that knowledge of the shared external environment is achieved gradually, that the early pre-verbal representations of objects, events, and situations acquire abstract representation by the utilization of verbal signifiers, and that functionally related referents and attributes organize themselves into inter-linked systems which have been termed schemata. The conceptual content of schemata in the verbal person appears to be semantically encoded, so that stimulus evaluation and response selection proceed through an analysis of verbally conveyed meaning of stimulus characteristics and implications, and the selection of equally meaning-determined responses which provide the best possible match at the semantic conceptual level of analysis.

To elevate semantic codes to the position of a dominant language by which experience from all sense modalities can be integrated does not imply that non-verbal sensory images either do not exist or do not contribute in stimulus evaluation and response choice. However, there seems little doubt that images become available as the result of preceding experience. This may be an external verbal stimulus or an internal conceptual one. If, however, concepts are validly defined by semantic labels, and if the image itself conveys meaning, then it should follow that images which respond only to a semantic stimulus are themselves definable only by another set of semantic terms.

The discussion of memory and knowledge structures and the language of their representational content has been directed almost entirely to the veridical and objectifiable environment and the sensory data it presents. We know, however, that memory schemata contain information which is subjective, which reflects affective and emotional responses and evaluations, and that affective, emotional, and interpersonal relationship data and evaluations may become generalized across situations and, therefore, across schemata. We also know that there are concepts about the self and about the relationship of self to valued others, that we have concepts about preferred goals and response outcomes, and that we conceptualize about alternative methods of reaching these preferred goals and outcomes. I am going to argue, therefore, that self- and self-related concepts differ in only three ways from general knowledge concepts: in type of encoded content or data, in terms of spread and elaboration of associative connotative structure, and in the degree to which affect is encoded as an associated attribute in cognitive schemata.

CHAPTER 5

Social determinants of cognitive structures

The data which are encoded in cognitive structures, and the knowledge which they represent in differentially elaborated cognitive-semantic schemata are both derived from interactions with an external physical and cultural environment. Although the physical environment on its own can provide the data for all spatial schemata, it is appropriate to label this environment 'social' for three reasons. Firstly, and obviously, because from infancy to old age no one is 'an island unto himself' (to mix two well-known aphorisms), and other people play the most significant role in providing, maintaining, or restricting interaction with physical reality. Secondly, because the range of available stimulation and its utilization in behaviour are governed by the culture patterns, role-playing opportunities and broad technological diversification of society, its subcultures and caretakers. Thirdly, and perhaps most relevant, the individual's knowledge of his environment is largely influenced by verbal and non-verbal communication from another person, or persons. It can be argued, of course, that not all perception is social perception. This is perfectly true if the term social perception is restricted to the analysis and influence of the behaviour of other people, or to the influence of social value norms. On the other hand, it is well known that a variety of sensory or perceptual deprivation settings, as well as experience deprivation, lead to impoverished or suboptimal response capacity in which even genetically pre-programmed perceptual skills such as size and distance judgements can become impaired. In this chapter I shall discuss the effect of socially mediated experience on the development of cognitive structures and on the schematic organization of the knowledge data which is encoded by them. I shall argue that the interaction between the individual and the environment is essentially an informational interaction, that the principal outcome of socialization and child-rearing strategies is cognitive development, and that communication plays a necessary role in attaining optimal levels of development. The early sections of this chapter, particularly, will demonstrate the presently existing gap between laboratory tests of cognitive processing theory and information processing concepts, and the acquisition of conceptual structures in a real-life developmental setting. My comments will indicate, I hope, that I regard the gap as bridgeable, and many of my assumptions as verifiable by properly focused experiments.

1 INFORMATIONAL ANALYSIS OF THE SOCIAL ENVIRONMENT

The present context dictates a heuristic economy. Somewhat dogmatically, therefore, the discussion must restrict itself to the most immediate environment: *people* and *objects*, and the relationships in which they may be found which lead to *events* or *situations*. Excluded, therefore, are the considerable informational attributes of climate and fluctuations of weather, of geographical topography, and of astronomy or cosmology, except in so far that they must be included under the general heading of educational information. Also excluded is a fine-grained analysis of the physical, ecological environment and its institutional structures except where they affect the characteristics of individuals, or where they may be given the status of objects. An assessment of the field of *Environmental Psychology* is excluded except when considering environmental stressors (e.g. Proshansky *et al.*, 1976; Stokols, 1978, 1979).

Individual people, objects, events, and situations are identified by overt or inferred attributes or characteristics, some of which acquire greater salience, or general descriptive or prescriptive importance. Attributes – whether central or peripheral – identify or define concepts. The larger the number of attributes attached to an object, person, event, or situation, the greater the amount of knowledge we possess about it whether it be objectively correct or false. The greater the amount of knowledge, the more complex the concept, and the more elaborated the schema or schemata in which it is functionally organized. The more elaborated the schema, the more complex the cognitive structures, their pathways, their decision nodes, and cross-referenced inter-modality associations. The greater these complexities, the greater the information processing demands of a stimulus situation and its response demands. Because a social environment is defined by the concurrent actions, goals, and judgements of individuals, in addition or in response to our behaviour, as well as by objects, events, and situations with social implications, a significant dimension of the social environment is its potential informational complexity. For example, if a schoolchild is asked to add up dinner money paid in by the children in his class for the last 12 weeks, this is a simpler task than if this child were one of a group of children each of whom had to make this kind of calculation *in a competitive setting of speed and accuracy.*

There are at least two significant differences between the concept of a common object and the concept of the same object when it forms part of a social event. Consider the difference between the concepts '*football*' and '*playing football*'. The attributes: *round, hard, brown, bouncy*, even allowing for the elliptical form of the rugby or American football, are likely to be shared. The additional concept '*playing*', however, does not merely elicit the prototypical or focal physical attributes of a particular activity, but the social and personal implications of that activity for one particular individual. These can include the innocuous associations of a satisfying social interaction with a shared competitive aim of playing well together and not losing a game, or they may centre on a highly technical analysis of passing strategy, ball control, or refereeing controversies as produced by a professional player. Let us take the case, however, where *'playing football'* is conceptually associated with ideal self-concepts of excellence and achievement, or, alternatively, with anxieties and doubts concerning competence, social acceptance and thus social status. Here the range of concept identifiers is appropriately enlarged to include informational data which describe social evaluations either objectively present, or inferred with uncertainty from objectively or subjectively ambiguous signals. Clearly, the cognitive structures of objects and events in a social context encode meanings and anticipations of outcome which exceed the basic requirement of category labels.

It follows that the informational complexity of the individual's environment is primarily defined by three factors: (i) the degree of conceptual differentiation offered by objects in the inanimate environment which require or invite interaction; (ii) the type and differentiation of interaction with another person or a group of individuals; (iii) the *subjective experience* of complexity which depends on individual differences in capacity to handle and process information.

As argued in Chapter 3, there are obvious difficulties in defining the terms information and informational complexity, and whichever unit of quantification is used it can be argued that anything more precise than an ordinal scale of ordering is not feasible here. This is consistent with tradition: six pairs of associates in a paired-association task contain less information than a list of eight word pairs, and simultaneously observing four dials on a piece of apparatus or machinery requires attention to more relevant information than the observation of only two dials. Similarly, a Piagetian type of multiple classification task in which, say, a series of identically shaped coloured drawings of a leaf have to be arranged in the most logical order, requires simultaneous processing of two dimensions of information: size and hue. An even more complex informational setting is embodied in the task assessing concept attainment used by Bruner *et al.* (1956). This task contained an array of instances in which four dimensions of information varied simultaneously: number of shapes, type of shape, colour, and number of borders. From these examples we can derive a two-dimensional definition of *social* information and informational complexity: number of stimuli simultaneously present, and number of stimulus attributes necessarily involved in and logically affecting decision-making prior to responding.

This somewhat gross but operational definition has a number of useful implications for a reassessment of the nature of environmental effects on the development and utilization of cognitive structures and conceptual operations. Rural life, or living anywhere in comparative 'social isolation' is said to be 'simpler' than living in a city, or by a heavy appointments schedule. Interpreting 'simple' or 'social isolation' in terms of amount of variable and simultaneous stimuli, objects, or events possessing multiple stimulus attributes, yields an information complexity definition for life style and social pressure. The simple and socially confined mode of living is a concomitant of the reduced number of objects, of other individuals, and of their interactions in this type of environment. Also, object and person attributes and their interactions are more reliably predictable because unexpected attributes rarely intrude. According to Berlyne (e.g. 1963, 1970) this constitutes a reduction in novelty and should lead to reduced levels of peripheral and central arousal. Moreover, this combination of cognitive and physiological events describes the reduction of stresses which is aimed for on vacation, or duing therapeutic interruptions of a busy life. Vulnerability to informational stressors arising in the social environment will be discussed in Chapter 8. We are concerned at this stage with the opportunities to profit cognitively from socially mediated environmental stimulation, and with the influence of ecological diversity, or of constriction.

Let us consider the constricted social setting first. The effects of sensory handicap could permanently impair the elaboration of cognitive structures unless special educational techniques were used to by-pass affected input channels. To obtain relatively normal levels of conceptual development in, for example, deaf children (e.g. Furth, 1964; McCay Vernon, 1967), requires personalized, often individual contact with a teacher, special techniques and, therefore, compensatory sources of information. The effects of sensory handicap can be similar to the results of gross social handicaps. Many studies summarized by Clarke and Clarke (1974), including those carried out by themselves, have shown that a state of intellectual pseudo-subnormality can occur in children who have been exposed to an extreme socially depriving environment. Such an environment was defined not only by neglectful and rejecting parental attitudes towards their offspring, a factor which will be considered in the next section, but by a home and living environment which lacked minimal comforts for sleeping and eating, as well as toys whether purpose-made, or contrived. The more adverse the environment the greater the cognitive effect of such subcultural environments. This relationship was established by finding substantially larger increments in IQs in children from the most adverse backgrounds, compared with children from somewhat less depriving homes, after long periods of residence in a subnormality institution. The principal reason for the deficit in cognitive development was the absence of a normal experience environment in which benevolent social interaction occurs and in which objects can be played with and manipulated in relation to other objects so that their general attributes may be discovered and compared and contrasted. The lack of normal play, especially with other children, would restrict knowledge of cause-and-effect relationships, and the acquisition of rule-governed behaviour. Animal studies carried out in Hebb's laboratory (Hebb, 1949) have provided comparable evidence. Dogs as well as rats reared in perceptually impoverished and restrictive environments with substantially reduced opportunities for exploration, for adaptation to unexpected or novel events, or practice in species-specific skills, showed large deficits in problem-solving and other adaptive behaviour when released from their confinement. These deficits were absent in litter-mates reared in normal conditions.

It seems valid to argue that these observations on children and animals reflect a suboptimal development of cognitive structures and knowledge schemata. In both cases there was a reduction in sensory input as well as a reduction in delivering and practising responses. Both types of reductions represent limitations in information received, encoded, analysed, and utilized in planning contingent responses. Concurrent deprivation of interactions with parents and peers leads to retardation of language development so that post-sensori-motor stages of development would be reached without an optimal symbolic labelling system. In addition, there is little doubt that this type of social environment would produce a positive feedback loop between low motivation, fear of punishment, and reduced activity.

Ecological or informational *diversity* have obvious contrasting developmental effects, except in those instances (to be discussed in the next section but one) where an enriched social environment is experienced as intrusive, overpowering, and thus aversive. A stimulating social setting, inviting and encouraging exploration of objects and situations, contains an abundance of opportunity for the discovery of object attributes, and cause-and-effect relations, and sensory information. Varieties of toys and articles of general use in the home present contrasting and similar informational data for the establishment of concept-bearing cognitive structures, elaborated knowledge schemata, and associations between functionally related schemata. Where an optimal social environment is paired with optimal opportunities for and practice in verbal interactions, structures and schemata achieve a new level of flexibility to proceed towards the acquisition of formal logical operations, and the acquisition and representation of higher-order, abstract social and personal concepts.

It is necessary to refer, at least briefly, to social group and to genetic factors which contribute to the availability and utilization of environmental information. Poverty, physical and psychological pathology, absence from school or work, overcrowding, family separation, or death, singly, or, as is frequently the case, in close causal relationship, will affect the content and quantity of information available in such environmental settings. It requires effort to overcome these disadvantages, either for the optimal development of children, or for the achievement of an adult social life experienced as satisfying. In the presence of many of the criteria of social disadvantage and deprivation for substantial populations, it seems to be as fully appropriate to point to the large number of individuals who have shown the capacity to surmount them, and to identify the reasons for this capacity, as it would be to aim for the reduction of disadvantage and deprivation.

Despite cogent critical assessments of the data base on which conclusions about the substantial contribution of genetic endowment to measured intelligence rely (e.g. Kamin, 1974), the available evidence nevertheless assigns a dominant role to biological endowment (see P. E. Vernon, 1976, 1979 for recent reviews). Since information held in cognitive structures requires biological material for the process of encoding, storing, and connection-forming, the capacity for relational conceptual processes must be, in the final analysis, a function of biological capacity and efficiency. Hebb (1949), who otherwise supported a sufficiency role for experience in cognitive development, clearly favoured the ultimate limitation of intelligence by genetic/physiological factors. His concepts of *Intelligence A* and *B* can serve us well to model the relationship between the internal representation of socially-mediated information and the availability of this information. Figure 5.1 tries to show in one particular though gross manner what may be involved if, as has been

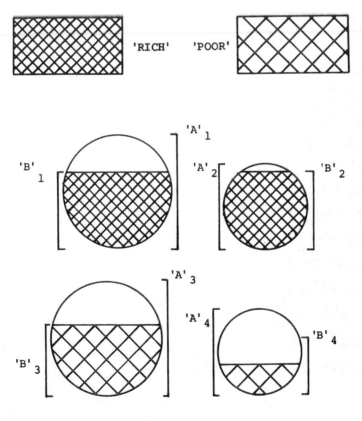

Figure 5.1 Encoding, storing and connection-forming capacity of contrasting physiological systems

argued, social environments differ in degree in informational complexity, and if physiological structures vary in degree of encoding and connection-forming capacity.

Let the two rectangles in Figure 5.1 be two environments differing in degree of informational variation and complexity as represented by the different density of cross-hatching. That is, environments differing in the number of referents to which the individual can and wants to relate himself, and the number of referent-defining attributes yielding knowledge generated by the interactions. Let the two pairs of circles represent the contrasting processing systems differing in capacity and efficiency. Systems 'A'$_1$ and 'A'$_3$ are genetically well endowed. Systems 'A'$_2$ and 'A'$_4$ are either less well endowed, or affected by intra-uterine or post-partum trauma. The index 'B' is used to represent the extent to which neurobiological characteristics are utilized in the development of cognitive structures and in knowledge representation in schemata. Three implications of the interaction are modelled here. The first shows the obvious – that an environment rich in information-bearing stimuli will produce more elaborated and more finely differentiated cognitive structures and schemata than an environment lacking in stimulus variability. Secondly, from the gap between the heights of 'A'$_1$ and 'B'$_1$ and 'A'$_2$ and 'B'$_2$ it may be inferred that the latter system received and was able to benefit more from social support and incentive to make optimum use of its more limited biological capacity, compared with the 'A'$_1$–'B'$_1$ system. The third implication highlights the most unfavourable situation: the interaction between low physiological capacity, a stimulus-impoverished environment, and lack of social inducement to profit optimally from a low-level-experience social setting.

Whereas the above discussion has centred on the diversity of stimulus objects, events, and situations, as well as individual interactions with them in the immediate experience area of home and family, there are more indirect sources of social information we need to consider. These sources belong to the macrosystem of social organization and social institutions. Their effects are mediated in two related ways: by direct contact, and by their influence on the agents of socialization. The latter will be discussed in the next section.

When we refer to the relationship between the social macrosystem and the development of an individual's cognitive structures, we are referring, of course, to an individual's concepts of institutions and organizations, as well as concepts of their functions for the smooth running and benefit of society at large. Awareness and comprehension of the functions and aims of hierarchically structured institutions depend on the capacity to integrate information concerning this, on direct contact with any aspect of institutional structures, and on secondary sources of information available through newspapers, radio, TV, and books. At least two fairly plausible propositions can be offered about the development of cognitive structures encoding this type of conceptual knowledge.

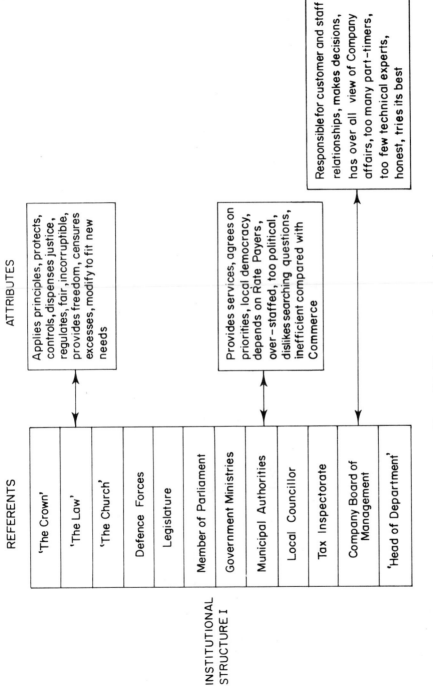

ATTRIBUTES

Applies principles, protects, controls, dispenses justice, regulates, fair, incorruptible, provides freedom, censures excesses, modify to fit new needs

Provides services, agrees on priorities, local democracy, depends on Rate Payers, over-staffed, too political, dislikes searching questions, inefficient compared with Commerce

Responsible for customer and staff relationships, makes decisions, has over all view of Company affairs, too many part-timers, too few technical experts, honest, tries its best

REFERENTS

'The Crown'

'The Law'

'The Church'

Defence Forces

Legislature

Member of Parliament

Government Ministries

Municipal Authorities

Local Councillor

Tax Inspectorate

Company Board of Management

'Head of Department'

INSTITUTIONAL STRUCTURE I

Figure 5.2 (*Continued over page*)

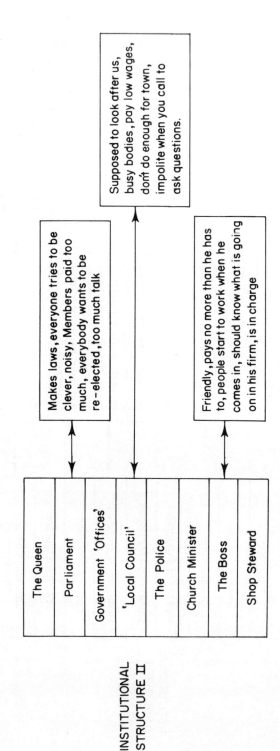

Figure 5.2 Fragments of two differentially elaborated referent-attribute structures representing social institutions

(1) The more restricted an individual life style by choice, tradition, misfortune, or general intellectual interest and capacity, the smaller, the more imprecise, the more undifferentiated and unelaborated his or her conceptual structures of institutions.

(2) The greater the amount of personal use and intrinsic conceptual interest in the running of society's institutions, the more differentiated and the larger the number of concept supporting referents and attributes.

Figure 5.2 offers contrasting illustrations of these propositions by reference to two hypothetical fragments of institutional referent-attribute structures, obtained from two hypothetical persons, which vary in level of differentiation and conceptual generalization. Although these examples can be thought of as saying nothing particularly new to the point of being self-evident, we must be aware of the special context in which the propositions are being considered. Firstly, individual personality and motivational characteristics are both influenced by, and subsequently interact with, various social institutions at some point of a life cycle. Therefore, the kinds of concepts about them will interact with an individual's characteristic forms of behaviour towards goal-achievement. Secondly, the more detailed, hierarchically structured and differentiated the knowledge data describing the functions and implications of social institutions, the greater the capacity to integrate this knowledge adaptively for the purpose of individual goal-achievement despite apparent obstacles. Thirdly, it can be argued, as I shall do later, that an informational analysis of social structures and institutions provides a more precise definition of social stress, that is, of stressors as they ought to be termed more correctly (see also Hamilton, 1979a, 1980).

2 SOCIALIZATION INTERPRETED AS COGNITIVE DEVELOPMENT

Socialization is an end result as well as an ongoing process. I define the term as the acquisition of knowledge and of behavioural skills which reflect the normative characteristics of an individual's family and his dominant peer groups. Knowledge and behavioural skills are acquired because individuals are born with a need to engage in activity which is experienced as intrinsically self-rewarding, because they facilitate socially independent activities, and because they lead to interactions which are experienced as pleasant and need-reducing. The types and levels of socialization are substantially determined by five major factors.

(1) The preferred mode of organized life of society, the individual's appropriate reference groups and their formalized rules for role behaviour and role-playing interactions.

(2) The degree to which institutional rules, knowledge and acceptance of rules and role-playing opportunities, and the capacity and willingness to transmit them, are present in the principal socializing agents.

(3) The ability of the child or adult to internalize, understand, and profit by what is transmitted.

(4) The power and appropriateness of techniques and strategies of socialization.

(5) The degree to which strategies and techniques employed by socializing agents communicate attitudes and evaluations experienced as favourable and supportive by the recipient.

Each of these five determinants operates through the transmission of informational data and their encoding along lines of subjective evaluation and meaningfulness. Let us consider each in turn.

(i) Society

In the earlier discussion of the representation of knowledge in long-term memory schemata it was argued that conceptual cognitive structures depend on experience. It follows that the more highly differentiated a society with respect to specialized institutions, codified and stratified rules of conduct, role prescriptions and ascriptions of status, the larger the number of concepts its members can potentially acquire. With rules for highly valued rewards and equally highly aversive sanctions, norm conformity is encouraged, if not induced. This is particularly true if societies or their subgroups are being subjected to pressure from outside, or to stressors from within the group in conditions in which the maintenance of a traditional way of life is threatened. By contrast to this 'closed' type of society, the 'open' society modifies its institutionalized rules. It widens the prototypical concepts of individual norms, provides for 'extenuating circumstances' in which previously established status and role-playing boundaries may be breached, and introduces new rules and conventions to identify 'exceptional circumstances' and permissible methods of dealing with them.

These considerations identify two independent dimensions which can describe the informational complexity of societies or their larger subgroups: the elaboration of a limited number of prescriptive rules of conduct, and the extension of the range of individual behaviour areas to which rules are made to apply. In both cases institutional changes increase informational complexity, and social adaptation requires an elaboration of schemata embedded in cognitive structures to maximize norm-conforming capacity. As an example of the elaboration of a limited set of rules we may cite taxation laws. The core concept is to contribute a percentage of earnings to be used for the needs of society as a whole. As a result of accountancy skills, tax-evasion strategies which are within the law have been developed. If these become too widespread, insufficient taxes would be collected to meet community requirements. As a consequence tax laws have been 'strengthened', that is, where tax-evasion loopholes existed, these were abolished by writing very specific subclauses into particular taxation-qualifying categories.

An example of the second dimension of institutional regulation may be taken from municipal bye-laws designed to cope with the ever-increasing flow of motor traffic. In older-established societies the new pressures on space could not be anticipated so that many roads are too narrow, road junctions are not designed for easy traffic-flow, and busy shopping centres and through-traffic arteries are rarely separated. In order to protect the rights of all road users and facilitate an efficient flow of traffic on existing and new roads, regulations have been widened in scope to deal as systematically as possible with the integrations of everyone's rights and needs. Figure 5.3 can serve as an example of different modifications of basic 'Rights Of Way' rules. The different traffic orders and road directions show how central social concepts have been expanded, and how norms for road usage behaviour have been extended to new contingencies. Particularly relevent to our discussion of cognitive development is the increase in the amount of information to be processed simultaneously, and, therefore, the increase in cognitive complexity of the environment for those who already use it independently, as well as for those whose task is the transmission of the norms of conduct and conceptual knowledge of object attributes and symbolic communication.

Figure 5.3 Elaborations of institutional regulations and information overload

(ii) Socializing agents

(a) Parental transmission of social information

It is agreed that the major influences are those of parents or other caretakers, the formal educational policies of schools, and peer groups or friends. Each one of them transmits aspects of the general culture pattern with specific contributions to conceptual knowledge dependent on the socializing role associated with them. Thus the unique contribution of home and parents is directed to the acquisition of skills serving the primary motives of eating, drinking, toileting, being independently active, and the early search for new information through exploration. The specialized contribution of the educational system is directed to the acquisition of formalized symbolic knowledge represented by language, numerical operations and implications, and formal concepts of biological, physical, and ecological events and interactions. The peer group reflects some of the effects of the above two influences and principally supplies feedback through its social interaction patterns. These lead to the acquisition of more elaborated concepts of norms and of conformity requirements, of the status implications of personal skills and capacities, and to modifications of conduct concepts learnt in the other settings which may or may not be at variance with them. In what follows I shall continue to employ an informational analysis of the influences mediated by agents since the direct as well as the implied relevance of any form of stimulation lies in the informational data which it presents to a skill-acquiring and response-generating behaviour system.

The influence of parents and other child caretakers operates along two dimensions: *knowledge* of rules, norms, conventions, and opportunities afforded by society and its subgroups, and *ability and incentive* to apply the knowledge. Knowledge of norms, etc. is encoded in the agents' own cognitive structures like any other knowledge acquired during their own periods of socialization. When they reach the novel phase of child-rearing, they will apply initially the procedures and skills retrievable from long-term memory which represent their own historical experiences organized in cognitive structures. Only subsequently may these be modified by changes in conventions and opportunities that have become available since their own childhood. For these reasons parental socializing knowledge lies on a gradient of cognitive elaboration. This ranges from few and minimally differentiated knowledge data, to a large number of relevant schemata encoding fine-grained differentiations incorporating constraints and facilitations dependent on sequences of events and contexts. It seems plausible to suggest, therefore, that the cognitive structures of socialization knowledge reflect individual differences in information content as modelled in Figure 5.1 and 5.2 for degrees of categorical diversity as well as for degrees of specification of referents by differences in number of attributes. This suggestion seems to be particularly strengthened by the consistently significant relationship between parental educational level and socio-economic group membership and socialization capacities and strategies (e.g. Bernstein, 1961; Hess and Shipman, 1965; Hamilton, 19721a). A simply and traditionally organized society, as argued before, is likely to have a smaller set of norms and role-playing expectancies than an open, complexly unstable (or dynamically stability-seeking) industrialized society. This will determine not only the number of necessarily acquired concepts, but the potential amount of stress-inducing conflicts between rules and conventions originating in interacting foci of personal and socially sanctioned goals. On this basis it may be argued that what is conveyed by socializing agents is not only information to encourage and guide diversity of behavioural skill, but different *levels of informational load*. These are presented to the child's processing system before he or she may be altogether ready to distinguish between mutually exclusive alternative instructions, and instructions with alternative implications depending on context. Two hypothetical extreme situations are sketched in Figure 5.4. The variations in cross-hatching the processing load factor have the same implications as those of Figure 5.1, and child-rearing and social adaptation referents are quantitatively conceived as shown by differences in the number of concepts.

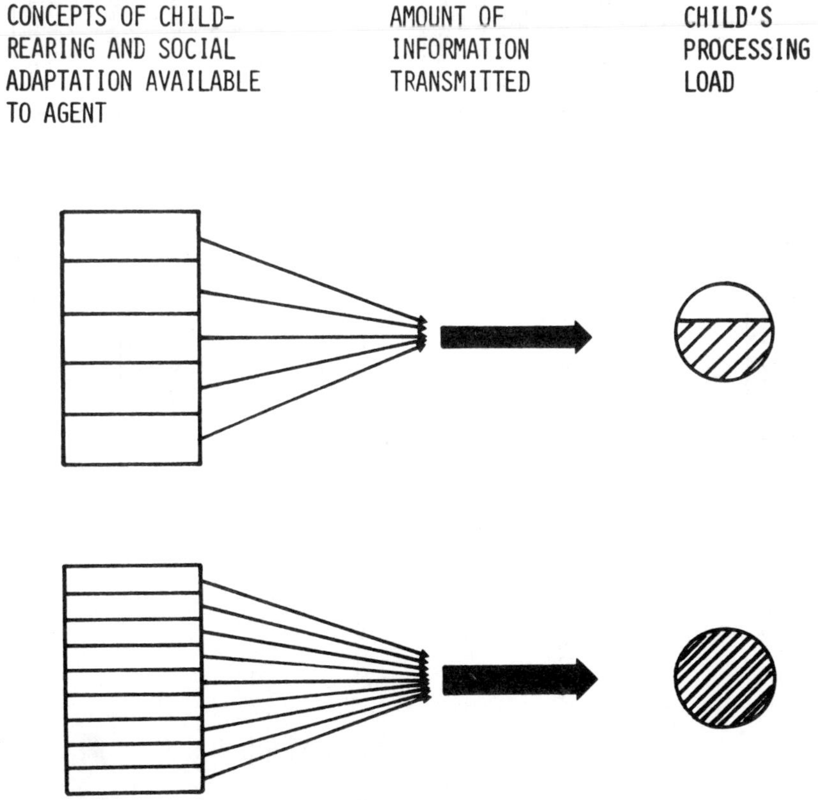

CONCEPTS OF CHILD-REARING AND SOCIAL ADAPTATION AVAILABLE TO AGENT

AMOUNT OF INFORMATION TRANSMITTED

CHILD'S PROCESSING LOAD

Figure 5.4 Child-rearing concepts and information transmission

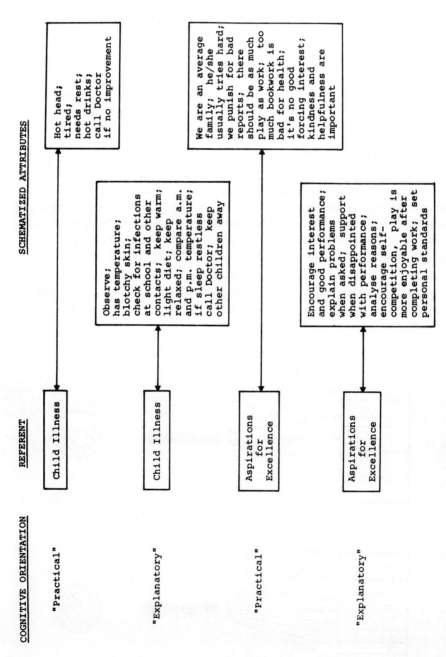

Figure 5.5 Differential normative conceptual structures applied in child-rearing

There are basically two concept areas involved: those representing knowledge of child and adolescent development, and those providing knowledge of social expectation. The first area encodes concepts of human biological rhythms, hygiene, 'milestones' and their aids, nutritional requirements, illness attributes, methods of control and their effects, skill acquisition and development of role-playing capacity, as well as complementary needs for dependence and autonomy. The concepts representing social expectation have cultural as well as caretaker sources. The parent or socializing agent may identify – that is through representation in long-term memory – completely with main or subgroup norms, may be substantially at variance with them, or transmit, as in the majority of cases, an attenuated version with individual foci of sharpening and/or elaboration. The conceptual categories involved include areas and levels of conformity and obedience generally, norms of self-control and regulation, number and level of 'ideals', and aspirations for excellence of and satisfaction from achievement. All of these contribute to a superordinate ethic of behaviour, and with the possible exception of achievement satisfaction fit naturally under the heading of morality, a topic to which I will return below.

An informational approach to socialization-relevant concepts is sketched in Figure 5.5. Two reference areas are show: child illness and aspirations for excellence as they may have developed in two social subgroups differing in complexity of the representation of normative structures. Socialization-relevant knowledge is assumed to be organized in schemata which encode the referent-attribute links which make up the subordinate conceptual structure defining the superior concept. Each attribute must be further defined by chunks of information with its subsidiary but relevant decision-making implications. As presented here, we would have to conclude that complex normative structures with their explanatory orientation contain and transmit potentially more information than more simply structured norms. Moreover, information from such a data base contains definitions which have implications for understanding the effect of concept attributes. Ability to apply socialization concepts effectively, therefore, requires their presence in the first instance, only secondly the capacity to transmit them in a setting experienced as favourable and supportive, and thirdly the incentive and ability to do so optimally.

(b) Schools as transmitters of social information

The specialized socialization role of the educational system is not the alternative that it provides for parental home influences. Nor does its contribution lie in its more formal authority structure, or the social power that it is able to exhibit by virtue of the authoritative knowledge skills which it has in its keeping. Its traditional and principal role lies in its capacity to develop general and specific conceptual structures which can serve as tools for the acquisition of working skills, and the development of conceptual operations and strategies from which higher-order, abstract, symbolic knowledge concepts can be derived. This is probably one of the major reasons for the progressively increasing positive correlation between the number of years of formal education and IQ (Husén, 1951). Since this correlation is not confined to culture- and/or verbally-loaded intelligence tests, additional factors are likely to be the transmission of problem-solving strategies and verification techniques, and of the sufficiency criteria of logical inference. Such skills are of intrinsic personal and social value. Moreover, they are sufficiently abstract and relational to be applied in fields other than educational or occupational achievement, such as social interaction and conceptual operations in the service of moral and ethical problem-solving.

Two major types of criticisms over the last 50–60 years in relation to educational procedures and aims are evidence of paradigm shifts in evaluating the goals of this socializing agency. The first, often associated with Montessori, Susan Isaacs, A. S. Neill and others, was that the standardization of a curriculum and of method of teaching wrongly assumed that free exploration and experimentation by children was educationally disadvantageous and retarding if carried out at the expense of formal teaching. The heyday of the 'Progressive School Movement' rapidly gave way, however, to assimilating *some* of their 'free activity' concepts into traditional curriculum planning of the state school system. A possibly excessive bias resulted in that the *doing* of a task was often considered as important as *doing it in a conforming manner to enable the results to be understood by another person.* It can be argued with some force that a letter or essay markedly deficient in spelling and syntax, or even a so-called 'abstract' painting or sculpture produced by a child, can present as a form of non-communication between individuals, that is, the very reverse for which compulsory formal education was designed. Perhaps it is not going too far even to suggest that the social implications of such free expression are akin to the communication difficulties of members of different language groups, or to the differences in verbal communication between socio-economic groups which were demonstrated so picturesquely by Bernstein (1961, 1971). I shall refer to this issue again when discussing the concept of creativity, without wishing to imply, however, that 'free activities' in schools are not to be encouraged some of the time.

The second and more recent criticism of educational socialization had a socio-political basis and was directed at the principle of grading children by ability for the purpose of effective teaching of standard educational and conceptual skills. It was assumed without any relevant research evidence that teaching mixed ability classes would be of intellectual benefit to lower ability children without affecting the natural conceptual progress of those with higher ability. It was claimed that this manipulation would counteract 'elitism' as an undesirable component of inter-group relationship, and that children of different social groups would acquire more veridical concepts of group characteristics other than their own. There is at present no reliable evidence that these aims have been or can be achieved for the benefit of all concerned.

The majority of admissions to British universities still come from a background of conventional schools with fathers or mothers in middle-class occupations, and North American evidence on university admission with lower qualifications than a Grade 12 School Leaving Diploma shows that lack of formal educational experience can be compensated for only rarely and with difficulty. The truism that seems to have escaped the social engineers is that concept formation has a historical and progressive basis. Where there have been difficulties in establishing the concrete pre-operational basis through lack of diverse experience, exploration, and home teaching and through imprecise or non-specific verbal communication, the most important factor in tapping intellectual potential is to discover which parts of the cognitive structures are incomplete or suboptimal, and to spend time on remedial work. To accept this, however, would have constituted an attack on the capacities of lower socio-economic group members, and an admission of *cognitive inequality*.

Although some children still leave school only partially literate or numerate *despite* mixed ability teaching in schools undifferentiated by status labels, unisex forms of dress, hairstyling, and musical taste have led to some fudging of cultural and social class boundaries. It could have been predicted on the basis of Asch's paradigmatic studies (1952) – but it was not – that shifts in behavioural habits would be in the direction of the normative influence of the majority. Therefore, where higher socio-economic group children are in the majority, their achievement orientation and ethical concepts would be more likely to be transmitted to the minority group. There is non-systematic evidence to support such a prediction. Since socio-economic group membership is most clearly defined by area of residence, the converse influence of a majority of lower socio-economic group children on higher group children has occurred too sparsely to make research worthwhile. North American experience on the effects of compulsory 'busing', however, will eventually provide some useful data.

The major cognitive effects of the educational phase of development, apart from the transmission of age-appropriate knowledge and strategies of manipulating it, are fourfold: (i) development of concepts of work assignments and schedules; (ii) elaboration of role-playing skills in interaction with peers, the 'other sex' (if this opportunity is absent in the home), and friends; (iii) and in the context of (ii), acquiring rules for conforming and non-conforming; and (iv) elaboration and differentiation of moral and ethical concepts. The development of relevant cognitive structures occurs in the setting and under the influence of two major factors: the level of conceptual-social development and maturity achieved in the pre-school years, and the dominant methods of applying positive and negative sanctions for inadequate performance or non-conforming in the school community.

It seems reasonable to assume – even in the absence of objective studies – that early conceptual structures defining 'school work' provide cognitive precursors for concepts of work in the adult economic world, and that this relationship is the same for other areas of adult development. Schematic structures encoding rewarding activity and play in the pre-school child have to be modified and interrelated with other schemata. These would have to contain the conceptual designations and requirement of an activity which is not necessarily immediately rewarding, and in which diversive exploration and creativity need to be associated by goodness-of-performance criteria. These performance criteria or standards are permanent memory data which encode the standards that are taught and which are elaborated and differentiated by externally or internally generated feedback of performance. In some respects, therefore, the growth of competence in dealing with scholastic demands is similar to the development of self-management skills in a conformity-oriented home setting.

The reorganization and elaboration of relevant schemata will be facilitated if a child enters school with an orientation towards competence, achievement, and enjoyment derived from intrinsic interest in exploring novelty. An approach orientation towards school work is strengthened if the control strategies of home and school are compatible.

More often than not this constellation of goals and expectations does not terminate in unilateral achievement-based status-seeking, unless the child is simultaneously operating on the basis of low self-esteem and expectations of social rejection through falling short of some standard of frequently illusory excellence. The most common outcome is a set of prototypical attributes defining the concept of work. These include an acceptable self-image of competence, enjoyment in solving problems, persistence, self-control, tolerating delay of gratification and the imposition of less desirable tasks, a completion orientation, and inevitably, an acceptance of authority's right to assign work tasks.

An extreme contrast is presented if a child enters school with poorly developed intrinsic interest structures, without a prior basis of competence in diversive play or performance, and with minimal favourable anticipations of school transmitted by parents. A positive interaction with a particular teacher might bring about substantial change in the child's evaluation of the new environment, but, as I suggested before, a remedial period of some duration may be required before concepts of knowledge acquisition, standards of performance, and enjoyment of competence change sufficiently to enable the child to make age-appropriate progress. Where a favourable teacher-child relationship does not develop the school work concept is likely to contain primarily negative and aversive attributes. The consequences are well-known: restlessness, disturbance of classroom routines, physical aggression, truancy, rejection of authority, and serious forms of delinquency. Work becomes something to be avoided unless it leads to something worse, or work is simulated in the hope that it will be considered adequate, or the simulation will not be noticed. In this setting potential abilities may remain unnoticed by the school, they may remain underdeveloped and unutilized, and a further basis for frustration-induced aggression, or social inadequacy, becomes established. The difference between the two hypothetical cases described would be inadequately designated by approach vs. avoidance concepts. The principal difference, I would argue, lies in the number of favourable attributes defining the work concept. These should originate from the amount of cross-referenced structures linking the work concept with favourable conceptual representations of other activities, and particularly perhaps from the number of available strategies for overcoming early intellectual difficulties of comprehension. Of great importance are the strategies for minimizing the awareness of temporary unpleasantness or aversiveness by an ability to orient towards more long-term, desirable goals.

Entering the school system provides the major impetus for the development of cognitive structures which encode the individual's opportunities to participate in large group activities. These include the constraints imposed by having to share these opportunities with others, and particularly the new wider range of activities provided by this setting. Opportunities for social interaction and novel activities provide, in the first instance, exposure to new and more complex stimuli compared with those experienced in the child's home. An important aspect of the stimulus setting is its context: the large number of persons, a more spacious environment with many rooms and passages, and being always in the company of others. Group tasks such as clearing up a room require adjustment to what another child is doing, and even sharing a small table with one other child for work or for meals requires taking notice of another person's needs, or intentions. If egocentric or egotistical behaviour has not diminished before entering school, this is the time when it usually gives way to matching personal goals to the social space and opportunity either provided or left unoccupied by others. Social psychology traditionally has made some theoretical distinction between concepts of role-playing, conformity, and co-operation. Thus, role-playing reflects a relatively conflict-free division of activity in a context of group relevance, conformity describes the closeness of a match between actual, and expected and normative behaviour, while co-operation refers to a state of interlocking activity towards a consensual group goal in which role-playing conflicts and conformity discrepancies are minimized. It can be argued, therefore, that a state of group co-operation is the superordinate dynamic process here. This process requires and also lends itself without much conceptual strain to a cognitive reinterpretation.

Role-playing is a problem-solving skill. Let us consider two examples. A class monitor is elected or designated to help the teacher in certain ways with relatively simple tasks which are part of the classroom routine; for instance, transporting the Class Register, and/or Dinner Money Register and cash from classroom to School Secretary or Principal; cleaning the blackboard for the next lesson and providing chalk; collecting set books at the end of a lesson or distributing them at the beginning. Routines have to be remembered and carried out within fairly narrow time limits. The skill involves problem-solving if obstacles arise in executing the routine on time. Other children may have hidden the chalk or the blackboard cleaner; the Secretary is not in her office to receive the Registers while the lesson about to begin is either important or requires boarding a bus for a swimming period. Clearly, the obstacles could be multiplied. The child with well-developed concepts of role requirements, conformity, and co-operation will find strategies of thought which will place a number of goals in a hierarchical order. So as to rejoin the group as quickly as possible, he may borrow blackboard implements from another class, or hand over Registers or money to the Head Teacher in person, both with suitable explanations. In either case problem-solving is based on past experience on what to do when trying to please all those dependent on his interpretation and skill of role-playing, and on valid deductions from correct premises. By finding alternative, conforming ways of discharging the responsibilities attached to his role, he is being co-operative. In the process, cognitive structures have been modified through an elaboration of contingency planning and rewarded behaviour. The key prototypical attribute added to the social interaction setting in this example is the concept of permissible and rewarded deviation from a norm.

As a second example we may take an able, only child, unaccustomed to taking turns with others, or providing a supportive role in activities of his own age group. The child was more intelligent and verbally skilled than most. On innumerable occasions there was disagreement with the rest of the group. Instead of participating in methods of group work decided by everyone else, this child stood on the sideline to provide a running commentary of criticism of the group approach, which indeed might be somewhat ineffective. Physical attacks and ostracism did not achieve full group cohesion.

While it is possible to create a 'happy ending' story, in this particular instance it may be more instructive to analyse why this child, in due course, had to be removed to another school. To be a deviant may be socially unproductive and even wrong if deviance is consistent across situations for largely irrelevant reasons. In the latter case it is certain to be socially and personally unproductive. Our hypothetical case, however, is intelligent and verbally skilled, and like many other able deviants may see a different, more interesting, efficient, and enjoyable road to a group goal. The developmental history enabled this child to be self-sufficient in problem-solving settings, and to attach great importance to unaided successes and to well-deserved parental praise. In this case, compared with the previous example, there is a substantial imbalance between highly elaborated *socially neutral* cognitive schematic structures, and those structures which respectively represent knowledge of other children's needs, and strategies for retaining individuality while subscribing to group consensus.

Before concluding this particular discussion, it is necessary to relate it to a child's two major reference groups: peers and friends. It is tempting to suppose that of the two hypothetical children described above, the first one has good relationships with most members of his peer group and more friends than the second child. All other things being equal this is a plausible infer-ence. The difference in friendships, however, may not be as substantial if we add the further hypothetical information that the 'difficult' child has many younger playmates outside the school who take great pride in their competent friend, who agree to take a subordinate position in decision-making, and who thereby elicit a warm and protective attitude from their competent and interesting friend. Since we have not argued that the social difficulties are accompanied by behavioural irresponsibility, all may indeed be well.

A further level of attenuation of the gross hypothetical differences may be offered. No reference has been made to an age factor. There is considerable research evidence that social conformity from primary school years to early adulthood is in the form of an inverted V (e.g. Iscoe *et al.*, 1963; Constanzo and Shaw, 1966; Landsbaum and Willis, 1971). That is, conformity is lowest in the early school years, then rises sharply in the 11–13-year age group when small close friendship groups or membership of gangs and teams are of great importance, and then proceeds to decline fairly regularly. The difficulty with this kind of evidence is that it is rather gross. For the purpose of a cognitive reinterpretation of social group behaviour it is necessary to know more of the kinds of groups, the types of group activities, and of the amount of individual differences in interests, abilities, and competence in activities in relation to which social dynamics operate. Another variable worth considera-tion is the choice factor: how many groups are available for social relationships, or whether there are in school special interest or activity groups to which children may belong, irrespective of age, if they can demonstrate competence.

The discussion of the development of socially relevant cognitive structures during the school years has concentrated on the concepts of work and social interaction. We must assume, however, that even the non-scholastic child acquires some general knowledge data and some capacity to make logically valid deductions from them with the help of verbal labels available to him. These general cognitive data and skills are integrated with response- and decision-making processes applied in other conceptual contexts. When at-tributes defining a referent are poorly elaborated, then the number of logical operations on them are fewer than if the referents were finely elaborated. Moreover, since children enter school with schematic structures developed in the home setting, pre-school elaboration of the extent and the contents of schemata will vary, and interact differentially with the evaluation and clas-sification of the new stimulus setting. Therefore, with different antecedents the behavioural end-result is a fairly complex function of early cognitive priorities and the subjective decoding of new and specific situational contexts. Special consideration needs to be given, therefore, to the influence of par-ental 'education' on the development of cognitive structures. This leads us to a reconsideration of a well-documented area of behavioural science. In the next section, too, we will examine the development of moral and ethical cognitive structures.

3 PARENTAL SOCIALIZATION STRATEGIES AND THEIR EFFECTS

A truly enormous literature has accumulated on this topic since the early fact-finding Berkeley Longitudinal Guidance Study and the work from the Fels Research Institute. Although most of the results derived from these sources employed correlational methodology, they have had a fruitful influence on subsequent more analytic research. It is not my intention to review this material in any detail. I have done so before (Hamilton, 1972, 1976), and the references I am citing will lead the reader to other reviews. Without implying any sort of negative evaluation, I will classify correlational work as reflecting a traditional approach to the topic. Subsequent strategies for the analysis of this area were able to benefit from the application of concepts from cognitive and information-processing theory, and the more recent views of the relevance of lexical and semantic labelling in the development of cognitive structures.

(i) The traditional approach

The relevant studies had two major aims: to investigate the relationship between parental characteristics and socialization strategies and, respectively, the development of intelligence, personality, and motivational characteristics of the children. The major parental dimensions were derived from either Sears *et al*'s (1957) influential book, or from Schaefer (1965), both of which drew on Macfarlane's (1938) parameters. The latter included socio-economic and physical status, social adjustment, ability, maternal concern, energy, and anxiety. The major maternal attitudes towards children employed in research were permissiveness–strictness, warmth–coldness, acceptance–rejection, autonomy–control, and firm control–lax control. One of the most recent reports of the Berkeley Study (Honzik, 1967), spanning 30 years of follow-up, shows that intelligence test performance increases progressively with early ratings of parental ability, maternal concern and energy, as well as with anxiety in the context of parental concern with achievement. Sons' IQs were higher with a close mother–son relationship and with fathers' occupational success and satisfaction. Sex-difference factors were present here, as elsewhere, in that daughters' IQs were positively related to a good relationship between fathers and daughters, and to parental compatibility. Not surprisingly, early ratings of children's 'happiness' were also significantly related to later intellectual competence. More narrowly conceived studies by, for example, Hurley (1965) and Bing (1963) have produced complementary results. Studies by Yarrow *et al.* (1974) produced substantial correlations between sons' IQs and the following maternal variables: physical contact, acceptance, positive emotional expression, emotional involvement, communication, achievement stimulation, offering, where and when appropriate, variety of stimulation in suitable amounts and intensity, positive affect, and responsiveness to vocalization and distress. Many other studies (e.g. Kagan and Moss, 1962; Douglas, 1964; Hindley, 1965; Moore, 1968) support these findings, and in addition point to the role of parental socio-economic status and education as mediators in parental attitude and socialization methods. With the exception of the Berkeley study, all other reports stress the adverse effect of anxiety experiences during, and as the result of, upbringing in the development of intelligence and behavioural performance in general (Sarason *et al.*, 1964; Hill and Sarason, 1966; Russell and Sarason, 1965; Weiss and Silverman, 1966; Hodges and Spielberger, 1969; Denny, 1966; Dunn, 1968). The evidence of these relationships is strongly supported by Kohn and Rosman (1973) in a study employing particularly powerful statistics to show the effects of social-demographic and socio-emotional factors on the cognitive development of 5-year-old boys. Social class was significantly associated with verbal as well as non-verbal intellectual capacity, but of special interest here is the finding that apathy, lack of interest and curiosity, and withdrawal are significantly negatively related to the cognitive measures.

The second traditional correlate of socialization attitudes – children's personality and motivational characteristics – has a long history in psycho-analytic theory (A. Freud, 1945), and in the study of the often comparable effects of overprotection (Levy, 1943) and of deprivation (Bowlby, 1951). Some of the important early maternal responses are those which correctly match various infantile need levels (Escalona, 1968), a generally high level of stimulation (e.g. Brody and Axelrad, 1971), non-routine attention (Ainsworth *et al.*, 1972), and expressions of positive emotion by affectionate warmth (Bowlby, 1951; Clarke-Stewart, 1973). The major effects of optimal strategies are evidence of secure attachment, an appropriately high activity level and independence in exploring. Obedience to verbal maternal demands was significantly related to maternal acceptance, co-operation, and sensitivity (Stayton *et al.*, 1971).

Particularly careful studies on nursery school children and their parents were carried out by Baumrind (e.g. 1967, 1971). School observation and home interview and observation data, subsequently submitted to cluster analysis, isolated three types of parental behaviour: authoritative, authoritarian, and permissive. Authoritative parents were warm, rational, controlling, demanding, and receptive to child communication. Their children scored highest on self-reliance, self-control, exploration, contentment, approach-orientation, and buoyancy. Authoritarian parents were firm, detached, controlling, and relatively unaffectionate. Their offspring were discontented, withdrawn, distrustful, and had poor relationships with their peers. Permissive parents were relatively warm, non-controlling and undemanding, but with some ambivalence, especially in fathers. These children were dependent, immature, and low on exploration and self-control. Elsewhere (Baumrind, 1972) argues that the three socialization styles and their effects on children are of primary relevance to adult socially responsible and independent behaviour. Instrumental competence as she calls it is optimal with the following adult practices and attitudes:

1. Modeling by the adult of behavior which is both socially responsible and self-assertive, especially if the adult is seen as powerful by the child and as eager to use the material and interpersonal resources over which he has control on the child's behalf.
2. Firm enforcement policies in which the adult makes effective use of reinforcement principles in order to reward socially responsible behavior and to punish deviant behavior, but in which demands are accompanied by explanations, and sanctions are accompanied by reasons consistent with a set of principles followed in practice as well as preached by the parent.
3. Nonrejecting but not overprotective or passive-acceptant parental attitudes in which the parent's interest in the child is abiding and, in the pre-school years, intense; and where approval is conditional upon the child's behavior.
4. High demands for achievement and for conformity with parental policy, accompanied by receptivity to the child's rational demands and willingness to offer the child wide latitude for independent judgement.
5. Providing the child with a complex and stimulating environment offering challenge and excitement as well as security and rest, where divergent as well as convergent thinking is encouraged.

(Baumrind, 1972, p. 222)

A more cognitive orientation towards behavioural competence and styles of behaviour is present in the theoretical position adopted by Harvey and his collaborators (e.g. Harvey *et al.*, 1961; Schroder *et al.*, 1967; Harvey and Felknor, 1970). This theory argues that stimuli possessing high personal relevance are evaluated by individually different belief systems which supply characteristic predispositions for response consistency. Belief systems are cognitive filters for the detection and processing of affectively involving events. The four systems determining conceptual stimulus analysis are: concreteness, negativism and anti-authority orientation, social sensitivity, abstraction and objectivity. These are short-hand labels and Harvey *et al.* define them in much greater detail. Basically these belief systems differ in the integrative complexity and relational elaborations of their cognitive structures and content. The differences will affect the type of preferred or possible stimulus analysis ('top-down' processes) and have their origin in developmental antecedents (Harvey and Felknor, 1970).

Table 5.1 sets out the pattern of functional characteristics defining a *concrete belief system*, and the pattern of socialization strategies which were found to be dominant correlates. This material was gathered from first-year students producing accounts of what they remembered of their relationships with their parents before age 12. While there is always selective bias in this type of retrospective study, we are able to observe a considerable measure of agreement with concurrent and the other retrospective studies discussed earlier.

Table 5.1 The Concrete Belief System and its Socialization Antecedents

Belief System Characteristics	Socialization Antecedents
Concepts poorly structured, poorly integrated and undifferentiated	Intra-family agreement on child-rearing techniques
Distraction by salient false cues	Consistency and fairness in a structured framework
Dichotomous evaluations	Concern with family reputation and religious beliefs
Snap judgements	Gender role differentiation
Dependence on external and institutionalized authority	Father strict, arbitrary, controlling and restricting towards sons
Norm-conforming	Mothers also control sons but show some warmth
Intolerance of ambiguity	Fathers punish but encourage dependence, and show less fairness towards sons
Rigidity and stereotyping in problem-solving	Daughters experienced more approach from both parents
Maintaining set	Physical punishment used frequently
Ritualistic acceptance of rules and conventions	'Explanations' relatively uncommon
Ethnocentric	

Source: After Harvey and Felknor, 1970

Whether we are considering infants, the nursery age group, or adolescents, the common element in all outcomes is the type and method of control. Essentially, control means parental participation by instruction, explanation, and guidance in the initiation and direction of behaviour by verbal and non-verbal methods. An interesting set of experiments by Hess and Shipman (1965, 1967) illustrated the role of control methods in cognitive performance tasks carried out by children in the presence and with the participation of their mothers. Three control strategies used by mothers assisting their children were isolated: the imperative, the subjective-regulatory, and the cognitive-rational. The first involves an authoritarian appeal to rule and norm enforcement – telling the child what to do – and led to low-level performances on several tasks. The last strategy emphasizes pragmatic logic and cause-and-effect thinking in performance, and was associated with the highest level of performance. Performance related to subjective-regulatory style was of intermediate competence, because this style, Hess and Shipman argue, encouraged inter-personal sensitivity, which in their experiments meant the child evaluating thoughtfully the mother's assessment of his problem-solving attempts.

Of great interest are the associated results which involve low IQ, low socio-economic status and poor verbalizing ability in mother-child pairs associated with the lowest performance. It seems plausible to suggest, as Hess and Shipman did, that the association between a restricted communication code (Bernstein, 1961), the imperative style, and poor cognitive performance is important. An unelaborated sentence content would clearly affect the transmission of social behaviour by parent to child. Moreover, in the context of the present thesis an imperative and restricted communication pattern would reduce the capacity for differentiated concepts and schematic structures.

In a discussion of the nature of maternal control techniques Schaffer and Crook (1978) have argued in favour of a tidy and hierarchical concept of verbal and non-verbal controls. While this omits any reference to an effective-emotional component which was considered a powerful factor in the outcome of socialization methods by other investigators, it has merit for two reasons. Firstly, it reminds us that obtaining a child's attention is a prerequisite for affecting his behaviour. Secondly, Schaffer offers a dimension of non-verbal controls. Here communication occurs through gestures and physical contact which need to be seen not only as a necessary ethological forerunner of the more fine-grain verbal communication code, but as a concurrent set of social signals (see also my Figure 5.6). As Schaffer *et al.* (1977) point out, rules for non-verbal mother–child interaction, 'turn-taking', and other forms of reciprocal mutuality seem to be available in the course of the pre-verbal second year.

Although Schaffer (1971) agreed that the cognitive processes of attention, perception, and learning operate in young children's interpretation of social stimuli, he does not present any analysis of the development of social cognitive structures. This type of analysis is also absent from the conceptualizations of the other theorists whose work I have discussed. What need to be supplied are cognitive mediating processes for the encoding of social stimuli and a concept-oriented analysis of the integration of functionally related classes of stimuli – as well as the effects of responding to them – in schematic organizations. Without appropriate conceptions of this kind, 'top-down' processes required for efficient social problem-solving cannot evolve in permanent memory.

This criticism seems to be equally relevant when evaluating the major theoretical views on the development and nature of moral and ethical behaviour. Although all of them, and even the social-learning approach, qualify more or less for the label 'cognitive', not one of them argues analytically about the relationship between norm- and social rule-conforming behaviour and the content of the permanent memory structures from which behavioural decisions are generated.

Bandura's (1977) recent reconceptualization of the roles of modelling and reinforcement (reward or punishment) in social behaviour is surprisingly non-behaviourist. Reinforcement is no longer an external control stimulus. Model and shaped stimuli, together with the characteristics of the social agent, are transformed into internal symbolic cues. These have the capacity to modify personal behaviour depending on situational context, as well as by reference to internalized standards and self-evaluative reactions. While it is refreshing to see learning theorists writing about the *anticipation of the consequences* of behaviour, to do so without ever saying at the same time that S–R theory was a false theory, is to deprive themselves of the praise and admiration of their contemporaries for a show of intellectual integrity. Bandura's Figure 6 (1977, p. 130) is a very good example of explanatory inadequacy if a stimulus is defined behaviourally. The illustrated series of unobservable judgmental processes as components in the self-regulation of an individual's behaviour is, in fact, a complex outcome of associating functionally related permanent memory data, and a set of serial matching processes in working memory between long-term information and the information implicit in, or inferred from, a situational context. In other words, moral norm- and rule-conforming behaviour is an inseparable function of cognitive elaboration and of cognitive power and skill, as well as of their limitations.

This kind of argument reduces the theoretical role of learning theory in socialization to contributions pertinent to reinforcement schedules and contingencies in behaviour acquisition. But even here the general validity of such propositions must depend on the cognitive content of the components of a self-regulating system. Thus, one schedule of contingencies may be optimal for habit acquisition in *Child A* with one particular set of antecedent experiences, but patently counter-productive for *Child B* whose profile of antecedents differs from that of the first child *on only one* of many variables. Somewhat superficially one may argue, therefore, that Aldous Huxley and George Orwell may have been able to offer skills to psychology which are not always clearly present in the last two generations of S–R theorists. In other words, rewards and punishments reside in the cognitive structures of the receiver rather than in the actions of the agent. This fact would account for the common ineffectiveness of measures of social control available to either caretakers or society in relation to delinquent or criminal acts. Furthermore, a more analytic view of the determinants of behaviour would predict that delinquency and crime are not necessarily due to either ignorance of consequences or to cognitively primitive moral thinking (e.g. Emler *et al.*, 1978). The 'conditioned reflex of conscience', as Eysenck (1970) called it, is not absent. There may be simply a high threshold for *disturbing* guilty thinking, or other goals of behaviour have a lower threshold.

The related cognitive-developmental theories of moral thinking and concepts of Piaget (1932) and Kohlberg (1969) can lay greater claim to the term cognitive. Their continuing importance, however, does not rest on their salient proposition of 'stages' of moral thought. Of principal importance are the *implications* for cognitive structuring of children's growing awareness of the effects of social interdependence, the existence of rules governing it, the reasons for having rules, and subsequently the integration of such rules in a system of principles. These are principles which a society evaluates as being ultimately just, fair, and good for the maintenance and progress of complex social organizations. Both theorists define the progress in moral thinking qualitatively. Progress is in terms of simple, external control concepts being replaced by complex and abstract concepts. These, in turn, derive meaning primarily from the logical cause-and-effect relationships which can be generated from an implicit integration of several hypothetical events and their outcomes. It can be plausibly argued, therefore, that changes in the encoded knowledge and meaning content of hierarchically ordered cognitive structures are only superficially described by a stage concept, and that the development of principle-oriented moral thinking can occur only when an individual can operate with propositional logic in relation to problems and issues generally (see also Langford and George, 1971; Tomlinson-Keasey and Keasey, 1974). Moreover, a rigid conception of stages of moral development is misplaced as much here as it is in relation to Piaget's other writings on cognitive development (e.g. Farnham-Diggory, 1976). As McGeorge (1974), for example, has pointed out the level of conceptual analysis applied to social rules is likely to be a function of past experience with a particular set of rules, the contexts in which they were relevant, and the experienced outcome of behaviour for a child or adolescent.

To place cognitive-developmental theories of moral and ethical thinking in the context of a cognitive theory of personality and motivation produces few difficulties. In the first instance there is substantial agreement that lax, inconsistent, punitive, and emotionally cold parenting reduces achievement orientation and social conformity. Secondly, low intellectual ability will restrict the capacity to elaborate the alternatives for self-regulation and diminish self-knowledge or insight into the effects of own behaviour on self and other. In this event, the major referents for socially approved actions will remain external control stimuli and their subjectively perceived attributes. *Optimal* moral development occurs in the context of the kind of favourable parenting discussed earlier and is associated with good self-esteem due to praise and encouragement of achievement, and relatively higher intelligence. The difference between these two sets of correlates can then be defined by three factors. Firstly, by the number of conceptual referents eliciting responses which are experienced and evaluated as just, fair, and good. Secondly, by the number of referent-defining attributes reflecting fine-grain sensitivity to stimulus variations. And, thirdly, by a functionally and internally consistent hierarchical organization of subordinate and superordinate schemata representative of referents, their attributes, and knowledge of the outcomes of previous strategies of responding to them. Thus the crucial elements of morality lie in the diversification of cognitive structures and in the type and degree of hypothesis-testing they are able to facilitate.

There are good grounds for arguing that the contribution of psycho-analytic theorists to the development and demonstrations of moral behaviour have been more directly cognitive than the theories discussed so far. This position can be taken for three reasons. Firstly, the subjective interpretations of early experiences in the family by a child result in memories and thought processes which necessarily exert a powerful influence on later and more mature memory structures. This must be so because no new experience can be responded to without its prior analysis by existing data codes which contain the information required for perceptual and conceptual identification. Secondly, because of the closeness and duration of parental influences, behaviour which is praised or punished will strongly affect the individual child's norms and standards encoded in memory by which he will evaluate the acceptability, utility, and outcome satisfaction of his potential responses. The choice and matching processes involved amount to what psycho-analytic theorists call the operation of ego-ideal processes – the critical part of super-ego control. Thirdly, the determinants of behaviour lying on a morality–amorality axis may defy self-knowledge, that is they are unconscious. Thus, the basic reasons for controlling or yielding to impulses towards or away from a goal which may have implications for personal guilt and/or social rejection, are more adequately defined here than by the more restricted concepts of reinforcement, or of maturation of cognitive operations. What psycho-analytic theories cannot discuss is the process of aggregation of functionally related classes of behaviour on the basis of labelled attributes and their organization into schemata. But their associationist approach comes very close to doing so. The theories' insistence on the importance of thought *content*, rather than the *mechanisms* by which items of content are acquired, makes them good candidates for an up-dating re-examination.

Inappropriate associations between relevant, irrelevant, and false evaluations of stimuli to which children were exposed from parental sources would, according to psycho-analytic theory, lead to irrational or ambiguous concepts. Unless further experiences in the socialization context are interpreted as strongly positive and favourable as the results of insightful parental guidance, and affectionate and tolerant handling, both types of suboptimal concepts will affect the child's dominant interpretation of later and novel experiences. The most common outcome is the emergence of anxiety about imagined punitive and harm-inflicting events, situations, and agents, and a strong disposition to focus on the control and avoidance of stimulus ambiguity. A strategy of categorizing stimuli into distinctive conceptual classes despite objective contra-indications from ill-defined, vague, reality-defying, or incongruent stimulus characteristics is used effectively in the control of anxiety. The studies by Frenkel-Brunswik (1949, 1954), Klein (1954), Gardner *et al.* (1959), and Witkin *et al.* (1962), employing the concept of cognitive control or style, have lent some support to propositions of an anxiety-avoidance interaction between external and internal stimulus demands. As discussed before the criterion measures of personality and motivation against which this interaction was tested did not always correlate significantly, however, with perceptual and conceptual response style adopted by subjects (see reviews by Vernon, 1973, and Hamilton, 1976).

In contrast, some early studies by myself (Hamilton, 1957, 1960) avoided the difficulties associated with projective test indices of anxiety and its control, by working with hospitalized neurotic patients. According to psychoanalytic theory the greater the evidence of defence against anxiety by neurotic subgroups, the greater the total cognitive and affective reservoir of anxiety. On the propositions that ambiguous stimuli present categorizing conflicts, and that conceptual uncertainty sensitizes anxiety and existing dispositions to control such experiences, two predictions were tested: (i) neurotic patients would exhibit greater avoidance of socially neutral ambiguous stimuli than a matched non-patient group; and (ii) the more severe and disabling the psycho-dynamic defences against anxiety the more pronounced the evidence of avoidance of stimulus ambiguity. According to psycho-analytic theory the most (unsuccessfully) defended neurotic subgroups are conversion hysterics and obsessive-compulsive neurotics. Both predictions were strongly confirmed in 12 test situations ranging from the classification of stimuli in a psycho-physical sensitivity setting, and of ambiguous drawings, to testing for apparent movement ('phi phenomenon').

Although predictive experimental work with criterion groups – whose selection forms part of the predictive framework – is an improvement on a simplified correlational methodology, it cannot precisely identify the crucial processes affecting research results. A new paradigm shift was required for a clearer identification of the short- and long-term effects of parental socialization methods. Information processing theory provided the tools for a more definitive approach.

(ii) The information processing approach

This paradigm, as discussed before, regards stimuli as potential transmitted information, that is, signals that can be decoded and acted upon by existing data that represent their meaning or response implications in permanent memory. Miller (1956) and Broadbent (1958) demonstrated that the capacity for processing the information in stimuli is limited at any given point in time. Miller, however, also argued plausibly that frequently associated stimuli form chunks of information in which a generalized abstraction can simultaneously represent a number of subordinate units. Chunking often implies some redundancy of information, and facilitates responding in more complex tasks in which there are also data with only little redundancy. Self-evidently, chunking cannot occur without prior exposure to stimulation and the acquisition of labelled representations of single stimuli. In any given area of stimulation or of induced or self-generated behaviour, the greater the amount of labelled information acquired, the greater the potential for chunking, that is, provided the required physiological efficiency for this process is available, and provided, too, an adequate symbolic labelling system can develop in the socialization setting.

Chunking, therefore, as well as the capacity to process decreasing amounts of redundancy, must be a function of elaborating and schematically ordering cognitive structures. This development is mediated by socialization agents and a child's own play and self-generated interests. Evidence that the capacities for chunking and handling low levels of redundancy depend on age, as well as on the adequacy of basic cognitive processes, has been presented by Osler and Kofsky (1965), and Hamilton and Launay (1976). Short-term working memory capacity plays an important role here for two reasons. Firstly, because the non-availability of chunking requires holding all discrete stimuli in memory while operations on them are carried out. Secondly, because chunking as well as redundancy depends on the ability to discover what may be 'chunked', and which choice operations are redundant.

Socially mediated information reflects two broad areas of experience. The first, with which we have been concerned so far, transmits knowledge of the common and shared objective environment, and of educational and logical skills. The second transmits the information contained in the socializing techniques and methods employed by parents and family members, teachers, peers, and friends. The theoretical positions previously discussed imply that social and behavioural control stimuli are generally chosen for their demonstrated effects, that is because the information they present to the child is interpreted as intended by the source emitting the signals. At the same time there does not appear to be available any systematic analysis of the conceptual structures to which they give rise. Whereas we have standardized tests of general and specific cognitive development showing peaks and troughs of competence and elaboration, comparable evidence for degrees of dominance and elaboration of socialization-related personality traits and goal hierarchies is not yet available to any significant extent. If we regard all behaviour as the outcome of goal-directed problem-solving, then cognitive structures subserving *preferred methods* (personality) *of achieving preferred goals* (motivation) play a distinctive and integrative role in the production of a task- or situation-relevant response. Moreover, such concepts may have – though need not have – the power of conscious self-concepts. In addition, they grow in complexity, elaboration, and adaptability in a manner which is difficult to distinguish from those of other concepts which are of lesser personal relevance.

Socializing information can be defined by two dimensions: amount of signals, and their relevance to the development of traits and goals. Amount of information is optimal if it satisfies the requirements of a child, and matches the overall context. The effects of low levels of interest, and of rejection and severe deprivation of affection have been discussed already. Excessive stimulation, especially if interaction has not been initiated by the child, can also have unfavourable effects (e.g. Wachs *et al.*, 1971). Ambiguous communication of parental attitude leads to conflicts of interpretation, and therefore to stimulus and response uncertainty. Ambiguous information may include internally contradictory messages, and the 'double-bind' contained in messages at different levels of production and analysis may generate considerable child anxiety (Bateson *et al.*, 1956). This last theoretical notion is difficult to test but unsuccessful attempts to do so (Schuham, 1967) cannot be regarded as having tested critical analogues of the hypothesized process.

We have identified the aim of social development as the achievement of personal effectiveness and competence in satisfyingly experienced role-playing, in association with, and by relating to, social interaction demands. This aim requires the development of strategies of behaviour towards preferred goals which facilitate the achievement of effectiveness and competence. Socializing information helps to create optimal behavioural strategies by the transmission of verbal and non-verbal signals which acquire, or have built-in, outcome expectancies. Frequency of contiguity between signal and outcome establish rewarded and rewarding behavioural concepts, and rules about when and how they may be optimally used. Ethologists have provided a great deal of evidence that some rules have phylogenetic as well as ontogenetic origins, and that the 'grammar' of human social behaviour may begin with universal innate responsiveness to non-verbal signals (see Eibl-Eibesfeldt (1979) and others, for a recent evaluation). These signals transmit adult approval or disapproval, emotional acceptance and affection or their opposites, protectiveness or lack of care, environmental safety or danger. Facial expression, gestures, postures, physical contacts, concurrent vocalization and their intensities, provide the sources of information. Observational evidence indicates that non-verbal stimuli form cognitive structures encoding generalizations which represent 'liking' or 'disliking', approach or avoidance. Other evidence, also too numerous to mention, indicates that responding to non-verbal signals is followed by progressively greater reliance on verbally transmitted information. Attention to non-verbal signals never ceases because this additional communication channel provides amplifying information which may be contradictory in the case of 'double-bind', or where 'looks defy words'.

The progress of sensitivity to social cues, the change from analysing and utilizing non-verbal to verbal cues, and their relationship to the development of symbolic schematic structures is modelled in Figure 5.6. The missing stage – verbal maternal signals – will be discussed later in Chapter 6. What we can see at this juncture is that frequency and generality of positively interpreted information will predispose towards the development of outgoing, explorative, achieving, and stable individual characteristics. An excess of aversively experienced information is likely to be associated with cognitive structures primarily encoding many types of social anxieties, timidity, isolation, frustration, and components of low self-esteem and social aggression.

Figure 5.6 also omits one other feature of parental signals to which attention has been drawn before – their possible ambiguity. Ambiguous information is insufficiently defined by reference to concurrent contradictions at a specific point in time. It is equally present in experiences of inconsistent parenting. This must be the case because a present stimulus can be interpreted only by reference to the implications of stimuli of the same category on an earlier occasion. Since all types of experienced stimulus ambiguity

111

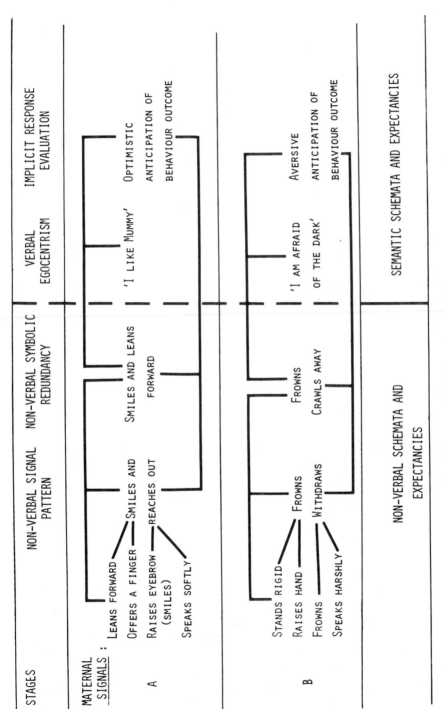

Figure 5.6 The 'languages' of children's symbolic structures

prevent a clear-cut classification of the event of which they form a part, and since non-classification of an event prevents a certainty decision about its outcome implications, information-processing requirements here are greater than in unambiguous settings. This deduction is made because difficulty or inability in identifying an event requires a larger and more prolonged number of memory operations of the search-and-scan type discussed by Newell and Simon (1972), and because the non-classification provides a focus for problem-solving deficiencies persisting long after the event.

Our discussion of the nature of socializing information transmitted by social agents has so far identified three components of cognitive structures which contribute to the information-processing demands on the cognitive system. They are: areas of 'specialization' or elaboration; ambiguity or uncertainty of information transmitted; and simultaneously presented information. The first of these exemplifies the emergence of a dominant and preferred behavioural approach to a social demand situation, and its goals. The second reflects inadequacies in the conceptual structures which provide degrees of predictive validity for the individual's choice of a particular response strategy. Both of these components operate on representations available in permanent memory. The third component is initially under external control. It reflects either differences in number of comments, exhortations, criticisms, or praise concurrently issuing from an authority source, or the complexity of task-related information which may lie along several dimensions simultaneously. Alternatively, processing demands result from a combination of both types of information.

This analysis makes it possible to adopt one type of fine-grained and definitive approach to the classical problem of the interaction between socialization experience and cognitive capacity. Given two children of comparable intellectual potential (which admittedly is difficult though not impossible to establish) presented with the same multidimensional task, we can argue that summation of information from conceptual and categorizing uncertainty and from the cognitive structures of a dominant trait, will differentially affect their ability for doing the task. The validity of this deduction rests on the evidence of processing capacity limitations of the cognitive system. It depends particularly on the previous arguments assigning informational status to processes involved in cognitive uncertainty and to the components directing behaviour towards preferred goals by preferred methods. As a corollary it can be proposed that task performance will be adversely affected by concurrent processing demands from the dominant individual characteristics if these become relevantly or irrelevantly but excessively involved in the task. Thus, the influence of socialization on personality and motivation and subsequently on cognition occurs not only because socializing experience is cognitive experience. This has been argued before by others (e.g. Feffer, 1970; Youniss, 1978) albeit within different frameworks and with less precise implications. The interactions with cognitive development, elaboration, and processing capacity occur because the information from all sources is represented within the same symbolic coding system and requires simultaneous handling by the same information processing components. Task performance ability, whether profiting from parental or school teaching, from self-generated play or constructive activities, is facilitated on the other hand by conflict-free anticipations of behaviour outcome. Constraints occur, however, in the presence of cognitive structures encoding social and probabilistic uncertainty, doubts about competence, and multidimensional goals.

These conceptualizations were tested over a number of years in several studies (Hamilton, 1972, 1976, 1979, 1981; Hamilton and Moss, 1974). The socialization variable was anxiety in children either inferred from maternal socializing strategies and attitudes or as exhibited in anxiety over school performance and the taking of tests and examinations. The first cognitive variable examined was conservation. In previous studies, directed at developmental antecedents of adult schizophrenia, impairments in the adequacy of this cognitive skill had been demonstrated in patients of average intelligence (Hamilton, 1966, 1972). Because of its importance in the development of related and later-maturing logical operations, I regarded conservation as a suitable cognitive skill on which to test the implications of an informational approach to the effects of socialization.

Conservation develops during the early years of maximum exposure and sensitivity to maternal influences, and provides the basis for adult knowledge of the invariance of objects, events, and ideas in the presence of misleading or irrelevant stimulus characteristics of the environment. It ranges from the concept of mother permanence to the concepts of mathematical invariances. (Conservation may even be involved in ambivalence – the child's dual perception of a loving and supportive mother, and her controlling restricting and punishing role.) Several studies suggest that infants develop the concept of the permanence of person before they develop inanimate object performance. Person permanence can affect the development of object permanence, and appears to be related to the quality of the infant's attachment behaviour towards his mother (e.g. Bell, 1970). Since person and object permanence are the first evidence of a conserving operation in the child, any maldevelopment at this stage may be a precursor of inadequacies or retardation of the conserving skill in later stages of cognitive development. If a child is exposed to socialization experiences which make it difficult to obtain certainty concerning maternal affection because it is ambivalently presented, or to experiences of rejection and loss of love, or to dominating control, a stress reaction may be elicited. In this event he may adopt a strategy of retreat from interactions with people and/or objects in an attempt to reduce stress. If these assumptions are correct, a child may be unable to learn and to accept the logical inevitability of certain events and conclusions, and his capacity for acquiring the skill of conservation (and other skills) may be permanently weakened.

Support consistent with this formulation comes from Goldschmid (1968) who found that children with higher levels of conservation tended to be more objective in their self-evaluations, were described more favourably by their teachers and peers, and were less dominated by their mothers than children with lower levels. Additional evidence was presented by Modgil and Lunzer (1971) who found that combinations of parental dominance, possessiveness, and ignoring their child were associated with depressed scores on Piagetian tests of conservation, as well as other basic cognitive skills. The theoretical basis of the project required a quantitative approach to the principal socialization dimensions as well as to conservation.

Maternal attitudes are multivariate and may be expressed overtly as well as covertly. In order to maximize the probability of obtaining valid assessments several techniques were combined and their results handled by regression analysis. In addition to a parental attitude questionnaire adapted from Schaefer (1965), the maternal test battery included Thematic Apperception Test plates representing actual or inferrable parent–child interaction situations, and a verbal and recorded descriptive sketch by the mother of the characteristics of her child and her attitudes towards him. It further included the presentation of several structured but hypothetical mother–child interaction situations and sets of prepared potential maternal responses to given forms of child behaviour. The following socializing dimensions were assessed: acceptance–rejection, control–autonomy, love and affection–hostility and anger, harsh–gentle, warmth–coldness, ambivalence–non-ambivalence, permissive–strict, and intellectual stimulation–non-stimulation. The TAT and child-description protocols were scored objectively for the unambiguous numerical presence of rejecting, negativistic, and punitive words.

The structured interaction situation technique employed a paired-comparison method. This is rarely used outside psycho-physical experiments, and was added here to improve the reliability of responses. For the acceptance–rejection dimension, the following hypothetical situation was one of those presented on typed cards: 'Supposing . . . hits you in the face because she is angry with you, how would you handle this?' Subjects were then given pairs of potential responses and required to say which of them would most likely reflect her reaction. Thirteen responses given in all pair-wise combinations were then offered. In the present example, the items for a girl were:

(1) Hit her back on whatever part of her body comes into the way of my hand.
(2) Smack her hand hard and give her an angry telling off.
(3) Hold her hands down firmly and tell her off angrily.
(4) I'd make sure that her father will deal with her.
(5) Lock her into the most unpleasant and uncomfortable room in the house/flat.
(6) I would show her that I felt hurt.
(7) Make her feel guilty about hurting the person who loves her.
(8) When she acts like that I would probably tell her that she is lucky that she has an understanding mother.

(9) Smile because I would be afraid to show my anger.

(10) I would tell her that since she does not see her parents hitting each other there is no reason why she should hit to get her way.

(11) Reason with her, and point out that violence can only lead to further violence, that we cannot always have things the way we want, and that arguments can be settled without fighting.

(12) Tell her that if she is angry about something, we could sit down sensibly together to discuss the reason for her anger.

(13) Tell her that I don't like being hit, but reassure her and don't punish her.

Preferences for reactions 1–5 and 10–13 demonstrate respectively acceptance and rejection, whereas choosing reactions 6–9 represents ambivalent and covertly unfavourable attitudes.

Detailed discussion of scoring and of the results is available in Research Reports (Hamilton, 1970, 1973) and can be only briefly summarized here. For validation purposes the test battery was given to 40 mothers of children attending a Child Guidance Clinic and 40 mothers of children attending a General Hospital or Dental Clinic. TAT and child-description material was scored by investigators who had not obtained the data themselves and without knowledge of subject group on the criterion stated above. Reliability of scoring was confirmed at almost 90 per cent.

Step-wise multiple regression analysis was used – checked by discriminant function analyses – to find a set of test parameters which would maximally separate the two criterion groups. To avoid subjective decisions in the selection of test parameters from a total number of 37, correlational and t-test analyses were carried out first. These showed that certain indices provided initial good evidence of group discrimination (i.e. scores on projective material and the paired-comparison test of acceptance–rejection), and of internal validity. The major discriminants came from the testing of covert maternal attitudes.

This block of indices, taken in all possible combinations, and with the step-wise addition and subtraction of indices from the paired-comparison tests of intellectual stimulation, warmth, and permissiveness, was submitted to differential weighting analyses. The weighted combination of 13 indices yielded a misclassification error of 7.5 per cent, using Mahalombis' D^2 index. Surprisingly the misclassification error from the projective probes taken on their own was only 13 per cent which was not significantly larger on calculation than 7.5 per cent. This result was disappointing primarily because it had been hoped either to exclude a projective test method which would always attract criticisms from objectively oriented researchers, or to minimize its role in a battery of selection indices. It was gratifying that the amount and type of information extracted from the TAT and child-description protocols so clearly fell into two groups that only 11 out of 80 protocols were misclassified with respect to subject group.

The tests yielding the lowest misclassification error with the addition of TAT plates and child descriptions were then given to 300 mothers of 7–8-year-old children in three schools. Two criterion groups of 40 mothers each were constructed on the basis of additive and weighted scores respectively representative of suboptimal and optimal child-rearing techniques and attitudes. Each maternal subject was also invited to tape-record a message to her own child in her own words in which she encouraged the child to take part in an experiment with the investigator. The length and content of the message were deliberately uncontrolled. To recapitulate: (i) suboptimal socializing was predicted to be reflected in suboptimal cognitive-ability – in this case in conservation testing; (ii) type and amount of maternal message was intended to reflect the preferred method of transmitting socializing information; and (iii) a history of unfavourable mother–child interaction, the experimental message, and the experimental task were predicted to generate performance-related anxiety in the child subjects leading to poor results in problem-solving.

Rank-order differences in maternal attitudes and strategies relatable to child competence needed to be matched by at least rank-order differences in task difficulty, if not by equal interval scale steps between problems. With rare exceptions individual differences in conservation have tended to be expressed by gross nominal scale categories, especially when one particular developmental level of this cognitive skill is assessed. Thus subjects' responses have been commonly classified as non-conserving, pre-conserving or transitional, and conserving, with additional categories of almost conserving or undecided (e.g. Lovell and Ogilvie, 1960). Alternatively, subjects' actual verbalized reasons for a conserving or non-conserving response have been used to differentiate them (e.g. Elkind, 1961). Apart from the difficulties attending the interpretation of verbal responses, this approach is usually confined to a limited number of test problems (at a specified level of conservation) which restricts the demonstration of the full range of individual differences. One of the main factors in this orientation was a perhaps unnecessarily rigid adherence to Piaget's concept of stages. Stages and levels of cognitive development inferred from verbal responses are of doubtful validity, and more objective indices of cognitive performance are desirable. The type of study reported by Wohlwill (1960) partly overcame this problem by extending the investigation to a wider range of difficulty embodied in conservation of number problems. This study had additional merit by virtue of the application of scalogram analysis to the difficulty hierarchy, thus permitting rank-order statistics and more discriminating demonstrations of individual differences to be carried out. Similar approaches to the scaling of cognitive development based on the stage concept have been attempted by Nassefat (1963) and Laurendeau and Pinard (1963). In both instances the level of cognitive development is derived from performance on a test hierarchy representative of stages of hypothesized progressively higher-order developmental structures as demanded by Piaget's conception of stages.

While this type of approach permits the empirical validation of problem difficulty, it is by no means certain that it is the most appropriate test of the stage theory, and it throws up many philosophical and physiological difficulties (Pinard and Laurendeau, 1969). For example, conservations of weight or displaced or occupied volume are more difficult than conservation of substance or quantity. What may be questioned is the largely tacit assumption that conservation at one particular stage of development is an all-or-none skill, and that we are dealing with discontinuities in cognition. That is to say, a child is either non-conserving, transitional, or conserving. Piaget illustrates his conception of an incomplete conserving operation by reference to changes in the response when a child is faced with the situation $A_1 \rightarrow C_1 + C_2 + C_3$ compared with $A_1 \rightarrow B_1 + B_2$ (Piaget, 1952). The transitional child conserves in the latter, but not in the former situation. An 'equal' response in the first situation, however, makes the child a conserver. The approach to the differential difficulty of conservation problems at one particular level of development presented here would hold that a child's conserving response in the situation $A_1 \rightarrow C_1 + C_2 + C_3$ does not guarantee that he will be able to conserve in situations containing multiple, heterogeneous deformations and redistributions. Supposing $C_1 \rightarrow D_1 + D_2$ and $C_3 \rightarrow D_3 + D_4 + D_5$, so that the comparison is between A_1 and $C_2 + D_1 + D_2 + D_3 + D_4 + D_5$. This extended conservation problem is predicted to be more difficult because a purely perceptual strategy will be approximate and inefficient, because more equations have to be handled, and because the inclusion of subsidiary conserving steps increases the information processing demands on the cognitive system.

From this analysis it can be concluded that an equational step in the presentation and analysis of a conservation of quantity or substance problem is a suitable unit for the quantification of informational load. Pilot studies confirmed that the number of units or steps are primarily defined by increasing the number of originally equal quantities, the number of distributions and redistributions, the number of parts formed thereby, and the number of so-called reversibility steps necessitated by a particular test question. By these manipulations equations could be generated to define systematically the informational content of problems. The greater the value of the above parameters, the larger the number of equations presented by it. The larger the number of equations involved in a problem, the greater its informational content.

On this basis the informational load of problems can be formalized by the statement

$$n(\text{steps}) = n_{C2} + \Sigma_i(m_i + p_i + 2q_i + d_i) + 1$$

where n_{C2} is the number of originally equal standard quantities, m is the number of parts resulting from distributions, p is the number of times given quantities were distributed or divided, $2q$ is the number of distributions of quantity necessary to deduce a conserving response, d is the number of quantities that were only deformed but not divided, and 1 is the equation

118

representing the solution statement (see Hamilton and Moss, 1974, for a detailed discussion).

Item analysis indicated that a minimal difference of 7 equational steps between adjacent problems in a series of progressive difficulty was required to reflect individual differences adequately on this task. Validation of the final test instrument was carried out on 150 children aged 7–9 years. Whereas the pilot studies had manipulated the difficulty parameter by laboriously adding vessels of different shapes, sizes, and numbers, or by actually forming plasticine shapes, concrete problem presentation of this traditional Piagetian type was retained only for the simplest problems in the new test. All other problems were drawn on heavy card with a full verbal description of the graphically shown distributions and redistributions, followed by the test question. Informational load and hypothesized difficulty increased from 3 to 68 equational steps. The average correlation between pass rate for problems and the n(steps) index was -0.941. This evidence of internal validity required support from concurrent validity, and an appropriate study was carried out.

The new test instrument was given to the children of the previously selected groups of optimally and suboptimally socializing mothers. Figure 5.7 shows

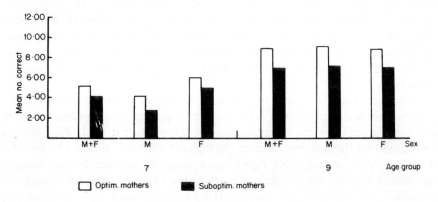

Figure 5.7 Conservation ability of optimally and suboptimally reared children
(after Hamilton, 1975)

the results for the groups of children which were controlled for verbal IQ, reading age, and socio-economic class. All the differences were in the predicted direction. An important associated prediction was tested in a repetition of the experiment one week later with a parallel version of the same test. On this occasion the investigators played the tape-recorded message of each child's mother at the beginning and at two further points during the session. This manipulation was designed as an analogue of an actual maternal participation in problem-solving. The predictions were that the children of optimal mothers would respond with greater effectiveness than the children of suboptimal mothers, and that performance might even decline for the latter group despite the operation of a practice factor. Figure 5.8 shows the results

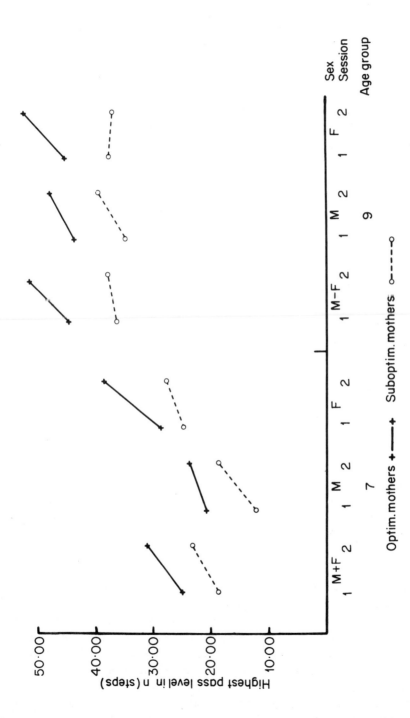

Figure 5.8 Effect of maternal participation on the conserving skill (after Hamilton, 1975)

of this manipulation, where Session 1 data are an alternative demonstration of the data shown in Figure 5.7, and where Session 2 data show the effects of the maternal message. The critical interactions between socialization group and performance were consistent with prediction and particularly strong for female subjects, and for 9-year-olds. Therefore, on the assumption that the test instrument validly reflects information-processing capacity, fine-grain differences can be demonstrated in association with ranked differences in socialization on a favourable to unfavourable continuum. Furthermore, groups of children without any evidence of behavioural problems respond differently to maternal messages which reflect their usual socialization background.

Five assumptions are tested in the cognitive/information processing approach to the effects of socialization on levels of cognitive skill. Firstly, that socialization is an information-transmitting process which affects an individual's preferred methods of obtaining preferred goals and behaviour outcomes. Secondly, that these behavioural preferences are themselves conceptual structures organized in progressively elaborated and differential schemata. Thirdly, that the amount of informational content of such cognitive structures is a function of dominant socialization experience, and particularly of its subjective interpretation by the young child or adolescent. Fourthly, because dominant experiences and preferred behavioural goals are cognitively coded, this type of long-term memory information can interact with the cognitive data, operations, and processes of affectively neutral responses in any situation requiring adaptation, including problem-solving. Fifthly, and consequently, types of socialization experience are able to interact systematically with cognitive tasks differing in information processing demands.

Our first four assumptions were tested only indirectly in the studies just described. We had to infer that types of optimal or suboptimal social stimulation correspond to the type of informational content of dominant cognitive structures of the recipients of given types of information. Studies reported in Chapters 6 and 8 were designed to bridge some of the gaps in theorizing and evidence indicated here. Our fifth assumption was simpler to support with additional evidence. Two closely related experiments were carried out to supply concurrent validity for the proposition that differential amounts of information were contained in the conservation problems of hypothesized systematically increasing difficulty. The predictions were that (i) high-scoring conservers would sort playing cards into categories of decreasing degrees of redundancy more quickly and with fewer errors than low-scoring or non-conserving children, and (ii) high-scoring conservers would show a matching superiority in a coding task with systematically increasing symbol substitution requirements. Details of these experiments are described in Hamilton and Launay (1976).

The experiment testing the first prediction has been described in Chapter 3 and the results were graphed in Figure 3.2. A particularly strong relationship was obtained for the predictions of differences between good conservers and others ($F = 4.03$, df. $= 8,336$, $p < 0.001$).

The second validation of the information load conceptualization of conservation was undertaken with a coding and recoding task. The experiment is difficult to describe briefly and the interested reader is referred to the source reference (Hamilton and Launay, 1976). The task required an increasing number of symbol substitution operations which defined its progressive difficulty. Primary stimuli – illuminated upper case letters on a display screen – were assigned the colour values red, green, or yellow. Subjects were given two response keys labelled 'yellow' and 'red' which they had to activate after applying a set of rules such as: 'yellow is more than red', 'two yellows are more than two greens', 'two reds are more than one yellow', etc. Two additional recoding stages were progressively introduced: representing letters by geometrical symbols, and assigning numbers to geometrical symbols. When recoding only letters into colours, the substitutional or operational steps equal the number of primary stimuli – letters. With three recoding stages 5 equational steps are required for solution. By varying the presentation of the number of primary stimuli and the number of recoding stages, an ordinal scale of problem difficulty could be devised ranging from 1–30 equational steps which needed to be processed before a problem could be solved. The experiment was carried out on the same subjects who took part in the informational redundancy study, and response time and errors were the dependent variables. Figure 5.9 gives the results for mean number of errors for a selection of difficulty points. (Because of a 'stop' criterion after two consecutive failures insufficient data were available to evaluate perform-

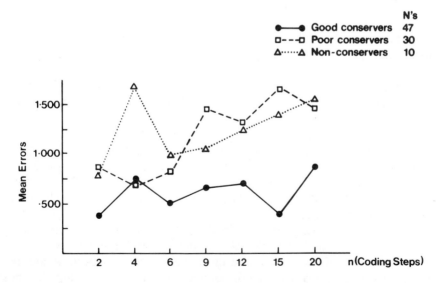

Figure 5.9 Coding and conserving capacity

ance beyond 20 coding steps.) The group, conditions, and group by conditions interaction effects were highly reliable and demonstrate the substantial superiority of the children with good conserving ability. Response time data were consistent but somewhat less reliable, partly because of the lower competence of the younger non-conservers in the early simpler problems, and partly because of the common speed-error trade-off. The experimental groups were comparable for socio-economic group and educational age-related levels. It is important to have demonstrated in both validation studies that the difference between the theoretically defined criterion groups increases with hypothesized task-difficulty which is precisely what would be predicted on the basis of an information processing load approach to the effects of unfavourable, anxiety-inducing socialization strategies and attitudes.

A further study was designed to demonstrate in a simpler and more limited setting the effects of different degrees of socialization anxiety on performance. Restraints in research funding, however, left an unfortunate but unavoidable gap: the relationship between an instrument measuring school and test performance-related anxiety and the indices of maternal child-rearing procedure could not be evaluated. An assumption was made that so-called Test Anxiety is a good reflection of socialization anxiety. The children who had previously taken part in the conservation study, and who were still available for experimentation, were assessed on Sarason et al's (1960) Test Anxiety Scale for Children (TASC). Task-difficulty in this study was defined by dual and simultaneous cognitive tasks with increasing amounts of informational content. The dual tasks were visual reaction time and digit span. A series of 3, 4, or 5 digits were read out for rehearsal and subsequent recall while subjects were set to respond to a visual signal. Reaction time was the dependent variable, and the results of groups differing in this type of social anxiety are shown in Figure 5.10. The main and interaction effects were somewhat less reliable than those obtained in some of the other studies. There was a clear-cut difference between groups, however, for the single task (digits = 0) to dual task *change*, but only a slight trend for the difficulty by anxiety interaction.

As evidence from our progressive series of studies accumulated, the potential source of favourable or unfavourable interactions between behaviour disposition and task performance came into focus. If both variables are defined as information encoded in a comparable or identical symbolic form, then the total amount of informational data should aggregate in short-term working memory in a test situation. If this conclusion is correct, then deficits shown on tasks are due to the overloading of this cognitive processing component, and to an inability to decode and hold information to be worked on. This inability or difficulty would be most pronounced if superordinate individual conceptualizations of a task assigned priority to meeting the most dominant goals of the personal behaviour system, rather than to the task itself. If social anxiety is task-irrelevant information, it can be predicted that

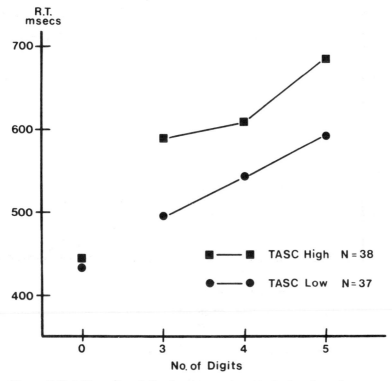

Figure 5.10 Effect of socialization/test anxiety on dual-task performance
(after Hamilton, 1976)

the earliest stage of working memory – iconic and early buffer stores – would
already show the effect of this source of interference.

In the final study involving new groups of children which I can report, very
short-term memory for letters was assessed. Following Sperling's (1960)
influential experiments, letter squares containing 12 letters were presented
at fast tachistoscopic speed (300 msec). This was slower than is traditional
because children are less practised in letter identification than adults or
students. The presentation terminated with a masking stimulus and a verbal
instruction as to which row or column of letters the subject was to recall. In
this partial report technique the number of correctly remembered letters is
multiplied by the number of letter rows or columns in the full display (see
also Chapter 3). Figure 5.11 shows the results of the experiment, which were
highly significant. It is worth noting, thus anticipating discussions in later
chapters, that concurrently obtained data on arousal levels and changes in
levels as reflected in skin conductance and heart rate did not co-vary with
group performances. On the other hand, however, poor memory and high
social anxiety were both significantly related to reading ability, though not
to verbal intelligence level.

This raises the further questions of why poor readers are anxious, to which

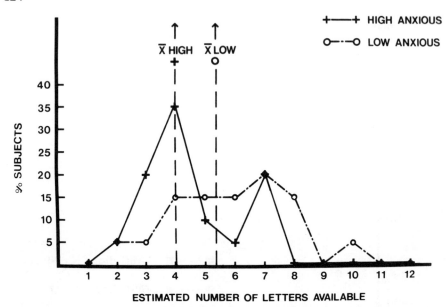

Figure 5.11 Effect of socialization/test anxiety on estimated number of letters available for recall (after Hamilton, 1979)

there may be an obvious answer, or the more complex question of why anxious children *might be* (though need not be) poor readers. I have probably cited enough evidence under the 'traditional approach' to indicate that unfavourable social and socialization factors will affect the development of educational skills. The information processing approach to the mediating operations and processes serves to identify, however, less gross, more fine-grained and more definitive analytic cognitive events by which individual effectiveness and competence may be achieved or diminished.

CHAPTER 6

The cognitive-semantic representation of motivation and personality

1 ANTECEDENT CONSIDERATIONS

In the last chapter I argued several propositions.

(1) That the socialization process is essentially an information transmission process.
(2) That the information transmitted is assembled and organized in functionally related cognitive structures.
(3) That cognitive structures encode individually preferred response dispositions and the goals towards which these are directed.
(4) That the development of characteristic preferred methods of obtaining preferred goals of behaviour outcomes involves the development of conceptual knowledge representations in permanent memory.
(5) That concepts of characteristic behaviour and its goals depend on referents and attributes which facilitate or constrain activities and behaviour outcomes.
(6) That optimal development depends on permanent memory structures encoding favourable self-knowledge such as acceptance, firm and affectionate control within unambiguous norms, communication of encouragement towards achievement, and explanations of difficult and conflictful situations.
(7) That interactions between the effects of socialization on personality and motivation and educational and intellectual development occur because all response-selecting events are cognitive events.

On these grounds it is possible to retain the traditional term 'dispositions' for behaviour characteristics and their determinants on certain conditions only. These must be consistent with cognitive specifications for social and intra-personal events, and for the transmission, elaboration, and depositing of the meaning and implications of stimulus and response-related information. These conditions and their elaborations can be embodied in a number

125

of *a priori* assumptions based on my analysis in Chapter 2, whose discussion will form the core of this chapter. I shall not necessarily argue these in the order in which they are listed here.

(1) Non-cognitive concepts of personality and motivation are substantially based on early scientific paradigms and are descriptive rather than explanatory.

(2) *Categorical* distinctions between personality and motivational processes are redundant.

(3) The evidence of unitary integrative behavioural acts requires evidence of the operation of integrative processes which can combine data from all behaviour-guiding systems.

(4) *Psychological* levels of analysis cannot usefully extend beyond cognitive processing constructs.

(5) Cognitive processing constructs are able to define preferences in methods of approaching or avoiding hierarchies of goals.

(6) Distinctions are required between cognitive *orientations towards* and cognitive *redefinitions of* personality and motivational characteristics.

(7) Since behaviour is governed by experience of preferred behaviour outcomes, cognitive processing constructs require symbolic data codes which can convey knowledge of outcomes.

(8) Because the organization and interpretation of all non-reflexive adaptive behaviour requires an analysis of stimulus meaning and of the implications of alternative responses, the required networks of informational data codes need to be semantic networks.

(9) Semantic networks representing the referents and attributes of personal goals and their precedence constitute semantic memories, which have established functional and adaptive utility over a large range of response requirements.

(10) The generalized utility of attributional semantic networks suggests that semantic memories relating to personality and motivation are organized in schemata.

(11) Where individuals possess highly elaborated, characteristic goal-directed semantic schemata with low retrieval thresholds, internal, self-relevant cognitive activities will affect the objective utilization of external stimuli

The approach which I am presenting here can be summarized by a number of inductive and quasi-deductive propositional steps. These steps are represented in the statements tabulated in Table 6.1 They are not intended to be logically pure syllogistic steps – the embedded concepts are too gross as well as too complex for such an exercise. Table 6.1 does reflect, however, my own reasoning steps in coming to the conclusion that the conception of personality and motivational characteristics as semantically coded cognitive structures is a plausible conception. It has the minimal merits (i) of being experimentally testable, (ii) of being consistent with a large body of psychological research, and (iii) of having been arrived at independently from other efforts to reinterpret what used to be called non-cognitive variables.

Table 6.1

All behaviour	is	Goal-directed behaviour
Motivation	is	Behaviour towards preferred goals
Personality	is	Preferred characteristic goal-directed behaviour
Preference	is	Choice and selection from alternatives by anticipating outcome
Choice and selection processes anticipating outcome	are	Problem-solving processes
Problem-solving	operates on	Information about stimulus attributes, definitions, and implications
Stimulus attributes, definitions, and implications	are	Long-term memory data
Fine-grained stimulus attributes, definitions, and implications	are	Fine-grained long-term memory data
Long-term memory data	are	Inter-related informational structures
Fine-grained information structures	are	Fine-grained conceptual data networks
Fine-grained conceptual data networks representing stimulus attributes, definitions, and implications	are	Conceptual networks supplying knowledge and meaning
Conceptual networks supplying knowledge and meaning	are the	Results of communication and instruction, and their encoding and elaboration in long-term memory networks
The medium of communicating and instructing in fine-grained stimulus attributes, definitions, and implications	is	Semantic language, its lexicon and encyclopaedia
Behaviour demonstrating and anticipating outcome of preferred characteristic methods of achieving preferred goals	is	Evidence of response selection by processes employing semantically coded concepts
Personality and motivation	are the	Results of operations on semantically coded conceptual structures

In subsequent sections of this chapter I will argue in favour of *cognitive structure concepts for affect, traits,* and *goals.* I will propose, furthermore, that the organizing functions of adaptive, characteristic, and preferred methods of action towards characteristic and preferred goals are usefully conceptualized by the concept of the cognitive schema. I will then turn to a consideration of the role of semantically coded information in the representation of the strategies and goals of behaviour.

Before I turn to the critical discussion, I would like to make one brief and one longer comment on two issues. Firstly, the implications of accepting the participation of expectancy-oriented mediating processes in animal learning. Such orientation seems to imply some kind of 'symbolic language' capacity for the analysis of input in terms of anticipation of the results of output in the higher infra-human species. This seems a plausible inference because in primates physiognomic and postural cues seem to be efficiently recognized as signalling the appropriateness of either approach or avoidance behaviour. Also, with the addition of a limited range of vocal signals, a relatively restricted repertoire of understanding stimulus meaning and response outcome expectancy seems to be present which is capable of facilitating quite complex adaptive individual and group relationships (e.g. Lawick-Goodall, 1971).

My second interpolated comment refers to the role variously assigned to consciousness in the self-regulation of behaviour. Like psychology, the concept of consciousness has a long past but a short history. It has been a key issue in the body–mind controversy and has remained a relevant parameter in accounting for and evaluating human behaviour. If the self-regulating processes governing behaviour towards goals take particular directions in order to achieve desirable rather than undesirable outcomes, then it is a plausible inference that the choice of a particular direction by the behavioural systems is a function of their having access to the differential outcomes of all alternatives. That is, cognitive processes have been able to match the implications of alternative actions with the goal to be achieved, and have selected the quickest, safest, and most satisfying method of doing so. Operations serving this end require interactions between working and permanent memory supported by sustained attention to the required end state. They also require serial and/or parallel retrieval from permanent memory of representations of past actions and outcomes towards goals of this particular class, in this type of context, with a given level of goal-approach or goal-avoidance intensity.

A great deal of recent thinking and writing on consciousness would be prepared to define these characteristics of self-regulating behaviour as evidence of conscious processes (e.g. Schwartz and Shapiro, 1976; Underwood and Stevens, 1979, 1981). In my view this conclusion is conceptually over-inclusive since it would lead to the generalization that all cognitive behaviour is conscious behaviour. This would lead to the plausible deduction that cognitive processes in dream-sleep are conscious processes, a deduction which is confusing and in general terms illogical, particularly if dream content cannot be reported. The proper antithesis here would be between brain-death and consciousness, since all cognitive processes depend ultimately on electrocortical activity, and since there is overwhelming experimental evidence for pre-conscious and unconscious cognitive activity (Dixon, 1981).

A necessary distinction must be made between *knowing*, for example, that the only way of avoiding being run over by an approaching car is to jump over a fence, and *knowing that one does or did know*. To know that one needs to jump over a fence includes a large number of internally computed but unreportable events which help to trigger a partially reflex action. They are not reportable because they either occur in parallel or in such rapid succession that they generate a retroactive inhibition or masking effect. If they are not reportable we are not aware of them, even though they have apparently communicated effectively with relevant components of the response-generating system. It is my view that to define this communication within the cognitive processing system and its interaction with the motor effector system as evidence of consciousness, is to deprive the concept of all distinctive relevance.

It could be argued that consciousness is essentially a working memory function. Working memory holds representations of a need state, of the goal required to reduce the need, while engaged in a rapid series of matching processes involving strategies available in permanent memory and the constraints and facilitations which define goal-access. A more restrained and more logical definition of consciousness would confine the concept to the ability to monitor these processes, and to the ability to report their major stages. This limited specification is a minor modification of Bartlett's (1932) concept of 'turning round upon ones own schemata', which can equally serve as a justification for the distinction between the conscious and unconscious processes maintained by psycho-analytic theorists. Whether we are dealing with an experimental task of remembering detailed aspects of a complex picture or story after a lengthy interval of time, or with the search for the determinants of a piece of unwanted behaviour, we would be able to say in both instances that the production of a 'missing link', after *knowing* which gap needed to be bridged, would facilitate the task. In both examples we may speak of *insightful problem-solving* in which reportable and therefore *conscious knowledge* of what needed to be found facilitates the selection of a missing piece of information, but where the *process* has defied introspection ever since it began to be studied systematically (Humphrey, 1951).

Consciousness in terms of awareness and monitoring of one's own thought processes can be regarded as counter-productive to efficiency. A processing system of finite capacity, and particularly its short-term working memory component, is interrupted in its search for and integration of information while self-monitoring, while at the same time rehearsing its currently held input. It is slowed down by a monitoring instruction and becomes less efficient in integrating the information which it has collected already for the execution of one particular response. In cybernetic terms Shallice (1972) has suggested that no more than one action system can become dominant at any given time. Eclectic information processing theory would say that volitional attention-demanding examination of the content of a memory store system prescribes a dual and, therefore, more difficult task for that system. The increase of information load would lead to slowness, loss of information and a reduction of optimal responding. Hence, *self-observation* of a habitual act slows it down and disrupts its smooth production, and self-consciousness impairs simple and, particularly, complex responses. We should conclude, however, that the critical definition of consciousness as self-monitoring implies guidance from a superordinate system which encodes methods and goals of behaviour which have general rather than specific application in the achievement of an acceptable total state of the individual.

An extensively documented monograph on the evidence for pre-conscious cognitive processes by Dixon (1981) appears to be consistent with these formulations. Dixon argues (i) that the *criteria* for conscious representation must apply to pre-conscious stages of information processing; (ii) that if stimulus meaning contributes to conscious awareness then analysis of meaning (i.e. semantic analysis) must have occurred before it enters consciousness; (iii) that stimulus meaning depends on access to unconscious permanent memory data *and its utilization before* it can be reported; (iv) that the capacity for monitoring sensory input is considerably greater than consciousness of the semantic processing applied to it; and (v) that semantically analysed but unreportable cognitive events must be able to influence all cognitive processes, including the content of consciousness. The logical and experimental support for these conceptualizations must lead to the conclusions that non-conscious processes are indeed cognitive processes, but that cognitive processes need not be conscious. Limitations of consciousness according to Dixon are not only affected by pre-conscious analysis of the subjective meaning and implications of stimulation (see also Chapter 9), but by the physiological characteristics of channel capacity for the transmission of information, and by the 'signal to noise' ratio of the information itself.

Two points may be added to Dixon's evaluations. The identity between reportable and unreportable processes is probably not complete when considering (a) self-monitoring, that is my own restricted interpretation of consciousness, and (b) the after-effects of stimulating emotively-toned information. Clearly, self-monitoring is a process that cannot be applied to data prevented from achieving salience in short-term working memory. As a result, the potential for informational analysis is restricted. The difference in processing potential as between emotively-neutral and emotively-toned processes resides in the implications of the content of the respective schematic structures themselves. For example, retrieving and then rejecting a concept or concept attribute because of its poor logical fit in response selection, has no further implications for the structures wrongly accessed. The search process simply continues until a matching process produces cues of an acceptable fit. If, however, an affectively loaded cognitive structure has been accessed, and if this structure is encoded with highly aversive attributes and behavioural implications, rejection of this information does not necessarily cease continuing activities on its contents and their associations. The response-generating system will indeed pass on to searching other (neutral) structures to fulfil the requirements of instructions from working memory, while the sensitized structures *simultaneously* attempt to cope with the stimulation to which they have been exposed by reducing their noxiousness (see Chapters 8 and 9 for elaborations of this notion).

2 TRAITS AND GOALS AS COGNITIVE STRUCTURES

I will now try to elaborate my propositions that personality traits and the significant goals towards which they are directed are long-term memory structures directing action by thought processes. These processes need not be available to awareness or self-monitoring, nor need they be a function of deliberate, consciously directed planning. Consistent with the position taken in the preceding chapter, I will argue that when a person engages in a particular form of action to obtain a particular end result, that person is engaged in problem-solving. To select behaviour method A rather than B or C indicates that a faster and more favourable outcome is expected by method A. This implies in turn that this manner of action has been successful more frequently. Knowledge of successful outcome must mean that the relationship between goal and behaviour is essentially no different from the relationship between using an object to achieve a purpose, for example selecting a hammer to drive in a nail as quickly and expertly as possible. I am suggesting, therefore, that the selection of trait-defining, goal-directed behaviour depends as much on conceptual knowledge representations as does the selection of a tool for its characteristic function. Knowledge of functional properties has been derived, however, from experience of its application in a context. Thus, knocking in a nail to hold two pieces of wood together without bending the nail or hitting and denting painted pieces of wood has been facilitated in the past by using an instrument that is relatively heavy, that has efficient lever characteristics, and a fairly broad contact surface.

Let us assume that the goal of behaviour method A above is to obtain an admission ticket to a heavily subscribed concert, film, or play. Possible oversubscription defines the context of the goal: barriers from competition with others wanting to reach the same goal, competition defined by early long queues, the latter being variously defined, depending on past first- or second-hand knowledge, by discomforts from standing for long hours, intermittent rain, and/or neglect of other tasks which are concurrent goals. Successful problem-solving involves the conceptual analysis of the contextual constraints and a selection of preferred forms of action which best fit the constraints. These will have acquired a dominant and characteristic position in the person's repertoire of actions by earlier yields of favourable outcome, and from subjective criteria of effort, competence, and need for cultural stimulation. The valued admission ticket in the present example may be gained either by submitting to all the demanding constraints by lining-up on the night before, by rewarding someone else for queuing instead, by answering an advertisement for the sale of tickets no longer required, or by using a friendship network ending at the door of the Box Office Manager and a complimentary ticket. Since we are describing the characteristics of a culture-seeker, it may be inappropriate to include strategies like falsely laying claim to a front position in the queue by one stratagem or another, or pretending that one has purchased a ticket, lost it, and claiming another!

Goal-directed problem-solving with the help of a behaviour repertoire has components which do not immediately fit into the cognitive analysis of trait–goal interaction. These are the emotional concomitants, the feelings or affective factors which are associated with the various forms of preferred actions available to a person, with the large variety of goals towards which they are capable of being directed, and with the success, failure, or postponement of goal-achievement. The discussion will start therefore with a reconsideration of the role and specification of affect. It will proceed to an analysis of the kinds of data that are usually sampled by questionnaires, and then to a unifying analysis of the trait–goal relationship within the framework of schematically organized cognitive structures.

(i) The representation of affect

My arguments will attempt to show that distinctions between cognitive and non-cognitive events are largely redundant in any discussion of cause-and-effect interactions between visceral and problem-solving events. This statement expresses the formal proposition that the primary contribution of affect to behaviour and goal-selection is a cognitive contribution, and that affective experience and self-regulating and state requirements are represented together as conceptual data in cognitive structures. There are three mainstays for the proposition.

(1) The categorical nature and implications of an affective state cannot be known to a person, or to his stimulus analysing and integrating system unless it is conceptually established and symbolically labelled.

(2) Avoiding or seeking a particular affect constitutes a goal even though the cognitive-semantic representation of this type of goal is gross and undifferentiated. Unless this were the case, expectancy and anticipation of affect could not form part of response selection.

(3) In generating and selecting preferred methods for the attainment of preferred goals, the data, or informational code of contributions from all experience categories, must have the same symbolic language to ensure integration.

When affect is cognitively defined, arguments about whether it precedes cognition or follows it become unhelpful and relatively meaningless. The utility and validity of my reconceptualization depends, however, on satisfactory answers to three questions: (i) are infants' affective responses cognitive responses; (ii) are visceral, physiological, and neurochemical events affect-specific; and (iii) how does our response system become aware of and initiate action following stimulation from affective events?

Recent necessary rereading in the area conveys an impression of effort, but also of conceptual confusion. Strongman (1978), for example, has commented on some 30 theories of emotion which often appear to present common denominators, but have not yielded a unitary concept. One major reason for this shortcoming is likely to be the use of an interchangeable terminology in the theoretical labelling of affective experience and events. Thus, autonomic arousal, feeling, emotion, emotionality, motivation, drive, and affect are infrequently differentiated with clarity. Pair-wise combinations of the labels, too, have been used, such as affective arousal or emotional arousal, or one or the other term has employed the remainder to signify subsystems. Izard (1977), for example, regards emotion not only as one subsystem of personality, but also as one type of motivation, the others being drive, affect–cognition interaction and affective cognitive-structures, Bindra (1968) and Leeper (1970), however, considered a distinction between motivation and emotion unnecessary.

Arnold (1969, 1970), Lazarus (1966, 1968) and Mandler (1975), on the other hand, put forward theories of simultaneous, or closely sequential, physiological arousal and cognitive appraisal for the production of an emotional experience, but only Mandler appears to give absolute precedence to the physiological arousal process. This may be regarded as a somewhat overinclusive position since arousal is required initially to *facilitate the direction* of attentional energy to any type of stimulus, whether external or internal, whether affectively significant, or affectively neutral. Arnold distinguishes between feeling and emotion by suggesting that the former adds to the appraisal-determinant of the latter an evaluation of the object or situation that has been appraised. From my own point of view, this is not a very useful distinction since an emotional reaction is hardly called for unless the cognitive identification of an event has 'good' or 'bad' implications for the appraiser. Considerably more important is Arnold's suggestion that appraisal is associated with the *memory of the affect* with which an object or event has been associated on previous exposure to it. This *must* be true, otherwise evaluative labels supporting feelings in Arnold's model, or the emotional reaction following appraisal in Lazarus' model, could not occur.

The consensus obtained from the majority of theoretical positions assigns a dominant though not as yet a primary role to cognitive processes. Schachter's experiments (Schachter, 1964; Schachter and Singer, 1962) are open, however, to that shift in emphasis. Although Schachter would probably no longer fully agree with all his earlier conclusions, his original epinephrine/social model studies strongly indicated that an emotion remains non-specific autonomic arousal unless the subject can attach affect-signifying verbal labels to it.

Definitions of affect are rare, and, as I suggested before, are lacking in unidimensionality. Izard (1977, p.65), for example, regards affect as a non-specific term which subsumes motivational states and processes, emotions, patterns of emotions, drives, and linkages and interactions with perceptions and cognitions. Kagan's (1978) conclusions on how affect has tended to be defined are similar. He lists changes in feeling states derived from internal physiological events, an immediately preceding stimulus which he terms a short-lived incentive event, linkage with cognitive structures, and the absence of physiological deprivation. These, he argues, are loose conceptualizations of the complex experience of detecting a change in one's feelings (or in those of another person). In a careful reanalysis of the development of emotion, Kagan suggests instead that changes in feeling state are primary sensations, and that these ought to be examined like other changes in sensory qualities.

Although Kagan regards cognitive events as important he does not go on to say that the person's analysis of changes in the experience of sensory quality is itself a cognitive process. This extension is justified, however, because changes in duration, intensity, periodicity, and suddenness of sensory events will be detected by hippocampal structures for transmission to higher centres. Hippocampal structures are pre-programmed to detect and respond to sensory discrepancy, where the sensing of discrepancy must involve a comparative process against a standard. That this is an early cognitive differentiating capacity is supported by studies such as those of Kearsley (1973). Here auditory stimulation of newborns with a slow-rise (gradual increase) of intensity elicited interest, whereas a fast-rise stimulation triggered an avoidance response.

Rapaport (1953), arguing from a psycho-analytic point of view, considered affect as signals. In the present context we can then say that the meaning of the signal for the newborn has binary characteristics. That is, it contains one bit of information, which yields either a 'good' or 'bad', or a 'liked' or a 'disliked' decision. The analogy here with Schneirla's (1959) A-type and W-type of arousal in response to, respectively, weak and high-intensity stimulation as fundamental response dispositions, appears to be a good one. Moreover, a biologically pre-programmed dichotomous response basis fits in with existing knowledge of the gradual differentiation of emotional expression as presented from Bridges (1932) onwards. This conceptualization is also reflected in Thomas and Chess' (1980) most recent evaluation of the implications of their New York Temperament Studies. Although Thomas and Chess consider that we are not yet able to apply developmental conceptual categories to stages in emotional development, they do relate emotional to cognitive development and thus tacitly accept the possibility that affective differentiation is cognitively mediated.

The initial answer to my first question is, therefore, that if newborns are capable of some form of cognitive analysis of emotion affect-inducing stimuli, older infants should be even more competent to do so. Since we have no grounds for challenging the evidence of approach-avoidance generalization learning from conditioning studies, the experience of pleasure or delight, and of displeasure or distress must in themselves have acquired a cognitive representation. This statement *must* be true because learning entails the *anticipation* of a particular behaviour outcome. As Bolles (1972) argued, it is not a response to a stimulus that is learned, but the *expectancy* of the result of the response. Anticipation and expectancy, however, are not limited to the sensory objective characteristics of the stimulus. They include memory of the affective experience of an antecedent event, which now becomes an inseparable component of one particular stimulus, and subsequently, of a class of stimuli.

A legitimate extension of this conclusion can be offered. Some adaptive systems have been shown to be more sensitive to unpleasant and distressing stimulation than to weaker and more gradual interest- or pleasure-generating stimuli, (e.g. Averill *et al.*, 1978). If that is a valid conclusion then there is a strong possibility that the affect-representing components, or attributes of cognitive structures encoding objects, situations, and other referents, will have a lower retrieval threshold on subsequent occasions when the relevant unpleasant referents appear in the stimulus filed. This is an example of a self-generated set or bias, as distinct from an experimental set, and appears to me to be a sufficient specification of the 'influence of affect on cognition' which was discussed in Chapter 2. In my rephrasing of the interaction we have here the dominance of one type of prototypical or core conceptual attributes over other attributes identifying, and thus defining, the same stimulus.

Let us consider my cognitive proposition for affect in relation to the infant's most important referent – the mother. The mother–child interaction and the child's experience of it has two components: the mother's characteristics, and the feelings or affect to which contact with them gives rise. At the same time we can consider this interaction at a somewhat later state of infant development at which conceptual classification of affect begins to be elaborated along several dimensions. At this stage, stimuli arising in the interaction may give rise to difficulties in classification, either because more categories are beginning to become available through sensory maturation, or because sensory and conceptual maturation enables the child to identify ambiguous maternal signals. A decision on this issue is less important than to demonstrate two frequently related results of these events for the encoding in memory of affective attributes defining the child's concept of mother. I have illustrated what is likely to happen in Figure 6.1 from the point of view of two issues. Firstly, we consider the stimuli which represent the socializing attitudes of three different mothers, and for this purpose ignore the feedback loops from child to the maternal referent. Mother 1 produces a majority of positively evaluated and classified stimuli, few with negative intent and implications, and none which are ambivalent. Mothers 2 and 3 produce an increasing number of aversive as well as ambivalent stimuli which generate

136

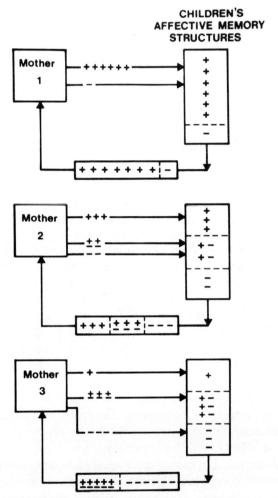

Figure 6.1 Development of differential cognitive representations of affect in children's permanent memory

an increasing number of negative and/or ambivalent affective conceptual attributes in the children's cognitive structures.

If we now regard Figure 6.1 as representing three mother–child *interaction* situations, and examine the feedback loops in each case, we obtain one particular demonstration of possible *reciprocal* interactions. I have deliberately overstructured this demonstration for situations where mothers would accept the child's response at its face value. Thus, for argument's sake, an increase in negative, that is resistant, rejecting, aversive, hostile, or ambivalent stimuli from the child will lead to an increase of maternal stimuli classifiable along the same dimensions. It is not relevant here to reach a conclusion on when a positive feedback interaction will cease, or with what final results. What is relevant, however, is the differential development or labelled affective attributes vis-à-vis a referent, and thus its stimulus characteristics. These generate behaviour that is consistent with the implications and meanings of attributes. The availability and utilization of such informational data, however, is evidence and a reflection of cognitive operations and processes on cognitively labelled affect structures.

My second question concerning the specificity of visceral, physiological, and neurochemical events in the experience of affect is more difficult to answer, and to do it justice really requires a degree of expertise in neurochemistry which I am unable to offer. Let me start by posing another question which does not appear to be phrased very often. How, for example, are we able to say that tomorrow we may be feeling anxious or depressed, because a bill for a large amount is likely to arrive by post? An anticipation concerns a future event, and cognitively expecting a feeling cannot be due to physiological events which have not yet occurred. It is likely that our anticipation will in fact generate a feeling tone which we can describe and which may fit the affect which is anticipated in response to the event of the next day. We are able to conceptualize the affect correctly, however, in the absence of precipitating physiological or neurochemical events. Unless we know what an affect is, and how one affect differs from another, we can neither report nor differentiate them. Inductively, therefore, affect must have representation in cognitive structures.

Like any other knowledge representations that we acquire about the world around us and of our self-experiences, the encoding in memory of affect requires an aroused and activated physiological system. A unilateral definition of the critical stimuli in terms of CNS, ANS, or corticosteroid reactivity would imply, however, that patterned activity in these systems, differing simultaneously in intensity, produces sufficient information to permit their labelling and the consequent differentiation of affects. We have sufficient evidence, however, that the difference between the *physiological* activity patterns of, say, fear and anger is too small to be cognitively and always reliably experienced as a significant difference (Malmo, 1975; Rachman, 1978). Malmo has also offered the opinion that the differentiation between *feeling states as reported from our own experience is much clearer* (my emphasis). At the same time it needs to be said that our dominant senses of vision and hearing are less involved in the sensing, interpretation, and labelling of our own physiological and neurochemical activities than they are in respect of external, environmental signals. This must mean that the biological signals of affect convey less information. If this is a plausible inference, it supports my earlier conclusion that the cognitive content of different types of affective physiological arousal is rather gross and unelaborated (Hamilton, 1979a, b). That is to say, the attributes of emotional experience and affect vary along relatively few specifying dimensions, each of them with only a small number of scale points. To this extent only, we may say that James was correct in attributing emotion or affect to the perception (or conception) of physiological changes.

Differentiation of affect by action pattern, facial expression, posture, gesture, and intensity of vocalization and touch are nevertheless universals in our species and other mammals. The important issue perhaps is whether distinctions are necessary between the innate capacity to generate different types of affect, and the facilitations and constraints which would determine their emergence and utilization. Balinese, Japanese, and Western cultures encourage the display of different emotional signs, and make different demands for expressive control at different ages. Modelling and incentive combine with individual levels of tolerance for arousal and delay, and the capacities for disguise and sublimation are learnt through their effects. Once affect is cognitively coded, it may require little or no hormonal activity to permit it being experienced, according to evidence collected from patients with various forms of decerebration. Some of these were nevertheless able to report feeling some general state of non-specific emotionality and arousal when asked to imagine themselves being sad, angry, or anxious. This, I would argue, offers no support for either James or Cannon, but is evidence of neurotransmitter events which have previously mediated in the encoding of affect experiences themselves, as well as their linkage to the representation of objects, situations, events, or persons which were associated with such experiences.

While there is now fairly good agreement between theories that cognitive events are a feature of affective experience, two types of argument continue to be favoured in support of a dominant role for physiological events. The first rests on the evidence of the close connection between a feeling state and its expression in motor behaviour including the facial muscles. The second argues that awareness of affect is not inevitable, and its presence need not be cognitively acknowledged despite behavioural evidence to the contrary. There is, of course, no good reason for assuming that efferent motor behaviour by-passes cognitive representations in memory structures. Quite the contrary if one considers what is required of a craftsman or an artist, or of a scientific author for that matter! Since, however, tactile and kinaesthetic sensing is usually non-dominant, any of its cognitive representations are likely to be gross. There can be little doubt, however, that they are as much present as is the feeling tone we term affect – because we can report on them. And that, I would argue, is evidence of their contribution to a cognitive schema which is involved in identifying and responding to any stimulus which is evaluated as significant by the person. But presence or association do not assign either dominance or primacy. To suggest secondly that non-awareness of an affective state argues in favour of its primacy seems to be like saying that a fast and successful avoidance action to prevent a motor car accident was possible in the absence of an even faster computation of the implication of significant visual signals from a carelessly driven vehicle, where neither set of events can be fully reported. Because we are not aware of all the stages of a search process trying to identify a stimulus pattern this does not mean that meaningful and relevantly directed searches of memory data banks were not carried out. A crucial omission in the thinking of neo-James theorists is the differential transmission speeds of the ANS and cortical response systems, an omission which continues to complicate discussions on affect and feeling.

A good example of the survival of an old theory is the interesting recent discussion on feeling and thinking offered by Zajonc (1980). This somewhat controversial paper makes a strong case for the non-cognitive representation of feeling preference – that perception of what is 'good' or 'bad', of 'liking' or 'disliking' is the immediate response of a system other than the cognitive system. I have not denied that feelings or affective preferences have *some* distinctive somato-sensory characteristics. The real question is whether a decision to label an event as 'good' or 'likeable' can be made in the absence of a preceding identification of the event to which the feeling is related. Even a self-generated feeling of 'contentment' must have a conceptual trigger. To be aware that we 'like' an event, and that it is a 'good' event, as well as to be able to report it, can only mean that conceptual classifying operations have taken place in an accessible part of the working memory system. This again must mean that emotional, affective feeling tones are in themselves cognitive data, albeit of a somewhat gross and undifferentiated variety, as I have argued already. It is possible that some people in some areas of experience and at some point in time will devote more energy, that is goal-related selective attention and labelling, to the elaboration of feeling categories or schemata than to the object or situation categories to which the feeling labels are attached. To gain access to these schemata, however, requires the prior recognition of an object or event that is diagnostic of a particular feeling category.

Thus, an adult emotional response is always a cognitive response whatever its physiological or neurochemical concomitants. Where a feeling tone is experienced without immediate awareness of its object, we may argue firstly in favour of the difference in salience of hierarchical feeling categories; secondly, we must utilize the distinction between 'appraisal' and 'reappraisal' (Mandler, 1979). Thirdly, the contextual importance of the event, and the time available to make the subjectively most acceptable response, may provide the clue for the *impression* that we are dealing with 'feelings without inferences'.

Experimental evidence is now beginning to accumulate that the representations of affect are conceptually differentiated. Averill *et al.* (1978), for example, starting with different premises, investigated self-attribution of emotion by having subjects judge potentially arousing stimuli (e.g. corpses or nudes) after these stimuli had been associated with failure or success on a problem-solving task. They found that after a failure experience nudes were judged more favourably and corpses as more disturbing than they were following the experience of success in problem-solving. These results confirmed the prediction that self-attribution of emotion is stronger when undesirable rather than desirable consequences are associated with it, and that ego-involvement is a potent factor. In the context of the present discussion this means primarily that there are strong links between one type of affect and others in different areas of behaviour which can only be mediated by processes that employ data coded in the same symbolic language. Isen *et al.* (1978) approached the issue of the cognitive aspects of affect by investigating the effects of inducing a 'good mood' in subjects on the evaluation of supermarket products, and on the recall of 'positive' material following success or failure in a game. Good mood-induction led to more favourable product evaluation, and winning a game was associated with greater success in the recall of 'most-liked' words compared with 'least-liked' words. While this study was concerned with studying merely the *effects of feelings* on the accessibility of cognitions, the authors themselves regard their findings as evidence towards a cognitive-state interpretation of emotion.

Several studies conducted in Bower's laboratory at Stanford and summarized in a recent paper (Bower, 1981), also support the proposition that affect is cognitively represented in adaptive processes which draw on appropriate memory data. Bower considers the following situations in which emotion influences memory and perception: free association, social perceptions, 'snap' judgements of other people, and the effect of self- or experimentally-induced mood states on memory for verbal material and personal history incidents which are congruent with an induced mood. The results of two studies are shown in Figure 6.2 (Bower *et al.*, 1978; Bower and Gilligan, 1979). These

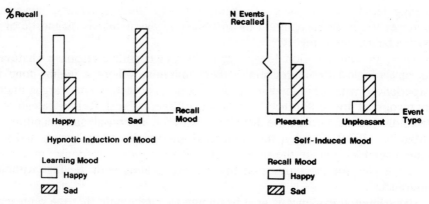

Figure 6.2 Mood-state-dependent memory (adapted from Bower, 1981)

are quite clear-cut. Sad or unpleasant mood-state recall facilitates recall of words and incidents connected with sad and unpleasant feelings, happy or pleasant mood-state recall biases towards the recall of words learnt during a happy mood, or the recall of personal incidents coded as happy. Bower accounts for the results in terms of an associative network theory in which mood or affect serves a memory unit which can prime and activate mood-congruent associations and response-selecting and -generating processes.

This is an important contribution to a unifying theory of human behaviour, and all the more welcome because it is proposed by a cognitive theorist with little previous commitment to holistic approaches. I will return to Bower's model in a later section of this chapter when considering the nature of memory data serving personality and motivational characteristics. In the same later section I will also consider in greater detail the results of a conceptually related experiment which I have recently carried out. This involved subjects who were within 30 minutes of receiving the results of their examination for a Bachelor Degree in Psychology. In the context of the cognitive model of socialization anxiety discussed in Chapter 5, I predicted that these subjects, compared with a control group, would remember anxiety words better than words denoting euphoria. I further predicted that this bias would increase in a second administration of the experiment only 15 minutes before the publication of examination results, and that the bias should be present only with a verbal and not with a visuo-spatial task. Although the obtained effects fell slightly short of prediction, they are in support of Bower's general proposition, and my own argument in the preceding pages that affect has cognitive representation (see Chapter 8 for further details). My own predictions, however, were somewhat more radical than Bower's in that the experiment was also directed at the nature of the symbolic language in which affect is coded. I will try to elaborate this later when considering the role of a semantic data code in the cognitive representation of personality traits and goal-directed behaviour.

If the differential experience of affect, emotion, feeling, or mood engenders differential conceptual labelling, then the development of affect-signifying cognitive structures should be similar to the development of other conceptual structures. That is, the development of awareness, reportability, and observational evidence of some degree of fine-grained differences in affect takes place along the same lines as the elaboration of attributes which define, specify, and identify objects or situational referents generally. The concept of a motor car, for example, with maturation and experience exhibits a progressive degree of differentiation and subclassification which is plausibly similar to the developmental sequence of emotion proposed by Bridges 50 years ago. Her model allows for the differentiation of a fundamental distress affect into fear, disgust, anger, and jealousy. The conceptual differentiation of a motor car changes from dichotomous classifications of big–small, nice–not nice, new–old, to subclassifications specifying manufacture, utility, acceleration times, top speeds, or social status implications. They are all information-bearing attributes of the referent motor car whose presence or absence defines the conceptual structure of the referent for people with different goals when purchasing a car.

Piaget's views (Piaget and Inhelder, 1969), and Décarie's (1978) reassessment of these, are not inconsistent with what I have said so far about conceptual refinement and elaboration of the cognitive representation of affect. When this school of cognitive development argues that cognition and affect cannot be dissociated and that they are two interacting functionally parallel systems, they must nevertheless mean that the stage sequences of sensori-motor to propositional cognition in the development of intellectual skill are matched by similar stages in the acquisition and maturation of affect-signifying structures. They do not discuss this plausible inference, however, mainly perhaps because they regard the study of affect as too difficult and as being subject to 'adultomorphism' (Piaget and Inhelder, 1969, p. 21). The Piagetian concept of 'decentering' appears as suitable, however, to explain how different multidimensional affective stimulus properties can combine in a complex conceptual structure, as in the analysis of, for example, conservation. Moreover, the evidence of progressive development of emotional sensitivity in interaction with others, as well as the larger number of possible combinations of types of affect, seems to require a normal concept elaboration approach to its cognitive representation. Plutchik (1980), for example, presents a 'psycho-evolutionary' account of emotion which points out that primary emotions in three-dimensional space can produce, with only four levels of intensity, more than 300 classes of emotion. Even some 80 different emotions at one intensity level are considerably beyond our capacity to label, however, with a single, purely physiological signifier.

If that is correct two conclusions relevant to my earlier questions would seem to have a measure of validity. The first is that it provides a plausible explanation of why the novelist's and dramatist's characterizations of individuals have continued to be so much more meaningful when trying to convey the feelings and affects of people depicted in novels or plays, and to allow us to empathize with them. They achieve this goal by presenting us with a large amount of differentiated information. This information is defined by a wide variety of semantic stimuli which are presented serially to working memory and provide, therefore, sufficient processing time to extract meaning from them with the help of permanent memory identifiers. My second conclusion is relevant to the traditional conceptual distinction between cognition and affect. If adult affect is in fact a very complex concept with multiple symbolic labels, whose description to another person requires time and verbal expertise, it may have seemed plausible to explain its different types and degrees by reference to patterns of physiological arousal and behavioural expression. Mandler (1975) has signified these patterns by the term 'warmth'. Without a cognitive conception, however, we cannot regard this specification of affect as sufficient or meaningful. And on the question of sequence I regard a James-type of statement 'I am anxious because I tremble' as only the second or third stage of a possible stimulus-identifying process because it needs to be preceded by the question 'Why do I tremble?'.

(ii) The data sampled by questionnaires

Questionnaires are self-report devices for obtaining evidence of individuals' usual or dominant response dispositions. Actual questions, or statements, in verbal form direct the respondent to specific areas of his personal characteristics, his goals, the ways in which he might respond, or has responded in certain situations, what kinds of feeling experiences are, or have been, associated with certain events or situations, or the intensity and persistence of the feelings. Because questions or statements can be phrased on virtually all issues, because a large number of subjects can be simultaneously investigated, and because these provide statistically important variations in scores which are objective rather than inferred data, the questionnaire methodology has become the most widely used technique in personality, motivational, and social psychology. Great care has been taken to satisfy the basic requirements of response reliability, test unidimensionality, and of the various forms of validity: concurrent, construct, or criterion. Safeguards against faked or misleading responses have been introduced with some measure of success. In the majority of cases, investigators know that the sum of responses to a questionnaire is no more than a gross sample of response characteristics or dispositions, and thus only a suggestive piece of evidence. I am not concerned here with an assessment of questionnaire methodology as such, or with a discussion of the logical and experimental difficulties of producing a valid paper-and-pencil test. My discussion needs to address two questions: (i) What cognitive processes are involved in responding to a questionnaire item? (ii) What is the nature of the data from which a response is generated? Although there is at least implicit agreement that responses are selected from a response repertoire, I find no evidence that there has been any systematic discussion *in depth* of what is actually *implied* by postulating a repertoire of responses.

To begin with, let us consider two examples from well-known questionnaires in the field of social psychology and personality. Item No. 25a from Rotter's (1966) original instrument for the study of internal vs. external control reads: 'Many times I feel that I have little influence over the things that happen to me'. Because it is the statement with the highest bi-serial item correlation, it can be regarded as the most representative stimulus for the assessment of the 'internal vs. external control' dimension. Responses would reflect, respectively, a particular individual's belief system, the role of such beliefs in expectancies of goal-achievement, and expectancies of the success of *characteristic* goal-directed behaviour. Our questions then are: What processes occur, and what kinds of data are examined by a respondent who affirms the statement? The instructions are that the response made should be the one the subject actually believes to be true in his case rather than the one he would like to be true, or the response he feels he ought to or should choose compared with a single alternative item which excludes chance, luck, or fate in the determination of goal-achievement.

The same questions concerning processes and data involved can be directed at a statement from a questionnaire used by McClelland (1961) in his 'Four-Country' study of achievement motivation. Item 4 reads: 'I set difficult goals for myself which I attempt to reach', where the response is selected from a six-point scale on the agreement-disagreement dimension. Both questionnaires induce a set of some sort for speed of responding, and attempt to reduce self-evaluation anxiety by stating that there cannot be any wrong answers. The methodological assumption here is that such instruction would facilitate the emergence of spontaneous, unpremeditated and, therefore, doubly valid responses.

Our reanalysis can usefully start by defining questionnaire administration and responding to each item as a problem-solving situation. A task has been given, and most commonly, since we are dealing with volunteer respondents, a serious effort is made to carry it out with a problem-solving set. The gross sequence of cognitive processes engendered by the task must be the following: visual-sensory input, identification of input and transfer to working memory, rehearsal of information in working memory, focusing of attention on and searching for conceptually fitting information in permanent memory, retrieval of required information, matching retrieved information with task information in working memory store, testing a tentative response and, finally, response decision and execution. The difficulty of the problem-solving task is reduced, of course, in the paper-and-pencil format, because the problem can be reviewed by rereading instead of having to hold it verbatim in working memory.

Let us turn to more specific aspects of the problem-solving task. A well-known difficulty attaches to the interpretation of parts of the question or statement, and of the implications of scale-point differences in the making of a response. Many questionnaires try to avoid potential ambiguities that arise with the use of words like: 'fairly', 'many times', 'often', 'usually', 'infrequently', etc. Where such items are present, however, respondents will need to define them in the context of their own past behaviour. This means, of course, that even where there is compliance with the directive not to spend too much time on any single item, long-term memory structures need to be searched for the correct criterion of frequency. This, in turn, may require a search for instances of relevant categories of past behaviour which are encoded in cognitive structures. In most cases this search process can proceed efficiently as a consequence of what we assume to be a functional organization of memory data in schemata. The process of responding can be fast because the concept of schematic organizing further assumes the presence of a higher-order generalization principle to which our earlier discussion has applied the terms unitization, prototyping, or diagnostic sign. Entry into permanent memory is to a specific instance of the behavioural domain, however, and the class of behaviour needs to be determined before previous preferred or obtained response outcomes become accessible. Only then does the generalized evaluation memory for the class and the instance become available.

It can be argued, of course, that when we are required to carry out a familiar task, such as in this case reporting on the frequency of a class of self-experience, there is a great deal of informational redundancy. Logically, however, and probably in practice too, subsidiary processes must intervene in determining the type and degree of redundancy, and actually establish that redundancy of information applies. In all probability, such additional processes are absent only for very simple and highly practised tasks. This situation is unlikely, however, to fit the questionnaire response setting of what one hopes is an experimentally naive subject.

Moreover, it is appropriate to refer to the possibility of individual differences in the handling, detection, and acceptance of redundancy. Almost by definition, information theory did not concern itself either with complex stimuli, or with the parameters of signal detection methodology – sensitivity and bias. It can be argued, however, that decision-making on whether a particular stimulus belongs to class X or class Y, involves a person's readiness to label the stimuli with certainty. Some people appear to be willing to do so for high degrees of perceptual or conceptual ambiguity with minimal doubt and considerable speed, whereas others require time to reach their criterion of certainty. In another context, this is the operation of the well-documented 'trade-off' effect of speed versus accuracy. Furneaux (1962), Eysenck (1977) and others, for example, have shown that subjects scoring high on an extraversion questionnaire are fast and make more errors on cognitive tasks than subjects scoring within the introversion range of norms. This trend might well apply to the more complex cognitive processes required when responding to questionnaire items, though I am not aware that actual data for this assumption are available. Observational evidence from my own studies suggests that test-anxious subjects take longer to complete their questionnaires, while being significantly slower on cognitive tasks, particularly when more than one of these has to be done at the same time (Hamilton, 1979, 1980). Because of the evidence of a medium-sized correlation between anxiety and introversion, many if not most anxious people also tend towards introversion, so that both these overlapping variables are likely to be associated with operating towards a narrow and more certain criterion of stimulus identification and response selection.

Individual and subjective requirements of certainty of judgements may be regarded as a general and superordinate permanent memory structure exercising an instructional influence on subsidiary input-analysing and response-generating processes. Depending on the degree of importance for the person of other, superordinate purposes or goals for whose achievement narrow certainty criteria have developed, care in stimulus analysis and response selection will occupy an early or a first position in a hierarchy of input-analysing processes. If certainty criteria are non-dominantly structured, responding to first or early stimulus associations may well be the rule. In that event, any comparison between individuals on an otherwise reliable and valid questionnaire will be affected by a factor other than that tested by the questionnaire. It is possible, however, that tendencies to respond prematurely to first impressions, impulsively, or without inferences, are variables which are embodied in the design of the measuring instrument. This may be the case where there are multifactorial assumptions about the nature of extraversion, or say, with behaviour-rating scales of mental subnormality.

This leads us on to a consideration of the role of permanent memory content in responding to questionnaire items. Affirming Rotter's most representative 'external control' item is the result of a generalizing inductive operation on a schema of personal ineffectiveness, powerlessness, or 'helplessness'. This induction will be based on instances which fit the proposition 'little influence on things that happen', subsidiary instances of 'things that happen', and dominant conceptual structures defining 'little' and 'influence'. Associated structures must encode the *circumstances* in which relevant events occurred in the life of the person. For a conceptual structure of 'little influence' to develop, the person's behaviour and behaviour outcome must have been coded by the person to have stood in a non-contingent relationship. The most obvious cases are those in which reward or achievement occurred in the absence of goal-directed effort, and where effort and application remained unrewarded. If, for a variety of reasons, such experience has been common over a short period of a person's life, and there occurs a diminution of effort, we refer to this outcome as lack of incentive or motivation – the individual stops trying. If this occurs for an extended period, it is plausible to assume that the behaviour outcome expectancies encoded in cognitive structures have raised failure expectancy to a dominant position in a hierarchy of expectancies.

This shift cannot occur with only brief exposure to non-contingency between response and outcome as suggested by theories of 'frustrative non-reward' (e.g. Amsel, 1962; Gray, 1971), or 'learned helplessness' (Seligman, 1975). These behavioural concepts do not adequately reflect all those cognitive processes working on long-term memory data structures as a result of which a history of elaborated experience yields a dominant 'external control' belief system. It is possible, of course, that a single traumatically experienced event may be a sufficient cause of demotivation, ostensibly supporting a single-trial hypothesis of learning (e.g. Solomon and Wynne, 1953; Eysenck, 1976). Our cognitive analysis, however, then demands an adequate definition of 'traumatic'. This definition cannot be a-historical, but must rest on assumptions about vulnerability to traumatic experience. In the simplest cases, vulnerability is to be defined either by already encoded anxieties about the possible future occurrence of aversive and adverse events, or by the availability of only a single or unilateral response to them. In either event, so-called coping responses, defensive or attenuating evaluative processes, are weak or absent. Furthermore, restrictions in response availability require additional definition by reference to differences in the *capacity* to generate elaborations of a stimulus situation in a wider social and personal context, and, therefore, differences in flexibility for the anticipation of response outcomes. These considerations are likely to suggest some of the reasons for the demonstrated relationships between submission to chance, luck, or other mythical beliefs and, respectively, intolerance of ambiguity (Frenkel-Brunswik, 1949), conceptual rigidity (Rokeach, 1951), and concrete thinking (Harvey et al., 1961, 1970). It may be useful to recall that these last two variables were additionally and negatively correlated with intelligence test scores, so that a further hypothesis of a positive relationship between intelligence and the elaboration of schematic cognitive structures can be regarded as plausible rather than fanciful (see Chapter 10 for an elaboration).

There is, of course, a level of cognition at which justifications for a belief in chance or luck in behaviour outcomes are the result of cognitive processes which have adopted a 'final analysis', statistical, or actuarial orientation. An 'external control' attitude here has clearly quite different implications either for vulnerability to traumatic determinants, or for intelligence, problem-solving, and conceptual and perceptual rigidity.

Our analysis of the problem-solving task prescribed by an item from an achievement motivation questionnaire can follow a similar line. Subscribing strongly (+3) to a statement about attempting to achieve difficult set goals again requires entry into long-term memory structures. These must fit instances of the proposition of 'attempting to achieve difficult goals', subsidiary instances of 'setting difficult goals', and 'achieving difficult goals', and dominant conceptual structures defining 'difficult', 'attempting', and 'achieving'. Level of aspiration research over the years (e.g. Lewin et al., 1944; Heckhausen, 1967) has shown that in the majority of subjects there is a close relationship between achieving and attempting to achieve goals, that is, goal-setting is generally determined by 'goal-discrepancy'. That is, evidence of underachieving operates against attempting or predicting a high level of performance, and overachievement raises the level of predicted performance in the direction of past achievement. The key conceptual structures are historically and developmentally determined. Evidence from the socialization studies discussed in Chapter 5 strongly supports the view that early encouragement and guidance of child behaviour in a setting of authoritative support and affection lead to the development of enterprising behaviour and attitudes, to a realistic appraisal of goal-difficulty, and to a goal-achievement orientation. While this relationship presents few problems if the associated behaviour outcomes have been largely success and reward, we still have to account for the frequent absence of effects due to failure in tasks undertaken by a child. The answer seems to be supplied by studies like those of Feld and Lewis (1969) and Sarason et al. (1960) which suggest that the conceptualizing of failure is closely associated with dominant and general self-evaluation characteristics and with the balance of fear of failure and approaching success motivation. This must mean that where self-concepts are largely defined by positively toned attributes and where the referents of the behavioural environment are represented in memory by attractive, desirable and interest-arousing signifiers, failure in a sequence of successes even with a simple task is not experienced and conceptualized as 'failure'. Dominant structures of high self-esteem in association with non-aversive explanations from a caretaker, in situations where a desirable end result was not achieved, prevent the establishment of anxiety in respect of non-achievement. Instead, the new knowledge of what is a difficult task will yield, with parental and later self-help, task-restructuring, new strategies, or the postponement of a particular goal until subsidiary skills are mastered.

Individual differences must be expected, therefore, in the induction of generalizations or prototypical core concepts from discrete instances of 'attempting' a task, 'achieving' it, and specifications of its 'difficulty'. Just as with concepts in general, availability, responding, and experience of behaviour outcome determine the individually best-fitting labelling of the total stimulus situation. As argued before, interpretative bias from self- and social-evaluation concepts determines the direction of experience-coding. The same bias affects subsequent elaborations of experience in the processes of integrating a current event with the existing schematic structures of functionally related past events. 'Top-down' processes, therefore, are not limited to the evaluation of an ongoing event in its context, they continue until the cognitive processing system decides at some level that a suitable tension-reduction stage of functionally important intepretation has been attained. There is the possibility that for some individuals this stage may never be reached if we regard a low threshold for fear-of-failure as appropriate evidence. By contrast, there may be either cognitive-affective denial of the possibility and implications of failure – although their representations in memory are potentially available – or 'attempts to achieve' have become associated with 'external control' structures. In the latter case, however, the demotivating state of powerlessness and resignation need not prevent a realistic appraisal of degree of difficulty of a task. It may affect only the reasons accepted for success or failure.

Predominance of denial response strategies, and of fear-of-failure (or of 'test anxiety' as it is often called), are likely to be associated with distorted and relatively undifferentiated concepts of 'difficulty'. With denial strategies we may expect to find a foreshortened scale of points on the concept dimension where 'very difficult' lies close to 'not difficult', so that the designation 'easy' may identify a task quite inappropriately. I am not aware, however, that there is at present any experimental support for this proposition. So-called test-anxious individuals, however, are known to perform well and with confidence on simple tasks (e.g. Spence and Spence, 1966; Spielberger and Smith, 1966; Sarason, 1975; Hamilton, 1979a, b), but not on difficult problems. On the basis of the same proposition, we may argue that there is again a collapsed scale within the conceptual dimension of 'difficult'. In this case, however, there is wide separation between the 'easy' and 'difficult' poles, bunching of scale differences at the 'very difficult' end, and relatively objective conceptual differentiation at the 'easy' or 'not difficult' extreme. In some respects my proposition refers to the concept of size of category (Hamilton,

1957; Tajfel, 1957; Bruner and Tajfel, 1961). The available evidence of individual differences here implicates not only the obvious role of prior stimulus experience, but also strategies of conceptual stereotyping, the influence of superordinate conceptual and affect-associated dispositions to label even unclassifiable stimuli, or strategies of classifying on fine-grained subsidiary and secondary criteria into multiple categories.

The discussion of the two questionnaire items from the standpoint of cognitive processing theory indicates that responding to them involves more than reflecting on past or future behaviour in a social context, or the recapitulation or anticipation of a feeling tone. Like any other task depending on available knowledge, self-knowledge requires more than perceptual processes, or the recall of episodic incidents in appropriate contexts, though both of these play a part in response determination.

A gross representation of the major cognitive processing events involved in responding to a questionnaire item is shown in Figure 6.3. I have omitted the specification of the actual operations required for a response such as those involved in stimulus identification, working memory storage, rehearsal for maintenance of an appropriate conceptual set, the necessary interactive checking stages, or hypothetical general processor functions. Figure 6.3 concentrates, therefore, on the general structures of a memory schema which, as I have argued, must be involved in the response selection processes of a committed respondent working to a high certainty criterion. The input stimuli are the conceptual propositions. These trigger principal diagnostic defining concepts which pass into a temporary working memory component where they operate as the cue for a search of relevant information in the memory schema. The schema encodes representations of all functionally related diagnostic concepts, the object, person, and situational referents to which the concepts apply in previous experience, and the attribute labels which the person has attached to the referents to signify the implications of the referents for the concept prototype or core. I have also shown that responses indicating goal-directed behaviour and anticipation of response outcome need to have a close link with action potentials, that is, executive motor responses in speech, written language, gestures, or other physical movements. These are likely to be part of the same schema, at least to the extent that codes for eliciting contingent efferent behaviour are present. Following Tulving (1972) Figure 6.3 indicates in an oversimplified form that actual instances of the disposition being sampled by a questionnaire item may play some role in the selection of a response by sensitizing some points at the referent and attribute levels to a greater degree than others.

Considering the relative speed with which even co-operative experimental subjects answer a questionnaire, the foregoing analysis may appear pedantic and artificial. In reply I would argue that self-concepts are more complex than the behaviour to which they give rise, and that memory structures are not simple stimulus-response links but knowledge data banks with an infinite amount of inter-related information. If that were not the case, we would be

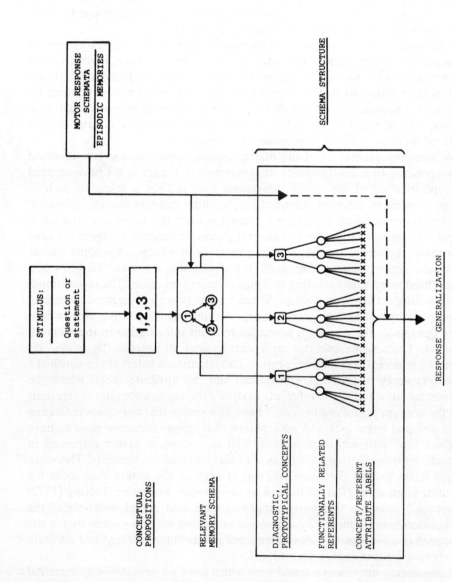

Figure 6.3 Cognitive processing events in responding to a questionnaire item

able to predict individual behaviour with far greater accuracy, 'complex-personalities' in fact or fiction would not exist, and questionnaire scores would have much higher correlations with actual behaviour and with criterion variables than they are able to produce.

My earlier comments, however, about 'first impression', impulsive, or low certainty bias approaches to response-making still apply. Thus, action- rather than thought-oriented people may be strongly influenced by memory data of a single, episodic event which lowers the retrieval threshold of one or the other dominant diagnostic or prototypical concepts encoding subsumed referents and their attributes. In this case the response may well be underdetermined and its reliability and validity may be low. Thus responses unduly influenced by single past events, rather than generalizations from several events, contribute to existing evidence of intra-individual inconsistency across situations. On the other hand, my example of the ideal, co-operative respondent implies that a great deal of memory schema content is actually sampled, albeit at two levels of consciousness, and that the response process is necessarily protracted. This level of delay is clearly unnecessary. Excluding unreportable scanning and matching operations which, as I argued before, are subject to retroactive inhibition or masking, there are semi-conscious cognitive work processes which transmit information to the human problem-solver that he is on the right track, as well as fully conscious self-checking operations examining concurrent working memory content. The propositional input and its principal concepts elicit their corresponding representations directly (otherwise input meaning cannot be established) and the set task focuses search only on selected content of one schema because redundancy decisions are inevitable in a selection process. This means that some of the referents and attributes shown in Figure 6.3 need not be sampled. For example, 'attempting to achieve difficult goals' excludes reference to practice, strategies, and goal-relevance, and 'little influence on things that happen' omits specification of goal urgency, task difficulty, or 'divine help for the deserving'. Although these are relevant concepts for the full representation of response disposition and self-evaluation, they also belong to other schemata which encode other goals and different areas of characteristic behaviour.

The analysis of the kinds of data sampled by the questionnaires considered so far can be extended without difficulty to all instruments of this type. The evaluation of an item and the selection of a response is always a problem-solving task even if items are phrased as simply as possible, or the task is reporting on the presence or absence of physiological signs in the respondent. On the other hand traditional type and trait theory usually requires direction to several behaviour areas which are hypothetically predicted to form more than one distinct pattern of inter-relatedness, where patterns are defined by factorial uniqueness or separation. Factorial uniqueness has frequently led to assumptions about the *identity* of factors and dominant dispositions, and about the functional *independence* of lowly correlated dimensions of characteristic behaviour. A good example is the EPI developed by Eysenck and his many collaborators over a number of years, and its various forerunners. This widely used instrument claims verified statistical independence of neuroticism and introversion–extraversion, that is between getting easily upset as shown by physiological signs of arousal, and responses to situations which engage various components of emotionality. I have previously regarded this independence as spurious and artefactual (Hamilton, 1959). It is certainly inconsistent with Jung's original theory which proposed many different, and not necessarily related, types of introversion or extraversion, and which identified the extreme ends of the I–E dimensions with the labels of neurotic diagnostic categories (Hamilton, 1976). Without a critically oriented substantial research project, and a close re-examination of all pertinent existing data, there cannot be an answer to what I would regard as an unproven issue. In the context of a cognitive analysis of traits, goals and their affective components it is not plausible, however, to separate the representation of affect from the referents with which they have become associated either by concurrent experience in an actual environmental context, or by subsequent elaboration and integration with functionally similar events, and the subsequent consolidation of the modified cognitive structures.

The real importance of the work that has gone into the Eysenck Personality Inventory, the different Test Anxiety Questionnaires by the Sarason brothers and their associates, the Taylor MAS, or the Spielberger, State-Trait instruments, and many others, is the hierarchical conception of the relationship between traits and personality type. That is to say that the introvert, anxious, or angry person is defined by patterns of response characteristics which are predicted and obtained for introverted, anxious, or angry individuals which then constitute the type. Each response characteristic constitutes a trait which can be further defined by subordinate patterns of dominant habits, and potentially, habits can be redefined by finer-grain patterns of responses. This structural conception has been particularly evident in the early theorizing of Eysenck (e.g. 1952; 1957), but does not appear to have progressed in any systematic way. In retrospect, this is not surprising, perhaps since structuring is no substitute for content orientation. This, however, has elicited dogmatic rejection from a generation of external-stimulus-oriented behaviourists. The startling progress in cognitive processing theory, however, following the rediscovery and/or rehabilitation of F. C. Bartlett, is establishing content-orientation as an appropriate genotypical approach to individual differences in behavioural characteristics, their preferred goals and response outcomes. This is clearly reflected in the recent developments in conceptualizing the representation and utilization of knowledge in memory which I discussed in Chapter 4.

It will have been observed that Figure 6.3 has adopted a hierarchical order for the representation of the processing events generated by a single questionnaire item. The assumption, however, that access to a level of conceptual referents must precede access to the attributes which define the referents is not fully borne out by the experiments on semantically oriented approaches to the structure of concepts (e.g. Smith, 1978; and the relevant discussion in Chapter 4). It can be argued, however, that no precise predictions for the organization of associative networks can be made, that is about which kinds of data have the closest and strongest links, without a very detailed knowledge of a person's previous responses and his idiosyncratic labelling of the whole event. The major reason for this statement is that modern semantic memory theory omits a discussion of the contribution of stimulation from affect, mood, or emotionality except as a facilitating or constraining interface in the structuring of associative bonds. Although Figure 6.3 has also omitted a clear specification of this factor in a schema, it is actually subsumed under the label of attributes, as required by my analysis in the preceding section. I argued there that the cognitive representation of affect, gross though it is, can be regarded as a necessary component of conceptual knowledge. The relevance and contribution of the cognitive information supplied by affect are inevitably assumed whenever we regard behaviour as being guided by *preference* whether for methods, or strategies, or for goals, or for the outcome of goal-directed behaviour. We give preference not only to what is utilitarian, and implying in any case a rewarding end-state of some kind, but to that which *maximizes* gratification. To that extent, the schemata which encode self-evaluation and self-images, concepts of social power, or self-esteem, are closely related to more general schemata which encode personal interests and preferred activities.

In Figure 6.4 I have sketched some of the cognitive and behavioural implications of affirming one representative item from an introversion–extraversion questionnaire: 'I prefer being on my own'. Here 'Crowds', 'Daydream' and 'Worry' are just three hypothetical referents which may be accessed by the principal conceptual component of the proposition 'on my own'. Below the referents I have entered for each of them a set of attributes acquired by and associated with each referent. These were deliberately chosen to reflect differences in conceptual processes that have preceded the registration of the attribute label. For 'Crowds', for example, I have confined myself largely to the results of direct experience and its description. For 'Daydream', the attributes 'own pace' and 'no criticism' represent a second stage in the identification of referents, namely, the implications and consequences of original and more primary attributes. This level of attribute labelling suggests a close link with, and a contribution to, the conceptual referent of 'Daydream' itself, as well as to the principal conceptual structure here of being 'on my own'. For 'Worry' I have taken the level of attribute labelling a stage further to indicate that the 'Worry' referent here is most likely not only a diagnostic concept for the principal conceptual structure of the stimulus item, but the core of two different and separate hypothetical self-image schemata encoding, respectively, social competence and social acceptability. Furthermore, there are good reasons for the assumption that 'Worry', in a generally anxious person particularly, is a schema in its own

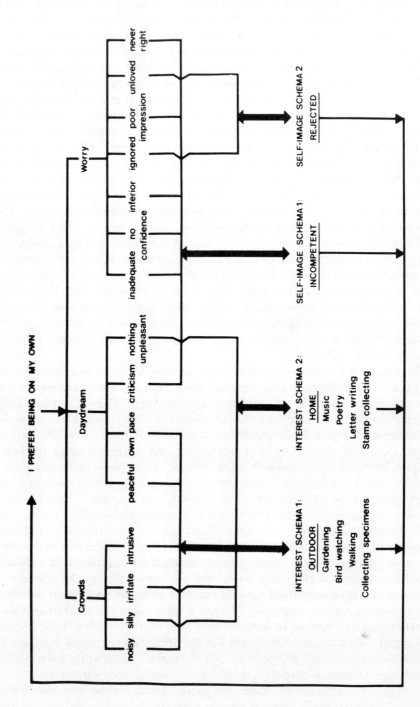

Figure 6.4 Interest and self-image schemata accessed by social introversion questionnaire item

right with its own extended organization of referents and their attributes. If that were not the case, the dominance of this disposition would be more difficult to demonstrate, and a 'Worry' response, whether verbal, motor, or autonomic would have higher thresholds and latencies.

Figure 6.4 also shows one plausible connection between self-evaluation and self-image schemata, and activity and interest schemata which reflect, and occur as a result of, the more general characteristics of an individual who affirms a preference for being on his own. In this case I have defined the 'Outdoor' interest schema by referents whose attributes are largely the converse of those given for 'Crowds'. It will be observed that this conception of the schema is close to Bartlett's original suggestion of an association of functionally consistent assemblies of specialized and elaborated concepts in memory, or attitudes as he termed them.

Since the analysis of the effects of social stress on behaviour has occupied a good proportion of my working life, it was perhaps inevitable, in the light of the model I am offering, that Figure 6.4 shows the most elaborated structure for a 'Competence' schema. Anecdotally, I cannot say that I was aware of aiming for this particular demonstration, but I am presenting this comment as a possible small piece of subjective evidence for the role of unreportable selection processes in conceptual operations and for the hierarchical structure of schemata.

A self-concept of competence develops in, and results from, interaction with others, or more specifically from carrying out tasks actually, or assumed to be assigned by others. Task performance occurs against standards of an end result and of criteria of adequacy and satisfaction implied or specified by task assignments. The criteria are represented in cognitive structures of the task or goal together with the subsidiary behavioural skills required for goal-achievement, and with representations of the evaluation by self and others of past performance. Experience in past behaviour of discrepancies between criteria of adequacy and evaluation of performance affect the structure of a superordinate self-esteem schema. A high discrepancy is likely to result in low self-esteem for which a diagnostic attribute of 'inferior' supplies an aversively experienced label. If an experience of 'inferior' occurs in a sufficiently large and frequent number of contexts, it is likely to be elaborated in its own right to become a principal cognitive structure, or a superordinate schema with its own subsystems of referents and attributes.

The neurological and cognitive dynamics implied by these propositions almost defy verbal description. This is because of their apparent infinite variability of combination and permutation, and because it seems as if referents or attributes can become temporarily superordinate schemata, and as if schemata can be destructured into their defining components each of which can assume the superordinate capacity of a schematic label. A system that can operate in this manner must be one in which fundamental units have both a specific label or signature, as well as the capacity to produce another signature or label in association with another unit. These capacities seem to be present in the atoms of organic and inorganic chemistry, and achieve their most outstanding expression in the information-bearing structures of the peptides. Conceptual analogues for behavioural science are at present not available, but Hebb's (1949) constructs of cell assemblies firing in phase sequence, and Pribram's (1971) proposals for a holographic model of neurological functioning are first approximations. The importance of the neurological constructs to date lies in their suggestions for the registration and coding of functionally related events by relevant cross-referenced classification or grouping, and hence for the organization of experience along subjectively coherent and even consistent lines. Hebb's construct of an assembly of information-bearing units and its numerous links between cells in some form of hierarchical arrangement is a system by which individual differences in set and selective attention can trigger both different and similar identifiers, depending on context. More recently (Hebb, 1974) has applied this construct to the emergence of a creative idea by reference to *randomly-firing* cell assembly groups which represent the cognitive data about the problem task. Only a small number of groups, however, contain the major relevant conceptual data, and they must assume a particular temporal order. Other assembly groups must make a contribution, however, otherwise they would not necessarily be activated at the same time. Some cell assemblies are clearly very specific in the information which they represent and transmit, others can represent information only in combination with additional assemblies.

Jusczyk and Klein (1980) have presented a favourable reassessment of Hebb's constructs. It is possible to apply their views to the conceptualization of one aspect of the self-concept schema of 'Competence' – a possibly principal cognitive structure of the self-attribute 'inferior'. In Figure 6.5 let components A–E represent cell assembly groups, where each group consists of subassemblies. They are assumed to represent information associated with and defining the conceptual structures of the five labelled behavioural situations, and more specifically expectancies of behaviour outcomes in their contexts. At the next level the two unlabelled circles represent negative experience generalizations and, following my earlier convention, may be called superordinate referents to which are assigned the attribute label 'inferior'. As already indicated by the feedback loop in Figure 6.4, stimulation of attributes may trigger further activity at the level of referents. In Figure 6.5 this is shown by a new and more complex level of activation of cognitive structures encoding subjectively associated experiences of 'Worry', 'Threat' or 'Danger' for, as in this case, a vulnerable individual. The quasi-synaptic connections between groups of assemblies show a simple pattern of interrelationships between super- and subordinate information-bearing structures, but provide no data on sequencing, or feedback. What I have wanted to indicate here, however, is the contribution to a single self-concept of knowledge and experience data from different areas of social activity, and its chain-effect on functionally related cognitive structures at various levels of organization.

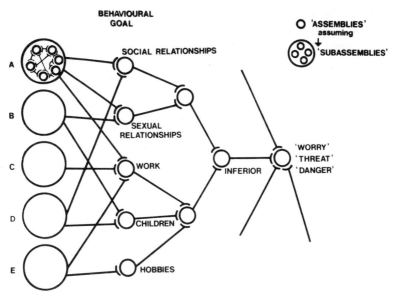

Figure 6.5 Hypothetical conceptual structure of 'inferior'

Summated scores obatined from questionnaire responses can offer, there-fore, no more than superficial evidence of a person's behavioural potentials while abstractly and artificially imagining the situations in which they might be displayed. The evaluation of an actual and urgent environment demand to respond would depend, however, on the conceptual analysis of the present situation, its context and dominant antecedent events. My analysis is grossly similar, therefore, to Mischel's reconceptualization of the nature of person-ality traits, and his criticism of the consistency implications assigned to ques-tionnaire data (Mischel, 1973, 1979). My position differs, however, from Mischel's in a number of respects, and aims for a more fundamental analysis of the cognitive factors in behaviour patterns, in stimulus analysis, and person–situation interactions. Although Mischel has abandoned a contentless S–R approach, I see no logical consistency when he persists in rejecting the unreportable preoccupations and thought processes which are treated in psycho-dynamic theories (Mischel, 1973), while granting scientific status to equally unreportable stimulus- and pre-response-analysing processes involved in person–situation interactions.

There are at least two additional inconsistencies in Mischel's propositions. Firstly, his categorical distinction between observable responses and the activities of the cognitive processing system without which behaviour would remain unsystematic and undirected, maintains the behaviourist's distinction between the differential theoretical importance of what is observed and what is unobservable. His own theoretical views require, however, a specific role for response direction in the cognitive structures involved in producing it. That must be implied by assigning substantial importance to anticipation of behaviour outcome or expectancy in generating a response, which, creditably, Mischel accepts. The second inconsistency, in the context of the model I am presenting here, and the most substantial distinction between a neo-behaviourist and a cognitive processing approach to personality and motivation, is Mischel's continuing categorical and conceptual separation of cognitive and non-cognitive behaviour. This separation is demonstrated not only when he discusses the interaction of cognition and personality in terms of an interface; it seems more clearly implied by the absence of a full cognitive analysis of 'social learning', *and* its affective components.

The concurrence between Mischel's and my own position on the superficiality of the trait concept and the questionnaire data from which this is derived will have become apparent in some of the foregoing discussions. I cannot agree, therefore, with Eysenck and Eysenck (1980) that Mischel has widened the gap between personality and experimental psychology – a distinction which will not be made in any case by many theorists. In fact, a recognition memory experiment by Cantor and Mischel (1977) supports very strongly the cognitive, experimentally-derived, position which I am also arguing here. They showed that the concepts of, respectively, introversion and extraversion are cognitively represented as patterns of functionally related attributes, just as patterns of different attributes define other concepts. Experiments by Hampson (1982) directed at the cognitive representation of personality traits rather than types which were studied by Cantor and Mischel are nevertheless consistent with a concept of the prototypicality of personality characteristics as represented in memory categories. Hampson's studies are even compatible with a semantic category model of person memory though they do not provide unambiguous support for it. Cantor and Mischel's, and Hampson's studies also support the view expressed earlier by Schweder (1975) that the traditional trait-rating procedures may produce spurious evidence of intra-individual consistency by stimulating the coherent and existing cognitive structures of the schemata towards which the questionnaire items are directed. High item-scale correlations, therefore, are a reflection of existing highly inter-related conceptual data and not necessarily evidence of personality consistency. And it needs to be remembered that this possibility was one of Mischel's most important explanations of the average low correlations between test–retest questionnaire scores, and experimental construct validity tests.

My own explanation of the modulating and attenuating influence of situational variability on findings of low intra-individual consistency across time and across situations would also differ somewhat from Mischel's, and certainly from the rather non-specific explanations offered by the recent espousing of a new 'interactionalism' (e.g. Endler and Magnusson, 1976a, b). In the context of the new model I would argue that with very rare exceptions 'situations' do not exist independently of 'persons'. These exceptions are most notably found in split-brain patients. For everyone else, 'the situation' is defined by the person's memory schema content, its elaborations determined by antecedent experience and evaluation from past behaviour outcomes, and by additional idiosyncratic data from the cognitive representations of situation-related affective experience.

If personality questionnaires do not provide reliable, consistent, or valid predictions of characteristic behaviour towards preferred goals and behaviour outcomes we need to examine the reasons for this deficiency further. If, moreover, the use of pre-determined response categories provides only for overstructured sampling of dispositions, we need to know not only whether free-responding provides us with evidence for the deficiencies in reliability, consistency, and validity, but also the reasons for the discrepancies between different types of test instruments. And if we accept the proposition that the personality and motivational characteristics of the individual are primarily available behavioural skills organized in functionally coherent cognitive structures, we must now ask about the nature of the data code which represents knowledge of behavioural preferences, of the effects of behaviour outcomes, and of hierarchies of goals.

3 THE SEMANTIC REPRESENTATION OF BEHAVIOURAL STRATEGIES AND THEIR GOALS

(i) Propositional framework

I will start the discussion by referring to one of the final points made at the end of the last section concerning the possibly superior reliability and validity of free-response self-descriptions. A study by Epstein (1976) required 30 subjects to keep records of their most positive and most negative experiences over a period of 30 days. Data were obtained in three forms for each incident: from a narrative, from an adjective checklist, and from the acknowledgement of 'response tendencies' representative of experienced general themes such as problem-solving or social withdrawal (negative), and problem-solving or pleasure-seeking (positive). As Eysenck and Eysenck (1980) quite correctly point out in their critique of Mischel's attack on trait theory and its measurement, Epstein's method of prolonged assessment of the consistency of individual response characteristics, that is traits, results in very high reliability coefficients.

I am less concerned with test–retest correlations, however, than with the data on which they were based. Epstein's method, I would argue, can be regarded as a variant of a verbal memory experiment. Apart from the retrospective (at the end of the day) verbal description of the most positive and most negative event of the day, the procedure required analysis and selective operations on 60 adjectives in the check list and on 66 'response tendencies'. To describe a past self-experience in verbal terms requires retrieval of the cognitive representations of the events that were stored when they occurred. Identification of positive or negative events depended, however, on applying meaning to them, in this experiment not only to determine their category, but to compare them with other events in the same category in order to achieve a scale from which the judgement 'most' can be derived. This conceptualization task pre-eminently demands fine-grained comparison processes which require a similarly fine-grained informational code in order to differentiate between degrees of presence of a given set of attributes. In this particular experiment, moreover, there was no need to depend entirely on self-generated verbal attributes encoding past experience since a lexicon of labels was made available simultaneously. The selection of a particular label or set of labels depends, however, on the previous matching operation between the meaning and experience of a past event and the label that had been attached to it at the time when it had occurred and had elicited its characteristic response. In other words Epstein's subjects needed to retrieve and semantically match the original experience. This, I would argue, is not feasible unless the original experience had been previously semantically coded on the basis of already existing semantic labels identifying appropriate referents and their attributes. It seems equally plausible to suggest that a written narrative is even more substantially determined by existing semantic defining labels which signify the content of the networks of cognitive structures, and of the schemata with their principal cognitive components, referents, and attributes in which the structures are organized. In the light of the recent explanatory trends of how concepts are obtained and remembered, which I discussed in Chapter 4, it seems fully valid to extend the proposition of the semantic nature of conceptual knowledge of external and impersonal objects, situations, and events, to the subjective and personal experiences which they engender.

The improvement in the reliability or *consistency* of measures of individual characteristics that can be obtained by methods such as Epstein's are subject, however, to some of the biasing factors advanced by Mischel in his critique of trait theory and measurement. In retest settings, particularly, there is a strong additional bias in favour of concept-identifying structures and labels which define the dominant task and the limited categories of self-description. It is also likely that daily repetition will have the well-documented overlearning effect obtained in list-learning generally. However that may be, it is of only limited relevance to the question of the *validity* attaching to free-response methods. For many years there has been consensus that narratives obtained from subjects, whether in pyscho-analytic session, from TAT protocols or in other settings, are not only difficult to quantify, but that their apparent low validity is largely due to difficulties and biases in extracting unidimensional, functionally related information.

There is other evidence, however, that narrations can supply important *and* valid data provided that their content is analysed operationally along hypothesis-derived pre-determined lines (e.g. McClelland *et al.*, 1953; Atkinson 1958). There is also more recent evidence that artificial intelligence models can generate information processing routines and subroutines which can match the interpretative requirements of psycho-dynamic theory. Colby (1975) and Faught *et al.*, (1977), working on models of paranoia, have suggested, for example, that a system of referents and attributes yielding principal cognitive structures of humiliation, shame, and self-blame can account for the dynamics of projection. Peterfreund's attempts to apply systems analysis to the rich content of self-reports (Peterfreund 1971; Peterfreund and Franceschini, 1973) show similar promise for a successful future attack on the validity problems presented by data with a large number of inter-connections, which are either specified, or implied but unexpressed. The study on the patterns of optimal and suboptimal maternal socialization strategies, which was discussed in Chapter 5, can serve as a reasonable example of how a less sophisticated method of operationally scoring TAT narratives can supply a level of criterion validity which could not be improved either by the addition of questionnaire-derived data, or by taking the results from objective instruments on their own. The application of more elaborate operational procedures to TAT protocol analysis has also been described (e.g. Foulds, 1953; Zubin *et al.*, 1965; Blatt and Wild, 1976) with not unfavourable outcomes for validity, especially in the field of psychopathology. There is a difference, of course, between free self-description and a TAT narrative. The validity of the latter is likely to be lower than that of the former because one cannot be certain to what extent projection operates, whether it operates evenly across the stimulus material, and whether it operates at all. To the extent, however, that all verbal reports about people, objects, events, situations and their interactions ultimately represent a respondent's permanent memory content, all narratives are projective. And what they project are subjective specifications of referents and attributes and their inter-connections which are organized in concept-specifying structures.

The most limited implication of this statement is that person-relevant concepts require a lexical and semantic transformation at the point in time when they need to be communicated in speech or writing. A less conservative view holds that self-concepts and their specification are coded in abstract propositional networks. In such networks temporal order and type and degree of relatedness supply the core of a concept for which lexical and semantic language adds a learnt set of signifiers which satisfy particular cultural demands for communication. The most radical approach to the data base of concepts is that where there are language, language skill, and learning capacity, perceptual and conceptual operations always involve semantic coding, and processes on semantic memory data. My reasons for preferring a radical model of the symbolic notation of memory and thought content have been argued to some extent at the beginning of this chapter. Those comments, however, require amplification. Let me summarize and to some extent recapitulate first the general conceptual framework of my model and the more specific assumptions derived from it for which I am trying to establish plausibility and, subsequently, offer some validity.

The basic proposition is that types and intensities of goal-seeking, and the consistent, characteristic way in which it is done, reflect response-selection strategies based on schematized information retrieved from one or several long-term memory stores. Unless motivation and personality are informationally defined, that is, by a comparable data code, we shall continue to be without plausible interacting structures which integrate conceptual data available from behavioural strategies, goal-preference, and response outcome. Since there is little disagreement that individually characteristic goal-seeking behaviour is substantially due to habit formation, this too, requires informational reanalysis. We may argue, therefore: (i) that reinforcement contingencies present information concerning behaviour and outcome to the central integrating parts of a processing system, and attach identifying codes to the information before channelling it to a long-term store; and (ii) that the information from habit-outcome contains adequate data from which on a subsequent occasion probabilistic expectancies of stimulated behaviour can be inferred. A necessary corollary holds that reinforcement and all its associated events and consequences are fundamentally cognitive data. Habit development and need-reducing expectancies will emerge if the analysis of the cognitive data by a central comparison process – including data currently held in working memory – yields a match with previously learnt, and initially biogenic, codes of pleasure and satisfaction. Individual differences in motivation and personality arise because of multiple interactions between subject and situational variables, because of inevitably idiosyncratic cognitive coding and integrating processes, and because the experience of what gives pleasure and satisfaction is, by definition, subjective.

This position does not logically destroy the behavioural specification of traits, or the utility of the concept, but inevitably assigns to a trait the power of conceptual structures with a number of infrequently stated implications. For example: the smaller and the more restricted the behavioural domain, the more constrained the opportunity for the development of social and personal interaction concepts, expectancies, values, and rules, and consequently the less differentiated the personality. The smaller the number of goals, the less complex the response system which selects characteristic ways of goal-seeking. On the other hand, an individual may emerge with relatively undifferentiated response-selection strategies, that is a small number of very dominant methods of goal-seeking, if these strategies have become excessively elaborated on the basis of one or several powerful prior experiences. This may occur because a cognitive event had elicited massive arousal which energized space- and time-occupying processes, which would have recruited further associations to the original stimulus. The resulting responses and subsequent response dispositions occur either as the result of a sequence of approximating cognitive matching processes with negative feedback characteristics (Miller et al., 1960), or as a sequence of search-match-and-scan operations along decision trees and pathways (Newell and Simon, 1972). Both process models propose methods and characteristics of goal-seeking, though with different degrees of specificity, and without reference to the nature of the symbolic, data-representing code.

In concrete terms, what is here proposed is that *characteristic ways of seeking adaptation or goals*, as in being dependent, aggressive, anxious, introvert, or competence-oriented, reflect cognitive schemata in which reside the outcomes of previously evaluated response strategies, the anticipated results of potential response tendencies, the concepts of self and others as they are relevant to a temporal hierarchy of goals, and the cognitive data deposited by previous experiences of pleasure and satisfaction. Thus, a characteristic aggressive way of goal-seeking reflects a response-selection strategy for which expectancy had predicted an optimum outcome for the goal and for satisfaction. If this aggression could be linked observationally to antecedent frustration, and if we also know the range of objects and people against whom frustration-instigated behaviour might be directed, we are able to make inferences about the cognitive elaboration of one characteristic way of goal-seeking. These inferences would include reference to substitute goals and displacement, to the number of response alternatives internally evaluated for probabilistic outcome, and to the cognitive load engendered by the consideration of behavioural alternatives and their objective adequacy.

We now add two assumptions. Firstly, that the kinds of processes just described demand a precise and rapidly available symbolization of their information in the form of semantic data supplied by the prior existence of an encyclopaedia of lexical terms. Secondly, that categorical distinctions between behaviour grossly described by traits, and the goals of that behaviour, are redundant because all trait-describing behaviour is goal-directed. This exercise yields a number of more precise formal propositions which express the substance of the model I am offering, and which amplify the statements tabulated in Table 6.1.

(1) All behaviour is problem-solving behaviour.
(2) All behaviour is goal-directed.
(3) Personality is defined by patterns of characteristic, preferred strategies and methods of reaching preferred goals and preferred behaviour outcomes.
(4) Response selection for the achievement of preferred goals and response outcomes is a problem-solving situation.
(5) Problem solving requires connection-forming and integrative processes between cognitive structures representing behavioural skills, goals, outcomes of previous goal-directed strategies, and situational constraints and facilitations.
(6) The unitary and co-ordinated nature of goal-directed behaviour requires a common system of symbols or codes for its connection-forming and integrative processes.
(7) The common system of symbolic codes represents the informational

content of functionally related cognitive structures and their organization in schemata.

(8) Cognitive schemata contain information for the identification of the meaning and implications of goal-relevant referents and their attributes, and of anticipated response outcomes.

(9) Fine-grained differentiation of the meaning and implications of stimuli and responses requires a fine-grained symbolic language with a high degree of in-built informational redundancy.

(10) Fine-grained symbolization of meaning with in-built redundancy is pre-eminently supplied by the semantic data of natural language, its lexicon, and its encyclopaedia.

(11) Semantic data in permanent memory represent the content of conceptual structures serving individual patterns of characteristic, preferred behavioural strategies, their preferred goals, and preferred outcome expectancies.

(12) The functional relatedness of semantic data codes in permanent memory is achieved by their organization in semantic networks.

(13) Individual differences in personality and motivation are ultimately defined by differentially elaborated, goal-directed semantic schemata.

(14) Where individuals possess highly elaborated, characteristic goal-directed semantic schemata with low retrieval thresholds, internal, self-relevant cognitive activities will affect the objective utilization of external, objective stimuli.

By singling out the role of semantics in establishing, elaborating, and refining the cognitive schematic structures in long-term memory, we are faced with many controversial core issues. Amongst these are what is meant by 'semantic', and how language signifiers come to substitute for existing non-semantic symbolic structures (e.g. Macnamara, 1977; Pylyshyn, 1977). We may agree with Bruner (1977) that the substitution of one signifier by another with a particularly good capacity for 'singling out', and thus for describing fine-grained differences, in a complicated series of associational cognitive and neurological events. These defy precise demonstration even in aphasic patients. But existing evidence, for example, of relatively unimpaired adaptive and problem-solving behaviour by the congenitally deaf (e.g. Furth, 1964; McCay Vernon, 1967), in no way undermines the proposition that semantic labels are the most frequently used and most economical representations of meaning and knowledge in the memory of individuals with unimpaired hearing. Quite the contrary, since the deaf are taught natural language symbols, albeit through other than aural channels. Hayes-Roth (1977a, b) has argued persuasively against non-lexical conceptual theories of memory, and it is of some importance that artificial intelligence theorists seem to share this view. For example, Findler (1979) accounts for the inadequacies of present machine translation programmes largely by the absence of semantic elaboration which derives from sophisticated encyclopaedic knowledge.

Thus, if we regard the definition of 'semantic' as the method and system of attaching meaning to a relational sequence of complex lexical terms and the concepts which they denote, we are able to argue that semantic labels organized in semantically coded schemata are a method and system for attaching meaning to complex stimulus and response areas. This is the case whether these are objectively and presently involved and conscious, or not. I believe that this conceptualization is consistent with psycholinguistic theory (e.g. Clark and Clark, 1977), and, in respect of pre- or unconscious processes, with Dixon's recent model (Dixon, 1981, p. 71).

There are many reasons, of course, why non-semantic factors in the analysis of meaning cannot be excluded: spatial reasoning seems to be a good example. It is quite possible that patterns of cross-referenced connections are pre-verbally analysed on the basis of the spatial patterns they describe (e.g. Waterman and F. Hayes-Roth, 1978). Inferences from these kinds of stimuli may not only be the forerunners of semantic labels, but may continue to be utilized during the development of very complex abstract knowledge to which lexical labels and semantic inferences cannot be immediately attached. There are no intrinsic objections to a dual-code theory of concepts as the discussion in Chapter 4 has already tried to show. In fact it is adaptively advantageous to possess both semantic and non-semantic representations of the same conceptual structure. For example, the difficult abstract concepts of 'justice', 'democracy', or 'happiness' probably achieve complementary definition by visual, auditory, or tactile data codes from episodic memories. Alternatively, concepts defining spatial or temporal separation such as 'next', 'before', 'after', 'above', or 'later' require relationship codes which in many cases never achieve fully semantic specification except in a meaningful, and therefore semantically coded context. A limited semantic specification may also apply to reference words like 'this', 'that', 'here', 'there', or to pronouns and grammatical tenses (e.g. 'deixis' terms). We need to be quite clear, however, that an image representation, once verbal learning has taken place, is an insufficient cue for goal-directed action without concurrent access to the meaning and implications of image stimuli. So-called verbal 'modals' or 'auxiliary modals' such as 'can', 'need to', or 'want to' are frequently cited as relational terms difficult to fit into a semantic theory of concepts. Their status of being 'relational', however, must imply that they represent a class of contingent proximity between a goal and the outcome of goal-directed behaviour, a relationship, that is, which can be semantically coded at appropriate stages of development.

While young children clearly operate on concepts before verbal labels are available to them (e.g. Nelson, 1977), and while an inadequately refined vocabulary appears to be responsible for overgeneralizations in children's perception and thinking (e.g. Clark, 1977), this may indicate only an absence of expressive capacity rather than non-availability. The same children can after all often appropriately point to referents which are vocalized by their mothers. The absence of a speech vocabulary in young children does not argue against Pylyshyn's (1977) notion of a pre-lexical language by which concepts are formed on the basis of their potential for action as well as their potential for expression. While a unity between verbal and non-verbal thought may well exist initially through the contingency between action and outcome at the perceptual level, evidence of language understanding at an early age favours the presence of specifically verbal knowledge. Words may not completely match or map concepts as Macnamara (1977) argues, but a full representation in any case requires the elaborated networks of attributes which have been discussed previously.

The nature of networks forms the basis of ongoing discussions between specialists in verbal learning and verbal memory (e.g. Collins and Loftus, 1975; Smith, 1978; Jusczyk and Earhard, 1980). There is general agreement that verbally labelled attributes assist in concept formation, and that verbal information is required to signify stimulus equivalence and the relationships between attributes (e.g. Rommetveit and Blakar, 1979; Zimmerman, 1979). There is also agreement that observational learning must precede lexical matching of the acquired knowledge (Macnamara, 1972, 1977; Whitehurst, 1979), and that, following Ogden and Richard's (1923) original analysis, semantic labels are required to differentiate referents and attributes from their alternatives to produce changes in meaning (e.g. Olsen, 1970). The concepts of semantic network theories of the representation of meaning, and of what is meant by 'understanding' continue, however, to evoke further theoretical controversy because of their lack of full precision. Great difficulties remain, for example, in conceptualizing *what* is actually implied by 'stimuli in context', *how* alternative stimulus identifications, verbal or non-verbal, can be produced, or *whether* evidence of semantic network *levels* has implications for the structure and functioning of human memory (e.g. Findler, 1979; Brachman, 1979). As I have suggested before, the nodes and choice points of propositional networks which can be mapped on to semantic structures may have not been sufficiently labelled in the past so that their obvious function in the representation of semantic complexity of meaning is inadequate (e.g. Newell and Simon, 1972; Anderson and Bower, 1973; Estes, 1976b). It is doubtful, therefore, that Schank's concept of 'scripts' to describe our knowledge structures for everyday activities (e.g. Schank and Abelson, 1977), as presently constituted adequately reflects the full potential of our analysing and action system.

Simon's more recent analysis of what is implied by 'understanding' (Simon, 1980b) considers several components that are necessary in deriving knowledge, meaning, and the capacity to communicate these to others (and to oneself, presumably). Among the required mechanisms Simon lists: facilitation of syntactical parsing of natural language; mapping incoming information into semantic memory; inferring meaning and means-ends relationships; matching processes *between* (my italics) semantic schemata and incoming information; recognizing and classifying instances of concepts; generating referents and attributes that match given relations; and significantly perhaps, mechanisms for finding reasons for the system's own actions (Simon, 1980b, p. 41).

Whatever our preference for one or several of the theoretical positions which have been mentioned, the role of the semantic representation of knowledge, meaning, and understanding cannot be denied. In the present model of the representation of personality and motivational characteristics I am giving precedence to a semantic schema representation of needs, goals, affect, and alternative behavioural strategies for the reasons embodied in the 14 propositions stated earlier. I do not see it as my function to take sides in ongoing controversies over *which* semantic or *which* multiple-code network model of memory is the most plausible. Even if semantic knowledge is not the only vehicle of memory and of information processing, the flexibility, the differentiating capacity and economy of semantic labels makes this system the number one contender for the encoding of functional knowledge and meaning. Semantic labels, their associations, and their variable hierarchical organization provide the most direct representational codes for the retention of personal and situational attributes. These attributes, by which an individual relates appropriately and predictably to the behaviour of others, can represent generality as well as specificity, temporal and conceptual distance as well as contiguity. The resulting *system* of labelled schemata thus encodes the person's characteristic goals and strategies of goal-achievement as well as his representation of environmental constraints and facilitations. Bartlett's and present-day concepts of the schema assume a further function that would have remained unstated, but for Piaget. He argues that the development and organization of schemata involve a process of logical conservation which ensures the invariance of the representational codes in all conditions of transformation (Piaget and Inhelder, 1973, p. 15). Any system which is able to overcome and ignore sensory information which would be misleading without utilizing contextual information (as even in the simple situations which test perceptual constancy and conservation of physical properties), must be a system which can employ general principles in stimulus evaluation and recognition. These must be deductive as well as representational. Because ultimately they subserve knowledge of functional meaning, they require superordinate symbolic codes by which to anticipate the outcome of a response. The preservation of invariance of meaning, however, is most securely effected by an informational code that is both invariant, *and* modifiable in a context. This is the function of natural language, and because language function is also directly observable I place this representational code in a central position for the acquisition, retention, retrieval, and selection of characteristic goal-directed behaviour.

For the purpose of structuring the major processes involved in the production of a preferred, characteristic response, let us suppose a person is faced with a difficult social interaction problem. He has the social skills, control of impulsiveness *and* time to plan his strategy so as to offend no-one, to achieve a group goal, and to be consistent with his previous strategies.

168

The progressive elimination of choice points in behaviour selection may be described, as was done by Newell and Simon (1972), as the elimination of irrelevant and illogical moves and subgoals by a search-and-scan strategy. In the most structured case of stage-by-stage deliberate and considered planning, the meaning and implications of alternatives will have been consciously, serially, and selectively attended to and tested prior to execution. To achieve the desired outcome, external stimuli must have been analysed to a set criterion and conceptualized in relation to dominant interpreting strategies. Therefore, it can be argued that these processes are not intrinsically different from those involving memory in problem-solving generally. Since, however, characteristically preferred methods of goal-attainment are to be utilized, the attentional and data-retrieval processes must reflect the involvement of data codes for the expression of individuality. Figure 6.6 illustrates in a very

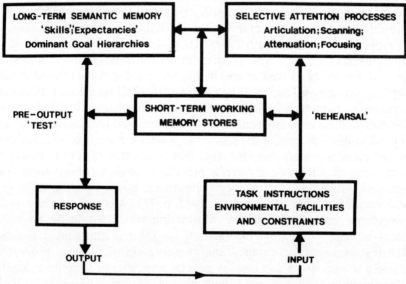

Figure 6.6 Model of an integrated cognitive processing system

general way the interactions that may be required between processing stages and subordinate operations to generate a socially competent and individually satisfying response. The long-term memory structures required for a response with social and personal implications contain the semantic information which identifies most precisely the meaning of facilitating and constraining aspects of the social stimulus field, as well as the prediction of response outcome for the person. To achieve a socially sensitive and personally rewarding solution to his problem, the individual avails himself of the information subsumed by an appropriate number of semantic schemata whose cross-referenced networks already encode superordinate social goal-achieving concepts and strategies. Depending on the individual's verbal capacity and the level of differentiation of his response-relevant schematic structures, we can obtain his introspective verbalizations of *why* he did *X* rather than *Y*, and *why* he used method *A* and not method *B*. Because of this capacity serious objections to the involvement of semantic information in goal-seeking behaviour are difficult to sustain. In the last analysis, however, the power and utility of our explanatory models depends on their falsifiability, and on experimental evidence consistent or inconsistent with predictions derived from them.

(ii) Initial experimental evidence

In Chapter 1, I referred to the experimental background from which the new model developed. I indicated that hypotheses derived from a cognitive-developmental approach to the study of the schizophrenic disorders obtained support from size-constancy and conservation studies, and that these findings in turn led me to investigations of the role of socialization anxiety in the development of the conserving skill. The negative relationship between the last two parameters was subsequently interpreted as the effect of information overloading on a limited capacity processing system. This reinterpretation required a cognitive approach to the analysis of anxiety because performance on various cognitive tasks such as problem-solving, word recognition, iconic memory, and dual tasks of increasing order of difficulty, on which anxious subjects performed worse, did not co-vary with peripheral arousal measures. The studies involved various groups of school children and university students and within each experiment were conducted on subgroups with, respectively, high and low scores on age-appropriate versions of a Test Anxiety questionnaire. These experiments are reported in greater detail in Chapter 8.

Two conclusions were drawn from the results of the several studies. Firstly, that anxiety is basically cognitive data in permanent memory which encode aversive expectancies of behaviour outcomes, and low-threshold pre-occupations with danger, social threats, and injury to self-esteem. Secondly, that low thresholds for this type of information facilitates its entry into working memory stages and processes while these are already utilized by the information processing demands of an externally presented task. It was also concluded that it interfered with permanent memory selection processes. This conjunction produces an excessively high load on processing capacity, and accounts for the demonstrated reduction in performance levels and speed of performance. Since the most pronounced independent variable differences between the experimental groups of all studies were defined by responses to questionnaire items, the most plausible explanation of these and similar studies had to be sought in those organized cognitive structures from which subjects deduced or induced their response to questionnaires. It could further be concluded, therefore, that the type and intensity of self-generated cognitive interference is a function of the content and elaboration of cognitive structures in memory schemata which encode subjective experience, a range of aversive objects, events, situations and persons and their attributes, and anticipation of aversive potential behaviour outcomes in the context of these referents and attributes.

If the content of memory includes largely semantic representations of characteristic preferred behaviour strategies, their goals and their preferred behaviour outcomes, three general predictions follow plausibly.

(1) Dominant personalty characteristics are associated with a more extensive trait-appropriate lexicon than non-dominant characteristics.
(2) Individual trait differences are associated with matching differences in trait-appropriate vocabularies.
(3) Experimental sensitizing of a dominant trait sensitizes the semantic structures of the trait. A number of experiments have been conducted so far to test these predictions which are minimal for a viable model.

Experiment 1: Dominant and non-dominant trait lexicon[1]

A dominant behavioural characteristic is defined by its appearance in many different personal and inter-personal situations and by its precedence over others. It follows that the characteristic is sufficiently well elaborated in its power of evaluating stimuli and appropriately fine-grained response modulation to deal with the largest possible number of non-identical situations. This must mean that one or several superordinate concepts are sufficiently well differentiated in their prototypical, diagnostic, or defining attribute structures to make subjectively adaptive generalizations possible. In the light of the preceding discussion on the role of lexical and semantic representations and labelling of concepts, a better-than-hunch prediction would be that dominant traits are associated with a larger trait-appropriate lexicon than non-dominant traits.

In a first study 24 male psychology students were administered the Edwards Personal Preference Schedule [EPPS] (Edwards, 1953), and percentile ranks on each of the 15 subscales were ascertained. For each subject the two most and the two least dominant scales were identified in terms of their percentile rank. Twenty-four hours later, each subject was presented with four TAT plates drawn from a set of 15, which were judged by two experimenters to be suitable matches for each of the EPPS scales. In order to maximize the match, each TAT plate was accompanied by a short verbal introduction intended to reinforce it. For example, to match the EPPS 'Achievement' Scale, TAT Plate 1 was selected (a young boy looking pensively at a violin in front of him) with the introduction that the boy in the picture wanted to be a famous concert violinist and was prepared to work very hard for this aim. For each picture stimulus subjects were required to produce in writing all verbs, adjectives, and adverbs suggested to them by the picture and its experimental verbal introduction. Dominant and non-dominant trait-appropriate vocabularies were assessed in randomized order. The results shown in

[1] This experiment was conducted by Carol Bernasconi.

Table 6.2 are largely as predicted with one notable exception for the least dominant trait.

Table 6.2 Association between EPPS percentile ranks and TAT-elicited lexicon

EPPS trait rank	Dominant		Non-dominant	
	1	2	14	15
Mean %tile	95	90	10	5
Mean lexicon	10.5	9.6	7.9	10.0

The combined lexicon for the two most dominant traits was significantly larger than that for the least dominant traits (p = 0.02) and Traits Rank 1 and 2 produced significantly more attributes than Trait Rank 14 (p = 0.01, and p = 0.02), respectively. Against prediction, Trait Ranks 1 and 2 did not produce significantly more attributes than Trait Rank 15. The correlation between verbal intelligence (Mill Hill Vocabulary Test) and size of lexicon was not significant. Differences between Trait Ranks 1 and 2, and between Ranks 14 and 15, respectively, were not predicted because of the deliberate closeness of EPPS percentile ranks.

The result seemed to encourage further work. In the next set of studies individual differences in trait dominance were selected as basic criterion, standard questionnaire techniques were employed for its assessment, and *memory* for trait-related words produced was added as dependent variables.

Experiment 2: Individual differences in trait-appropriate lexicon

Two traits were investigated – anxiety and anger – with number of words produced and number of words remembered as predictor variables.

(a) Anxiety[2]

Two experiments were carried out on small groups of school children and on university students, respectively, with substantial differences in scores on two different Test Anxiety Questionnaires (S. B. Sarason *et al.*, 1960; I. G. Sarason, 1972). It was predicted that highly anxious subjects can report a larger number of objects, events, situations, and people which make them anxious, and that these referents are defined by a larger number of verbalized attributes and response dispositions than those of the low anxious. Criterion groups of extreme-scoring participants were asked to report separately all those objects, situations, and people which they regarded as either pleasant, or worrying. Each of the referents produced was then submitted to a lengthy routine of questioning by asking 'Why?' as often as possible to elicit the fullest account of pleasant or worrying attributes associated with the refer-

[2] This experiment was conducted by Leslie Abbott.

172

ents. Representative results obtained for the 'Worry' referent from two children are shown in Figures 6.7 and 6.8. The overall results were consistent with the predictions, but fell short of significance. (Mean number of referents and attributes produced were: High Anxious 23.6, Low Anxious 17.5.) The results from the student group were statistically reliable with high anxious subjects producing a larger number of anxiety referents and associated defining attributes (N's = 7.7, p = 0.006).

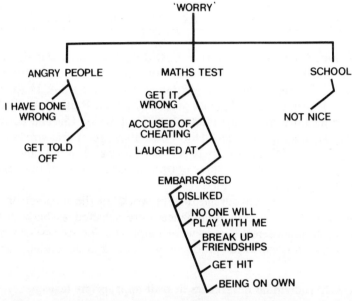

Figure 6.7 Semantic network of 'worry' from a low anxious child (age: 10.9 years, reading age: 9.1 years, verbal IQ: 90, test anxiety score: 11)

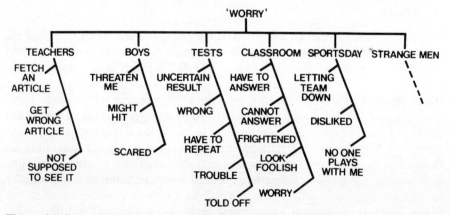

Figure 6.8 Semantic network of 'worry' from a high anxious child (age: 11.1 years, reading age: 11.1 years, verbal IQ: 98, test anxiety score: 21)

Because the free production method is substantially influenced not only by verbal fluency but by suppression of material considered undesirable by subjects, a more indirect approach was made to the semantic networks of anxiety. In this next experiment 26 different student subjects, respectively high and low anxious, were asked to produce as many attributes as possible for three referents: 'Worry', 'Pleasant', and 'Apparel'. Because of the control categories the experiment could be described to subjects as being concerned with verbal fluency. The words produced were subsequently inserted randomly into lists of altogether 50 attribute words each, in their appropriate classes, prepared by the experimenter, and the new lists were presented 24 hours later in a recognition memory experiment. It was predicted (controlling for the number of words originally produced) that high anxious subjects would identify significantly more 'worry' words as having been originally produced by them than low anxious subjects, and that this bias should not apply to 'Apparel' or 'Pleasant' words. The most important results and the significance of between-subjects and between-conditions differences are shown in Figure 6.9. Whereas high anxious subjects had produced initially

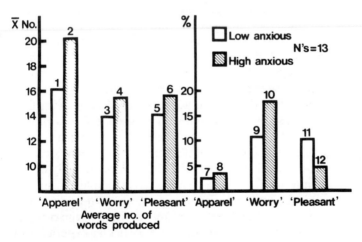

Figure 6.9 Production and recognition of anxiety and control words (significant differences: $p < 0.05$, 7–9; 9–10; $p < 0.01$, 2–4; 2–6; 8–10; 10–12)

more 'Apparel' than either 'Worry' or 'Pleasant' attributes, at the recognition stage they identified significantly more 'false positives' from the 'Worry' than from either of the other two attribute lists. Although low anxious subjects also falsely identified more 'Worry' than other attributes words as their own, they showed no significant difference in 'false positives' between 'Worry' and 'Pleasant' list words. Whereas the low anxious subjects appear to have had a general affective set, the high anxious subjects had a lower threshold for words denoting anxiety, as predicted. While this does not constitute conclusive evidence for more elaborated semantic schemata encoding anxiety, it is consistent with the model under discussion.

(b) Anger[3]

There is no question but that anger is experienced as an emotion and feeling tone, just as anxiety is experienced as a set of physiological signs and signals, and that the two subjective experiences are generally distinguishable. It has been argued already, however, that their physiological distinctiveness is not strong enough to determine unilaterally the subjective labelling of the two emotional states (Malmo, 1975). It may be proposed, therefore, that anger, just like anxiety, refers substantially to the experience of cognitive events. With respect to anger these encode activity blocking by constraints or restraints, prevention of goal-achievement, frustrating agents or agencies, or stimuli which are discrepant with a person's usual conception of himself, his ability, and his social role-playing opportunity and competence. The cognitive structures of anger will also have representations of preferred methods and strategies of responding to anger-inducing stimulation, and hierarchies of anger-inducing objects, events, people, and situations. As for anxiety, it can be argued that the conceptual structures of anger depend on lexical markers of its concepts and of the emotional experience itself, and that semantic networks and the size and retrieval thresholds of an anger lexicon will describe individual differences of this trait.

This definition differs from those advanced by others. Averill (1979), for example, in a very interesting account with a substantial historical descriptive bias towards antiquity, points out that the study of anger as compared with aggression has received relatively little attention in behavioural science. It seems all the more surprising, therefore, that Averill actually nowhere offers a clear-cut definition. He refers to it as an example of an emotion, or motivation of 'passionate' intensity, as a 'complex syndrome', or as playing a 'transitory social role'. This is only a slight variation of the orthodox stance: that an anger emotion is the consequence of particular experiences which are cognitively defined, or that processes of cognitive rationalization operate to provide *post hoc* reasons for feeling angry. Although Averill agrees that anger 'involves' appraisal of events labelled as unjustified or avoidable (Averill, 1979, p. 70), he fails to see that such labels, and those mentioned above, are the necessary components of the concept of anger which distinguish it from the similarly arousing conceptualizations of emotions such as anxiety or euphoria.

On the other hand, Novaco's (1979) proposals for a cognitive model of anger arousal, also applicable to clinical practice, could appear on superficial examination to be identical with the interpretations which I have offered above. This model departs from those presented in earlier sections of this

[3] This experiment was conducted by Frances Bayley.

chapter, however, in two significant respects. Firstly, it regards arousal and its cognitive labelling as anger as *consecutive* events, and in that sequence, whereas I regard them at the most as concurrent. Novaco's interpretation, therefore, is in the James tradition. Secondly, the model as presented fails to make it clear that without an anticipation or expectancy of frustration, annoyance, insult, and assault, that is cognitive expectancy, these definitions of experience would not be available. Cognitive expectancy, therefore, implies the presence of goal-directed response patterns defining the antagonistic response of anger. Novaco agrees, however, that the cognitive labels of anger may require some form of semantic signifiers, and therefore adopts a position quite closely related to mine.

Three predictions were tested in our initial experiments:

(1) Subjects scoring high on an anger questionnaire should remember an 'angry' prose passage better than subjects scoring low on the questionnaire, and should also remember more anger target words from an 'angry' than from a 'non-angry' prose passage.

(2) High angry subjects should list a larger number of referents eliciting anger and a larger number of defining attributes and response alternatives than low angry subjects, thus exhibiting a larger and more elaborate semantic network structure.

(3) High angry subjects would give more anger-related words than low angry subjects when asked to produce such a list, and in a recognition memory setting would remember more of them and additionally respond with a larger number of 'false-positives'.

An Anger questionnaire with a four-point response scale was developed which was based to some extent on the instrument recently produced by Spielberger (1980). Item analysis for internal consistency resulted in the retention of 35 statements representative of goal-blocking, acting-out responses, and emotion label statements, with an average inter-item correlation of 0.75. From an initial pool of 35 subjects, 8 high scoring and 8 low scoring subjects were retained as criterion groups for the experiments.

The first prediction, that high angry scoring subjects (1) would remember a larger number of anger target words than low angry scoring subjects (2), was confirmed: Mean (1) = 12.13 (SD = 1.89), Mean (2) = 7.38 (SD = 1.68), $p < 0.05$. The between-group results for the 'non-angry' passage were not significant. Also, as predicted, high scoring subjects remembered more anger than non-anger target words, but the difference just failed to reach significance.

To test prediction (2) that high angry subjects would show a more elaborate semantic network structure for anger than low angry subjects, the previous two criterion groups were tested individually. They were asked to report all those objects, events, people, or situations which made them angry. Each referent produced was then submitted to a lengthy routine of questioning by

176

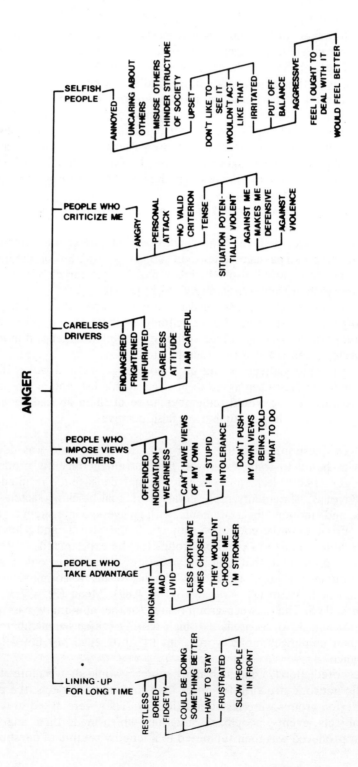

Figure 6.10 Semantic network of low angry subject (verbal IQ: 112, age: 20 years, anger questionnaire score: 27)

asking 'Why?' as often as possible to obtain the fullest account of the anger-denoting attributes which had been produced. There was no time limit.

Prediction (2) was confirmed for referents as well as attributes. High angry scoring subjects offered significantly more anger-appropriate referents than low angry subjects ($p < 0.01$) and also more attributes ($p < 0.05$). Representative semantic networks for anger are shown in Figures 6.10 and 6.11. The two examples are nearest the mean for their respective criterion groups.

Prediction (3) was tested in the following manner. For each subject the anger-denoting words were extracted which were given by subjects during the enquiry for attributes associated with referents in the network experiment. Also available were lists of articles of clothing which subjects additionally had been asked to produce during the previous experiment. The two lists of words were then randomly inserted into lists of 50 words each, in their appropriate classes, with the balance of words added by the experimenter. These two new lists were presented 24 hours after the previous experiment as a recognition memory task. Subjects were required to say which words they had previously produced themselves.

A portion of the results is illustrated in Figure 6.12. Low angry subjects produced significantly more 'Apparel' than 'Anger' words ($p < 0.05$), and high angry subjects produced significantly more 'Anger' words than the low angry subjects ($p < 0.01$). This difference applied separately to referents as well as to attributes. This result is shown in the left-hand portion of Figure 6.12. The high angry also *recognized* significantly more 'Anger' words than the low angry ($p < 0.05$). The right-hand side of Figure 6.12 plots the results for 'false-positive' recognitions. Although the difference in 'false-positives' for the recognition of anger words between the criterion groups fell short of reliability, it was in the predicted direction. However, the high angry gave a significantly larger number of 'false-positive' responses for 'Anger' than for 'Apparel' words ($p < 0.05$), whereas the 'false-positives' for the low angry subject went non-significantly in the opposite direction. Prediction (3) thus received no more than partial support. The results are not related to verbal intelligence assessed with the Mill High Vocabulary, and word fluency is controlled by virtue of the near-identical word production score for 'Apparel'. (The term 'false-positives' is parenthesized to indicate that signal-detection methodology was not applied in any of the experiments cited in this section).

The results of our series of initial experimental probes seem to be consistent with the new model and with the first set of general predictions. Dominant personality and motivational characteristics clearly have some association with the ability and readiness to produce and remember trait- and goal-defining verbal referents and attributes. Several alternative explanations, however, require consideration. The first of these would try to account for the results by reference to the effects of peripheral or electrocortical arousal. The induction of high arousal is held to facilitate performance most probably

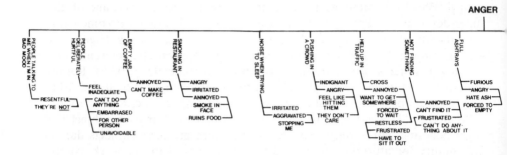

Figure 6.11 Semantic network of high angry subject (verbal IQ: 112, age: 20 years, anger questionnaire score: 40)

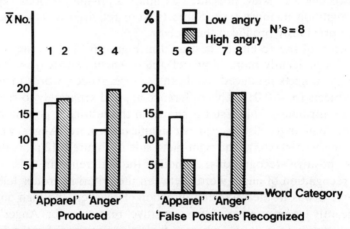

Figure 6.12 Production and recognition of anger and control words (significant differences: $p < 0.05$, 1–3; $p < 0.01$, 3–4)

through the focusing or narrowing of selective attention (e.g. Warburton, 1979, for a recent summary).

Two rejoinders can be offered against the full relevance of this alternative explanation. In relation to anxiety other experiments show (see Chapter 8) that there is only a weak basis or no basis at all for explaining the cognitive performance of high anxious subjects by high peripheral arousal. In none of the other studies was the dominant and/or criterion trait manipulated in order to induce a state of so-called emotional arousal. If arousal was induced or raised, then it was a general task performance arousal. With task-focused selective attention this should have affected all production tasks equally, which it did not, as well as accuracy of recognition. Accuracy of recognition was assessed in the 'anger' and 'anxiety' experiments by recording errors of omission in recognition performance. No significant between-group, between task, or between-group within-task differences were obtained in the 'anxiety'

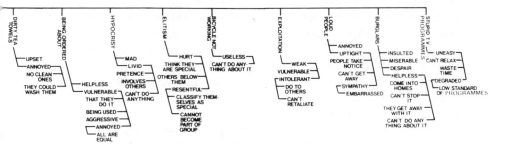

experiment. In the 'anger' experiment, high angry subjects made significantly more errors of omission for anger words than for apparel words, and low angry subjects made significantly more omission errors for apparel words than the high angry subjects. These data, therefore, do not give support to a role of differential task-performance arousal in our results.

A more potent rejoinder to an arousal explanation would take two forms. Firstly, if arousal facilitates selective attention, it may be asked which stage of the cognitive processing sequence decides on where the attentional focus should be, and what conceptual basis (because that is what it must be) is used for the decision. Bower's recent model (1981) of the relationship between mood and memory would be relevant here if our subjects had been emotionally aroused by hypnosis or imagination, because we could then argue in favour of facilitation through emotion-dependent or -linked semantic memory networks. But emotion induction/manipulation of this type formed no part of the experiments. Let us suppose, however, that emotionality indeed had been experimentally induced. We must then ask how this would help to explain finding a more highly elaborated semantic network of referents and/or attributes not only for the high anxious and high angry subjects, but also for dominant compared with non-dominant traits.

A further objection to the interpretation of the experimental results could be statistical and refer to the absence of significant ANOVA interactions between levels of anxiety and anger, and performance measures. Two answers can be offered. In the first place, the differences in the personality criterion groups were all within the normal range of each dimension, and there was no induction of the trait. Secondly, very substantial differences on *several* problem-solving tasks of *increasing order of difficulty* would have been required to demonstrate significant first- or second-order interactions. Again, it might be argued that the predictions were in any case tautological – that subjects would, of course, produce and remember anxiety- and anger-related linguistic referents if they were highly anxious or highly angry. Apart from the fact that the experiments distinguished between referents and their attributional signifiers, this objection misses the point of the model. When anxiety and anger are conceptualized as affect, emotions, or even behavioural traits, there are absolutely no *a priori* grounds for predicting differences in semantic networks. Such a prediction requires a cognitive reinterpretation of that which is aversive and threatening, or that which is frustrating and experienced as aggressive or frustrating. To label such events or agencies, requires conceptual analysis and appropriate identification by conceptual structures encoding the experience-defining signifiers. And without such structures it is difficult to see how people can become anxious or angry in response to stimulation, particularly in complex and frequently ambiguous social settings.

Although much more, and more fine-grained, work will need to be done, the present results plausibly support the prediction of the role of language in preferred behaviour towards preferred goals and outcomes. The results are also consistent with current views on the nature of concepts, and that lexical and semantic performance depends on the presence of verbal markers and semantically coded meaning in permanent memory. And what primarily matters is not temporary emotional arousal, but the presence of *those* conceptual signifiers and semantic labels which are descriptively associated with that state. The more frequently an emotional response has been experienced, and the larger the number of events that induced it (since there is no emotional experience without an emotion-signifying event), then the larger, more elaborated, and more differentiated the particular emotion concept in the individual's long-term memory. To this extent an emotion concept is little different from the concepts that encode professional skills or aptitude for social relations. And, of course, we accept that a lawyer has a larger lexicon and a more elaborated semantic network for 'law' than a non-lawyer, and that a social worker can produce more referents and attributes for, say, 'handicap' than a non-specialist. An anxious or angry person is just a different kind of specialist.

The present model extends the discussion from semantic networks closely *associated* with an emotion as recently argued by Bower (1981), to a *semantic definition* of the signifying components of emotion. Figure 6.13 makes a graphical comparison between Bower's concept (left diagram) and my own elaboration in which I have retained some of Bower's terms for ease of cross-reference. Whereas the studies reported by Bower and his associates (Bower, *et al.*, 1978; Bower and Gilligan, 1979) have employed hypnotic emotion-induction, ours have excluded it. Subjects came to the experiment emotionally 'cold' and without the activation of dependence and suggestibility which are likely to be associated with different emotions and their cognitive structures. If a 'cold' experiment elicits supporting evidence of lexical and semantic elaboration, then it seems more plausible to speak of the effects of cognitive events (task instruction or ease of memory access) on the retrieval and selection of emotion-signifying verbal labels, than of the effects of mood-state on memory category search. If, however, some areas of cognitive content are individually more meaningful than others, that is, if they are dominant and elaborated, then the retrieval threshold for that content area

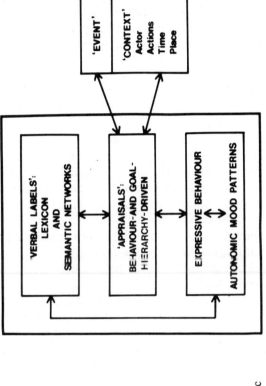

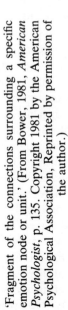

'Fragment of the connections surrounding a specific emotion node or unit.' (From Bower, 1981, *American Psychologist*, p. 135. Copyright 1981 by the American Psychological Association, Reprinted by permission of the author.)

Figure 6.13 Cognitive-semantic components of one behaviour- and goal-appropriate emotion

will be lower. Because memory search yields emotion-related cognitive representations which are necessarily associated with electro-physiological or psycho-pharmacological components of the appropriate emotion, a positive feedback factor is not excluded here. In a 'cold' experiment, however, it can only be secondary, and to *discount a primary cognitive induction* in adult emotional behaviour (e.g. Izard, 1977; Zajonc, 1980) seems to be implausible.

In a natural and developmental context positive feedback between arousal and conceptual operations is likely to contribute to the cognitive-semantic labelling and coding process, because the more intense and persistent an emotional or mood experience, the more likely it will be to generalize to conceptually adjacent objects, events, and situations. On the basis of the preceding argument, these will attract additional verbal labels subsuming meaning, relevance, and outcome information for the person. Thus, the more dominant a personality trait and the major goals towards which it is directed, and the higher its demonstrated salience in an appropriate context, the more elaborated the schematic cognitive structure and the more numerous its lexical and semantic signifying labels.

There is as yet, of course, a substantial gap between the available empirical data and the theoretical framework offered here. There are also enormous difficulties in the selection of the most useful experimental strategy to close this gap apart from basic, concurrent, developmentally-oriented cognitive-linguistic studies. We need to minimize the extent of *post hoc* inference from experimental data, and avoid the common criticisms of low validity and reliability of questionnaire scores and of projective protocols obtained from subjects. One 'strong' method would be to select criterion groups on the basis of cognitive-semantic networks which appear to be concomitants of dominant and non-dominant traits and goals. This would be followed by an experimental manipulation designed to induce characteristic goal-directed behaviour, with predictions derived from the semantic network structures previously obtained.

A difficult question remains. If words signify objects, people, events, and situations, and semantics describe their meaning and implications, how are meaning and implication identified in an adaptive situation? I am not now referring to my earlier and deliberate restriction of the definition of consciousness as the ability to 'read-off' working memory content. We need to search for an agent or agency, a system or its process, by which semantic information is recognized as being of a particular class and conceptual implication so as to connect it and relate it to semantic information of an associated class and its implications. For the recognition of isolated words, Morton (1969, 1970) has proposed a so-called 'logogen' system of word availability. A logogen is a process rather than a word, and a device for collecting evidence that a given stimulus word is present in a lexicon of words. This process depends on frequency of usage and contextual settings in which a word has appeared (see Morton, 1979 for a simplified recent discussion). The majority of studies in this area of work with fairly simple stimulus situations has been concerned with speed and accuracy of word recognition, with finding missing words to fit a gap in an incomplete sentence, or with the identification of words from a jumbled arrangement of letters. The logogen system, therefore, is one particular inference system operating at the lexical level of analysis, whereas semantic interpretations, according to Morton (1979), such as relating words to referents or attribute structures, occur in a functionally separate cognitive system. This is not the place to discuss the validity of a proposition which argues in favour of separate systems for closely related processes, partly because of supportive evidence from the small number of clinical cases in whom brain dysfunction appears to lead to differential impairment of either language or cognitive function (Coltheart *et al.*, 1980). What we can argue, however, is that just as word recognition depends on word context – defined by previous usage, previous contextual settings, as well as by task set – so the recognition of stimulus meaning depends on a meaning context. Just as word recognition depends on the availability of a word in an established lexicon, so the recognition of meaning depends on its availability in an *encyclopaedia* of meanings.

Behavioural dispositions, preferred goals and goal-outcomes are acquired because their meaning and implications are interpreted as positive and desirable for the person. If these meanings and implications are semantically coded in the permanent memory component of the cognitive system, then the recognition of a *personally important* stimulus-in-context cue requires a higher-order process rather than a logogen process, but one that is analogous to it. Just as a logogen process engages comparatively simple search-and-matching processes, so the expression of characteristic motivated behaviour and the maintenance of its coherence requires search-and-matching processes that reflect the response systems' overall goals. This is implicit in slower reaction times in complex situations, and in the even slower responses where stimuli-in-context are excessively complex, ambiguous, or appear to contain mutually exclusive information. When a search-and-matching process requires the retrieval of meaning and implications rather than the retrieval of words, we may well wish to coin a new term for it. The neologism 'semantigen' may be suggested for the present, to identify that process by which the identification of semantically coded meaning and implications is achieved of stimuli-in-context associated with, and relevant to, characteristic goal-directed behaviour.

We may propose that the units on which the 'semantigen' process operates are the generalizations implicit in the organization of attributes around referents which yield the principal conceptual components discussed earlier in this chapter and which were structurally modelled in Figure 6.3. The process is primarily an attentional and working memory search process which is guided by the task requirements and instructions held in working memory. The goal of the search process is to find units in all accessible cognitive structures which the stimulus-in-context cues have labelled as functionally related. Among the instructions in working memory are the dominant superordinate goals of the system with representations, respectively, of economy of effort and gratifying effects of outcome. With these constraints and facilitations, a 'semantigen' process will search the encyclopaedia of stimuli-in-context, and their representation of meaning and implications, with individually different degrees of exhaustiveness. The process will include the 'Test' stages first proposed by Miller *et al.* (1960), and will be concluded, therefore, if meaning representations in working memory are optimally matched by the identified implications of a potential response, that is, its semantically coded response outcome. Essentially, therefore, a 'semantigen' process operates on the verbal specifiers of semantic schemata and their dominant label or labels. These would have to include, however, representations of rewarding motor behaviour, and of the effects of need-reduction.

The level of abstractness of the process is demonstrated by the effects of altering a single word in a phrase or sentence. The *method* of cognitive analysis that results in a changed interpretation and response, however, is difficult to objectify by existing symbolic systems of notation whether they be arithmetical, chemical, or mathematical. But developments in science have always yielded new languages to describe the complex results of reductionist thinking. The interaction of biologically, socially, and cognitively induced processes in human behaviour will eventually yield an appropriate system of notation which defines the sets of rules which govern behaviour. A body of formalized rules would then yield a grammar of characteristic, preferred behaviour toward preferred goals and behaviour outcomes. Predictability and consistency of behaviour would reflect the operation of the behavioural grammar and its internal coherence. Coherence does not require full consistency because rule-governed behaviour of a dynamic system must include rules for when not to apply a conventional grammar, otherwise it would not be dynamic.

The model offered here retains distinctions between personality, motivation, and cognition *only for types of responses and goals to be achieved*. The expression of individuality and uniqueness does *not* occur as the result of cognition acting on personality and motivation, or personality and motivation acting on cognition in the manner of an interface between two separate functional units. Individuality and uniqueness are more appropriately defined as the outcome of the processes of integrated cognitive analysing systems which organize the direction and manner of behaviour. Integration is achieved by relating the *meaning* of existing need states to the *meaning* of variable environmental facilitation or constraints through a process of labelled inferences and interpretations which can be 'understood' by all significant components of the responding system. This process requires lexical and semantic codes, process systems for identifying and relating them, and memory structures in which meaning labels have been stored during preceding periods of developmental experience.

PART III

RETROSPECTIVE AND PROSPECTIVE APPLICATIONS

Introduction

In the next four chapters I will examine the implications and relevance of my major propositions for some current approaches to personality and motivation, and for some cognate behavioural domains. Clearly, I have to limit myself to issues in which I possess a certain amount of competence. For that reason I am compelled to omit any attempt to present a physiological or neurochemical infrastructure for the cognitive-semantic model of goal-directed characteristic behaviour. This must be left to a future collaboration between specialists in all appropriate areas, if the task is thought to be worthwhile. Inter-disciplinary research is fortunately on the increase, and we are beginning to see useful results for theory building from such interactions. O'Keefe and Nadel's (1978) recent work on spatial representations in the hippocampus is a good example, as well as the multivariate informational analysis of human stress which Warburton and I offered fairly recently (Hamilton and Warburton, 1979). This can be regarded as a first step in encouraging theorists and experimentalists in physiology, neurochemistry, cognition, personality, and social interaction to search for an integrative model of an adaptive system which deals more often with chunks of information than with discrete stimuli.

It would be entirely presumptious of me to attempt to integrate what is after all a set of molar concepts concerning the relationship between language, thought, and action, with existing and alternative theories of the nature and cognitive representation of language and grammar. The gap between ongoing analytic studies of verbal comprehension and sentence structure, and the semantic codes of concepts required for engaging in rewarding behaviour is substantial. If what I am offering here arouses interest, competent researches will try eventually to bridge the gap.

I will confine myself, therefore, to issues to which I feel I can contribute. I shall try to relate the model which was introduced and elaborated in the preceding chapters to the effects of anxiety on performance tasks, to the analysis of individual's susceptibility to 'stress' experience, to the role of intelligence in semantically coded self-concepts and to a selection of problem areas in society which affect the smoothness of national life and international relations. The label 'retrospective' in the title of this section refers particularly to the discussion of anxiety and stress vulnerability. My earlier cognitive reinterpretation of anxiety as informational data coded in and retrievable from permanent memory (Hamilton, 1975, 1979b) was a cognitive interference and overloading interpretation without reference to the nature of the conceptual 'language'. Similarly, my previous attempts to reinterpret 'stress' in informational terms as 'stressors' summating to an unacceptable 'strain' and 'load' for the cognitive processing system (Hamilton, 1979a, 1980), stopped short of identifying the means by which stimuli assumed the role of stressors, or the nature of vulnerability to stressors. Chapters 8 and 9, therefore, show my own conceptual route to the cognitive-semantic model of personality and motivation. These chapters are offered in its support by drawing attention to relevant experimental results which preceded its formulation.

CHAPTER 7

Some implications for some currently dominant models

I am confining myself here mainly to some general considerations because a comprehensive comparative and integrative exercise would require a separate volume. Apart from that, a full-scale integrative exercise is premature in the absence of a great deal more finely-focused experimentation, and is probably beyond the capacity of a single worker. At this stage, therefore, I will deal only with a restricted number of issues that arise more immediately from the statement of the new model and its present level of experimental support. Some of these issues are complexly inter-related and it is not easy to discuss them in isolation, or to make definitive suggestions for integration.

1 SOCIAL COGNITION

The critical reader will have experienced some cognitive discomfort from an early stage of my presentation. It could appear that the semantic model of personality and motivation is overdetermined by excluding abstract and non-verbal symbolizing systems and structures, and that its plausibility may be limited to the characteristics of highly verbal and introspective members of sophisticated societies. In defence it can be argued that non-verbal societies do not exist, and that the role of associative and propositional networks has been acknowledged. It is necessary, however, to maintain the distinction between structures and functions, between signifiers and that which is being signified, and between knowledge and knowing the implications of knowledge. I am inclined to make two somewhat extreme assumptions: (i) expectancies of outcome in *infra-human* organisms require the presence of some symbolic signifying system which conveys conceptual or quasi-conceptual knowledge; and (ii) the personalities and motivations of *pre-historic* man and of *pre-literate* societies were less differentiated than ours are today. The first assumption is a plausible hunch derived from the present assumptions concerning the role of expectancy in animal behaviour, and I am not competent to argue it further. The second can be sustained by the irrefutable evidence of the diversification of human goals, and of the modulating and moderating influence of social, goal-related behaviour outcomes on the phylogenetic primary drive system. As argued earlier in Chapter 5 in relation to the effects of social complexity on socialization strategies, it is plausible to assume that with an increase in the number of socially desirable goals and formalized constraints governing their availability, there is a matching increase in concepts and cognitive structures. And the greater the number of goals and goal-conflicts, the greater the need for finely differentiated behaviour strategies to achieve maximum pay-off at minimal cost. This interpretation implies not only that motivation – preferred goal-attainment – is primary, and personality – preferred characteristic strategies of attainment – is secondary, but that behavioural differentiation and its resulting individual differences depend extensively on the socio-cultural environment, and on individual capacity and competence to conceptualize and utilize it appropriately.

A broad 'educational' approach to the conceptual structures underlying goal-directed behaviour must assume that their development is related to age as well as to intelligence. A carefully conducted comparative study on more than 300 children by Livesley and Bromley (1973) provides good evidence for this proposition. The subjects, aged 7–15+, were asked to describe eight people known to them, four whom they liked and four whom they disliked. Each description was for a man, a woman, a boy, and a girl. A high intelligence and a low intelligence group were constructed from comparable verbal tests. The investigators' analysis of two core variables – number of trait names used and number of 'central statements' about referents – shows that both age and intelligence are significantly related to differentiation of person-description. 'Central statements' were defined as abstractions and generalizations of person characteristics such as personality traits, general habits, motives, values, and attitudes and social orientations. Such person-descriptions were significantly more frequently obtained from the higher intelligence and older research groups, and tended to be a substitute at times for the mentioning of trait names. Livesey and Bromley suggest that this may be one of the reasons why the relationship between trait names and intelligence was not as significantly high as the relationship with age, and that it might account for the drop in trait names produced by the oldest group.

Cognitive-developmental evidence requires support from models of superordinate cognitive strategies which can account for the accentuation or articulation of different types and amounts of information up-take, and for the classification and organization of perceptual and conceptual data. Here we are now less concerned with the cognitive controls which were discussed in Chapter 2 than with cognitive style, to use the original term. The elaboration component of the semantic model of personality and motivation relates to two assumptions which need to be discussed here: (i) that stimulus and concept articulation vary on a dimension of simplicity–complexity; and (ii) that simple as well as complex conceptual structures may acquire different degrees of rigidity and stereotypy.

Simplicity–complexity, extensively researched by Bieri (1955, 1966) and many others (e.g. Crockett, 1965), is a concept as well as a measure of cognitive differentiation. It refers not only to the number of conceptual categories which are employed to describe a given person, object, event, or situation, but particularly to the number of intervals or scale points on a dimension of attribution. Wegner and Vallacher (1977) proposed that information about people, for example, is frequently in the form of general attributes which lie on scales of attribute strength. These would then require a differentiated lexicon to conceptualize that which is described by a scale point. Specific attributes are unarticulated by definition, they apply only in restricted instances, but they can also vary in strength and, therefore, require conceptual differentiation to represent variation. We have already seen that age and intelligence affect type and differentiation of attribution. In addition, however, we must consider the role of the more central characteristic to classify and subclassify percepts and concepts. In the field of the social dynamics of inter-group hostility and intra-group identification Tajfel (e.g. 1969) has shown in a number of experiments that out-group and in-group attitudes are influenced by a superordinate goal of conceptual coherence, by assimilation of group-values and norms in childhood, and by simplifying categorization of stimuli having complex implications. Hamilton (1957, 1960), adopting a rather different theoretical basis, obtained evidence that anxiety can restrict the number of cognitive categories people are willing and able to use, thereby reducing the subjective complexity of stimuli. This strategy, however, need not be evidence of generally restricted cognitive structures and of undifferentiated representation in a semantic memory store. Since the subjects of many of the relevant experiments were reasonably intelligent adults, the reasons for oversimplifying the identification and labelling of stimulus input are discomfort and/or aversiveness associated by an individual with cognitive complexity. Superordinate goal structures could determine, therefore, strategies for the avoidance of cognitive uncertainty which inevitably occurs in the presence of multiple defining attributes. One such superordinate goal structure is intolerance or avoidance of ambiguity (e.g. Frenkel-Brunswik, 1949; Rokeach, 1951; Hamilton, 1957, 1960).

Stereotyping refers to overgeneralization and constriction in the attribute structures of conceptual schemata; *rigidity* refers to degrees of unmodifiability of existing structures. Again, cognitive strategies of stereotyping and rigidity are normally and positively related to the progress of and capacity for cognitive development generally. Both aspects of social cognition are not necessarily present only in the problem areas of group relationship. A bland judgement that an event is 'good' or 'bad', or a person is 'liked' or 'disliked' *is* a stereotypical response. This response occurs, however, after processing the representations of a small or a large number of attributes fitting the core concept. Generally, the complexity of the available attribute structures is determined by the factors discussed earlier. Ease of access to available information would depend, however, on objective or subjective pressure to respond, and particularly on the differential accessibility of individual attributes.

Multidimensional scaling techniques (as well as factorial analysis) have been employed frequently to demonstrate the ways in which individuals organize the attributes of a conceptual structure around a core concept. This exercise may usefully describe the degrees of differentiation of a concept by the number of attribute dimensions employed to define it, and it may adequately represent a conceptual stereotype. Co-occurrence, however, does not necessarily provide a clue as to whether the stereotype is 'good' or 'disliked'. A study by Rosenberg *et al.* (1968) which was directed at identifying the dimensions of impression-formation may serve as an example. In the dimensional space defined by the concepts 'good/bad-intellectual' and 'good/bad-social', the attributes 'serious' and 'naive' are roughly equidistant on the 'good/bad-social' dimension with a scale-value of near-zero, but at opposite ends of the intellectual dimension. Purely statistical inference, therefore, would not lead to the conclusion that the attribution of 'naive' might yield a 'bad' and 'disliked' *social* stereotype. If the schematic structure of 'naive' were further investigated, however, particularly in relation to social sensitivity referents, a quite different structure would emerge, and a 'bad-social' label would attach to a naive individual or group. Since an intellectual interpretation of 'naive' contributes to the final classification, this must then mean that evidence of statistical independence or orthogonality can be theoretically misleading.

Considerations such as these are part, of course, of Mischel's formidable criticisms of the trait concept. Whereas stereotyping reflects the result of imposing cognitive economy for a variety of reasons such as decision time, social conformity or avoiding uncertainty and anxiety, the co-occurrence of attributes in the definition of a concept can reflect the effects of stereotypical verbal learning. But this level of analysis is again too simple because of substantial evidence that negative and unfavourable attributes tend to be more highly differentiated, because negative attributes appear to be more influential when evaluating other people, and because their conceptual modifying capacity has been shown to be greater than that of positive attributes (e.g. Kanouse and Hanson, 1972). Various explanations from social psychology of the reasons for this effect in terms of differential salience or of dissonance effects seem less generally useful than Kogan and Wallach's (1964) conclusion that costs of behaviour are subjectively more important than gains. But there must be individual differences determined by the degree to which costs enter into decision-making. Distinctions must also be maintained, however, between conceptual category width (Pettigrew, 1958; Tajfel, 1957) reflecting cognitive strategy in general, and the number of categories employed by a storage and processing system (Hamilton, 1959). Differentiation operates in both situations, and the rejection of exemplars or attributes from a category does not mean that the category itself is undifferentiated. In fact, a recent study (Huang, 1981) showed that narrow categorizers possess better differentiated *semantic* categories. This sort of evidence provides some of the much-needed support for the propositions of the present new model that concept specification benefits from semantic elaboration. Another recent paper (Rothbart, 1981), on the relationship between memory processes and stereotyped social beliefs, suggests that out-groups are perceived as less differentiated and more homogeneous than in-groups. Rothbart's actual experimental results, however, showed only superior memory for stimuli which generally *confirmed* events that were expected, whether they were negatively or positively slanted. Which dimensions of classification are most salient and most likely to be used in stereotyped attribution is still an open issue in social cognition. There appears to be, however, a growing consensus (D. L. Hamilton, 1981) that the affective signature of trait labels contributes significantly to an imbalance of costs and gains observable in behaviour.

This raises another question, however, of why that should be so. A fundamental explanation would start from a hedonistic principle of behaviour control, and would argue that the avoidance of costs takes precedence over gains. If as a result of a developmental history and of genetic vulnerability the avoidance of costs acquires strong salience, appropriate conceptual attribute structuresnwill reflect the heightened tendency to anticipate costs by a more fine-grained differentiation of situational and subjective implications of stimulus events. Self-concepts of social rejection and incompetence, of threats to physical integrity and self-esteem, as well as concepts of significant persons in the individual's past and present life can constitute, therefore, the basis of more numerous and more intrusive negatively evaluative attributional structures. A hedonistic conception of goal-directed behaviour also implies not only that positive self-evaluations are important, but that this aim may require substantial focusing on negative self-attributes (e.g. Ickes *et al.*, 1973). This occurs in order to modify them, or to minimize their associated aversive affect (see the earlier discussion on affect in Chapter 6).

The interpretation of personality and motivation by response dispositions encoded like any other concepts in semantic permanent memory networks, provides a rational and economic vehicle to explain the original data of cognitive style and control theorists (e.g. Frenkel-Brunswik, 1951; Klein, 1954; Witkin *et al.*, 1954; Gardner *et al.*, 1959). It elaborates previous explanations of these findings which referred either to integrated cycles of informational analysis (Bruner, 1951), or to the role of an 'executor' system (Neisser, 1967), or to special instances of selective attention (Erdelyi, 1974), or to the role of parallel, ongoing self-monitoring processes (Forgus and Shulman, 1979).

2 PSYCHO-DYNAMIC CONCEPTS

(i) Kelly

The proposed cognitive-semantic model of personality and motivation bears only superficial similarity to personal construct theory (Kelly, 1955). The emphasis here is on the *method and language of the internal representation* of sets of coherent response dispositions, and on the range of coded goals, expectancies, preferences, and stimulus analysing strategies which characterize a person or a group of people. It has greater affinity, therefore, with the notion of conceptual belief systems which derive from the effects of socialization and developmental antecedents on cognitive strategies and concept elaboration (Harvey, *et al.*, 1961; Harvey and Felknor, 1970), which have been discussed in Chapter 5. Although Kelly's theoretical views were originally favourably received (e.g. Bruner, 1956), and although they have generated a considerable amount of research (e.g. Bannister, 1970, 1977), the repertory grid scaling technique, which was developed concurrently, has found wider acceptance than the theory itself. It is probable that the increasing sophistication of social attribution theory and of analytic cognitive processing theories provides a relevant explanation for this outcome. Objectively considered, constructs are imprecisely defined conceptual structures. Despite their clinical richness and their contribution to pattern-directed analyses of related and unrelated conceptual referents and their constellations of attributes, the construct approach seems to detract rather than add to psychodynamically oriented efforts for the elucidation of unobservable thought processes. What Kelly's successors have gained by limiting the extent of probing conceptual structures to the use of the grid technique may have been lost by restricting the number of referents which could be subject to enquiry. On the other hand, Kelly's concept of hypothesis testing as a dominant strategy for adaptive behaviour is, of course, similar to my own suggestion that personality and motivational characteristics are the end result of a problem-solving process. I am suggesting, however, a specific system of data processing by which problem-solving can occur. This may eventually negate the somewhat unkind conclusion that at present the repertory grid technique is yet another example of a test in search of a good theory.

(ii) Psycho-analytic theory

Let me turn to implications of the model offered here for psycho-analytic theory. This must be no more than a cursory exercise, not because I have ever shared in its rejection, but because a comprehensive comparative analysis is quite beyond the scope of this volume, and possibly beyond my own competence. Although the Freudian variant has been the most influential, its crucial propositions are shared by eclectic and *less* physiologically conceived theoretical developments. We ought to use the plural 'theories', rather than the singular, because we are dealing with groups of propositions each of which is a theoretical statement. If for no other reason than this, a number of past somewhat dogmatic criticisms have really been misplaced. I will restrict my comments to three issues: the core propositions of such theories, the nature of the data at which the propositions are directed, and the relationship of the propositions to those of other, and ostensibly irreconcilable, theoretical conceptions of behaviour.

Depending on the orientation of the theorist, we obtain different lists of the basic and most important concepts. There are two reasons for this.

(1) Rejectionists will tend to list concepts which are difficult to test experimentally, and for which attempts at validation have been unsuccessful.
(2) There appears to have been a fairly general failure to distinguish between theoretical core concepts and their corollaries.

Corollaries, however, depend very much on the specificity and adequacy of the premises, and if these are too general, precise deductions are not possible. This, of course, has been the principal difficulty of this body of theory. Although infantile sexuality has been frequently selected as the most distinctive statement of psycho-analytic theory, it is properly a corollary from more general statements of the organizational structure of personality and motivation. Similarly, I would argue that oedipus and castration complexes, symbolism in dreams and humour, and slips of the tongue or of the pen are corollaries – plausible deductions – but less important in absolute terms than the basic propositions. Popper's (1959) requirements of the scientific process are not inconsistent with this statement. The falsification of a hypothesis requires revision of its theoretic premise only if premise and hypothesis are stated with sufficient precision. The problem with all psycho-dynamic propositions, however, has been the absence of precise propositions about mediating processes through which general and dynamic functional properties of the person can express themselves in actual behaviour.

There may well be some agreement about the core propositions. My selection is confined to only four: unconscious deterministic processes; the significance of salient experiences in childhood for adult motivation; processes which are capable of protecting the individual against intolerable subjective experiences; and the functional continuity between so-called normal and abnormal behaviour. Now, if it is conceded that there is some merit in my suggestion in Chapter 6 that affect necessarily has substantial cognitive representation, then, more than ever before, *psycho-analytic theories are cognitive theories*.

Our recent liberation from dogmatically oversimplifying S–R theory enables us to look once again without horror and professional status anxiety at *unconscious and unobservable events* in the complex, adaptive, hedonistically-oriented human processor. In such a context unreportable events are neither non-existent nor without importance in the selection and expression of thought and action. We need to consider only laboratory tasks in which personal implications are minimal: learning and recall of word lists, memory for unfamiliar prose passages or complex pictorial displays, dichotic listening phenomena, or solving anagrams. The subjects are usually unable to say why some stimuli are better remembered than others, why they are grouped in recall in the way they were grouped, how some stimuli entering a non-attended ear intrude into concurrent 'shadowing' processes, or how anagram solutions are actually obtained. The unreportable processes and operations involved in these examples were required for performance, however, and must have occurred. Their conceptual status as unconscious processes and operational strategies is no lower, or higher, than those unreportable events which at times may prevent us from hearing a derogatory remark, or those which must have played a role in displaying a socially unacceptable, and immediately unrewarding form of behaviour. Admittedly, these are more complex examples, which in some respects could be used as an argument against a hedonistic concept of goal-orientation. On the other hand, however, complexity defines not only multiplicity of external stimulus cues, but primarily internal representation of multiplicity of goals, goal expectancies, behavioural alternatives, and occasionally unadaptive shifts in a hierarchy of goals. Such shifts must be internally determined by the emergence of a particularly strong cognitive-affective schema into a position of salience. The reasons for the shift in goal salience must lie, however, in a temporal and temporary conjunction of dispositions and expectancies which were sufficiently intrusive as to prevent a self-protective series of testing operations concerning the type of behaviour outcome they would engender (see also Dixon, 1981).

Impulsive and unpremeditated behaviour can be regarded as evidence of conflict between the priorities of satisfying a number of goals simultaneously to achieve optimal pay-off, or of satisfying an intrusive goal of releasing the tension from a particular goal-related cognitive-affective signal. There is no special difficulty in a cognitive-semantic reinterpretation of conflict. Problem-solving generally requires at many stages the comparison and testing of competing solution strategies. It can actually be argued that all combinations of Miller's (1944) original approach-avoidance decisions may be involved if, for example, what is required is not only a correct solution, but the most efficient and elegant solution in the shortest possible time. This, of course, would require pre-knowledge of outcome of each step towards solution, processes for which semantic representations of knowledge are indispensable according to my argument. If behavioural adaptation through its goals and its goal expectancies is basically a problem-solving task, then conflicts involving alternative self-images and self-evaluations differ from other conflicts primarily in terms of goal-hierarchy position and in terms of content. As proposed before, however, self-relevant concepts are by definition and by experimental data from self-description and self-attribution studies more complex than other concepts. As a result, the number of retrieval, matching, and selection processes prior to responding are likely to be more numerous and especially so in highly differentiated persons. In the presence of a large number of simultaneous as well as serial decision processes, while holding in working memory the goal to be achieved, retroactive inhibition or cognitive masking seem to be inevitable. Thus, although a large number of cognitive events have taken place and have been utilized, most remain unreportable to oneself or to others.

There can be, therefore, no intrinsic objection to unconscious processes *per se*. Similarly, it is really quite difficult to sustain objections to the proposition that the content of unreportable cognitive data is the outcome, in the last analysis, of subjective direction in the elaboration and associative connection-forming of experienced events. *All* concepts and their schematic structures are affected by subjective strategies and idiosyncrasies, which reflect individual experience over a long period of time. Events or experiences which were unusual, unexpected, and additionally elicited strong affective responses at any point of the developmental history, are likely to induce prolonged cognitive processes, partly, of course, because of the prolonged and strong effect of peripheral and electrocortical arousal. For this reason, if for none other, significant events thus defined will contribute disproportionately to the dominant signature or prototypical label of objects, persons, and the situations associated with them. Since in the majority of cases our conceptual structures are remarkably modifiable over many years, Freudian 'fixations' with pathological implications are the exception rather than the rule. This is partly reflected in population statistics of the incidence and prevalence of behavioural abnormality. In any case, *positively experienced* significant early events, too, are likely to impair selective concept development where they are experienced as subsequently unobtainable, objectively through death or separation from the appropriate agent, or subjectively through untested fantasies. These experiences can be encoded as aversively as actual negative events.

Since there is no evidence that any living organism ever engages freely in *absolutely* unrewarding, threatening, or painful activity, there are no logical objections to extending the application of self-protecting and self-promoting behaviour strategies from actions to processes prior to action. That is, cognitive processes involved in identifying stimuli, and in encoding, attenuating, articulating, elaborating, and retrieving, are fully capable of preventing available information from reaching the working memory stage in such a form that it can obtain the status of threatening knowledge. Initially aversive information resides in external stimuli; only subsequently will the memory codes of classes of aversive stimuli sensitize the cognitive processing system to the probability of their occurrence. Sensitization will affect external scanning and focusing strategies so that either less potentially threatening information enters the recognizing system, or it enters it with insufficient strength to outlast the limited holding-capacity of early durable buffer stores. If potentially aversive information succeeds in penetrating this first self-protective barrier, it is likely to be submitted to further identifying processes which establish its meaning. This is regarded generally as a matching process. Now, if the identifier to which penetrating stimuli have gained access is part of a self-protecting schema, it will simultaneously exhibit its defensive capacity. Depending on the previously rewarded strategies, identification of stimulus class and its implications will be followed by either denial, or disguise of the aversive information. For denial to succeed, the identification process must then retrieve additional information that instructs the system to refrain from further processing, and to assign to the stimulus the status of a schema with low retrieval bias, or to direct it to memory structures representing classes of stimuli which have attracted a non-processing label in the past. In a posthumously published monograph, George Klein (1976) describes these processes as being due to the prevention of adaptive feedback, and their result as the development of dissociated schemata.

The concept of repression shares with the concept of gravitational force one important characteristic: neither can be directly demonstrated. They are constructs and their reality and presence need to be inferred from evidence of the actions and effects which have been predicted for them. Fortunately for the physical sciences, gravity effects are visible and need not, though they often do, require sophisticated instrumentation. Repression as a protective cognitive strategy is non-visual and extremely difficult to demonstrate and operationalize. Moreover, the required logical distinction between repression and unconscious processes has not always been maintained. While protective denial processes are clearly intended to be unreportable and unavailable to self-knowledge, only a proportion of unreportable, unconscious processes are concerned with cognitive data from which the person is meant to be shielded. These data and their implications vary from individual to individual. What is highly aversive and threatening to one is mildly unacceptable to another. Moreover, interactions between the perceiver, events, situations, and the involvement of other persons in the distant or near past, make it virtually impossible to test for repression in a standardized and 'open' setting. Thus verbal learning and memory tests with words assumed to be associated with experiences of danger, or threat of injury to the body or to self-esteem, are relevant tests of the concept only where there is independent evidence that such dangers are an important component of a person's cognitive structures. Such experiments need to control in addition for verbal learning capacity in general, and they need to manipulate by instruction the known outcome for subjects with different performance levels. One of the most recent and somewhat strident attacks on psycho-analytic theories (Eysenck and Wilson, 1973) is largely based on tests of the theories in which these considerations play little or no part. At least one of the studies these authors used to demonstrate the invalidity of the concept of repression is actually consistent with it. Levinger and Clark (1961), for example, found that words which achieved the highest emotionality rating prior to learning also showed the highest forgetting rate after four months.

If the net is thrown wider, and a large number of studies employing quite different experimental methodologies are examined, the evidence in support of a repression concept is no worse, and often also no better than other behavioural concepts to which theorists appear to be less sensitive. An objective and scholarly re-examination by Kline (1972) of a large number of published studies leads him to conclude that the balance of evidence supports the validity of a protective denial process. Of particular interest are studies initiated by Dixon (Dixon and Haider, 1961; Dixon, 1971) which showed that subjects tend not to report threatening information presented in only one-half of a stereoscopically viewed field (see also Dixon, 1981 for a massive array of other evidence).

Although denial and disguising processes are separate concepts, *disguise* of aversive information requires suppression of the undisguised stimulation so that it cannot intrude into the chosen protective strategy. While it is assumed that threatening repressed information remains unmodified because the protective strategy is a non-processing one, this does not apply to Anna Freud's other defence mechanisms (Freud, 1945). Disguise of an aversively interpreted stimulus requires the integration of this information and its attributes into schematic structures which do not generate aversive identifications, or do not generate them to the same extent, or with the same implications. In many respects the cognitive dynamics of disguise by *displacement* are the simplest. Assuming that we have sufficient corroborating evidence, it can be concluded in appropriate cases that a person who is excessively frightened of a motor car accident on the way to work is anxious about significant aspects of his working situation. Alternatively, a person who shows excessive anger with a domestic animal in response to events which generally do not elicit it in other people, or in himself on other occasions, protects himself against awareness of unwanted characteristics in another object or person which are inconsistent with the desirable characteristics of the same object or person.

Many years ago, Miller (1948, 1959) proposed a stimulus generalization model to explain conflict resolution. Arguing from findings that the strength of avoidance and inhibitory responses is greater than the strength of approach responses, he stated that inhibitory responses and the responses with which they compete generalize to situational contexts similar to those in which they were originally learned. Furthermore, the strength of the generalizing response is a function of the degree of similarity between an original and a new situation. Applying this proposition to the above examples, we can say that there are fewer threatening implications for self-esteem or job security in being afraid of an accident compared with a negative self-assessment of professional competence. Equally, expressing anger and physical aggression towards an animal has a smaller number of undesirable consequences for personal relationships, and their usually rewarding outcomes in thought and interaction, than attacking a spouse, an offspring, or a colleague or superior at the place of work.

Although displacement has been incorporated into social learning theory, its generalization principle derived from learning theory has not yet been conceived as a set of cognitive events. Similarity between objects, people, events, and situations is determined by the degree to which their attributes are shared, by the frequency with which interaction with them is followed by comparable outcomes, and by the frequency with which processes assessing comparability have been carried out in the past in general problem-solving to achieve preferred behaviour outcomes. The cognitive components of the affective response, however, remain undisguised, and play an overriding role in the selection of the object of the anxious or angry response. Miller's conflict paradigm led to a further prediction, however, in respect of strong conflict between responding and response inhibition, namely, that in such conditions the generalization gradient is extended backwards to less and less functionally similar responses. In this event, occupational anxiety may be expressed in some focal phobia, and anger may find its outlet in hostility towards social out-groups, such as ethnic minorities.

The notion of substitution of one goal for another, and the assumption that stimulus generalization is a key process, require a number of premises. A displaced response must be 'safe', that is, it must not induce greater anxiety or anger than the one for which it substitutes. It must be appropriate, in that it is reasonable in respect of the functional characteristics of the substitute and its constituent schematic structures. The attribute structure of the new referent must already contain information that is consistent with the identification and expression of anxiety or anger. Moreover, the elaboration of the cognitive structures of the new goal object, its principal concepts, and its associated schemata, must be greater for anxiety and anger than for information incongruent with these affects. In the above examples this means that a cognitive basis for fear of car accidents and for leaving the protective security of one's home has existed prior to the appearance of a disabling behavioural abnormality. It also means that there are pre-existing attributional dispositions to be angry with a domestic animal, and with minority groups. The substituted behaviour achieves stability because its pay-off is greater than its costs in terms of experienced discomfort and anticipation of aversive outcomes.

In some respects it can be argued that repression and displacement are classification and reclassification processes. In the case of repression, a superordinate 'not-to-be-processed' attribute label assigns the stimulus material, whether externally or internally generated, to a 'not-to-be-processed' class of experience. Such a process was foreshadowed by Dollard and Miller (1950) when they termed this type of cue-producing response a 'not-thinking' response. While the focus of their important book was an attempt to specify the complementarity rather than the incongruity between S–R theory and psycho-analytic models of personality development and the pathological directions this can take in certain contexts, Dollard and Miller appear to have been among the first to anticipate the role of semantic memory stores in these events. The cue-producing response in an S–R chain was conceived by them as a verbal mediating process. By applying the same verbal label to different cues, generalization is facilitated, whereas labelling the same cue differently on separate occasions can specify conflict. There is still general agreement with these authors, as argued a number of times before, that culturally influenced communication and explicit teaching affect the acquisition of verbal knowledge, and through it the implications of stimulus labelling for behaviour.

We can, and have, taken this proposition further by saying that verbal labels and their semantic elaborations *are* the basis of conceptual operations for the expression of characteristic preferred behaviour towards preferred goals and goal-achieving outcomes. If that is a valid assumption then the concept of repression assumes the prior presence of available and accessible semantic identifying conceptual structures. These can recognize a range of stimuli as belonging to a class of experiences which an individual has previously labelled by highly aversively-toned attributes, and by an additional 'not-to-be-processed' instruction imposing a very low retrieval threshold. Displacement, on the other hand, requires access to groups of cognitive structures which are differentially consistent with the identification of aversive stimulation, and the conflict in which it would result. The recognition of conflict-arousing anxiety or anger in the context of schemata simultaneously encoding positive and desirable attributes for the same referent requires the search for cognitive structures whose semantic meaning labels are unilaterally negative and aversive, or where such labels are in the majority. Recognition of the danger of unmodulated behaviour expression must have occurred. Its subsequent accessibility in memory will be reduced, however, in proportion to the degree of relief that is experienced as a result of the substitution of a 'safe' goal. The maintenance and stability of the substitution will be a function of the goodness of the logical fit of this act of self-deception which in turn will affect the degree to which the labelling of the relief from conflict will be experienced as adequate relief. Experience of relief is here knowledge of positive response- or goal-outcome, that is positive reinforcement. Reinforcement, therefore, is a cognitive set of events which affects the relationship between referents and labelled attributes in schematic structures.

There is some justification for regarding *the process of projection* as an extreme example of displacement, at least, of the *source* of the cognitive-affective stimulation. The experience of anxiety or anger has been placed within the stimulus-analysing and response-generating system of another person. Recent studies in the fields of attribution theory and impression formation are fully consistent with the classical psycho-analytic view that the ascription of affect, thought, action, and intention to others depends on the availability in the ascriber of similar or functionally identical behavioural dispositions. Even outside the range of severe psychotic disorder, insight into who is the actual possessor of the behavioural characteristics is often securely prevented. Three reasons for this are the most plausible. Firstly, that which is projected is so noxious that only radical protection against self-awareness is the solution to the problem. Secondly, the projecting person's conceptual system has developed dominant and largely aversive cognitive structures representing the facilitations and constraints offered by objects and people in the social environment. Thirdly, if self-awareness of the problem would normally yield aggressive thought processes, including self-criticism, and the demeaning consequences of guilt accompanied by intropunitiveness, then placing these dispositions within the cognitive system of another reduces the possibility of self-aggression and lowered self-esteem. If the behaviour and intentions of another person are then attacked and produce in turn various forms of counter-aggression, justification for the deviant attribution process is obtained which will support its stability.

Again there is a dual defence of denial-repression and of disguise, and cognitive structures are transformed *by an exchange* of referents while retaining their attribute structure. To facilitate this process, it is necessary that the projecting individual has already structured a vulnerable self-esteem system in which representations of real or imagined minor stigmata have been organized in relatively unmodifiable principal conceptual data. Moreover, the assembly of attributes defining socially important referents is dominated by ambivalent and often incongruent signifiers. If the avoidance of aversive self-perception has the higher priority required by a hedonistic principle of behaviour, then soliciting support for personal shortcomings is more threatening than attributing these to those agents which are already represented negatively in existing schematic structures. These structures will then be strengthened by the responses of the unfairly attacked other person, a process not unlike a self-fulfilling prophecy.

The concept of *reaction formation* presents rather more difficulties in the present context. The kind of evidence needed to confirm a supposition that overt behaviour is the very opposite and mutually exclusive expression of suppressed and unreportable behaviour dispositions is difficult to obtain. If we accept, tentatively, the clinical-therapeutic reports of its validity, we have to account cognitively for two different forms of the protective disguise. The first and ostensibly anxiety-free variant may be described by excessively inoffensive, weak, and submissive behaviour even in the face of objective provocation. The second type of expression may show an excessive preoccupation with propriety, or with ostensibly objective protection against danger, or with minute attention to the details of any task. Not meeting the self-set goals leads to anticipations of threat and doom. Psycho-analytic theory argues that these behaviours disguise, respectively, anger and resentment in respect of social frustrations, and dispositions towards unmodulated expressions of strong basic needs with sexual or aggressive foci. This may or may not be a correct interpretation. It is certainly correct to say, however, that like any other dominant characteristics, they have become established because they and their goal-outcomes have been experienced as desirable and rewarding most probably by the associated reduction of anxiety. The cognitive similarity between the different types of reaction formation seems to reside in classificatory strategies, and in the degree of bonding between functionally related conceptual structures. The uniformly inoffensive person, by definition behaviourally interprets all social signals as uniformly unexceptional. He shows no evidence of possessing any other or intermediate evaluation categories. The moralist indicates that his behaviour selection processes derive from only one schema of propriety with many highly differentiated referents. The compulsive checker exhibits, again, a somewhat absolute criterion of behavioural adequacy. In each case, however, the dominant and reportable stimulus-analysing strategies indicate an excessive bias towards subclassification of the stimulus characteristic and implications of objects, events, or persons in their environment which elicit the dominant response. From this it is at least plausible to conclude that the schematic structures serving the dominant response are highly differentiated, but that those serving a mutually exclusive response are gross, undifferentiated and include highly aversive equally undifferentiated attributes. Categorical separation between opposites, as well as biasing excessive cognitive elaboration of subjectively acceptable conceptual structures, may then serve to maintain the 'split' between overt and covert dispositions, and between objects, events, etc. and their cognitive-affective implications. Although I am well aware of the shortcomings of this argument, there is some evidence from earlier studies carried out by myself (Hamilton, 1959, 1960) that obsessive-compulsive neurotics – the pathological category assumed to employ the reaction-formation defence – are significantly fine-grained classifiers, and that their evaluative categories are relatively immutable.

The implication of a cognitive-semantic model of personality and motivation for the psycho-dynamic proposition of a *normality–abnormality continuum* is not difficult to demonstrate. Essentially, behaviour classified as abnormal by society or by self-report is supported by cognitive structures. These either encode preoccupations with aversively experienced expectancies which are intrusive and uncontrollable, but maintain a realistic awareness of the environment, or they distort objective reality and self-experience and present their decision processes in incongruities of logic and behaviour. As I will argue again in Chapter 9, vulnerability to aversive experience will determine the degree to which an adaptive balance between objective and subjective evaluation is struck in interpreting types and intensities of individual goals, in assessing capacities to elicit and assimilate socially relevant information, and in processing the types of feedback from own behaviour. In general terms, the distinction between normality and abnormality, and between categories of abnormal behaviour, is a quantitative distinction. It may require complex indexing as provided by a regression equation or by profile analysis. In both cases, however, each parameter is already, or potentially, quantifiable, and whatever test instrument is used, each parameter reflects the outcome of decisions by an information processing system. If this system operates, as proposed, on semantic meaning structures organized in functionally and subjectively organized inter-related schemata, positions on a normality–abnormality axis are defined by quantifiable differences in the elaboration of referent-attribute structures. If developmentally early aversive events prevent the consolidation of primary and relatively primitive inferential skills, then the objective representation of the external world and the individual's position in it may become subject to flaws in inferential analysis. The semantic distortions that occur as a consequence will diminish the capacity to think and act as the majority of people do in situations in which consistency and predictability are statistically high.

Although psycho-analytic theories are content-oriented and assign a dominant role to functionally related associations, they give no clear indication that content implies the presence of concepts, and conceptual structures which, like personally neutral concepts, convey knowledge and meaning. While the theories have been developed from and utterly depend on verbal and verbalized evidence, there has always been a large gap between the highly elaborated therapeutic interpretation of verbal report, and the explanations of behaviour in terms of relatively gross drive constructs. These constructs by-passed for many years the implications of person–environment interaction. As a consequence they actually assigned a greater role to the arousal factors of behaviour than to either the cognitive processes that induced arousal, or the selection processes which direct behaviour to express or reduce arousal.

(iii) Murray

Murray's (1938) concepts of personality and motivation avoided some of these shortcomings by introducing a system of many *needs* representing underlying physiological processes akin to drives and types of arousal which respond to and are directed by *press* arising from objects in the environment. Here 'press' (he never used the plural) refers to the implications of external stimuli for the person. Murray proposed that a 'thema' is an organized behavioural unit which represents the interaction between 'need' and 'press'. The significance and utility of Murray's concepts today lies in the complexity of motivational structures for whose analysis he developed the Thematic Apperception Technique, and in his concept of the 'thema'. The semantic data of the TAT supply a wide and differentiated range of dominant themes in the respondent's evaluation of people, objects, events, and situations which are elicited by the ambiguous features of the stimulus material. Verbalized evidence of consistency and inconsistency in the identifications which respondents assign to the subjects, objects and their interactions in their story construction yields evidence of some validity of at least some dominant conceptual structures. It can be argued with a certain amount of conviction that Murray's themas are identical to the modern construct of schemata, without which self-knowledge, meaning and implications of external events, and the problem-solving processes required for adaptation cannot occur.

These processes require three stages: data identification, context analysis, and data reanalysis and modification in the light of context, all of them 'top-down' conceptual operations. Since the TAT plates were selected to elicit protocols reflecting different motives while providing opportunity for eliciting the same motive in different contexts, hierarchies of goal-directed behaviour as well as the interactions and conflicts between different goals can be demonstrated. In parenthesis we may add that the original stimulus material is now proving to be epoch-bound, because many respondents refer repeatedly to 'old-fashioned' features in the display. We also need to note again that outside a clinical-therapeutic setting, TAT-elicited material requires validation by an additional, more objectively controlled, methodology.

With these provisos, however, two conclusions are justified.

(1) Matching a story to the perceived visual stimulus provides a sample of the cognitive-semantic conceptual structures available and accessible in the respondent's permanent memory. The selection of themes, of characters' dominant goal strategies, goal-achieving expectancies, and constructed goal-outcomes can only reflect what is already represented in existing and appropriate schematic organizations. To the extent that these dispositions are capable of verbal report with usually more than a semblance of internal cohesion and logical structure, to that extent the memory data from which it is drawn employ a semantic data code.

(2) Evidence of consistent and elaborated themes in the protocols permits the conclusion that particular behaviour and goal-achieving strategies are dominant characteristics of the person, at least within the context of a particular dyadic social setting. Evidence of multiple dispositions towards the same or functionally similar goals, or inconsistency in evaluating a same or similar goal and in the choice of preferred goal-directed behaviour, leads to an assumption of conceptual complexity. Complexity here is defined by multiple schema interaction, and consequently, by complex semantic attribute structures defining, in turn, complex relationships between referents which depend on context. Since inconsistency refers to alternative and possibly mutually exclusive preferences, it also serves to define some types of conflict.

Theoretically, conflict can occur if only two mutually exclusive attributes define a referent together with the additional general information from the experience of dual affect, and this possibility could argue against the interpretation of conflict by cognitive complexity. A minimally elaborated principal conceptual structure containing insufficient fine-grained subclassifying attributes can be regarded as complex, nevertheless, for two reasons. Firstly, and with perhaps lower plausibility, it can be argued that persevering with conflict-resolution with such an inefficient schema will increase the cognitive strength of affective cues as the result of delayed problem-solving. Prolonged analysis of just two behavioural alternatives, both judged to be unacceptable, will prevent full analysis of new stimulation to which adaptation is also required. The attempt to process this additional information, which may be unrelated to the original decision conflict, will tax the temporarily limited processing capacity of the cognitive system. As a result, further conflicts may arise either from experiences of processing overload, or from the results of evaluating as inadequate a response made under pressure. Secondly, internally generated complexity develops by recruiting for conflict resolution, minimally or superficially relevant conceptual structures which possess a higher level of elaboration and differentiation. If this occurs, a response is made on false premises, though admittedly under pressure from aversive cognitive-affective cues. Socially it may be evaluated as inappropriate, counter-productive, incongruous, or bizarre, because it appears gross and impulsive rather than sensitive in a logical as well as a behavioural action sense. The reason for the presence of underelaborated conceptual structuring will lie not only in restrictions of experience opportunity during earlier periods of personal development, but equally in the influence of denial defences on previous exposure to this class of stimulation. If there is some merit in these generalizations, one rather interesting and challenging deduction can be made about the development of severe psychopathology. It can be predicted that types of neurosis and psychosis are a partial function of intelligence. However unacceptable this connection may be to 'progressive' socio-political thought, I will refer to it again elsewhere.

Let me return to some of the basic theoretical issues and assumptions of the semantic model of personality and motivation. The acquisition and transmission of knowledge occurs as the result of communication and interaction between people, and between people and objects, events, and situations. This includes the acquisition of self-knowledge. What I have proposed is that the system of symbolic signifiers, the symbolic language by which societies and individuals in societies communicate, is the same symbolic system through which knowledge, meaning, and implications of meaning are encoded in the individual's cognitive structures. That is, all experience is potentially capable of being transformed, or translated, into natural linguistic symbols which through temporal or cause-and-effect association with one another acquire extended semantically coded meaning. In some respects, what I am suggesting is similar to acquiring the language operating in a new country of residence on the basis of competence in another language. For often many years the foreigner has to translate verbal input into the symbols of an older information-storing system. The analogy is far from complete, of course, since actions and their perceived relationships can induce appropriate behavioural responses without verbalization. There is some evidence, too, that many manual skills may be efficiently performed without one being able to communicate verbally the conceptual knowledge required to do so (Bainbridge, 1979). On the other hand, unless fine-grained representations of conceptual knowledge in some symbolic form are available and accessible, the same concepts required in a different context with changed implications cannot be productively utilized.

McGuigan (1978) has recently presented a reanalysis of electromyographic, oculographic, and EEG concomitants of cognitive activities. He concludes from these '. . . that mental processes *are* the activation of selected neuro-muscular circuits . . . (and that) independent measurement of mental activities is not possible' (McGuigan, 1978, p. 63). It is a truism, of course, that all behaviour requires a functioning neurophysiological system. It is equally true that all functional neurophysiological activity depends on neurochemical events, in which, in turn, various nucleic acid constituents and interactions play a determining role. This ultimate level of reductionist explanation is scientifically proper. At the same time, the undisputed contribution of biological events is insufficient for explanations and predictions in a far-removed, more molar setting operating with a different information-bearing symbolic system. Ultimately perhaps, behavioural science and its biological substructure will require a mathematical language to describe its processes, to serve as an economic alternative to semantic specifications of conceptual structures and their content.

CHAPTER 8

A cognitive-semantic model of anxiety

For the benefit of those readers who will probe selected chapters only, let me briefly recapitulate the experimental steps preceding the anxiety studies I am going to discuss and which in turn led to the semantic model of personality and motivation. Step 1: evidence that schizophrenics of average intelligence were low on Piagetian conservation. Step 2: Normal young school children brought up in a suboptimal socialization climate assumed to generate social anxiety showed a low conservation skill as tested on tasks with systematically increasing information processing requirements. Step 3: An informational load interpretation of conservation task difficulty was validated. Step 4: Low performers on a conservation test were slower in a dual-task setting. Steps 2 to 4 have been discussed in some detail in Chapter 5 and resulted in a tentative processing capacity model of anxiety-induced performance deficits (Hamilton, 1975, 1976).

1 INADEQUACY OF AROUSAL EXPLANATIONS

The processing capacity model of anxiety-induced performance deficits was a tentative one because of the small number of experiments, because the effect of suboptimal mothering on socialization anxiety was inferred rather than directly demonstrated, and, particularly, because the dominant mediator of other theories – arousal – was not concurrently tested and controlled. For reasons which are amplified below, arousal is regarded as a necessary *general* mediator because the interpretation of a laboratory test situation requires initially, and primarily, *cognitive* processes. What needed to be shown, therefore, was the relative independence of the aversive cognitive preoccupations of a subject, and his arousal level, and changes in level. Let me clarify some of the doubts that attach to propositions of the fundamental and overriding importance of the arousal variable.

Although temporary co-variation between measures of anxiety and of physiological arousal can be demonstrated, correlations between them are generally low (for recent summaries see McReynolds, 1976; Hockey, 1979). There are also substantial individual differences in the objects and situations

208

which will either elicit reports of anxiety or evidence of arousal (e.g. Saltz, 1970). As already argued before, subjects' arousal response must *follow upon the identification* of what is threatening to them, and this cognitive process is considerably faster, for example, than the autonomically mediated transmission of pain (Melzack, 1973). Thus, cognitive identification precedes arousal, except to the extent that any stimulus generates arousal by eliciting an orienting response (Sokolov, 1963; Pribram and McGuinness, 1975). When arousal mechanisms are triggered by the identification of an aversive stimulus, they fulfil primarily an energizing role for the emergence of avoidance responses, followed by further analysis of the meaning of the stimulus (Mandler, 1975).

A postulated feedback relationship between two discrete processes of anxiety and arousal contrasts markedly with the more influential models of the interaction between a monistic process of stress with performance, such as the 'noise' model, and the postulated similarity between the behavioural/ cognitive effects of white noise and incentive rewards (Broadbent, 1971), or an axiety-drive model (e.g. Spence and Spence, 1966). The concept of an anxiety drive has received substantial support from findings of an inverted U-shaped relationship between level of anxiety and a variety of easy and difficult learning and problem-solving tasks (e.g. Mueller, 1976; Eysenck, 1977). This relationship is explained by drive-determined differences in association-forming, and, depending on the strength of the anxiety drive, by changes in interference due to the eliciting of competing responses. The theory is external stimulus oriented, it defines competing responses only as those engendered by task demands, it does not distinguish between these and the effects of competition from internally generated task-irrelevant affective responses, and it makes no distinction between the effects of emotional-physiological and cognitive components of anxiety. Explanations of how the demonstrated unfavourable drive-performance interaction is mediated were never fully worked out, except that arousal and activation have been proposed as factors accounting for individual differences in the consolidation of perceived material, and thereby for differences in learning and memory (H. J. Eysenck, 1973; M. W. Eysenck, 1977). While this form of drive theory offers a mediating process, it is still a generalized arousal-performance statement based on the Yerkes–Dodson model.

This model has always been descriptive rather than explanatory: it does not specify cognitive as distinct from physiological mediating processes and, for ethical reasons, has not been derived from systematic, *extreme* variations of either general emotionality, arousal, or anxiety, applied to human subjects. Therefore, with respect to the right-hand side of the inverted U curve, it offers only circular logic: poor performance is due to high arousal and high arousal leads to poor performance. An apparent exception to this may be the type of study reported by Sjöberg (1977) in which arousal measured by heart rate and blood pressure was raised by physical exertion. It is doubtful, however, that this type of stress provides a valid analogue for arousal-stress functionally related to anticipated injury, or insult to self-esteem.

Easterbrook (1959) provided the first step in the search for mediating processes, although here too no distinction was made between cognitive and physiological factors in performance decrements. Restrictions in the range of cue-utilization in states of high emotionality, arousal, or anxiety were postulated to be due to changes in attentional strategy. Because of the general acceptance, however, of the proposition that emotive/arousal states of the organism facilitate the emergence of competing responses, this type of explanation is more suitable for explanations of *optimal* performance through the *exclusion of task-irrelevant* cues, than for explanations of poor performance in which excessive competing responses play an interfering role according to the drive-arousal model. In the simple form in which the model was stated, it actually defines processes working in opposite directions: arousal restricts the range of cue-utilization, and simultaneously energizes competing responses. This impasse can be overcome in only one way: the two processes must operate on different kinds of data. For this we assume that Easterbrook's model applies to external stimuli, and that the Spence/Eysenck propositions apply to internal self-generated stimuli. Walker's suggestion (1958, 1967) of a consolidation process, utilized by Eysenck (1973) to buttress his theory of introversion–extraversion, then becomes an internally generated process of encoding stimulus class and meaning by associating it with other appropriate cognitive schemata. Since, however, the experimental subject is also personally concerned with the social evaluation of his performance, high arousal-drive will generalize to schematic conceptual structures encoding preferred behaviour outcomes. This will be the case, particularly, for individuals with highly elaborated structures encoding anticipation of aversive outcomes for self-esteem and social evaluation. For these subjects, therefore, high emotionality, arousal, or anxiety *increases* rather than decreases the range and amount of information presented to a processing system through a combination of task- and affect-relevant information. Arousal and drive provide the energy for the retrieval of competing responses, including unpleasant expectancies, and while the physiological events increase in intensity with an increase of retrieved aversive data, their effect on performance is indirect. The information which *perception of the effects* of high arousal and drive conveys to the processing system at the same time is undifferentiated and small as I have suggested before, although differences in affective tone, intensity, and persistence will be appropriately represented in attribute structures.

2 DERIVATION OF COGNITIVE MODEL

In view of these interpretations of the role of arousal, a capacity model was proposed to account for the adverse effect of high anxiety on performance which is relatively independent of arousal and is consistent with findings of information processing limitations demonstrated by cognitive processing theory (Hamilton, 1975; 1976). While this owes much to Broadbent's (1958) original theory of the single-channel, limited-capacity human processor, it assigned a more substantial role to internally generated information which reflects individual consistencies in the behavioural manner of achieving goals, types and hierarchies of goals, and strength of goal-seeking. Predispositions to avoid experiences with aversive content and implications provide a store of long-term memories which are available for retrieval when stimulated. The greater the predisposition, the greater the store of elaborated generalizations, the lower their retrieval threshold, and the greater, therefore, the response bias towards a primary operation of identifying and avoiding aversiveness. Multiple-channel, parellel processing concepts would seem to be required to accommodate shared processing priorities, and to account generally for all the existing evidence of personality–cognition interactions. This view appears to be consistent with Broadbent's more recent statement about parallel events at different *levels* of a processing system (Broadbent, 1977).

The cognitive model of anxiety elaborates the 'costs' of information transmission in conditions of information overload (Miller, 1960), as well as the *unspecified* interfering role assigned to self-preoccupation (e.g. Mandler and S. B. Sarason, 1951; Wine, 1971; I. G. Sarason, 1975). A system already processing externally presented data may be easily overloaded if the same, or additional, data need to be scanned and interpreted for evidence of social and personal dangers. The greater the informational complexity of the external task, therefore, the greater the total work-load effects on anxious subjects: the information is additive. Thus, processing capacity becomes inadequate or unadaptive when the sum of externally generated task-relevant information, added to the sum of internally generated task-irrelevant information encoding anxiety, exceeds the total processing capacity reserves of the system. The most likely major points of interference, saturation, and masking effects are the short-term memory components of the analysing and integrating system, and particularly its temporary hold stages.

The cognitive reinterpretation of anxiety can be formalized by phrasing sets of 'postulates' and 'deductions' without, however, necessarily meeting all requirements of syllogistic purity. These formulations are shown in Table 8.1. They can be restated in quasi-mathematical terms because the informational load of anxiety as well as the difficulty level (information processing demands) of an externally presented task can be quantified with varying levels of precision. Preoccupation with cognitive data representing degree of anxious anticipation of behaviour outcome can be grossly estimated by questionnaire scores, by elaboration of attribute structures defining stimulus aversiveness, or by responses to a manipulation of environmental stressors. Task difficulty can be manipulated by increasing the number of components of a task as was done in the conservation experiments described in Chapter 5, by imposing severe time limits on task execution, or by requiring more than one

Table 8.1 Inductive and Deductive Steps Towards a Cognitive Model of Anxiety

	'Postulates'	
The cognitive processing system	is	An information processing system
An information processing system	is	A space and time limited capacity system
Problem-solving	requires	Information processing
Information	is	Cognitive data
Characteristic goal-directed behaviour	is	Problem-solving behaviour
	'Deductions'	
Problems with high information processing demands	make	Heavy demands on a limited capacity processing system
Characteristic goal-directed behaviour	requires	Information processing
Anxiety	is	Goal-directed behaviour
Anxiety	is	Cognitive data
High anxiety	makes	Heavy demands on a limited capacity information processing system
High anxiety plus tasks with high information processing demands	make	Excessive demands on limited cognitive processing capacity

task to be done simultaneously where one or both of them can additionally vary on a number of dimensions.

Elaborating Kahneman's (1973) concepts of the distribution of finite amounts of processing effort, we can write an expression for successful task performance. This states that problem-solving is feasible if

$$APC + SPC > I_e + I_i$$

where APC is average processing capacity, SPC is spare (reserve) processing capacity, I_e is externally presented task-relevant information, and I_i is internal information generated by the task. I_e and I_i can be expanded so that

$$I_e = I_{ep} + I_{es} \text{ and } I_i = I_{ip} + I_{is} + I_{i(c)}$$

Here I_{ep} is primary external cues; I_{es} is secondary external cues – both task-relevant; I_{ip} is internal representations of primary task cues and I_{is} internal representations of secondary task cues. $I_{i(c)}$ is complex and requires additional expansion so that

$$I_{i(c)} = I_{i(Cp + s)} + I_{i(A)} + I_{i(RSO)} \text{ where}$$

$I_{i(Cp + s)}$ is the task-relevant competing responses postulated by arousal-drive models for primary and secondary task cues, $I_{i(A)}$ is the information represented in cognitive structures encoding aversive expectancies – that is anxiety

– , and $I_{i(RSO)}$ is the informational load exerted by restructuring strategies and operations of the cognitive system in its attempt to handle diverse demands on its capacity and load-bearing tolerance.

In the experiments reported below which were conducted by my assistants, students and myself during the last five or six years, $I_{i(A)}$ was assessed by questionnaire scores, and $I_{i(Cp + s)}$ was manipulated by systematic changes in task difficulty, variously defined. In every experiment in which arousal was monitored and performance stressors were introduced it was predicted that the anxiety variables, and not arousal levels or changes in level, would explain the experimental results. Some of the studies have been reported and discussed previously in other publications (e.g. Hamilton, 1980, 1982) but for the sake of completeness will be considered here again.

3 TESTS OF COGNITIVE MODEL

One of the experiments, not previously reported, was carried out on children and employed a methodology previously discussed in Chapter 5. Children exhibiting different levels of skill in the conserving capacity were shown there to have matching levels of competence in a coding and decoding task (Hamilton and Launay, 1976) (see Figure 5.9). In that experiment informational complexity was defined by the number of substitution steps required for solution. In a subsequent experiment subjects aged 9–11 years were drawn from the pool assembled for the socialization effects project, and according to the classifying criteria discussed in Chapter 5 were divided into two groups: those who were thought to have been exposed to socialization stress and anxiety (SSA), and those who were not thought to have been exposed to it (NSSA). Educational achievement and intelligence levels as well as socio-economic group membership were controlled. The coding task was presented first as a single task, and subsequently in a dual-task design. The second, simultaneous task here was counting backwards in 3s from 100 while attempting to solve each coding problem. Three variations of each difficulty level of the coding task were presented.

The group results in terms of solution times for all problems, correct or incorrect, are shown in Figure 8.1. It was predicted that the SSA group, because of interference from their social anxieties, would perform worse on both tasks. This prediction was strongly confirmed for the dual-task setting, but less clearly for the single task. The negatively accelerating curves obtained in the dual task clearly represent a learning and adaptation factor. Whereas the group assumed to have been relatively free of anxiety eventually reached the performance level they had shown in the single task, this was not the case for the group exposed to socialization stressors. In terms of the previously formulated and formalized relationships between performance level and task-induced processing load, it was concluded that the SSA group was exposed, respectively, to a dual and to a triple task. The extra task was the handling of fears of failure and social censure which in their case would

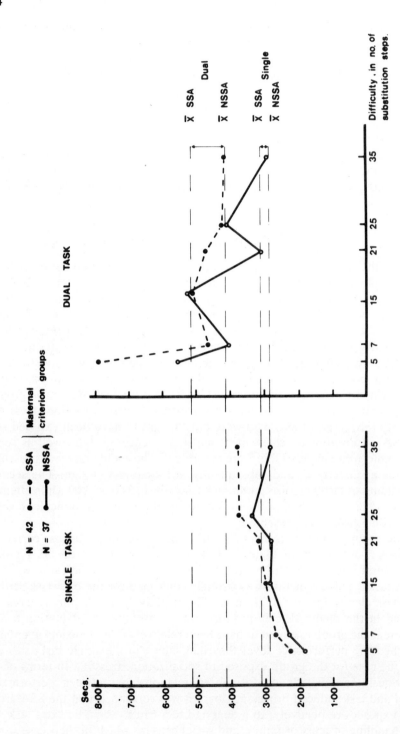

Figure 8.1 Effect of social anxiety on speed of serial substitutions in single- and dual-task settings

be likely to intrude into the test situation and occupy space and time in the information processing system.

Let me now turn to a block of experiments in which cognitive and physiological arousal explanations were pitted against each other. The first of these was an adaptation of a dual task first used in an experiment with children involving simultaneous testing for visual reaction time and digit span (see Figure 5.10).[1] Subjects were 24 students divided by median-cut into high and low anxiety groups on the basis of scores on Sarason's Test Anxiety Scale (Sarason, 1972b). After 10 practice trials with visual reaction time, they were presented with a series of digits. This was followed by the 'ready' signal for the reaction time test, a randomly variable signal-anticipation interval, the visual signal, response to signal, and finally digit recall. Subjects were adivsed to rehearse the digit string until they had made their response to the visual signal. The task was presented with two variations: without feedback on goodness of performance, and with false feedback of a poor performance. The reaction timer was coupled with an oscilloscope and a variable but pre-set programme by which a fictitious difference between subjects' performance and performance of an assumed normative sample of subjects could be displayed on the oscilloscope screen. This visually displayed knowledge of results was in 90 per cent of the trials not in individual subjects' favour. This was termed the 'stressed' condition. Skin conductance as a measure of arousal was monitored throughout. The results for the two anxiety criterion groups of 12 subjects each replicated the previous results obtained from anxious and non-anxious children, in that high anxious unstressed subjects were generally slower than the low anxious.

In order to examine the differential contribution of the criterion variable – test anxiety – and of arousal to the results, the two groups were again divided by median-cut into high and low arousal subgroups on skin conductance levels obtained in the 'stressed' condition. The measure of arousal was the range-corrected index for output θ (Lykken and Venables, 1971). The experimental results with this manipulation are plotted in Figure 8.2. Single-task performance (number of digits = 0) was identical for three of the four groups; the odd one out from the low anxious group indicates a superior concentration, or readiness at that stage. Three findings are prominent.

(1) High anxious subjects with a high arousal index perform better than high anxious subjects with lower arousal in the 'stressed' condition.
(2) For the most difficult tasks (number of digits = 6 and 7) a combination of low anxiety and high arousal yields the most efficient performance.
(3) The high anxious–high arousal group performed significantly worse than the low anxiety–high arousal group despite a virtually identical arousal level.

The results show that arousal facilitates performance even for anxious sub-

[1] Both these experiments were conducted by Gilles Launay.

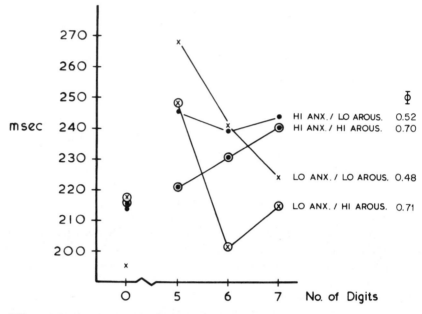

Figure 8.2 Visual reaction times while rehearsing digits – anxiety × arousal criterion groups with false feedback of poor performance (stressed). *N*'s = 6 (after Hamilton, 1980)

jects, and more importantly that the criterion group differences cannot be explained by differences in arousal.

The next experiment studied the effect of anxiety and anticipation of an electric shock on speed of visual word recognition.[2] Lists of words were constructed which were either anagrams, or nonsense words, differing in assumed difficulty by the number of letters they contained. These were arranged in pairs and shown on a memory drum with a constant exposure of 5 seconds for each pair of stimuli. Two lists of 48 stimulus pairs were prepared; one list was presented without a stressor, a second list was given in conditions in which subjects might reasonably expect a single electric shock at some point during the procedure. At the beginning of the 'stressed' session subjects were given the choice of opting out from the electric shock procedure. None withdrew, however, and they were then invited to select, by operating the controls of a signal generator, a level of shock which was painful but just tolerable. This was done after it was first demonstrated by the experimenter. Shock could be expected, if it were to occur, immediately after a buzzer signal. No shock was administered, however, to any subject at any time. The manipulation was required to generate arousal in low and high anxious subjects, and was successful as shown by significant changes in skin conductance between the two experimental conditions. Subject groups

[2] This experiment was conducted by Annemarie Robinson.

of 10 each were constructed again by a median-cut of scores on Sarason's Test Anxiety Scale. Stimulus word pairs required either a 'same' response (e.g. mxe–mxe; dreab–dreab; dondiam–dondiam), or a 'different' response (afk–hiq; xrolk–yefot; rhoakjs–slywunp). Skin conductance was monitored during both experimental sessions.

The results showed that task difficulty was varied successfully. There were no significant differences in the 'unstressed' condition between high and low anxious groups. Threat of shock, however, led to significantly slower response times for the high anxious for 5 and 7 letter word pairs. This result obtained even though the skin conductance arousal levels of the experimental groups were nearly identical in the 'stressed' conditions. This argued against mediation of results by arousal. But an additional analysis of data was made: dividing the criterion groups into high and low arousal subgroups on the basis of skin conductance levels when anticipating electric shock (i.e. the procedure adopted in the dual-task experiment just described). The results are illustrated in Figure 8.3. They confirm conclusions already reached after the dual-task experiment.

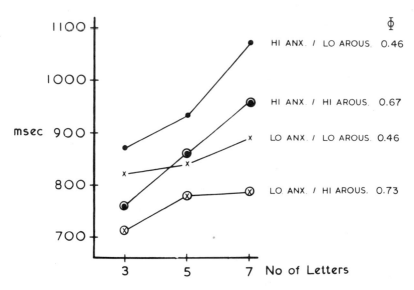

Figure 8.3 Word recognition times varying word length, anxiety × arousal criterion groups (stressed). N's = 5 (after Hamilton, 1979)

(1) Low anxious subjects perform more efficiently on a cognitive task compared with high anxious subjects even if their arousal levels are identical or nearly so.
(2) The difference in efficiency tends to increase with an increase in task difficulty.
(3) Heightened arousal in anxious subjects facilitates rather than impairs performance.

Since it would be unreasonable to hold that threat of electric shock is not anxiety-inducing in the cognitive sense for subjects already admitting to heightened susceptibility to anxiety, and since the same subjects produced heightened arousal in response to a threat *and* an improved performance with it, arousal cannot be the dominant factor which impairs the performance of anxious subjects. There must be other reasons for improved performance and a later experiment was designed to find them. It was clear by now, however, that the conception of anxiety as cognitive data and the analysis of its effects with tasks of systematically increasing difficulty, was a promising line of investigation.

Research emphasis was now directed at the design of a task which would be sufficiently difficult for intelligent adults, which would require the results of several intermediate cognitive operating steps to be held in the working memory component of the processing system, and which would satisfy a criterion of systematic increase in difficulty. It was decided to attempt an adaptation of the conservation task devised for children which was described in Chapter 5. The construction of that task (Hamilton and Moss, 1974) and its validation as an information processing task (Hamilton and Launay, 1976), suggested that mathematical expressions could be substituted for the pictorial and verbal commentary stimuli describing the distribution of mass. Figure 8.4 shows an example of one of the problems described by Hamilton and

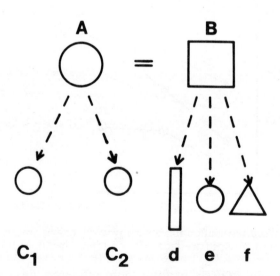

Figure 8.4 Example of item from pictorial conservation test (adapted from Hamilton and Moss, 1974)

Moss (1974). By substituting actual mathematical expressions for the visual display and verbal commentary tracing the distribution of materials, the task presented in Figure 8.4 could be rewritten as follows:

$$A = B; B = d + e + f; A = C_1 + C_2; \text{Is } d + e + f \lesseqgtr C_1 + C_2?$$

Applying the formula expressing difficulty given in Chapter 5, it can be shown that 13 steps are embedded in the problem which have to be taken to obtain and verify the correct response. Similarly, it can be shown that the problem illustrated in Figure 8.5 requires 30 steps for solution.

$$x = y$$
$$x = a + b$$
$$a = e + f + g + h$$
$$y = c + d$$
$$d = i + j$$
$$i = k + l + m$$

$$\text{Quest.: Is } e+f+g+h \lesseqgtr k+l+m+j+c \ ?$$

Figure 8.5 Item from mathematical version of pictorial conservation test

A number of validation studies were undertaken to verify the sensitivity of newly constructed problems to absolute and individual differences in information processing capacity. The results of one of these, in which Test Anxiety was manipulated by questionnaire scores as well as by ego-involving instructions, is shown in Figure 8.6.[3] The linear trend of task difficulty and the anxiety × difficulty interaction were both statistically significant. The correlations between arousal and performance, and between arousal and anxiety, did not differ significantly from zero. Although the predicted interaction between anxiety and performance deficits was disproportionately determined by the most difficult problem, this was most probably due to the small difference between the number of processing steps required for the early, easy problems, This deficiency was easily rectified in subsequent experiments. It is possible that the high anxious subjects were slower because they carried out more checking, though enquiry could not confirm this. If extra checking did take place, it could have been the result of subjects getting lost in the sequences of substitutions, so that they had to retrace their steps. This is precisely what would be predicted, however, for subjects working with interference from task-irrelevant cognitive data, with the possible focus of interference in working memory integrating processes.

The next stage in the research programme had to concern itself with the

[3] This experiment was conducted by Amanda Praill.

220

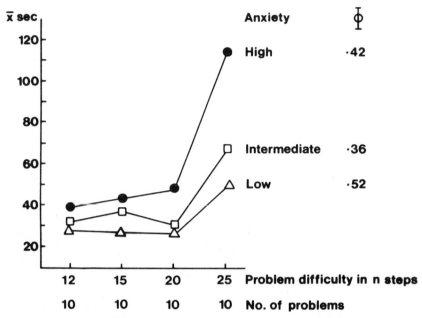

Figure 8.6 Anxiety and problem-solving performance solution times. N's = 8
(after Hamilton, 1979)

unexpected improvement in problem-solving of high anxious subjects in conditions of induced physiological arousal. Arousal-drive theory would have predicted an additive relationship between high test anxiety and arousal level manipulated by physical and self-esteem threats. A possible explanation would involve mediation by high achievement motivation which has been shown to be substantially related to performance anxiety (Hill, 1972). In that case exposing high anxious subjects to ego-stressors would generate energy reserves through activation of failure-avoidance goals to enable them to improve their performance even with difficult tasks. This should be possible only, however, for relatively short periods. If the time allowed for problem-solving were to be reduced, however, which is really another type of stressor, this extra coping effort would be of limited utility since in these conditions high anxious subjects would be deprived of adequate processing time as well as of processing space for short-term memory and selective attention operations.

An experiment was designed, therefore, to test for the interaction between problem-solving and anxiety in a counterbalanced design to enable the effects of ego-stressing and non-stressing instructions, and of experimenter-pacing and non-pacing to be assessed in all possible combinations.[4] The main predictions were that the effects of ego-stressing would be smaller than the effects of restricting problem-solving time by pacing, that this effect would be

[4] This experiment was conducted by Reine Le Gall.

stronger for high anxious subjects, that it should be particularly strong at a new and higher level of problem difficulty, and that arousal would not account for the results. Thirty-two student subjects were randomly assigned to groups in which the order of the sequence and combination of conditions was balanced for high and low anxiety subgroups. Ego-stressing was induced by creating dissonance between the self-evident difficulty of the problems and a statement that students find them easy. In the non-stressing instruction the difficulty of the task was emphasized as well as giving reassurances about insufficient solution time and the possibility of errors. The time limit in the paced method of problem administration was set at 70 per cent of the mean time for problems at each level of difficulty obtained in pilot testing for subjects commencing with the paced condition, or 70 per cent of subjects' own unpaced performance which preceded the paced condition. Arousal was monitored throughout the experiment, in this instance by heart rate. Parallel versions of the problem-solving test were designed and administered.

A selection of the results of this study is shown in the next three figures. The solution times of the criterion groups and their arousal levels for the stressed and unstressed conditions are illustrated in Figure 8.7. Heart rate

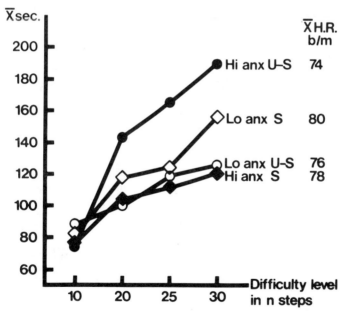

Figure 8.7 Unpaced solution times for blocks of three problems per difficulty level. N's = 8 (U–S = Unstressed, S = Stressed condition)

arousal is unrelated to the performance of the criterion groups and ego-stressing, as before, improves the response times of the high anxious. The introduction of a new difficulty level of 30 steps for problem solution was clearly effective in separating high from low anxious subjects. From the large

222

number of errors made by the low anxious when unstressed and their improvement when stressed, it was concluded that this group was relatively unmotivated when given non-stressing instructions. This interpretation was supported by other data.

Figure 8.8 shows the effect of experimenter-pacing on errors. The main effect of increased errors from pacing was highly significant, and as predicted high anxious subjects made significantly more errors when pacing was added to the ego-stressing instruction particularly on the most difficult problem set, and compared with the high anxious subgroup in the U-P/S condition. As before, heart rate arousal did not co-vary with performance. Figure 8.9

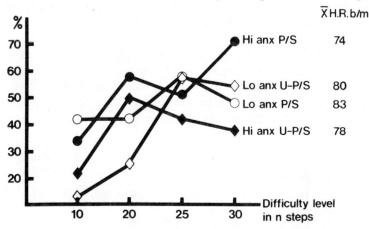

Figure 8.8 Errors and heart rate for Paced/Stressed (P/S), and Unpaced/Stressed (U-P/S) conditions. *N*'s = 8

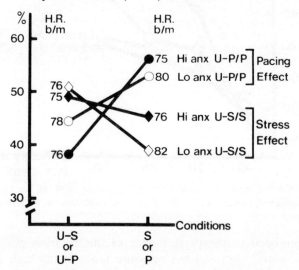

Figure 8.9 Grand mean percentage errors for combined problem difficulty levels. *N*'s = 16

summarizes the results across all levels of the difficulty factor (which in every analysis was the most significant main effect) in order to demonstrate the discrepancy between stressing by instruction and by pacing. The slopes of the graphs indicate that pacing had the most impairing effect on the high anxious group as predicted. Furthermore, at difficulty level n steps $= 30$, slowness of processing was paired with lower error rates only for the low anxious group and for the high anxious only when unpaced.

The most plausible explanation of these results needs to be in terms of time and space limitations in cognitive processing for the high anxious, who by prediction are also processing task-irrelevant aversive information. Evidence for this interpretation remains incomplete, however, until even more difficult tasks can be designed which produce an even higher load on short-term working memory and selective attention, and until the effect of systematically increasing the *period* of paced problem-solving at these higher levels of difficulty can be assessed. Moreover, evidence must be made available to show that *all* task-irrelevant motivational preoccupations deplete the data processing capacity of the cognitive system. One type of this evidence was aimed for in the study discussed next.

If instructions to subjects were to require them to rehearse for subsequent recall visually presented erotic material at the same time as being engaged in a difficult problem-solving task, we have a test situation which is somewhat analogous to placing high and low test-anxious subjects into an ego- or self-esteem threatening situation while engaged in a similarly demanding problem-solving task. If, however, sexual preoccupation is not only less aversive but consists also of less finely differentiated and elaborated cognitive structures in long-term memory than has been proposed for cognitive anxiety, then the interference or intrusion effect should be less marked than the interference from cognitive anxiety. Conversely, if what matters is a consistent and stubborn intrusion effect from a second task whose content occupies a high position in a hierarchy of characteristic goal-directed dispositions which has been deliberately stimulated, then the sensitization of 'eroticism', as it may be called, should have an effect that is similar to that of ego-threat on anxiety.

Twenty-one male undergraduate students were given Sarason's Test Anxiety Scale and a questionnaire elaborated from items intended to measure sexual interests previously published by Eysenck (1976b). High- and low-scoring subjects were assigned to four criterion groups which were given the two parallel problem-solving tests previously described in counterbalanced order. The instructions were relatively stressing in that they asked for great care, and fast and error-free performance. After completion of the first set of problems (pre-intrusion task) subjects were required to examine eight numbered photographs each depicting a man and a woman engaged in erotic play, and to place them in rank order of degree of being sexually arousing. They were then asked to rehearse for subsequent correct recall the ranked number of the pictures with the advice that rehearsal of content would help

224

them to do so. The second set of problems was then administered with the same instructions as before, and this was followed by the request to recall the *ranks* of the previously ranked erotic pictures. Heart rate was monitored throughout, and exposure to the ranking task led to a significant rise in beats per minute.[5]

Some of the findings of this study are shown in Figures 8.10 and 8.11. Figure 8.10 confirms again the slowness of high anxious subjects. The 'eroticism' subgroups, however, which were undifferentiated for anxiety, performed very similarly to the low anxious group before they were exposed to

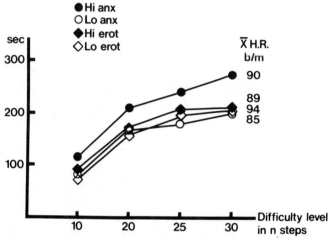

Figure 8.10 Mean pre-intrusion task solution times, anxiety and eroticism groups, blocks of three problems. *N*'s = 7

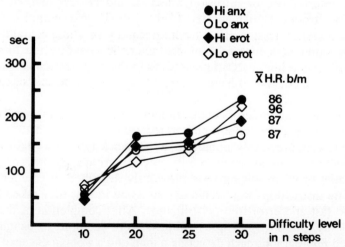

Figure 8.11 Mean post-intrusion task solution times, anxiety and eroticism groups, blocks of three problems. *N*'s = 7

[5] This experiment was conducted by Linda Inglis.

the erotic material, and there were no significant differences between the 'eroticism' subgroups. Figure 8.11 gives the solution times after the sexual material had been inspected and ranked and while subjects attempted to remember the rank order of their sorting exercise. The anxiety main effect is now no longer present, but a significant difficulty factor for the 'eroticism' groups now appeared which was absent for the pre-intrusion task. In other words, after exposure to erotic stimuli, and with an ongoing rehearsal of that material, successive problems took progressively longer to solve. As a corollary it may be suggested that the absence of a significant post-intrusion main effect for anxiety was due to the motivational irrelevance of the sexual material for subjects differing in test anxiety rather than 'eroticism'. No systematic peripheral arousal factor was obtained relatable either to sexual arousal, or to problem-solving capacity, or an interaction between these. If Lacey is correct (e.g. Lacey, 1967), then sexual arousal and heart rate deceleration during problem-solving should work in opposite directions, and electrocortical, or tomographic measures (e.g. Lassen, et al., 1978), may have to be employed in more definitive experiments.

The evidence from this experiment is not conclusive. The difference between high and low 'eroticism' groups describes a pattern only roughly similar to that of high and low test-anxious subjects for solution times and errors in problem-solving. Four reasons can be offered for the deficienceis.

(1) The level of erotic interest shown in the questionnaire was not fully reliable.
(2) The attempted simulation of cognitive interference in respect of interference from erotic preoccupations was only partially successful.
(3) Sexual arousal at any level of the behavioural system is dampened not only by competition from problem-solving effort, but as the result of achievement motivation operating while being observed during task performance.
(4) The ceiling of task difficulty was still too low.

The last study to be carried out in the effort to distinguish between the effects of cognitive loading by anxiety and the effects of arousal dealt with the test difficulty issue by designing a problem difficulty level of n steps $=$ 40. In addition, however, a pharmocological manipulation of arousal was introduced. Because of the generally unreliable correlations between peripheral physiological arousal – such as skin conductance and heart rate – and behavioural measures of affect, and between peripheral arousal and performance measures, it has always seemed likely that electrocortical arousal was the principal mediator of these interactions. Evidence accumulating in recent years has suggested that focal selective attention required for cognitive tasks depends on the release of corticosteroids in the brain, and their effects on cortical desynchronization (e.g. Warburton 1977, 1979). Drug-induced variations in central arousal, therefore, should be related to performances requiring selective attention, vigilance, and separation between relevant and irrelevant information. Administration of nicotine produces increased desynchronization and can be predicted, therefore, to lead to improved performance in cognitive tasks. Such results have been obtained in a number of studies employing different experimental strategies (e.g. Warburton and Wesnes, 1978; Warburton, 1981; Warburton *et al.*, 1982). In this framework it can be argued that performance deficits normally associated with high anxiety could be reduced by the administration of nicotine if electrocortical arousal is indeed the dominant mediator of information selection and integration.

A new study was designed to test this prediction, and to compare the effects of nicotine and of cognitive desensitization (or 'inoculation' e.g. Horowitz, 1979) on anxicty.[6] Thirty-two student subjects were divided into high and low test-anxious subgroups and in two sessions were administered parallel versions of the problem-solving test previously described. The first session was given with self-esteem threatening instructions. Prior to the second session *four different treatments* were given to four subgroups consisting of four subjects each within each anxiety criterion group. They were: (i) a nicotine tablet; (ii) a placebo, both tablets given in conjunction with a general talk on issues in behavioural science while the tablets dissolved; (iii) a talk on behavioural science; and (iv) a talk explaining the development and effects of test anxiety, anxiety-reducing comments on subjects' performance in the first session, and other comments minimizing the importance and difficulty of the task.

Only a selection of the results can be considered here. The introduction of a yet more difficult problem requiring 40 solution steps was only partly validated. In the no-treatment session only low anxious subjects were slower and made more errors at this level of difficulty compared with n steps $= 30$. The difficulty main effect and the interaction between session and difficulty, however, were highly significant. The interaction between anxiety, session, and difficulty was also reliable. Performance levels for the second session were affected, of course, by practice. This effect could expect enhancement from high anxious subjects for whom familiarity, even without knowledge of results, would reduce the threatening aspects of the test.

The overall interaction between type of treatment, anxiety, and test difficulty was reliable. Although nicotine was associated with significant reductions in solution times, the intervening talks and particularly the cognitive manipulation of anxiety were substantially more significant. This result is shown in Figure 8.12 for the combined criterion groups, indicating that the effect of desensitizing anxiety was more than twice as strong as the effect of nicotine. Plotting these results separately for the two criterion groups under four different treatments as in Figure 8.13, it is apparent that three of the treatments produced greater effects for the high anxious subgroup. The

[6] This experiment was conducted by Gillian Noake.

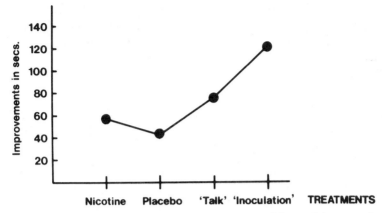

Figure 8.12 Effects of different treatments on problem-solving speed, high and low anxious subjects combined. N's = 8

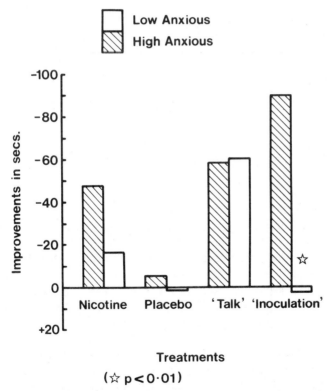

Figure 8.13 Effects of different treatments on problem-solving speed, high and low anxious subjects. N's = 4

general talk had a greater effect on the improvement of the low anxious in the second test session. The reasons for this are not immediately clear, but since the improvement occurred in both groups, some insight into what may have been involved in the experiment may have become motivating for all subjects. The only statistically reliable difference, however, applies to the effect of attempted anxiety reduction by discussion for the high anxious, and operated most clearly at difficulty level n steps $= 30$.

Although the pharmacological manipulation by nicotine had some of the effects predicted from central arousal theory, a placebo effect was also observed in some of the comparisons. The most plausible conclusion from the experiment, however, is that a cognitive manipulation of the assumed cognitive content of anxiety helped to reduce the number of unfavourable and aversive stimuli preoccupying high anxious subjects while engaged in another task. In these circumstances anxious subjects are no longer significantly impaired in the availability of processing space and time compared with non-anxious subjects, unless anxiety is of the clinical-pathological type and level when more skilful and prolonged cognitive intervention would be required. Because not all predictions were fully confirmed, because independent arousal measures were not taken, and because of the small number of subjects in the treatment × anxiety groups, replication of the reported results is highly desirable.

4 FURTHER EVIDENCE FOR SEMANTIC CODING OF ANXIETY

At this stage of the research programme it became inevitable that the *nature* of the interfering cognitive data which impair the performance of anxious individuals needed specifying. It was at this point that the propositions of the semantic memory codes of personality and motivational dispositions were first stated. The two experiments which are described next, therefore, preceded those experiments on the semantic representations of dominant characteristics already presented in Chapter 6. Because they were primarily concerned with the semantic representation of *anxiety*, however, they are reported in greater detail at this stage, rather than before.

The first of these two experiments proceeded on the proposition that if anxiety is substantially a reservoir of cognitive-semantic structures consisting of assemblies of referents and attributes signifying aversive implications of objects, events, situations, and people, then verbal processes should be sensitized when anxious subjects are placed in a test situation. Three major *a priori* assumptions were made.

(1) High test-anxious subjects when placed in a test situation would be more set or sensitized to anticipate aversive outcomes for their performance and thus generate in appropriate behaviour structures a state of defensive preparedness. If anxiety is, as argued, a set of cognitive structures organised in semantic schemata, then the assumed sensitization should affect particularly the dominant hemisphere.

(2) Dominant hemisphere analysis of verbal stimuli is necessary when stimuli possess low imageability.

(3) Monaural stimulation is transmitted to the contra-lateral cortex.

Assumptions (2) and (3) were considered justified in the general context of the model despite continuing controversies over right-hemisphere activity during verbal tasks, whether EEG records give valid evidence of task × hemisphere activity interactions (e.g. Davidson and Erlichman, 1980; Gevins *et al.*, 1980), or whether single-hemisphere activity can be tested only with a dichotic task (Kimura, 1967). Evidence, however, is accumulating that the left hemisphere is dominant for voluntary verbal monitoring (Milner, 1981), and that it controls self-generated speaking and manual signing (Kimura, 1981). It is possible to argue, therefore, that the verbal hemisphere plays a dominant role in goal-directed behaviour which is guided by knowledge and meaning of goal-outcomes.

A monaural study was designed in which the stimulus material was high-frequency nouns and adjectives, balanced for imageability and non-imageability, with subjects required to identify correctly 'noun' or 'adjective' by pressing appropriately labelled response keys. Imageability, response hand, input channel, and word type were fully counterbalanced across trials and subjects.[7] A simple task was chosen to minimize inter-hemispheric interaction, but in the knowledge that the *impairing* effects of high anxiety in normal populations is most aparent in complex and demanding response settings. Twenty undergraduate students took part in the experiment, divided equally into high and low anxious subgroups. It was predicted that high test-anxious subjects when stimulated via the right ear would be significantly faster in classifying high-frequency, low-imageability words than low anxious subjects. That is, if anxiety is semantically coded, and if subjects are placed in a situation in which performance anxiety is induced by instruction, then the operations of high anxious subjects' verbal hemisphere should be sensitized and possess a higher state of response readiness than their contra-lateral hemisphere, or the verbal hemisphere of low anxious subjects. Figure 8.14 shows that the null hypothesis was rejected with a considerable degree of confidence. The interaction between stimulus ear, imageability, and anxiety was highly significant. Follow-up monaural studies with low frequency words were in the same predicted directions without, however, reaching significance for an anxiety effect.

A similarly designed dichotic task also failed to reach acceptable levels of reliability for the predicted main effect. However, the presentation of anxiety-signifying words on the unattended channel lowered the response time of the high anxious albeit at the expense of a higher error rate.

In the absence of concurrent arousal measures or a significantly more difficult semantic task, it is tempting to account for these results by reference to a Spence-type of high drive and low level of competing responses (Spence and Spence, 1966). Since none of the previous studies involving test anxiety

---

[7] This experiment was conducted by Simon Gelsthorpe.

230

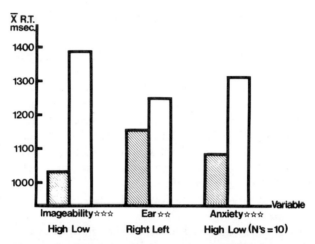

Figure 8.14 High-frequency word classification times, monaural presentation, high and low anxiety groups. *N*'s = 10 (** *p* < 0.01, *** *p* < 0.001)

had shown a systematic arousal effect, and since a drive concept without cognitive mediators can no longer be sustained, it seems more plausible, however, to regard the present findings relating right-ear advantage and low imageability to anxiety as the effect of a verbal processing factor. It is quite possible, of course, that the *a priori* assumption made above concerning the sensitization of semantic anxiety schemata in high test-anxious subjects in a test situation is misleadingly oversimplified, or that hemispheric asymmetries are the result of pre-perceptual information processing events affected by an interaction between verbal ability and the differential allocation of attention (Schwartz and Kirsner, 1982). This would be consistent with evidence that anxious neurotics score higher on tests of verbal ability (Payne, 1973), and that introverts generally score higher on written school and university examinations (e.g. Furneaux, 1962; Wilson, 1977). Consistent with both interpretations is a dichotic study by Nielson and Sarason (1980). They employed the shadowing technique with sexually explicit material presented to the unattended ear and found that high anxious subjects became more aware of this material and exhibited more interference in shadowing material presented to the attended ear than low anxious subjects. Although there is now some evidence from studying shifts in gazing that the right hemisphere may have a special role in processing affect (e.g. Schwartz *et al.*, 1975), more recent experiments suggest that at certain levels of anxiety left-hemisphere processing takes over from right-hemisphere operations (Tyler, 1981).

Laterality studies are difficult to validate and anxiety is difficult to induce in the presence of ethical restraints. The most recent study in the current research programme was concerned, therefore, to find a socially normal situation in which high anxiety is a natural feature, and to test the cognitive-semantic model of anxiety by the traditional verbal learning method. The situation chosen was the imminent publication of university degree examination results. Psychology students were asked to volunteer for an experiment to be carried out half-an-hour before the results were posted up. It was anticipated on the basis of evidence from past years, however, that students with the highest level of anxious anticipation would not check their examination results in person, but would depute friends to do it for them, and to 'break the news gently'! As a consequence the subject sample would be biased towards the low anxiety end.

The experiment consisted of two list-learning sessions – the first 30 minutes before the publication of examination results, the second 15 minutes before. The material to be learnt consisted of words given in some of the previously described studies which for other subjects had been descriptive of 'anxiety' or 'worry', and 'anger'. A new set of words signifying 'euphoria' was specially produced. Two lists of 24 words each controlled for word frequency, containing 8 words for each of the affective categories, were constructed after a Q-sort by two judges aimed at unidimensionality and unambiguousness of items. The subject groups were 8 examinees (experimental group) and 10 control subjects one year removed from their degree examination. Each word list was presented twice in a different order over 4 minutes, followed by a pattern-recognition task, followed by verbal task recall, and finally by pattern-recognition memory. The pattern-recognition task served as a buffer, but simultaneously would give some evidence of non-verbal memory capacity. The two groups were tested one week apart at the same time of day in group session, and then 24 hours later for delayed recall. The experimental material was projected on a large screen, and some control over visual angle was achieved by an appropriate arrangement of seats. The predictions were that the experimental, high anxious group would (i) remember more anxiety-signifying words for both learning sessions; (ii) remember more anxiety-signifying words the closer they were to the time of the publication of examination results; (iii) remember fewer euphoria-signifying words in the last session; (iv) recall more euphoria than anxiety words with delayed recall; and (v) that spatial pattern recognition would be unaffected. The results for the verbal tests are shown in Figure 8.15 and are generally consistent with prediction albeit short of statistical reliability, except for prediction 4. The difference for anxiety words recalled as between session 1 and session 2 for examinees and controls was just short of that required for a 5 per cent level of confidence. Similarly the difference for euphoria words demonstrated the tendency of the examinees to recall fewer of these words at session 2. Employing the criterion of group differences in the recall of 'false positive' words, the experimental group produced near-significantly more anxiety than other words. For the delayed recall, only 8 control subjects participated. As predicted, the examinees recalled a significantly higher percentage of euphoria than of anxiety words ($p < 0.005$).

Although the short-delay results were disappointing, they are consistent with the cognitive-semantic model of anxiety, and of personality and moti-

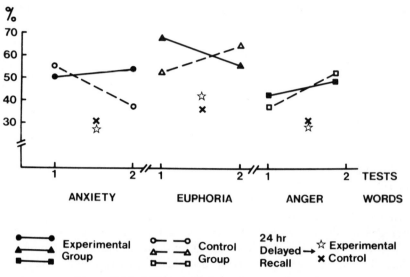

Figure 8.15 Affect-state-dependent word recall

vational dispositions generally, and in view of the anticipated non-partici-
pation of very anxious subjects (including those who had to sit their
examination papers under special stress-reduced conditions), this outcome
was not totally unexpected. New and larger scale studies are planned, therefore, to avoid biased subject selection. These would have to include non-
verbal recall tasks, because pattern-recognition memory, which was unimpaired in both groups of the study, does not have the required non-verbal
performance match.

The delayed recall results are less consistent with Bower's (1981) mood-
state dependence model than with my own. Bower's model would predict
that delayed recall would be affected by subjects' emotional state in the first
two experimental sessions, that is, by remembering the context in which the
word lists were learned. This model would predict, therefore, that the anxious
examinees who were expecting their degree results would remember a higher
percentage of anxiety words 24 hours later. This they did not do. The
cognitive-semantic model of personality and motivation would predict the
opposite: the current motivational state with its relief from expecting aversive
outcomes would affect recall performance, with euphoria a better description
of the current state than either anxiety or anger. For at least two subjects,
relief was tempered by disappointment in that they did not perform quite as
well in the examinations as they had hoped. The word lists did not contain
attributes which would describe depression, but it is worth noting that the
total number of words recalled by these subjects was smaller, and that the
word 'sad' occurred three times, as well as the words 'indifferent' and
'satisfied'.

Although most of the experimental studies were carried out on small numbers of subjects, they show an initially gratifying level of internal consistency and complementarity. Several conclusions seem to be valid. Physiological arousal is a *mechanism* for the activation of cognitive and other behavioural events and operates in all adaptive (and maladaptive) processes. Arousal *facilitates* cognitive activity, but only indirectly determines the content of cognitive structures by threshold values that link together experiences and their objects which have generated prolonged and raised physiological and biochemical activity. If anxiety impairs cognitive processes without a direct contribution from arousal, then the impairment is associated with cognitive factors. If verbal and semantic processes differentiate between individuals respectively high and low anxious, then verbal and semantic representations of a subjective concept of anxiety are likely to contribute to the demonstrated performance deficits. If it is agreed that anxiety is a personality and motivational characteristic predisposing towards particular interpretations of stimulus meaning and expectancies of behaviour outcomes, then this predisposition resides in verbal and semantic representations in permanent memory. This premise led to the semantic investigations of dominant traits, anxiety and anger, reported in Chapter 6 and to the development of the general model outlined there.

Complex societies require complex problem-solving from their adult members, the ability to discover the core of problems and to integrate divergent approaches. If problem-solving can be impaired by dominant self-relevant, but task-irrelevant, thought processes then it is socially desirable to minimize interference from this type of cognitive intrusion. If it is correct, as I have argued, that preoccupation with characteristic and preferred behavioural strategies towards preferred goals and goal outcomes imposes additional information processing demands on the cognitive system, and if these demands and those of social adaptation are additive, then tasks and preoccupations become stressors. The readiness of an individual's cognitive system to retrieve task-irrelevant but intrusive information would then define the system's vulnerability to stressors.

CHAPTER 9

The cognitive structures and processes of stress vulnerability

1 PROBLEMS OF DEFINITION

There are several levels of difficulty associated with the meaning of the term 'stress'. The first and perhaps simplest is a common lack of distinction between stress as a stimulus or agent, and stress as a response, effect, or outcome. A second difficulty arises from the common and generally valid distinction between neurochemical, physiological, and physical stress, and psychogenic stress. A range of theoretical and methodological problems is present, thirdly, in the common practice of equating stress with excitement, arousal, and drive. Finally, we have a persisting, so-called, philosophical or quasi-philosophical controversy over the precedence and comparative deterministic importance of neurochemical and cognitive appraisal sources of stress.

Ambiguity over stress as an agent and as an effect can be resolved by distinguishing between stress agents and stressor effects (Selye, 1976, 1979), or between stress and stress response, with an intermediate response of strain (Warburton, 1979). An appropriate reference to physical and engineering science, from which the term is borrowed, reintroduces the terms strain and load so that, by Hooke's Law, stress can be defined by the effects of load on strain (Eysenck, 1973). This relationship in physical science is monotonic, however, and it has been argued that non-linear relationships between strain and load may describe this relationship better for humans and animals. To avoid further problems of definition, it has been suggested that the term stress should be abandoned, and that instead we should rephrase the agent-effect sequence in terms of stressors acting on a system which responds with strain, where the sum of strains constitutes the total load of demands on an adaptation-seeking organism (Hamilton, 1979a). This relationship is sketched in Figure 9.1 together with the required feedback loop between load and stressors to indicate that load signals will add to, or diminish, the stressor components depending on the ability of intervening processes to

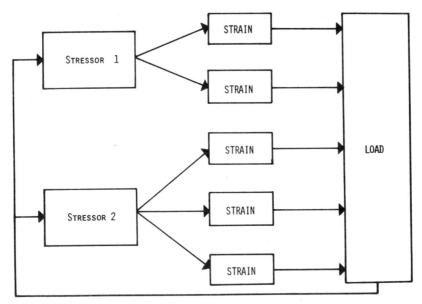

Figure 9.1 Components of the 'stress' reaction

reduce the impact of the stressor-strain effects. These interactions require elaboration of the nature and sources of the stressors.

Physiological models of the stress response emphasize the role of cate-cholamines, adrenalin, and noradrenalin released from the adrenal medulla, and of corticosteroids released from the adrenal cortex, in preparing the system for action against stressors. Although these agents tend to be released together, one acting primarily on body tissues, the other on the neurochem-istry of the cortex, the precise reasons for their correlated release are not yet fully understood. Strain arises here from excessive demands on the neuro-chemical system to produce and release hormones, and particularly from the demands for and depletion of blood sugars to energize behavioural system activity which is stimulated and maintained by corticosteroids. Both effects contribute to the load factors on the system which will be exhibited by performance decrements, by *fatigue*, and by changes in body chemistry with unfavourable secondary effects. Although there appears to be general agree-ment among investigators that these neurochemical events occur whether the stressors are physiological, physical, or 'psychological', there is more than a possibility that this position veils important distinctions, particularly those affecting the interaction between thought processes and the adreno-cortico-trophic system. Thus, it is more than likely that corticotrophic release will be differentially affected by (i) a painful boil on some part of the body, and (ii) transmission and understanding of an associated medical diagnosis that the boil is a manifestation of a rare and serious disease process. In the latter case, stressor-strain effects from physiological events are compounded by the effects of a noxious piece of self-knowledge. This triggers cognitive processes encoding danger, threat, and anxiety, and the appropriate neurotransmitter processes which they initiate and with which they have become associated previously when exposed to potential danger.

It is not difficult to find the reasons which have led to the application of synonymous meanings and behavioural effects to stress, emotion, arousal, excitement, and drive. Grossly conceived they all describe states of high activation of the person, where excitement is the most superficial descriptive with few theoretical implications. Arousal has the most general application because peripheral and electrocortical arousal are by definition and by neurochemical processes inevitable components of stress and emotion. Parts, however, do not equal the whole, even though arousal is a necessary concomitant of sympathetic ANS activity which forms part of the stressor response. Moreover, our earlier discussion has already argued with some force (viz. Chapters 5, 6, and 7) that arousal is no more than a necessary rather than a sufficient factor in the behavioural effects of affect- and stressor-strain-induction. The equating of drive and arousal has always seemed particularly odd and inadmissable since drive is at least partly situationally and goal-determined, whereas arousal is at most a concomitant, or an energizer of adaptive goal-directed behaviour.

The last problem of definition which has been selected for consideration cannot be dismissed as a non-issue in behavioural science. Clearly, there are stages in a stressor-strain adaptation process when neurochemical and cognitive events are not only concurrent but when they are involved in a positive or negative feedback relationship cycle. Unless our primary concern, however, is the effect of tissue injury, viral infection, or pharmacological manipulation on what Selye called the general adaptation syndrome of the organic homeostatic system, a stand needs to be taken on the matter of 'first cause', or the trigger of stressor-strain. The position taken here, and in the earlier discussion, is that the physiological and neurochemical systems are not activated until sensorily received information is identified as belonging to a category of events which, initially by biological blueprint, determine approach or avoidance behaviour. Thus, a deaf infant responds to high-intensity noise neither with motor behaviour indicating distress, nor with peripheral or electrocortical arousal mediated by catecholamine or corticosteroid release. Similarly, a peaceful Sunday afternoon siesta in a sunny garden remains uninterrupted and sleepy with its concomitant state of high cortical synchronicity (de-arousal, unstressed), until a telephone call intrudes with information of a personally aversive and/or distressing nature. Here the resulting physiological events and the release of neurochemical stress hormones are a consequence of, and neither a concomitant nor a cause of, the initial cognitive experience of threat, danger, or distress.

Two contra-arguments can be defended, however, with some degree of logical and experimental justification.

(1) The intensity, duration, lability, and habituation of physiological and

neurochemical processes will necessarily affect the individual's ability to generate physical actions and cognitive reinterpretations of the initial stimulus meanings by which the experienced stressor-strain effect may be reduced.

(2) By genetic blueprint, by a history of response demands, and by their interaction, physiological and neurochemical systems exhibit individual differences in the capacity to assist in and maintain a level of stressor-strain activity and levels of peripheral and central arousal which are experienced as optimal by the person, and as socially adaptive by an observer.

These arguments, taken as propositions, represent simultaneously biological definitions of vulnerability to stressor-strain, or of what is often termed diathesis.

In the context of a cognitive-semantic reinterpretation of personality and motivation, stressors require cognitive conceptualization. It is worth noting, perhaps, that this is one of the rare situations in which the definitions of the layman and those of the specialist are in close accord. Stressors are stimuli which are interpreted by a person as signifying aversion, disquiet, discomfort, threats, dangers, or distress to an unacceptable degree either singly or in any combination, but whose experience in these terms cannot be immediately avoided. The identification of these experiences, and the behavioural strategies and thought processes which they engender constitute the strain effect on an information processing system which attempts to reduce the stressor effect. I have suggested elsewhere (Hamilton, 1979a) that at least four processes affect the behavioural and cognitive strategies, and thus the sum of strains defining the load on the adaptive system. They are: the previously acknowledged energy allocations of the physiological and neurochemical systems to facilitate adaptation; the presence and elaborations of cognitive structures encoding aversive and/or distressing expectancies; the cognitive work involved in the interpretation of situational complexity which forms the setting for the strain-inducing information; and finally the coping and defensively-oriented cognitive restructuring processes which need to be applied where the other processes fail to reduce stressor-strain and load to a subjectively acceptable level.

This analysis has confined itself so far to stimuli or events that have actually occurred. An alternative, and additional source of stressor-strain resides in the anticipation of stimuli or events which, when they do occur, may generate a not fully predictable number of identifying responses interpreted as aversive, threatening, or distressing. A major mediator here is stimulus uncertainty. On the basis of evidence from a great deal of experimental work (e.g. Jones, 1966; Broadbent, 1971) we conclude that uncertainty – and its resulting stressor-strain – is greatest when the probability of stimulus occurrence is at the 50 per cent level. If we are now dealing not only with one but two or more probable events each of which engenders various types and degrees of aversive experience, stressor-strain from uncertainty will describe an in-creating function. Because we are unable to say at present whether the triple interaction described is additive or multiplicative, we can speak only in terms of a nominal scale. Table 9.1 shows the hypothetical effects for stressor-strain

Table 9.1 Hypothetical Relationships Between 'Uncertainty' and Stressor-strain

Events	Stimulus expectancy	Probable no. of distressing implications	Stressor-strain and load
One	High	Small	0
		Large	+
	50%	Small	0/+
		Large	++
Two	High–High	Small	+
		Large	+++
	50%–50%	Small	++
		Large	++++++
	50%–High	Small	++
		Large	++++
	High–50%	Small	++
		Large	++++

and adaptive load generated by the number of probabilistic events, two levels of event uncertainty, and two levels of the probable number of aversive or distressing interpretations that may be applied to the probabilistic events and certainty levels.

Although my discussion is primarily concerned with negative, undesirable, and unfavourable stressor-strain effects, reference to positive and desirable stressor-strain experience must be made. Sporting activities, with or without a competitive factor, are enjoyed and deliberately chosen by many people for a variety of reasons. Many, if not all of them, are physically demanding and have strain and fatigue effects on the physical, physiological, and neurochemical systems. These effects are here deliberately sought out and the end-state of exhaustion is frequently experienced as pleasurable and/or satisfying. What matters, of course, are the goals that have motivated this behaviour – the expectations of health benefits, obtaining evidence of a motor skill, of endurance, or of social acceptance by other members of a team. This argument applies equally to intellectual/cognitive activity and the enjoyment of demanding problem-solving tasks engaged in for the purpose of diversion and entertainment, alone, or in the company of others. And it applies, of course, to constructive hobbies with their demands on planning and skill. What is important, therefore, for the definition of stressor-strain and load is neither the stimulus *per se*, nor the stimulus-in-context, but the interpretation of these within a framework of individual goals, and the labelling of stimuli, context, goals, and the strategies required to achieve them. These interpretations, however, are determined by the content of existing cognitive structures and the assemblies of referents and their attributes in functionally-related, schematic organization. Thus, cognitive prominence of fear of failure, low frustration tolerance, or defining personal social accepibility in terms of high level of competence, will transform a pleasurable experience of stressor-strain into an aversive and disturbing experience. There is no evidence to suggest that these divergent experiences are due to different levels of physiological arousal or corticosteroid release. On the contrary, and as discussed before, without a cognitive orientation it is difficult to differentiate affective states.

When stressor-strain is experienced aversively performance skills decline. If physiological and neurochemical events cannot account for the qualitative differences in experience, a corollary to a cognitive definition of stressor-strain is required to account for performance changes. Our earlier discussion of the effects of anxiety on performance, and of the cognitive-semantic elaboration of dominant personality traits, preferred goals, and goal-outcomes, provides the basis for an additional defining element. Negative and undesirable behaviour and goal expectancies dominant in a hierarchy of expectancies, have lower retrieval thresholds, are irrelevant to task performance and, by definition, have led to greater cognitive elaboration. If the probable level of the expected outcomes is maximally uncertain (50 per cent), but their cognitively coded implications are numerous, then unfavourable goal and behaviour expectancies add to the information processing load of a system already engaged in what started off as a primary task – playing a game, solving a puzzle, or constructing an object. In this event it becomes possible to define stressor-strain in terms of the level of load exerted on an information processing system. In other words, and as is already implied by Table 9.1, the addition of task-irrelevant cognitive processes to operations on task-related stimuli converts a qualitative conception of stressor-strain into a quantitative one. Figure 9.2 attempts to structure this amplification of the definition of stressor-strain. The effects of cognitive overload and stressor-strain on post-task performance experience and on task performance are shown in the upper half of Figure 9.2; the effects of an unstressing situation are shown in the lower half. The widest definition of a task can be applied here.

Fewer problems attach to the definition of *vulnerability* to stress, but present conceptions are of limited utility for a cognitive orientation. Clearly, however, the term focuses on unfavourable responses to stressor-strain and load. Genetically and physiologically oriented approaches to vulnerability are represented, for example, by the New York child temperament studies of Thomas *et al.* (e.g. 1968), and the Copenhagen and Mauritius 'at risk' studies of schizophrenia by Mednick, Schulsinger and their associates (e.g. Mednick *et al.*, 1975; Venables *et al.*, 1978). Sociological approaches to vulnerability such as those by Rutter and Quinton (1976) and Rutter *et al.* (1970, 1976) and by Brown (1979) and Brown *et al.* (1973) focus on the role of social and socio-economic circumstances in the aetiology of so-called psychiatric disorders, as does the review of 50 studies by Melvyn Kohn

240

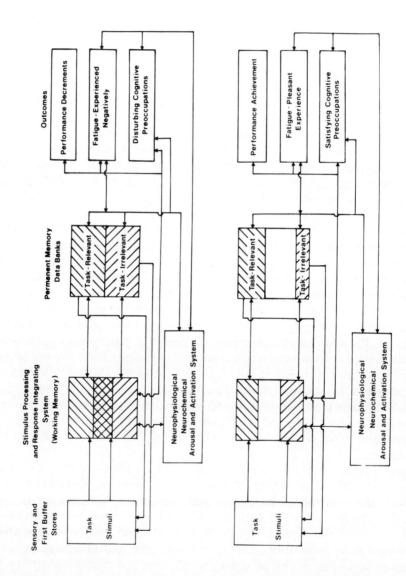

Figure 9.2 Cognitive processing analysis of behaviour with and without stressor-strain

(1976). Kohn's approach emphasizes, however, the effects of experienced deficiencies in social power and influence and therefore embodies the effects of cognitive events. Whereas the physiologically-oriented studies minimize the role of environmental experience, the sociological studies give an inadequate role to physiological processes. With fairly little effort, however, both approaches can also be labelled psychological. If we were to delineate areas of special expertise more precisely, one could equally well argue that neither approach is central to psychology. Psychology's special expertise lies in the *processes* that convey and control meaning, purpose, expectations, and self-direction of behaviour in the social context, whereas the approaches mentioned exclude an examination of cognitive processes, cognitive operations, and their selective strategies. For that reason analytically orientated socialization studies are more informative and of greater explanatory importance. As examples we may cite the detailed observations of Escalona (1968) on the development of early need satisfaction, the long-term study by Murphy amd Moriarty (1976) of the gradual development of coping capacity in Topeka children, and the careful work of Diana Baumrind (1967, 1971) on the analysis of interactions between parental child-rearing strategies and their associated outcomes for children.

To the extent that the cognitive processing system interprets events as aversive, and that excessively aversive events will be coded and interpreted as stressful information, to that extent the ground is prepared for the development of vulnerability. Vulnerability, therefore, has the dual definition of sensitivity to respond unadaptively to a high information load from stressors, as well as the readiness to interpret isolated stimuli and events as stressors. There is some value, therefore, in Zubin and Spring's (1977) proposal that vulnerability and an acute behaviour disorder may reflect a kind of trait-state relationship. Like many other suggestions, however, this one does not define vulnerability in terms which make possible more concise statements of the *nature* of vulnerability, and of why certain events precipitate adaptive incompetence.

2. VARIETIES OF STRESSOR-STRAIN VULNERABILITY

It is conceptually difficult to distinguish between stressful experience and the predisposition to be stressed. One is tempted to describe the relationship as two sides of the same coin, or as a reciprocal interaction. There is a grain of validity to both suggestions in that they imply that vulnerability provides a low threshold for experiencing events as stressors, and that a history of stressor-strain increases the probability that subsequent events of the same or a different category will be experienced as stressors. This relationship is the basis of all theories of psychopathology, whether stressors are regarded as primarily physiological and neurochemical, or as psychogenic or cognitive, or as their combination. A reciprocal interaction description, however, is not fully valid since success in overcoming, or coping with, stressful experience provides a person not only with the experience of that success but with some knowledge of the strategies that helped to achieve it. Effects of this kind will serve well until the nature or the amount of stressors arising in the person–environment interaction change in a substantial way, and when only relatively limited physiological and cognitive resources are available to reduce stressor-strain experience. Resource limitations are the most likely major cause of prolonged and progressive maladaptation to stressors, and since cognitive methods of coping develop only gradually over years, the effect of conditioned physiological stress response to aversively experienced events must initially be stronger than the influence of stressful cognitive associations.

From this analysis it follows that physiological vulnerability – and its genetic basis – provides the necessary condition for future psychopathological states. These cases account, however, for little more than 12 per cent of the general population, whereas even quite intense stressor effects can be over-come by the majority of individuals. It is likely that full adaptation is more apparent than real if one considers that adaptation must usually involve some form of compromise between preferred personal states and external con-straints. Examples are compromises between goal-directed behaviour and some type of risk-taking; between accepting bereavement, childlessness, or impediments to professional advancement and the still present memory struc-tures of the objects, persons, or events which are no longer available; or between handling a large number of simultaneous demands on attention and problem-solving inadequately and selecting only some for the efficient ap-plication of available effort. Since the whole information processing system has participated in stressor-strain reduction, memory data representative of the mismatch between an ideal and a possible but unachieved state will have been encoded. This situation may be described as *residual conflict* which will remain benign unless new, functionally related stressors appear on the scene and deposit their own residual conflict with additive effects. So-called stress tolerance, therefore, is not a static disposition or capacity, but has incre-mental function. Moreover, tolerance to stressor-strain exhibits two types of incrementation: lowering resistance to strain with consequential progressive decrements in adaptation, or increasing resistance by recruitment of re-sources after receiving feedback from initial decrements in adaptation. Neither response need be linear over time (Hamilton, 1979a).

Despite residual problems encountered in analysing the relationship be-tween stressors and vulnerability, it can be helpful to impose some kind of structure in terms of types and areas of operation. *Stressors*, for example, can be considered separately as originating in and from physiological and neurochemical events. Among these are tissue injury, pain, fever, fatigue, extreme temperatures, intense and especially intermittent noise, and sleep loss. A second category, and that which approximates most closely to the general (and lay) concept of stress, is defined by the nature, number, and intensity of aversively labelled anticipated outcomes, implications, and ex-pectancies associated with an actual or a future event. These are the psychogenic stressors which present the information processing and adaptive system with associative data that are unpleasant, threatening, or somehow dangerous for the person. Whereas this information is internally- and self-generated, the origin of a third category of stressors is primarily external to the person. This is defined by the complexity, simultaneity, and duration of response requirements presented by occupational tasks and demands implicit in social interactions.

Vulnerability, or sensitivity to stressors, can also be defined by reference to major areas of operation. Physical/organic integrity, for example, may be an identifiable focus of stressor-strain experience. Here we can demonstrate, however, that categorical distinctions between stressors which may be useful for conceptual structuring, are unhelpful in the analysis of stressor effects, and of the dispositions by which stimuli become subjectively identified as stressors. Physiological and neurochemical stressors will indeed interact with organic resources in the counter-shock and resistance phases of Selye's adaptation syndrome. Equally probable mediators in many persons, however, are stressor responses concerned with behavioural efficiency in the work and social context, and with the implications for longer term goals of physical health *and* behavioural efficiency of an acknowledged state of physiological impairment and strain.

A further category of vulnerability for plausible differentiation may be labelled social integrity. This category of response predisposition is most likely to be sensitive to the cognitive implication structures which represent and evaluate the goals of the social self-image, its status and role-playing ideals, its competence, its acceptability to others, and the continuing utility of existing preferred behavioural strategies for the attainment of these goals. I have argued at some length elsewhere (Hamilton, 1979a, 1980) that the core of differential degrees of vulnerability to socially interpreted stressors is likely to be found in anxieties and in avoidance strategies associated with social isolation. A third plausible category of vulnerability can be constructed by isolating sensitivity to being overloaded with demands on executive systems required for skilled performance at work, at leisure, or in social interaction. Although work performance is likely to be most often interpreted in a social evaluation context and therefore is subject to social stressors and thresholds of social vulnerability, there are occasions when these factors are minimized. For example, work pressures are self-created when prior to leaving home in haste in order to arrive at the office punctually, an appointment needs to be entered on a memo pad, windows have to be closed, house and car keys need to be taken, an unexpected phone call has to be answered, and the front door needs to be double-locked before shutting it. Each one of them is cognitively and skill-wise simple. Compressed into a short time, however, and with preoccupation with the content of the telephone message, we may arrive at work not only lacking in a desirable calm and collected state, but without the house key and with nagging doubts as to whether every window has been secured. To account for the omissions and commissions we argue that short-term working memory and its tool of selective attention have been overloaded with the result that tasks to be done were insufficiently rehearsed before being 'masked' by a subsequent working memory input. Even in this hypothetical example, however, it is likely that social stressors and social vulnerability intrude with processes determined by the preferred goals of punctuality and calmness. These in turn involve generating physiological stressors which together with the energy demands of the series of simple tasks will be experienced as a load factor with the most likely consequence of fatigue.

Since my main concern is the analysis of cognitive structures and processes in stress vulnerability, let me turn to brief considerations of a number of features which initially are objective and unavoidable functions of stimulus situations, and which only subsequently engender individual differences in response strategies leading to stressor-strain, or its absence. One of these features – stimulus uncertainty – has been discussed already, and in the context of response uncertainty due to multiple response outcome implications. At this stage, however, let us confine ourselves to situations representing those features in which outcome implications are affectively relatively neutral, an infrequent condition, of course, if these features are an important component of vulnerability.

Let me start with *decision-making*, and let us assume that a limited period of time is available to engage in one of three equally desirable and equally unobjectionable activities, any one of which can be carried out equally enjoyably at any other time without special advantage or disadvantage. Although this degree of personal non-involvement is extremely unlikely, it permits us to focus on decision processes which are purely task-oriented with the single constraint that the activity chosen can be completed within the available time. Although N. E. Miller would have termed this a triple-approach conflict, this would be inappropriate since my specification excludes motivational and emotional strains, and is concerned with choice processes and the cognitive work, or information processing activities determining choice, decision-making complexity, and cognitive processing load. The steps involved would have to include considerations of the following critera: accessibility of task; whether it interferes with another person; availability of implements or material; amount of preparatory work in the context of time available; attention to detail and quality of performance required in the context of time constraint; and others which the motivated reader may wish to supply.

Now let us compare the decision-making processes presented by three alternatives and a minimum of five criteria to meet the time constraint, with the processing requirements of only two, or those of four alternative activities. Clearly, the greater the number of alternative tasks, and the greater the number of criterion categories, the longer and the more involved the comparison processes to find that optimal combination of criteria which enables the ostensibly rational decision to be made. Since it is unlikely that the number of alternative tasks available at any given period is as unlimited as the criteria applied to the choice process, the decision-making process will depend substantially on the last variable for the specification of decision-making difficulty or complexity. In that event the crucial contribution to the process is made by the availability and accessibility in memory of differentiating and elaborating conceptual structures which define the alternative tasks and their requirements. The more finely elaborated the concepts, the greater the number of potential criteria, and if accessible, the greater the cognitive work load. And what we can now add is that the more equal the degree of conceptual elaboration of alternative task requirements (and the greater the habitual preference of the decision-maker for the application of exhaustive rational criteria to decision-making), the more unlikely that a decision will be reached before the time available for the task has run out! I shall return to decision-making processes in the context of decision-making conflict and adaptive coping processes (e.g. Janis and Mann, 1977). The preceding comments have been intended to illustrate what may be called 'structural complexity' and its potential as a stressor in terms of its information processing load.

A second example of 'structural complexity', defined by objective and integral features of a stimulus situation, is stimulus ambiguity. This term has several related definitions. The most general refers to a signal which is unclassifiable because of its lack of sensory determination or clarity. For visual material we manipulate this in the laboratory by subthreshold tachistoscopic exposure speeds, by defocusing or blurring, by figure-ground contamination, or by superimposition of one stimulus on another. Auditorally, we manipulate clarity by 'white noise', by volume control, by superimposition of one stimulus on another, or by acoustic distortion. Many of these manipulations have a naturally occurring prototype, and many of the stimulus degrading effects can be produced by non-attention, or split attention. Unless there is a pre-attentive directive bias by instruction or contiguity (Broadbent, 1977a, b), stimulus identification is impaired, though stimulus class may be determined. Stimuli which are presented in a degraded form by intervening optic filters so that individual letters are missing from a displayed word require identification by higher order or an 'upper' recognizing system from whose activities stressor effects arise (Broadbent, 1971; Broadbent and Broadbent, 1976). This, of course, is the system and the level which encodes preferred modes of behaviour, their goals, and preferred outcomes.

Laboratory studies are often concerned with simple stimuli which are usually presented in isolation from others and without interference from social contexts. Stimulus ambiguity usually resides here in identifying one exemplar of one or several classes of stimuli. Multiple stimuli, however, are usually embedded in real-life exchanges of information with their demands for optimal adaptation. The complexity of these information processing demands requires analysis along several dimensions. Schroder *et al.* (1967), for example, suggest that differentiation, discrimination, and integration of information is required to impose structural organization, and in order to make optimally efficient inferences or deductions from complex stimulus situations. The greater the number of elementary stimulus dimensions, the greater the degree of differentiation along each dimension, and the more complex and elaborated the schemata which integrate the information from stimulus dimensions and their fine-grained differentiation, the greater the structural complexity. In that event also the higher the probability that ambiguity at several levels of analysis will impose a stressor-strain load on the processing system. Shalit (1977), in a study of the relationship between structural ambiguity and coping capacity, added the dimension of positive or negative emotional evaluation associated with the other dimensions of complexity. Multiple-scaling analysis applied to the results of over 300 published studies indicated that degree of differentiation and affective loading of situations most clearly defined structural complexity and ambiguity, and that these dimensions were negatively related to effectiveness of coping.

The addition of an affective loading dimension to the sources of stimulus ambiguity recapitulates the relationship between the implications of a probable event and their effect on stressor-strain load shown in Table 9.1 It introduces, moreover, the effect of conflict between alternative outcomes for the person that are implicit in stimuli capable of eliciting multiple identifications and interpretations. If fundamentally and developmentally considered, conflict is defined by choices between simultaneously desirable and undesirable goal-outcomes which have not resulted in solution without a residual cognitive problem of classification, we can argue that an individual is vulnerable to the structural complexity of stimulus ambiguity. It has been previously suggested (see also Chapters 5 and 6) that anxiety may be the major response to ambiguity. The reasons given were that ambiguity presents decision conflicts which are magnified by cognitive-affective memory representations of residual conflicts, and which have been associated with, and have led to, anxiety (Frenkel-Brunswik, 1949; Hamilton, 1957). Stimulus ambiguity, therefore, is synonymous with response ambiguity since problems of stimulus classification are a direct function of response class differentiation and its contribution to the stimulus-identifying process. If ambiguity and its informational complexity are sources of stressor-strain, then feedback from the load-registering system will initiate cognitive strategies to reduce the effect of those identified outcomes which would increase vulnerability to such classes of events. I will comment on these strategies below when discussing coping processes.

Other sources of stressor-strain vulnerability are experiences of hopelessness (Lazarus, 1976) or helplessness (Seligman, 1975; Miller et al., 1977). Evidence of incapacity to resolve difficult personal or social issues, or evidence or persistent non-contingency between effort and behaviour outcome is frequently followed by a state of demotivation and exhaustion. Two sets of processes are to be held responsible: the relationship between stress hormone secreton and glucose depletion, and the problem-solving, adaptation-seeking search processes of the cognitive system which precede and accompany them. There are probably only two situational events in which hopelessness and helplessness are absolutely and objectively justified: a medical verdict of an inevitably terminal illness, and the imminent execution of a sentence of death. In all other cases the depressing interpretation of the outcome or implication of events depends on the prior presence of expectancies of undesirable, unfulfilling, or unrewarding effects of behaviour. Because of the presence of such negative anticipations, it is likely that the person's problem-solving work is conducted in a conflicting setting where parallel processes representing negative outcomes compete for space and time in the working memory component of the processing system with the search for an adaptively experienced solution. In this event, a state of non-responding can be regarded as a self-fulfilling prophecy.

One further category of stressor-strain vulnerability deserves mention. The concept of 'environmental stress' has emerged to describe the unfavourable physiological and cognitive effects of certain ecological and technological by-products of complex societies. Among these we find: population density or crowding, noise, and pollution, technological innovations imposed on non-technological populations, elaborations of institutional organizations and their regulations (already discussed in Chapter 5), design of housing complexes on the basis of efficiency and space-utilizing criteria, restrictions in recreational space, the anonymity of central and local bureaucracies, the power structure of industrial relationships, and the demands of repetitive work performance in situations inducing excessive and unavoidable degrees of fatigue (e.g. Proshansky et al., 1976; Cox, 1978; Stokols, 1978; Payne, 1979; Rohmert and Luczak, 1979; Sarason and Spielberger, 1980). Although what is now termed the field of 'environmental psychology' has exhibited a marked growth trend, it is reassuring that the modes of 'transaction' between persons and environment are interpreted largely in cognitive terms. Stokols in his *Annual Review of Psychology* article even appears to be willing to regard the affective component of interpretive, evaluative, operative, and responsive modes of interaction as cognitive events (Stokols, 1978, p. 259). This interpretation is fully consistent with the conceptualization offered here, but it has one obvious implication for terminology: environmental stress requires rephrasing as environmental stressors. Not only are there individual differences in the degree to which ecological and technological situations and events are *interpreted* as aversive, threatening, conflicting, or disorganizing, differences which permit valid application of the concept of internal versus external control (Rotter et al. 1972). There is also convincing evidence that physiological and neurochemical *response thresholds* interact with the aversive interpretation of environmental stimuli, to produce susceptibility to varieties of cardiovascular disease (e.g. Rosenman et al., 1975; Glass et al., 1977).

3 STRESSOR-STRAIN AVOIDANCE, OR 'COPING'

The major sources of discomfort and distress are stimuli which are interpreted as inducing experiences of anxiety, anger, frustration, loss, and conflict. Conflict in this case refers to the inability to select the most stressor-reducing response strategy, in the context of an irreversible event or situation, with the available decision-making resources, and with a disposition of having to respond. Avoidance or coping behaviour are strategies in action and thought to reduce experiences of anxiety, anger, frustration, loss, and conflict by evading or withdrawing from the noxious stimuli, by modifying the distressing interpretations which were associated with them, by denying the occurrence of the stimulus or its interpretations, or both sets of events, or most adaptively by searching for additional information which would reduce the stressing interpretations of the stimulus and its experienced aversiveness.

Let us consider the reality-oriented adaptive strategy first. In their discussion of pre-decisional cognitive activities of different patterns of decision-making, Janis and Mann (1977) label this the 'vigilant' coping pattern. A vigilant responder searches for alternative responses, for new information, clarifies goals, evaluates implications of old and new response strategies, assimilates information with acceptable implications, and engages in planful implementation of new strategies while prepared for new contingencies. These response patterns have three prerequisites: modification of action and thought must lessen the 'risks' to which the individual has felt exposed, there must be 'hope' that this goal can be achieved, and there must be time to engage in all these cognitive processes. This style of undefended conflict resolution is likely to be confined to situations or issues in which either stimulus analysis predicates relatively low 'risks', and relatively high 'hopes', or where vulnerability in terms of residual conflicts is low. Alternatively and additionally, the style requires the presence of some general resources such as those provided by health and energy, by problem-solving capacity, by awareness of sources for social support, and by existing cognitive structures representing self-confidence, anticipation of favourable outcomes (e.g. Folkman et al., 1979), and a generally low susceptibility to interpret stimuli as stressors. Life-stress research has indicated (Rahe, 1968, 1978; Rabkin and Struening, 1976) that major negative changes in, for example, life style, social responsibility, or personal status have an adverse effect on physical health (see also Johnson and Sarason, 1979 for a recent review and elaboration), and that low socio-economic status and its implications are significant components in depressive reactions (e.g. Brown, 1979). The effect of such stressors is not confined to the reduction of physical and physiological energy. In the context of an information processing conceptualization of stressors, strain, and load, these factors become intrusive cognitive data presenting the individual with additional sources of aversive experience and decision-making demands. The degree of interference from this type of susceptibility is in turn a function of the extent to which in preceding periods of life history a repertoire of stressful, that is aversive, threatening, thwarting interpretations has been acquired and conceptually structured in functionally related assemblies of referents and their attributes.

The reality-oriented, vigilant strategy of adapting to stressor-strain must pre-suppose an adequate level of *resilience* to physiological and cognitive effort. To experience this effort as tolerable, the adaptation-seeking cognitive processing system is likely to have available memory representations of the effects of past, and at least partially, successful effort outcomes. These are, that stressors are episodic, often can be managed very quickly, and sometimes are of relatively low intensity and duration. Subsequent evidence of resilience and efficient reality-oriented coping can be interpreted with some justification as evidence of habituation to or of extinction of an aversive avoidance response. Some investigators have used the term *inoculation* to describe a growing capacity of tolerance to stressors (e.g. Murphy and Moriarty, 1976; Horowitz, 1976, 1979; Janis, 1982). In terms of a cognitive-semantic model of personality, motivation, and affect, inoculation implies a restructuring of the concepts involved in the identification of stimuli as stressors. This is likely to take two forms.

(1) Aversive signifiers attached to referents will become attenuated so that less intense experiences of affect are encoded by less extreme semantic attributes.

(2) Schematic organization of referent-attribute structures will acquire either new or stronger associative links with structures already encoding self-knowledge of capacity and competence, and of satisfaction over the outcome of past efforts in functionally related areas. What occurs is not so much a matter of 'getting used to' the stressor affect in the lay sense, cognitive restructuring must actually *reduce* the physiological tone of the stressor.

Just as vulnerability is likely to be the result of incrementation from residual conflicts, so resilience and inoculation are likely to develop in a step-wise progression over a number of years, almost in the manner of a desensitization programme, but with implication for changes in conceptual content rather than merely assumptions about the weakening of mechanical links. Murphy and Moriarty's (1976) informative report of their longitudinal study of Topika children provides a great deal of data pertinent to the development of resilience in children. Although many of the variables studied were assessed observationally rather than experimentally, the investigators were exceptionally well-qualified observers, reliability data were obtained, and the large number of fine-grained assessment categories are testimony to the differentiating ability of the personnel. The following child behaviour categories (among others) had very significant positive correlations with resilience at pre-school age: range of areas of enjoyment; 'feeling good to be myself'; realistic evaluation of people; insight into social situations; reality testing; capacity for free-wheeling attention; flexibility in adapting means to a goal; synthesized thinking, affect, and action; freedom to translate ideas into action; intuitive approach; creativeness and originality; overall activity level; speed of orientation; accepting substitutes; ability to accept affective warmth; positive self-appraisal; wanting to 'grow up'. Correlations which remained significant at a later pre-puberty stage included: affective coping capacity; pleasure in own body; flexibility in adapting means to a goal; frustration tolerance; using environment selectively; ability to ask for help when needed; wanting to 'grow-up' (all categories selected and adapted from Murphy and Moriarty, 1976, p. 381). Among the assessment variables which correlated most strongly with psychiatric assessments of vulnerability were: (for boys) spread of affect; difficult peer relationships; tendency to hurt oneself; and (for girls) feelings of rejection; tendency to hurt oneself; evidence of tension load; and non-social environmental difficulties.

It is useful, I think, to refer to the remarkable closeness of Murphy and Moriarty's criteria of stressor-strain tolerance, and those most frequently cited by non-specialists. And if objections were raised because of bias endemic in all observational studies, and especially those in which observers operated with the concepts of psycho-dynamic theories, comparison between these results and those obtained by Baumrind (1967, 1971) are salutory. The match between Baumrind's data, obtained from objective observation and rating procedures, which describe the optimally socialized child and his antecedent experience of parenting strategies, and Murphy and Moriarty's resilience data, is probably adequate to confer more than face validity on the Topika results. Comparable results were obtained also by Krohne (1978, 1980) on German children and parents. His studies showed that a combination of undefended coping strategies and low level of test and general anxiety in children were significantly related not only to the socialization antecedents of strong parental support, non-restrictive rearing, consistency and praise rather than punishment, but that this combination was associated with superior ability in cognitive and educational testing.

Three further comments are pertinent, the first two of relevance to the question of whether unilateral reality-oriented adaptation to stressors is plausible without disguising some of their most threatening components. Firstly, vulnerability is probably a necessary stage of all developmental skills, from the exposed state of the neonate, to exposure at all later stages to novel stimuli and progressively more complex demands on competency. It is likely that the early findings of Levine (1957, 1962) of the effects on subsequent stress tolerance of stressors applied to young rats have their parallels for the human species. It is plausible to suggest, therefore, that there is no resilience without prior stressor-strain vulnerability. Secondly, the detailed documentation of the behavioural characteristics of the 32 Topeka subjects, none of whom were specially protected from normal as well as unusual stressors, indicates that undefended coping is a quite exceptional state. A fully reality-oriented adaptive strategy of stressor-reduction as implied earlier on is, therefore, equally exceptional unless some of the prerequisites, also cited earlier, apply. The third comment in this context must refer to the high intelligence level of the Topeka sample. Predictions can be derived from definitions of intelligence and from definitions of cognitive and information processing capacity about the availability of alternative and/or substitute goal-directed responses, flexibility in generating these, and the ranges of attention and activity which they might serve. From such considerations we may plausibly infer that serious problems encountered in coping, and the adoption of gross defensive strategies, are generally less likely in the presence of good intelligence. In support we might cite the Terman study of highly gifted children (Terman and Oden, 1959), and epidemiological studies (e.g. Hollingshead and Redlich, 1958). I will return to this issue at a later stage.

Let us now turn to those stressor-strain avoidance and coping strategies where it is not difficult to identify degrees and levels of cognitive-affective disguise, or denial of aversive and distressing stimulus interpretation, and of their implications. These strategies, like others, are learnt on the basis of their experienced effect, and to some extent people can be instructed in techniques that achieve stressor-strain reduction for conflicts which are available for introspection (Meichenbaum, 1977). Moreover, if the state of living always involves exposure to stressors, it is probably correct to argue that stressor-reduction, or coping capacity, has more powerful implications for health, morale, and social functioning than *experience* of stressor-strain itself (Roskies and Lazarus, 1980). The most common technique most people adopt when faced with, for example, important interviews or examinations is to separate the cognitive and social demands of the situation from its aversive, frustration, or conflicting implications for the person. This can take the form of direct self-control and self-instruction, or being primarily affected by external direction to objective features of the situation. These strategies have been described by Mechanic (1962) in relation to student counselling, by Lazarus (1974) in his analysis of the reaction of medical students to a first experience of autopsy, and by Lazarus (1966) and Koriat et al. (1972) in studying the stressor-reducing effects of instructions to be objective and rational while observing and reporting on films depicting infliction of physical injuries. Although the effects of the strategies are limited to specific temporal events, and although actions are controlled by the person himself, they do not prevent a subsequent relinking of task- and affect-related cognitive structures and processes. They transform what Janis and Mann (1977) termed a possibly hypervigilant coping pattern, in which the person is flooded by the probability of aversive consequences, into a vigilant, or reality-oriented pattern.

There is a number of problems with this simplified approach to stressor-strain avoidance which also apply to coping strategies with long-term effects for veridical, reality-oriented adaptation. A process of detachment or separation of task-relevant from task-irrelevant processes requires specification. It is possible to argue that a detaching self-instruction, or an external cue facilitating it, represents a shift in focused attention as a result of having one task in working memory followed by another. This could function like a masking effect in laboratory studies when a second stimulus follows upon a first before this can reach a better consolidated phase in a processing sequence. Since physiological and neurochemical arousal processes are likely to have been activated in the examples cited above, these may directly influence 'cortical recurrent inhibition' (Walley and Weiden, 1973) and thus facilitate the masking effect. The function of stressor-strain avoidance for optimal adaptive capacity, however, is not only the inhibition of superarousing cognitive events, but a reduction of arousal itself. There are one or two lines of evidence that support the orientation I have adapted throughout: that cognitive events will affect arousal and that this is the primary sequence. Studies comparing experienced and novice parachutists have shown that the former show elevated arousal strain at a more distant point, and to a lower level, of preparation for a jump sequence than the latter (Fenz, 1964, 1975; Ursin *et al.*, 1978). This effect of a preparatory set is also shown in a study by Averill *et al.* (1977) in which subjects reported a diminished stress reaction when they utilized a warning signal of an impending electric shock.

Negative feedback between cognition and arousal is important not only for subsequent demands on energy allocation, but because (i) the maintenance of arousal is known to determine the development of the somatic disabilities of anxious and psychosomatic patients, and (ii) maintenance of a high arousal level plays a role in autonomous cognitive work on those conceptual representations which initially stimulated arousal. If Walley and Weiden (1973) were correct in their suggestion of the close relationship between arousal and masking inhibition, this could explain why many anxious patients with somatic symptoms have little or no insight into the sources of their anxieties, and also why a drug-induced Beta-adrenergic blockade of somatic signals has no effect on mainly cognitively anxious patients (Tyrer, 1976). On the other hand, maintenance of arousal by individuals who are sensitive to their own arousal signals, that is 'high autonomic perceivers', provides facilitation for what has been termed the 'incubation phenomenon'. This concept has been advanced to explain the maintenance of phobic thought processes in the absence of exposure to the objects of phobic anxiety (Eysenck, 1968; Borkovec, 1976). Thus, any kind of conscious control to be fully adaptive needs to be paralleled by damping of autonomic and electrocortical arousal. A close examination of the important and seminal coping studies by Lazarus (1966), utilizing a film of subincision initiation rites, shows that subjects classified as denying an aversive reaction to the stimulus had significantly higher skin conductance levels than non-deniers. This indicates (i) that severe forms of control for the reduction of stressor-strain may be ultimately maladaptive, (ii) that denial like other types of inhibition is an energy-demanding process, and (iii) that arousal in denial has similar functions to arousal required for work. It must follow that all forms of stressor-strain avoidance or coping reduce the total information processing capacity of the cognitive system at any phase of a sequence of operations.

The earlier reference to crude jokes, by which some medical students reduce the stressing effect of first exposure to a corpse and the dissecting task, has suggested already that there is an antagonistic relationship between humour and stressor-strain. Physiologically, humour and wit provide a non-aversive outlet and release for an adrenergic tension state which is then experienced as intrinsically pleasurable. In a social context it attracts approval when it is interpreted as reducing a concurrent stress reaction, it adds to the status of the initiator, and provides evidence of group belongingness to those who share in the experience. This shift in the allocation of resources required for stimulus interpretation and response selection relocates the focus of electrocortical arousal processes from structures encoding stressor-strain, to those required for a novel interpretation of strain-reducing stimuli. Novelty here can reside in a high degree of incongruous juxtaposition of stimulus elements, it can be provided by transforming threat into aggressive ridicule not accompanied by anxiety over the response this might elicit, or by creating analogies to the source of threat that temporarily distort and, therefore, diminish its impact.

The capacity to interpret events with humour and wit is clearly a cognitive capacity, a point made lucidly and amusingly by Dixon (1980) in an all-too-brief review. Dixon states quite pertinently, and consistently with the approach adopted here, that the stress reaction consists substantially of an information overload from aversively interpreted stimuli, and that the person seeks stressor-reducing interpretations of the information input in order to gain control over its threatening implication. As he points out, the effect of generating a threat-diminishing interpretation is not unlike Archimedes' 'eureka' experience: the sudden emergence of a satisfying problem solution.

There is little that is controversial in a therapeutic concept of 'a sense of humour' even if its coping effect is only temporary, and in the nature of a diversion. Its strain-relieving and energy relocation effects will minimally buy time in which additional aids to problem resolution may emerge from within or without. On the other hand, modern cognitive processing theory has not yet concerned itself with the analysis in depth of the data base of humour and wit. Recent attention to applied aspects of human memory has provided evidence that humour can have the opposite effects of distraction and of salience in the recall of information and messages (e.g. Chapman and Crompton, 1978) depending on the type of material, its method of presentation, and the degree of intensity with which the intruding humorous message is presented and experienced.

These kinds of findings suggest that the antagonism between stressor-strain and humour must be due in part to an inhibitory effect, either of the retro-active type, or of an arousal-mediated type (e.g. Walley and Weiden, 1973), or of the combination of both types of inhibitors. Such a mechanism facilitates two effects: it reduces the physiological and neurochemical stressor-strain signals, and it stimulates alternative cognitive processes. In combination these effects diminish the cognitive threat element of the stressor, and lower the retrieval threshold of alternative analysing and interpreting conceptual structures. The stressor-reducing capacity of humour requires three further assumptions in order to make the case for its adaptive effects.

(1) Aversive and threatening interpretations of an event must not be so numerous and persistent that they occupy the full quota of capacity available in the cognitive processing system.

(2) Dependent on (1), the *capacity* to construct an incongruous or ridiculous combination of elements must be available.

(3) Previous experience of this strategy for meeting stressor-strain must have been encoded as rewarding and pleasurable.

Points (2) and (3) have a necessary further implication. Incongruous, aggressive, or witty distortions of a threatening object, event, person, or situation require sufficiently elaborated referent-attribute structures in a flexibly organized system of schemata so that attributes can be temporarily transferred to a novel context and a new schema can be established. Gross so-called extravert humour and its common focus on sexual, eliminatory, or aggressive themes, compared with the so-called introvert humour and its cognitively more complex and sophisticated play on words, meanings, and logical bizarreness, tells us something of the difference in cognitive complexity between personality structures generating stressor-strain, as well as those involved in constructing the humorous diverting or distracting tension-releaser.

A brief detour to the possible coping functions of dreams seems justified. There ought to be little disagreement with the statement that dreaming is a cognitive process. It presents sequences, or episodes of events, objects, situations, or people signified either by attributes only, and/or by their interactions, to which the dreamer may or may not attach an affective experience. In the absence of feedback from reality-testing, logical constraints on time sequencing, or internal contradictions, displacements, confabulation and condensations do not have to apply (McKinnon, 1979). Whether any theory of symbolism applied to dream interpretation has any validity is not relevant to the basic statement, but only to propositions about the motivational components, that is goal-directed efforts, of dream content. Since the original observation by Aserinsky and Kleitman (1953) and Dement and Kleitman (1957), the relationship between rapid eye movement during sleep and dreaming has received multiple confirmation, but to explain image or imageless dream as the *result of* occulumotor impulses (Hobson and McCarley, 1977) seems neither plausible nor reasonable. It leaves out of account the predominantly auditory dream imagery of the congenitally blind (Blank, 1958), dreams with primarily conceptual content, or how *meanings and implications* attached to visual dream images in the normally sighted can be generated solely by a motor system. Moreover, an interesting longitudinal study of children's REM dreams extending over the Piagetian pre-operational, transitional, and concrete operational developmental stages suggests that dream frequency, content complexity, self-representation, and the involvement of affect, match the growing conceptual development and integrating capacity subsumed by the stage theory (Foulkes, 1981). Elswhere, Foulkes (1978a, b) argues that since REM dreams are less bizarre than dreams recalled after normal waking, there is likely to be greater continuity between dream thought and waking thought than has been acceptable hitherto. Foulkes offers two further propositions: (i) dreams could be considered to possess 'deep structure' and to be operating to a grammar of rules so that dream image structure reflects a sentence structure; (ii) forgetting of dreams is a cognitive workload phenomenon where the constructions of a dream sequence occur without sufficient space and time and volitional control for working memory rehearsal prior to more permanent storage.

If aversive, distressing implications generated by referent-attribute structures provide the cognitive core of stressor-strain, and if tension-reduction cannot be effected during waking hours, what is the possible contribution of dreaming to coping? As a first comment we recapitulate that the new model regards the motivational features of the stressor-strain response as a conceptual, and therefore cognitive problem-solving task, a position which is echoed by Foulkes (1978b) when referring to motives as representational data. With maintenance of arousal from an unresolved problem there are two extreme outcomes: sleeplessness in which dreaming plays no role, and deep, non-REM sleep through the joint action of fatigue and the possible thought-inhibiting action of arousal on mid-brain sleep centres. Aside from the possibility that sleeplessness will provide the additional time required for problem-solving, we could argue that non-REM sleep provides the cognitive system with the kind of respite which we have associated above with one of the effect of humour.

Turning to dream-sleep we have two possibilities. Dreaming may exacerbate the overload on the system by producing variations and elaborations of functionally related stressful referent-attribute structures. Alternatively, without interference from time pressure, it may continue work on the stressor-strain avoidance problem by symbolically, that is functionally, associated dream events and contents. In relation to the first point there is interesting experimental evidence that REM dream deprivation by waking of patients diagnosed as endogenous depressives has a similar therapeutic effect to medication with the anti-depressant imipramine which also reduces REM sleep (Vogel, 1975; Vogel et al., 1975, 1980). These findings support a suggestion that perseverative preoccupation with stressors even in dreams is counter-productive. It is possible, of course, that this conclusion applies only to REM sleep, to individuals with severe behaviour disorders, depressive psychosis, or only to so-called destructured dreams in which rules of logical connection and sequence are not operating (Foulkes, 1978b).

Repetition compulsion in dreams in which the same aversive themes may recur over many years, is not associated necessarily with behaviour pathology. Moreover, repetition compulsion in thought content in the waking state is capable of contributing to adaptive coping in that it can gradually desensitize the individual until the aversive experience and content can be integrated with appropriate schemata in permanent memory. Experiments by Horowitz (1975, 1976) support this interpretation; he also uses the term 'dosing' to describe such a gradual process. All the evidence for the second alternative, the problem-solving contribution and stressor-reduction effects of dream work, is non-experimental, subjective, or anecdotal. There are no intrinsic difficulties remaining, however, to engage in objective studies in which the cognitive-semantic representational dream content can be related to the conceptual structures of stressor-strain interpretations of waking life, by examining matches between their respective networks of referents and attributes in the context of selected schemata.

In this Section I have deliberately used the term 'avoidance' as a label for the responses following the experience of stressor-strain. This general term provides a conceptual continuum for types of coping strategies varying in degree of acknowledgement of stress-inducing cognitive data. Its behavioural connotation side-steps the element of ambiguity that attaches to 'coping'. Although this concept has been fruitful in the hands of Lazarus (e.g. 1966, 1974), it has some of the features that have been present in the unelaborated use of the term stress. One of its most recent definitions as efforts to manage, tolerate, or minimize demands and conflicts which tax or exceed a person's resources (Lazarus and Launier, 1980), compared with its conception as the consequence of mediating cognitive processes (Folkman *et al.*, 1979), assigns to coping the dual functions of agent and outcome. Our chief concern, however, is with processes that reduce stressor-strain so that it is more useful to regard coping as those processes which facilitate such reduction. Since overt behaviour follows upon cognitive analysis, coping *is* the essential antecedent cognitive processes.

The discussion has so far focused on avoidance strategies which temporarily or more permanently *minimize* stressor-strain while maintaining full awareness of those events, etc. which induce its aversive stimulation. The majority of strategies, however, employ processes which control the experience of aversiveness by a manipulation of the stressor stimuli themselves so that the full impact of certain informational data does not reach the level of actual or potential self-awareness. We have referred already to the principles of processing economy and redundancy which impose their own selective and generalizing strategies on excessive simultaneous stimulus input irrespective of the cognitive-affective nature and implications of the data. I have also discussed earlier (*viz.* Chapter 2) the functions of protective cognitive styles and cognitive control systems by which anxiety-inducing perceptual and conceptual processes are thought to be attenuated. Attenuation can take several forms and it can also vary along a number of independent dimensions. One dimension is the continuum of partial to full avoidance, another can be described as a partial- to full-processing continuum. The first refers to sensory stimulus input control, the second describes the degree of interpretive and labelling analysis applied to the outcome of input control. Interacting dimensions are provided by set or bias – whether stressors are anticipated, or whether they occur without preparatory signals, and whether the person has only one or several sources of stimulation to respond to at any given moment at which the stressor may also occur. Sudden onset of a stressor stimulus while the analysing system is working on the solution of another task, and in the context of a system which is susceptible to this class of stressors may have serious effects. It will leave the person either open to a flood of highly aversive cognitive-affective data, or trigger an avoidance response which will prevent a reanalysis of the stimulus either at the sensory, or at the interpretive, or at the encoding stage, or at all stages.

Although I have previously distinguished between levels of stressor-strain avoidance by referring to either denial or disguise, the latter lies logically and cognitively on a denial-process continuum. A wealth of terminology has been applied to identify this, and to grade the intensity of the process. This attempt has not always succeeded in distinguishing between outcome-defining concepts such as 'self-deception', 'turning away from reality', 'repudiation', or 'disavowal'; and process-related concepts such as 'ignoring', 'distorting', 'rejecting', 'repression', 'misrepresenting', 'splitting' (thought from affect), or 'scotomizing' (sensory inhibition). There is no empirical basis at present for grading or ranking the outcome- or process-defining forms of denial except by the effects of the coping strategies for the person. A coping solution can be defined as *ad hoc* or temporary, or as planful, or long-term. These distinctions appear to be missing from the majority of coping models, although they are major concepts in psycho-analytic theory and its derivatives, all of which emphasize the importance of reality-testing and the positive benefits of objective stimulus analysis. This position has been misinterpreted frequently by the false deduction that *all* stressor-strain denial processes result either in a future heightened level of vulnerability, or lead to pathological forms of behaviour. What matters here, of course, is the level of pre-existing vulnerability as defined by the elaboration and hierarchical position of referent-attribute structures conceptualizing aversiveness for the individual, their availability to self-inspection, and the threshold of associated electrocortical arousal. If this is correct, and if it is possible to force types and levels of denial into an at least nominal scale, then the personal utility of coping and avoidance strategies can be defined. This definition would be in terms of the assimilation and integration of stressor stimuli into functionally appropriate schemata which through restructuring establish informational links with other schemata encoding these strategies themselves *and their effects*. That is, coping must result in changed concepts.

One additional aspect needs to be considered if a denial strategy is to have a durable effect. Denial of stressor-strain-inducing stimulation proceeds not only on the basis of existing identifiers which supply knowledge of its aversive meaning, but also under the influence of the goal-directed denial operation itself. To prevent future exposure to stimulus meaning *and* its denial, the content of both operations needs to be classified as unwanted because of its aversiveness, and to be encoded appropriately. This is likely to be achieved by attaching non-processing 'instructions' to its classification. A 'safe' form of denial, therefore, requires this as well as disguising, distorting, negating or defocusing processes which may be termed the information restructuring strategies and operations of the internal stimulus analysing system. These are indexed as I_{RSOi} in Figure 9.3 which schematizes the required activities.

My analysis here differs from the cognitive control process analysis presented by Erdelyi (1974) in two important respects. Firstly, as argued before,

$$I_{RSO_i} = \left(\begin{array}{c} \text{Distorted} \\ \text{Recognition} \end{array} \xrightarrow[\text{OR}]{\text{AND}} \text{Negation} \xrightarrow[\text{OR}]{\text{AND}} \begin{array}{c} \text{Selective} \\ \text{Recognition} \end{array} \xrightarrow[\text{OR}]{\text{AND}} \begin{array}{c} \text{Retrieval of} \\ \text{Substitute} \\ \text{Structures} \end{array} \right)$$

$$+$$

NON–PROCESSING 'INSTRUCTIONS'

Figure 9.3 Hypothetical processes operating in denial of stimulus meaning

selective attention is neither an executive controlling process nor the main determinant of a repressor type of cognitive control. This last function belongs to the response strategies already encoded in permanent memory. Secondly, I have argued that the identification of a stressor cannot occur without matches between a stimulus and its representational data retrieved from permanent memory, that is, the same system that decides whether the stressor-strain impact is tolerable with a given level of vulnerability. Whereas Erdelyi has suggested that the interruption of working memory processes by a denial strategy prevents rehearsal of what is in short-term storage and thus prevents storage in permanent memory, my preceding discussion must regard this suggestion as implausible. In the first place, I have drawn attention already to data which show that denial need not lead to a reduction of arousal. Since arousal must have a cognitive focus either as an antecedent or as an effect, and since the chain of events started with the recognition of a stressor stimulus, it is more reasonable to suppose that arousal associated with denial is due to continuing cognitive work on the stressor-strain-inducing stimulus. A further difference from Erdelyi's view of the nature of the denying processes concerns the proposition that the retrieval of non-processing 'instructions' by attentional scanning at the behest of a task in working memory has no subsequent effects on the conceptual structures of which these instructions form a part. A non-processing 'instruction' should be conceived as an attribute, and like other principal attributes it may be weakened or strengthened by events that stimulate it. To expose an adaptation-and/or protection-seeking system to information which might grossly destabilize it, is like forcing a non-swimmer afraid of the water into it, or like abandoning a phobic patient in the centre of town during the rush hour. The psycho-dynamic conception of the effects of such exposure are more reasonable here than the hypothesized effects of behaviour-therapeutic flooding. Controls threatened by attack will tighten and recruit further controls, so that dangers of a break in a denial defence are likely to be met by additional defensive work. This work, however, must be confined to restructuring processes in permanent memory – that component of the system which stores the expectancies which define vulnerability.

An additional consideration and its role for different levels and degrees of stressor-denial requires some illumination. I am referring here to stages and foci of stimulus analysis. As Breznitz (1982) has pointed out, denial may be a sequential series of operations where each step tests whether a given system needs to apply it, rather than a single avoidance operation. For example, if stimulus-analysing processes signal the presence of threatening information, the restructuring operations of denial could start by testing whether the information is actually present. They would then test whether it is threatening; whether it has personal relevance for the receiver; whether the threat is immediate; whether its aversive implications are justified; and whether the receiver is vulnerable to, or can cope with this potentially threatening information. This analysis is similar to the appraisal-reappraisal sequences which are central to the coping processes as conceived by Lazarus.

In the context of a cognitive-semantic model of personality and motivation, however, this approach has more complex implications. In the first instance, each step, apart from the first which attempts to disconfirm the presence of external signals, requires an analysis of stimulus meaning. Meaning responses are extracted by a search process from existing representational data banks consisting of referent-attribute structures. Since their content and implications are relevant to the task data held in working memory, this task is amplified and thereby increased. This is an incremental process since each of the above testing steps, if confirmed, adds potentially aversive information to the task held in working memory. Simultaneously, however, superordinate cognitive structures encoding the characteristics of a subjectively required state of experience and behaviour outcome contribute their own task demands with their focus on stressor-strain reduction and/or avoidance. Denial-oriented restructuring strategies and operations begin when a match between stimulus characteristics and retrieved identifying attributes signifies aversive behaviour outcomes. Depending on the hierarchical dominance of these structures – determined by the severity and elaboration of attributes possessing aversive notation – defocusing, disguising, distorting, or rejecting operations will commence at an early, or at a later stage of input analysis. The later the stage, the more difficult the task of preventing threatening information from affecting all aspects of cognitive processing. In that event, the greater the vulnerability to its implications, the greater the likelihood that the processing system, personal awareness, and decision-making will

260

acquire, and be swamped by, the aversive and distressing cognitive-affective data of anxiety, anger, frustration, unresolved conflict, etc. If tests for aversive personal implications and vulnerability have acquired high priority in an analysing sequence – the hallmark of a person susceptible to stressor – or if the stressors consist of information signalling extreme danger to any member of the species, denial defined as 'refusal to acknowledge', 'disowning', 'disavowal', or 'repression' is likely to operate. As suggested before, however, this strategy does not imply that aversive information has been prevented from entering the permanent memory system, or that this system is prevented from carrying out further operations on it.

The difference between levels of denial and its processing stages at which any of its variants begin to operate can be illustrated by comparing results from psychological laboratory studies which conform to ethical standards, with results from studies investigating the effects of actual serious physical illness. In Allport and Postman's (1948) studies of rumour, we find one of its distortion components in experiments on high and low prejudiced white subjects. One procedure involved the description from memory of the scene reproduced in Figure 9.4, and its serial reproduction from one subject to another within these criterion groups. The results showed that the high

Figure 9.4 Test picture for investigation of perception and memory in prejudice. From The Psychology of Rumor by Gordon Allport and Leo Postman. Copyright 1947 by Henry Holt and Company, Inc. Renewal © 1975 by Holt, Rinehart and Winston. Reprinted by permission of Holt, Rinehart and Winston, CBS College Publishing

prejudiced subjects displaced aggressive and personally demeaning features from the white on to the black man in the picture. There was no denial here of threatening information *per se*, nor of its cognitive-affective aversive implications. Vulnerability to the dissonance and incongruity between task and beliefs must have been high, however, in order to bring stimulus interpretation into line with pre-conception, but not high enough to deny its aggressive aspects. Dixon's experiments which were mentioned before (Dixon, 1958, 1971; Dixon and Haider, 1961), on the other hand, show the operation of the most powerful strategy: of denying by refusing to acknowledge the presence of information *per se*. Findings that the presentation of *unacknowledged* threatening stimuli to one eye can affect luminosity thresholds for the other eye in stereoscopic vision, moreover, are evidence that stimulus analysis and its resulting interpretation is continuing with permanent memory participation.

An intermediate position in the level and focus of denial is occupied by the original tachistoscopic experiments on sensitization vs. repressor recognition strategies (e.g. Bruner and Postman, 1947 and many others). In a hypothetical example given elsewhere (Hamilton, 1982), I have tried to show how the presentation of the word 'failure' to a test- and examination-anxious subject can result in a perceptual response of *'feature'*. In this example, there is incomplete denial of the phonemic and graphemic characteristics of the threatening stimulus. There is sufficient distortion, however, in support of the need to deny personal affective relevance and vulnerability to it. Psycho-dynamic theorists might conclude that the partial recognition of word structure is evidence of so-called 'leakage' (Spence, 1982) or of a 'sliding' distortion (Horowitz, 1979).

Most interesting results have been obtained in studies with cardiac patients. These suggest that denial need not have long-term unfavourable consequences for adaptation and the overall integrity of the individual, either as implied by psycho-dynamic theories of the development of neurosis and psychosis, or by physiological models of the development of psychosomatic disorders. Follow-up of patients who had suffered coronary thrombosis produced evidence that as many as 20 per cent denied that they had had a heart attack (Hackett *et al.*, 1968; Croog *et al.*, 1971; Hackett and Cassem, 1974), and that high deniers had a greater chance of survival after intensive care. Hackett *et al.* defined high denial as patients' unequivocal statements that they had not been anxious at any time during their stay in hospital, or in any earlier period of their lives. What seemed to be important was not a temporary state, but an integrated and internally consistent pattern of minimizing or rejecting information which would mediate aversive stressor-strain. Their approach to the possibility of death was hearty and fatalistically accepting, they displaced fear of death on to others, and showed a history of risk-taking, somewhat reckless adventure, and of a strong and invulnerable self-concept. Such data suggest that the cognitive processing systems of such patients does not have to work constantly on anxiety-denoting associations with low thresholds for accessibility and retrieval from permanent memory, or to be stimulated into decision-making and conflict-solving operations on all the issues arising from a serious illness. The major mediator of superior resilience to physical deterioration, all other matters being equal, may be the self-controlled level of cardiovascular activity of this type of person. Lacey's studies (e.g. Lacey, 1967; Lacey and Lacey, 1958) have presented reliable evidence that attention, particularly to arousing stimuli, produces cardiac deceleration, whereas problem-solving is associated with cardiac acceleration. It is likely that in the absence of prolonged periods of preoccupation with the implications of illness and/or death, there will be fewer shifts per hour between deceleration and acceleration so that more resources can be devoted to the healing of heart damage with better facilitation for the action of medication.

While the recovering cardiac patients appear to deny the cognitive-affective relevance of information, its aversiveness and their vulnerability to it, the studies were not designed to elucidate the presence of these cognitive factors. Equally interesting experimental studies on patients with a positively identified cancer were concerned to show that denial is never complete, and that the effects of denied aversive information may nevertheless suggest that its implications have been correctly identified. In a study by Schmale and Iker (1966) some 60 women at risk for cervical cancer entering hospital were interviewed prior to biopsy with the double-blind method. The hypothesis was that a positive diagnosis following biopsy would be associated with a high rating score on a scale of 'hopelessness'. Hopelessness was defined by such criteria as: depressive mood in various settings; social interests and attitudes yielding little evidence of enjoyment of success; and mismatch between achievement and response to it. More than 70 per cent of the sample were correctly diagnosed for cancer as positive or negative on the hopelessness ratings alone – a statistically highly reliable finding. The most plausible explanation of this result must be that at some level of analysis the confirmed patients must have processed information, that is symptoms, that was more likely to be consistent than inconsistent with a disease process, and with interpretations of that information which induced the moods and attitudes elicited in interview.

A more recent study by Spence et al. (Spence, 1982) adopted a more analytic approach to the association between denial and a disease process. They postulated that derivatives of a cancer process might appear in 'lexical leakage': the balance between words signifying hope and words signifying hopelessness. Analysing the language of women at risk for cervical cancer, Spence et al. found that positively diagnosed patients tended to use a more extensive lexicon of words signifying hopelessness according to a criterion list of words produced by actual terminal cancer patients, than patients with negative biopsy results. Subdividing subjects into deniers and concerned patients, and dividing the words used by patients at interview into those related to cancer and those which were not (a task carried out by independent raters), the investigators established that the use of cancer 'marker' words was significantly more common for the less defended group than for the deniers. Moreover, positively identified cancer patients using denial defences show a dominance of unrelated words, which tend to dilute or disguise the implications of lexical terms which otherwise predominate in positively diagnosed patients. Spence suggests somewhat speculatively, but plausibly, that deniers diminish the impact of signifiers of aversiveness by separating lexical terms which in the context of the same sentence would supply the very meaning against which the denier erects a defence.

The relevance of this study for the model I am presenting is fairly clear. Denial at any level is concerned with the avoidance of aversive meaning and the knowledge derived from it. Meaning and knowledge reside in concepts of objects, events, situations, issues, of other people, and of oneself, which supply a system of referents defining our life space. The implications and subjectively experienced characteristics of each referent define its functional role for all adaptive, decision-making, and evaluative responses. This role is prescribed by constellations of attributes which signify the effects to which preceding interactions with referents have led. Whether these effects are objective and match the experience of others, or whether they are subjective and idiosyncratic, does not affect the method or notation by which the effects are stored in permanent memory. If actual or anticipated experiences can be verbalized then lexical and semantic symbols must represent these experiences and their referent-attribute structures. And it is more plausible and economic to conceptualize a direct link between signifiers and the concept specification which they serve, than to regard their verbal expression as the result of a secondary, intervening process of translating non-verbal symbolization into semantic form. The greater the anxiety associated with pain, illness, disfigurement, sexual enjoyment, or death, the higher the probability that cognitive-semantic structures encoding these event-outcomes will be activated, and the higher the probability that they will intrude and participate in conflict-solving processes.

Stressor-strain arising from self-knowledge and/or a medical verdict of terminal illness, or other evidence that personal extinction through violent assault, or a nuclear war, is highly probable or imminent, makes the ultimate demands on avoidance and coping capacities. By definition, it is unlikely that this level of adaptation will be required more than once in a lifetime of the majority of individuals. Even this contingency, however, will be met with differential strain reduction depending on the presence of conceptual structures which can minimize, attenuate, or overcome the implications of ultimate aversive attributional signifiers. Their effectiveness may not facilitate survival, but they can make the prospect of death acceptable. This again requires an organization of stimulus-identifying and response-generating schemata that is optimally cross-referencing, and continues to possess sufficient flexibility to undertake the required restructuring strategies and operations. Consequently, an optimal level of adaptation – defined by the

264

absence of panic, uncontrollable anger, depression to the point of immobility, or incongruous substitute activities – requires interactions and integrations between aversive and non-aversive representational conceptual structures. The cognitive aspects of stressor-strain avoidance or coping can be defined most comprehensively, therefore, by the relationship between three factors: restructuring capacity, the level of elaboration and thus dominance of aversiveness-signifying referent-attribute structures, and the probability of an event occurring whose aversive implications are accessible and/or retrievable from storage. This relationship is sketched in Figure 9.5. Each three-dimensional configuration shows the relationship between stressor-strain avoidance,

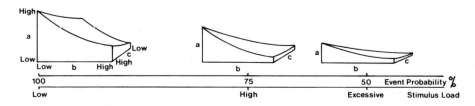

a   Coping capacity
b   Stressor attributes
c   Restructuring and integrating capacity

Figure 9.5 Cognitive factors determining coping with stressor-strain

or coping capacity (a) and schematic integrating and restructuring capacity *(c)*; the relationship between coping *(a)* and the space- and time-occupying cognitive structures encoding the elaborated stressor-identifying attributes *(b)*; and thirdly, the effect on coping *(a)* of the interaction between integrating and restructuring capacity *(c)* and the size and dominance of stressor-identifying structures (b). In the light of the foregoing discussion, it is further proposed that this group of relationships is subject to the stressor-effects arising from the number of simultaneous stimuli requiring adaptive responding, and to the probability level of occurrence of stimulation. The influence of these variables on stressor-strain control is diagrammed by horizontal displacement and the progressive reduction of dimension (a) – coping capacity. Since event probability and degree of simultaneous stimulation are independent, complete graphical representation really requires all relationships to be conceived in a three-dimensional field which for the sake of clarity has been omitted. As far as I can judge it, this generalization of coping processes can accommodate all the factors previously cited as cognitive mediators of stressor-strain, the coping facilities of humour, dreaming, partial disguise, full denial, as well as the pressures from stimulus ambiguity, simultaneous tasks, and event uncertainty. It would not be surprising, however, if important consideration had been omitted in this first attempt to treat coping with stressor-vulnerability as cognitive-semantic processing events.

To conclude this section I have constructed a hypothetical semantic network of referents and attributes. This illustrates how an integrated system of event-related schemata could achieve an adaptive coping state following the experience of a bereavement in a time span and in a manner which would exclude the possibility of labelling it abnormal. The system of depressive and alternative semantic network structures shown in Figure 9.6 has been limited by considerations of space to a selection of referent-attribute structures and superordinate schemata. Depressing referents are assumed to have been elicited by asking a depressed woman whose husband has died recently to list the objects, events, situations, issues, or persons which signify the foci of depression. Taking one referent at a time the hypothetical enquiry would try to elicit those attributes which determine the depressing label of each referent. This procedure was adopted in the actual studies illustrated in Figures 6.9 to 6.12 which compared the semantic network structures of high and low anxious and high and low angry subjects. The hypothetical structures of depression have been elaborated in Figure 9.6 in two ways. Firstly, it is assumed that a further enquiry has been conducted with the subject or patient to elicit what Beck (1976) called alternative views of the depressing referents, by asking if any aspects of the original referents were less or non-depressing. These hypothetical alternatives are listed to the right of Figure 9.6. The second elaboration compared with the analyses made in Chapter 6 shows the interaction between schematic attribute structures encoding vulnerability and their alternatives representing adaptive structures. Adaptation will be mediated by the restructuring strategies and operations applied to low threshold depressing structures through the addition of positively experienced stimuli, and the goals and goal-achieving outcomes which they represent. These, however, are at variance with the restrictions on behaviour mediated by the referent-attribute data signifying grief. Some of these, like the experience of 'Nights' in the given example, will have no alternative attributes available for some time. The restructuring strategies and operations required for grief-avoidance and coping may be any or all of those cited in the preceding discussion and in Figure 9.3. Adaptive coping is predicated in the hypothetical example by the availability in permanent memory of conceptual identifying experiences and attitudes in respect of children, work, and previously underutilized interests. It is the presence of such alternative, competing, and attenuating referent-attribute structures which is most likely to supply the sufficiency criterion for the absence of pathological solutions and outcomes, and consequently for coping.

4 PATHOLOGICAL STRUCTURES AND PROCESSES

I will confine myself to two limited aims: the plausibility of applying the semantic network concept to the development of some neurotic and psychotic cognitive structures, and reference to one set of mechanisms by which the probability of a long-term adaptive cognitive structuring process changes into

266

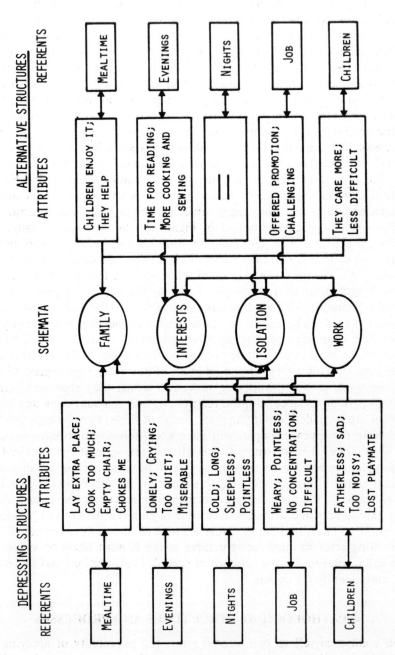

Figure 9.6 Hypothetical semantic network structures in adaptation to bereavement

the high probability of a maladaptive and potentially pathological process. An extensive treatment of theories of the development of behavioural abnormality is not only precluded by the more general object of this book, but I have also presented fairly recently reviews and cognitive interpretations of the major explanatory dimensions shared by most current models (Hamilton, 1976b, 1979b). These interpretations took two directions. They defined anxiety-based neuroses as the presence and low threshold of excessively elaborated cognitive structures encoding aversive and threatening information. Psychosis, by reference to its dominant category of the schizophrenias, was defined by the dominance of weak conceptual structures, in the presence of anxiety-signifying attribute assemblies, and information overload effects arising from a combination of poorly differentiated, unintegrated concepts together with processing precedence applied to subjectively aversive information and its avoidance.

Anxiety-based neurosis pre-supposes the presence of vulnerable, stressor-sensitive schemata, that is, schemata encoding what I have previously termed residual conflicts in the experience areas of physical danger, social isolation, or performance competence. In terms of the cognitive-semantic structure model, this proposition implies that neurosis (as well as psychosis) is the outcome of an incremental process rather than the result of 'single-trial', traumatic negative reinforcement. In a state of generalized anxiety with its multiple foci, aversively experienced conceptual information is mediated by an increase in the number of aversion-signifying attribute labels attached to an increasing number of referents. This process need not be determined by action or contact in the external environment – symbolic operations involving self-generated expectancies or goal-directed behaviour are sufficient. All that is needed is a stress hormone system with low action thresholds and low inhibitory capacity, and the reverberation of one major residual conflict impervious to coping solutions. Interactions between these factors favours the operation of two self-fulfilling prophecies.

(1) External reality-testing is avoided because this would lead to the retrieval of aversive response anticipation – consequently conceptual structures cannot be modified.
(2) Attempts to falsify aversive anticipations of behaviour outcome by reality-testing are vitiated by concurrent response characteristics such as timidity, lack of confidence, tenuousness, or confusion from competing thoughts and goals.

Each of these factors, if sufficiently intense, will lead to additional awareness of physical stressor-strain signals such as tachicardia, chest pains, sleeplessness, headaches, etc. which will become threateningly and dangerously interpreted in their own right. Clinical evidence supports this cognitive interpretation of anxiety neuroses in most respects (e.g. Beck *et al.*, 1974; Beck and Rush, 1975). The spread of anxiety to a wide variety of stimulus classes and the breadth of stimuli within classes to which it becomes attached is reflected in the high scores of such patients on appropriate questionnaires such as the Manifest Anxiety Scale. Without aversively coded referent-attribute structures, in which aversiveness is semantically labelled, neither clinical nor questionnaire evidence could be properly provided.

When anxiety is focused exclusively on the avoidance of a single class of objects, an event, situation, or person, we refer to it as phobic anxiety, and to the behaviour restriction as a phobia, particularly if inadequate and implausible justifications are given for its presence by the patient. This last conceptual refinement is a logical requirement in order to distinguish, say, between a plausible fear of snakebite in open heathland and making a detour to avoid stressor-strain from the probability of that event, and an agoraphobic condition in which the person refuses to leave his home *in the town* to reduce this threatening expectancy. The former anxiety is reasonable, the latter is not. Thus, desensitization therapies applied to so-called snake-phobias – a reasonable expression of phylogenetic aversion – are misleadingly labelled (e.g. Bandura *et al.*, 1969). In the majority of *clinical cases* no rational explanations can be offered for the extreme avoidance behaviour; patients agree that their behaviour may be irrational, and they cannot account for its presence. Psycho-dynamic and S-R theories have agreed, albeit by citing different mechanisms and processes, that stimulus substitution has occurred by referring, respectively, to protective displacement, or to conditioned stimulus generalization. In many instances the external focusing of anxiety is paralleled by evidence of so-called secondary gain – the achievement of other preferred states or goals.

Where the source or sources of aversive expectancy are disguised or denied, the cognitive-semantic model assumes that restructuring operations and strategies have been applied to conceptual schemata and linkages between them. If severe anxiety was unaccountably experienced on the way to work, stimuli associated with the journey are likely candidates for aversive attribute labelling if the significant stimulus was an internal one with a 'non-processing' attribute briefly accessed in permanent memory, and immediately rejected. Many available case histories indicate that the onset of a phobia is not sudden, although it may progress rapidly. This suggests that the restructuring operations applied to schema content, and associations between schemata, have an incremental effect in which exposure to the original stimulus setting plays no role because restriction of movement prevents further contact with it. Under the influence of the basic source of aversive expectancy, we might almost say that the affected person thinks himself into a phobia, where the phobic stimulus becomes the referent which receives the attribute specifiers of the unacknowledged source. What Eysenck (1976a) termed an enhancement or incubation effect in the maintenance of a phobia without further exposure to the unconditioned stimulus, therefore, cannot be just an arousal-driven strengthening of an S–R bond. It is a problem-solving operation in which the person searches for a coping solution to inescapable knowledge of threat and danger.

The critics of psycho-analytic explanatory concepts may well be correct that the focus of danger need not be associated with sexual or aggressive conflicts. I have at least one example from my own earlier clinical experience, however, that is consistent with a Freudian-type model. An agoraphobic of 10-years standing, a skilled craftsman without any impairment of high average intelligence and general behavioural competence, was entered into a desensitization programme. All other therapies had failed, and the new technique was at that time receiving enthusiastic support from theorists and practitioners for whom unreportable, unconscious, and ostensibly untestable processes were anathema. After 10 weeks of progress to unaccompanied long journeys on the Underground, to the marital home, and to a place of work for imminent employment, the patient had to be informed that his therapist was leaving. The next journey by car with the patient elicited a severe panic attack in which he threatened to jump out irrespective of heavy traffic, and, when this was prevented for obvious reasons, burst into uncontrollable sobs. The first-ever direct question of why he was so afraid was then put. He replied explosively that he was afraid of sexually assaulting young girls. There was no case history record of this motivation, and for the reasons already mentioned, there was no opportunity to follow-up in therapy the implications of this new evidence. I gather that he was discharged from hospital, however, some years later.

An anecdote does not constitute a theory but a collection of matching observations provides an acceptable basis for testing its plausibility. The moral of this particular story is clear: an S–R model of sympton development is untenable without reference to facilitating cognitive processes operating on referent-attribute structures and those functional associations which encode susceptibility to stressor-strain.

I will comment only briefly on the implications of this proposition for obsessive-compulsive and hysteric neuroses. The ruminations and high-intensity rituals of obsessive-compulsive patients provide particularly telling evidence of the elaboration of anxiety-defining aversive referent-attribute structures. In this context it is unlikely that the association between the generally higher intelligence of this neurotic subgroup and its dominant behavioural abnormalities is fortuitous. In the absence of a well-differentiated system of cognitive structures, their principal concepts, and their constellation of attributes, there would be no basis for these patients' fine-grained specifications, elaborations, and rationalizations of action and thinking routines. Since their experience of aversiveness has no external focus, it cannot be avoided. Its effects can be reduced only temporarily by symptomatic behaviour. The probable reason for this is that sets of parallel cognitive structures encode both the basic irrelevance of the coping strategy, and, at some level of accessibility, memory structures holding those representational data from which the *knowledge* of irrelevance is obtained. Self-knowledge of irrelevance is further indicated by the well-documented perseveration, intrusiveness, and severity of the most common coping attempts. If psycho-analytic theory is correct that the coping strategies of this group of disorders include the separation between the physical-objective features of the principal source of anxiety, and memory of its associated affect ('splitting'), as well as the capacity to transform one particular goal and its outcome into one that is mutual exclusive ('reaction-formation'), then the obsessive-compulsive neurotic is not only fundamentally the most anxious, but also exhibits the most (unsuccessfully) severe defences against stressor-strain.

By comparison, the histrionic, attention-demanding, explosive hysteric personality has a less complicated coping system, and relatively focused concepts of anxiety. Again, however, the chosen coping strategy is relatively counter-productive, since the preferred behaviour elicits responses of withdrawal, aversion, and rejection in others. The condition develops on the basis of an inability to recognize that the sources of anxiety – the probability of social isolation, degree of experienced insecurity and of being unloved – have acquired excessively aversive attribute structures. Coping, by denying the requirement of *unrealistic* levels of support and reassurance, prevents identification of available cues that indicate that social props are available, albeit not to the degree to which the idealized concepts demand it. That is, selectively processed attributes do not match those stored in referent-attribute structures.

Conversion hysteria, with the exception of fugue and other dissociate states which are often subsumed under this category, occurs most frequently in association with average and below average intelligence. This provides *a priori* grounds for the prediction that stressor-strain avoidance strategies and operations are likely to be more limited by virtue of less finely differentiated conceptual structures, fewer concepts with a smaller number of semantic defining attributes, and reduced ability for cross-referencing between schematic organizations. It is plausible, therefore, to regard the physical expression of denial of anxiety and conflict by sensory and motor symptoms as the most naturally available defence where cognitive restructuring capacities are low. In those cases in which any evidence of anxiety is absent (*belle indifference*), the degree of secondary gain accepted and demanded is likely to be in proportion to the unacknowledged need to avoid aversive self-knowledge. More commonly, however, anxiety is freely expressed in relation to the disabling physical features and their implications for a normal life. Again, however, the verbalizations are conceptually relatively gross, and thus a reflection of undifferentiated memory representations. Some fairly recent experimental findings (Bendefeldt et al., 1976) provide support for observational clinical evidence that conversion hysterics have difficulty in maintaining vigilance and focused attention. This can only mean that these patients' processing system is engaged on other tasks. Bendefeldt's experiments confirmed that as a group conversion hysterics exhibit greater short-term memory incapacity compared with other neurotic subgroups, which became enhanced when testing took place under stressing conditions. This rather sparse evidence suggests nevertheless that this type of patient employs a level of denial which requires continuing strengthening by preoccupation with other, task-irrelevant stimuli.

A considerable degree of intellectual enthusiasm has been generated by Seligman's studies and theorizing on what he and his associates have termed 'learned helplessness' (e.g. Seligman, 1975; Miller and Seligman, 1975; Maier and Seligman, 1976; Miller et al., 1977). Although there have been some critical reappraisals of this concept and its theoretical elaboration (Abramson et al., 1978) some additional points could be usefully added. The basic statement is that reinforcement and responding are experienced as non-contingent or independent. This ignored the fact that one-third of the dogs in Seligman's (1968) original experiment did escape from shock, and that fundamentally the experiment can be classified as a conflict experiment. Insoluble conflict, however, frequently has been shown to lead to either non-responding (e.g. Maier, 1956), or to oscillating behaviour (Miller, 1948). Moreover, the experimental paradigm is closely similar to so-called 'frustrative non-reward' for which Gray (1981) has proposed a complex physiological theory of *anxiety*. Another example that does not fit the theory can be observed in the study by Miller and Seligman (1975) on students scoring respectively low and high on Beck's Depression Inventory. High-scoring *control subjects* not submitted to either escapable or non-escapable noise performed worse in an anagram task than any other group in any pre-treatment condition. This must suggest that an inescapable aversive intrusion can have facilitating effects. I have mentioned before that this possibility was suggested by Foulds (1952, 1956) many years ago, and that the most plausible reason for long response latency and poor performance in depressives needs to be sought in preoccupation with task-irrelevant, rather than relevant cognitive processes (see also Hamilton, 1982c).

Although learned helplessness is considered as a negative cognitive set variable (Miller et al., 1977), it limits the set to an *outcome* of experiences of helplessness or hopelessness *rather than to the wide variety of antecedents* of this expectancy. In the absence of in-depth considerations of what is meant by depression this is not surprising. The experience of loss, and the overt grief responses in the example of adaptive coping discussed above, need have no relationship with a non-contingent relationship between behaviour and outcome. The majority of people faced with the high probability of bereavement are fully aware that they can have no possible influence on the course of a terminal illness. In order for an experience of loss or severe disappointment to become transformed into a clinical reactive depression syndrome, hopelessness, helplessness, and self-concepts of incompetence must have been present before in cognitive structures which have incrementally encoded demotivating attributes defining these experiences. In psychotic depression, the self-attribution of worthlessness, and reproach, represent an incongruent and somewhat impervious generalization of existing referent-attribute structures. Although it is true that this outcome is due to a cognitive learning process, and that feeling helpless is one of its features, there is no parallel here between depression and Seligman's concept. In the absence of a full consideration of the cognitive content of overt depressive behaviour to which Freud (1917) contributed a far-reaching analysis, the theoretical link between depression and learned helplessness seems to be based largely on semantic affinities and analogies.

Let me turn briefly to a consideration of the cognitive structures of a paranoid psychosis. Clinical discussions tend to concentrate on descriptions of delusions and hallucinations, usually with somewhat vague reference to developmental precursors, and with often no more than paying lip-service to a defensive mechanism of projection. A notable exception is Cameron's conceptualization of the paranoid's pseudo-community (Cameron, 1951; 1959): a system of cognitive structures by which the patient attempts to reconcile social reality with his own internal interpretations of its features. Cameron's precursors of paranoid cognitive structures and the behaviour which they generate are: deficient social learning and social skills reflected in difficulties of applying valid attributes to the motives, attitudes, and intentions of others; anxiety, anger, frustration, and conflict resulting from these difficulties; withdrawal from optimal reality testing; preoccupation with developmentally primitive goals and goal-conflicts; and predispositions to employ denial and projection defences. A perceived mismatch between reality and phantasy experiences, according to Cameron, leads to feelings of estrangement, hyper-vigilance to find associative links between incongruent experiences, increased self-reference, and, via the testing of explanations of incongruity, to delusional cognitive structures.

Applying the cognitive-semantic model, it can be inferred that the dominant cognitive restructuring strategies and operations here involve the transposition of aversive and aggressive attributes from self-concept referents to the referent structures signifying other people and/or external situations. I would argue that this reorganization of schemata content identifies the processes of a projection defence. This process and its validity are difficult to demonstrate experimentally (Kline, 1972), and studies which have attempted it, have failed to do so (Holmes, 1978). Holmes' rejection of the concept of projection, however, is subject to the same criticisms which I have previously applied to experimental studies of repression. Unless a subject is predisposed by excessively elaborated aversive expectancies which functionally match the theoretical antecedents of projective defence, and unless independent criteria of projection are applied, the concept and process cannot be said to have been validly tested.

Projected aggression is an insufficient explanation of paranoia, however, since it does not immediately account for the second major sign, megalomania, nor for repressed homosexuality. Colby's (1975) concepts of the role of antecedent cognitive structures of humiliation provide one method of linking the delusions of power and those of projected aggression. Humiliations and lowered self-esteem are experienced when there is a mismatch between an ideal self-concept and evidence from reality-testing. This may occur when a young child identifies strongly with the same-sex parent and then receives evidence from his goal-directed behaviour outcomes that he cannot produce adult role-playing competence. If ideal self-concepts of incompetence are narrowly defined but highly elaborated, anxiety, anger, frustration, shame, and conflict may be the result. Since this information is equally unacceptable, and particularly if the result of perceived incompetence is experienced as even more aversive, comprehensive denial processes will be searched for.

Since paranoids as a group are commonly of above average intelligence, facilities for major concept restructuring strategies and operations are available. At least two variations can be identified. The first takes the form of a homosexual type of solution, by making an excessive loving attachment to the same-sex parent. To the extent that this minimizes subsequent stimulation by anxiety, anger, etc. from same-sex parental competence and power, this restructuring process is not unlike the defence of 'identifying with the aggressor'. If this transformation, with progressive social learning, becomes conflicting a second restructuring phase, initiated by guilt and shame, will turn this love into hate as being a more comprehensive solution to experience of stressor-strain from this source.

The second variant is almost entirely self-concept directed. The misleading interpretations which signify incompetence to the vulnerable individual need not only be transformed into attributing the blame for shortcomings to another person who then becomes the rightful recipient of anger and aggression. This was argued by Colby (1975), and as a process was transcribed into a computer program by Faught et al. (1977). Social withdrawal, which amounts to cutting-off or reducing corrective information feedback, may in fact be the simplest and most natural avoidance strategy. In this event, the original favourable self-concept of competence can be elaborated and strengthened without external interference. A reaction-formation-type of defence will transform referent-attribute structures of shame, guilt, and humiliation into structures signifying personal power and superiority. When in the process of adult role-playing demands evidence of incongruity between self-concepts and social reality can be successfully denied no longer, extreme falsification of information, that is delusional megolomanic restructuring, will be strengthened. This process is not unlike Alfred Adler's overcompensation syndrome, which, however, excludes fewer aspects of reality. Because of the larger number of restructuring phases and the multiple avoidance processes megalomania is not only the most severe paranoid state, but it is unlikely to occur without a considerable spread of effect to many behavioural areas and their demands for rational interpretation. It is also worth noting that the conceptual transformations just described are doubly projective: first – projecting power and aggression on to another person or persons, and reinternalizing those same characteristics into self-concepts; and second – projecting anxiety, guilt, and humiliation on to external objects because they are now incongruent with the newly acquired grandiose self-concept.

A hypothetical example of the objects of paranoia, their conceptual signifiers, their antecedent self-attributes, and the transformation of referent-attribute structures in searching for a coping solution, is illustrated in Figure 9.7. This shows possible semantic network structures for the two major variants of paranoia: persecutory and grandiose. The left side of Figure 9.7 presents hypothetical structures in which antecedent stressor-strain conceptualizations are encoded. The paranoid 'solution' structures are such as might be elicited in a clinical interview, or by interaction with the referents cited here as examples, or, following hospitalization, in interaction with nursing staff, or other patients. No special claim is made for the exclusiveness or sufficiency of the example. The main purpose is to indicate that conceptualization of self, of others, and of planning strategies of behaviour with preferred goal-outcomes, requires conceptual notation from which implications, meanings, and expectancies can be derived. The present example is concerned with those concept identifiers which as antecedents and as responses to them generate a high intensity level of stressor-strain and of vulnerability.

The last issue to which I wish to redirect attention concerns the processes and mechanisms by which the core or prototypical label of a concept is changed. This issue is not addressed directly in concept formation studies generally, nor does it appear to have been considered in situations in which the label of a conceptual core changes into its opposite. That this process occurs is a corollary, however, of a cognitive-semantic model of personality and motivation, in that a change of meaning labels is required to describe behavioural change. A number of examples can be listed.

(1) A change from approach to avoidance behaviour as in a phobia.
(2) The reaction-formation component of an obsessive-compulsive cognitive structure in which, say, obsequiousness becomes a substitute for domination.
(3) Severe depression when a loving and supportive person is responded to as if he or she were incapable of offering these characteristics.
(4) The hypothetical case of paranoia above in which the anticipation of attack or the delusional implications of power become substitutes for anxiety, frustration, shame, etc. associated with the same referents.

Where conceptual prototype labels signifying behaviour change into mutually exclusive lebels, we are dealing with a discontinuous, categorical property – a change from one state into another. Zeeman (1976, 1977) has proposed that changes in behaviour from one state to another as a result of stressor-strain load may be analogous to the changes in state of physical objects, such as beams under tension, or bridges subjected to overload, which Thom (1972) has described as examples of elementary 'catastrophes'. A catastrophe occurs when an equilibrium of forces acting on smooth surfaces breaks down. Thom

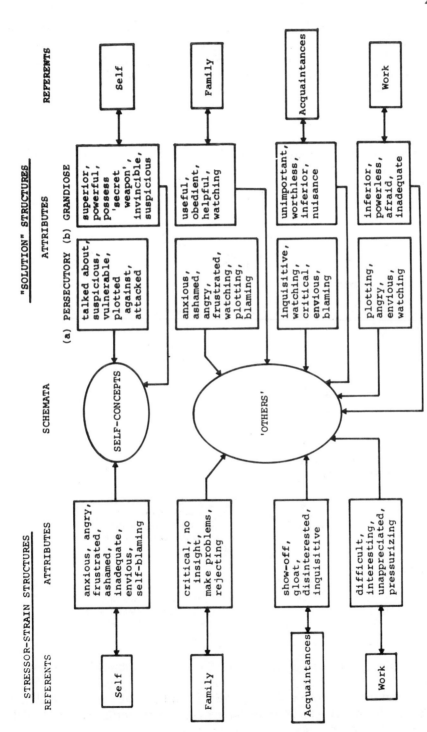

Figure 9.7 Hypothetical semantic network structures in persecutory and grandiose paranoid 'solutions'

proposed seven possible abrupt changes in equilibrium each of which is mathematically defined by an increasing number of variables and interactions between them. Zeeman's application of this methodology to psychology has been confined to bimodal and opposite distributions of behaviour as in fight and flight, fear and rage, or anger and self-pity. This is one type and level of conflict. Another is one that interests us here: the opposing energy sources mediating recognition–non-recognition, affirming–negating, accepting information or denying it, or approach-avoidance.

A non-mathematician cannot possibly explain the new model adequately, and certainly not its proofs. The effects of opposite forces acting on a smooth surface can be illustrated, however, as in Figure 9.8. The so-called 'cusp

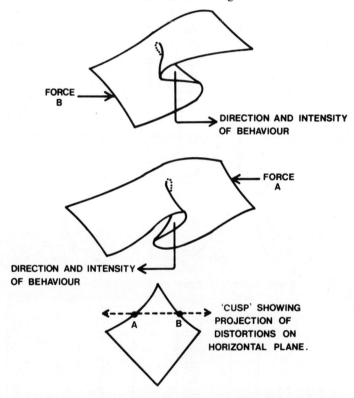

Figure 9.8 Two 'behaviour surfaces' showing forces and behaviour of equal and opposite directions in a dynamically sensitive system (A 'cusp catastrophe' freely adapted from Thom, 1972 and Zeeman, 1976)

catastrophe' shown here is just one of the seven possibilities proposed by Thom.

The changes in conceptual prototypical identifiers cited above which are implicit in the model I am offering, have a number of prerequisites for which I have tried to make a case in earlier chapters.

(1) They require the notion of a unitary symbolic language for the coding, integration, and retrieval of information that signifies knowledge and meaning of the external objective world as well as its subjective interpretation by a person.
(2) They assume that the actions of that person depend on a choice from responses with different anticipated outcomes and different degrees of satisfying expectancies which are coded in the same language.
(3) They further require that concept signifiers, and the preferred behavioural strategies and goal-outcomes they serve, can change incrementally in response to residual conflicts and cognitive-affective experiences of discomfort and disquiet.

In the presence of these prerequisites we have a system in which functionally associated incremental changes involving more than one cognitive structure can summate and thus determine a novel conception, perception, or experience of an existing referent. Concurrently, the referent acquires new labels and meanings. When these in turn are experienced as stressor-strain-reducing, other changes in referent-attribute structures follow and thus provide for the emergence of internally consistent pathological coping solutions. My assumptions describe a system which seeks adaptation, either in the Piagetian sense of assimilation and accommodation, or in the physicalistic sense of forces in equilibrium as required by thermodynamic laws, or field forces of energy. It is a system which seeks stability. There are many criticisms of catastrophe theory as a theory *per se* and its application to issues in the social and biological science (e.g. Marmo and Vitale, 1980). The most important criticism from our point of view has been that psychological phenomena do not meet the basic required assumptions of Thom's theory: a stable dynamic system with identifiable processes of continuity and differentiation. The theory may indeed be bad, and the mathematical equations may indeed raise further (rather fruitless) philosophical discussions about the insoluble difference between quantitative and qualitative concepts of reality, *and* its experience. The critics' concept of the human cognitive-affective information processing system, however, is patently false. Stability need not be a once and for always state, and the logic of the term 'dynamic' is that stability has self-rectifying capacity. It simply happens to be the case that these capacities are the pre-eminent characteristics of the human processing system. In that event, catastrophe theory, or some future modification, may well provide a paradigmatic clue of how to quantify *those processes that are subsumed by concept formation, as well as those* that would predict its direction, in the formation of optimally adaptive, or pathological, cognitive coping structures and processes.

CHAPTER 10

Implications for the role of intelligence, and for social conflict

This brief chapter will be strong on speculation but rather short of empirical data. I could have devoted the space to the application of the cognitive-semantic referent-attribute model of personality and motivation to a further representative sample of the large number of traits which are discussed in our standard textbooks. Instead, it seemed to me more challenging to examine possible implications of the model in relation to some socio-politically sensitive issues which are rarely, if ever, discussed in a cognitive context because they are bound to be somewhat too complex for fine-grained analysis. These also happen to be issues to which psychology has made, and continues to make, empirically based contributions, many of which our enthusiastic social engineers and political masters tend to view, largely incomprehendingly, with suspicion, horror, or hostility. By what I would regard as a fairly plausible process of induction I will argue in favour of two propositions.

(1) The differentiation of preferred characteristic behavioural strategies for the achieving of preferred goals and goal-outcomes cannot exceed the general cognitive differentiating capacity of a given individual.
(2) Conflict within and between social groups in the final analysis is the result of coping processes required by the presence of vulnerability to stressor-strains which lack adequate restructuring strategies and capabilities.

The conceptual gap between these propositions and those which are focal to the present model is acknowledged. The extrapolations in this chapter, however, are not intended as a formal test of the plausibility of the model.

The first propostion has been referred to already in some of the preceding chapters. The second is derived from discussions in Chapters 5 and 9. I am not concerned here with taking positions on nature-nurture controversies either in relation to intelligence, or in respect of anxiety and aggression. Furthermore, my exercise does not require me either to promote or to denigrate the customary tools for the assessment of intelligence and of traits. The limitations of questionnaires have been discussed earlier, in Chapter 6, and the limitations of intelligence tests are well-known to their designers, and to those who have been trained to use and interpret them. Instead, it seems worthwhile to try and extrapolate from the implications of cognitive-semantic interpretations of personality and motivation to the conceptual operations involved in problem-solving both generally, and in relation to the handling of group interaction crises. The starting point for this task is my earlier defining statement that characteristic goal-directed behaviour towards preferred outcomes reflects *antecedent* problem-solving processes and capacities.

1 INTELLIGENCE AND THE REFERENT-ATTRIBUTE STRUCTURES OF GOAL-DIRECTED BEHAVIOUR

Among the specialists there is no misconception of the underlying complexity of the concept of 'intelligence', not even where for the sake of brevity they refer to it without further definition. It is neither a unitary entity, nor 'a ghost in a machine' (Ryle, 1949), and intelligence cannot be a 'cause' of anything. Properly defined, the results of its subsumed structural components and the processes in which they participate can be regarded as 'effects'. This applies clearly to the earliest attempts at definition: Binet's reference to the capacity for judgement; Spearman's analytic concept of the deduction of relationships and the eduction of correlates; or Thorndike's quasi-physio-logical reference to the capacity for association-forming. An effect-orienta-tion is equally present in Piaget's definition of hierarchies of progressively inclusive accommodating schemes, and in Hebb's 'intelligence B', the repo-sitory of environmental stimulation in cognition-mediating cell assemblies. Guilford's (1967) model of the 'structure of intellect' makes the point even more specifically by its suggestion that intelligence needs to be defined by the interaction between operations of the cognitive system, representational knowledge codes on which they operate, and principles or strategies by which groups of knowledge data are organized. Guilford's terms for the three categories of cognitive activity are, respectively, operations, contents, and products. Although information-oriented cognitive processing theory does not regard Guilford's 120 categories of intellectual processes as exhaustive or sufficiently process-oriented, it is useful to list them as in Table 10.1 because of their implication for our discussion of traits and motives. The parameters within each of three categories are conceived in ascending hier-archical order reading from top to bottom, but again cognitive processing theory would regard the evidence for this as inconclusive and the attempt as overstructured. The product or organizational principle of 'implications', for example, is likely to be involved in all levels of grouping strategies as a process of induction and generalization. At the same time, some success has been achieved in mapping the structure-of-intellect parameters on to types

Table 10.1 The Parameters of Guilford's Structure-of-Intellect

Operations	Contents	Products
Cognition	Figural	Units
Memory	Symbolic	Classes
Divergent production	Semantic	Relations
Convergent production	Behavioural	Systems
Evaluation		Transformations
		Implications

of learning as suggested by Gagné (1965). An interesting and somewhat amusing result of one such attempt (Merrifield, 1966) was the demonstration that S–R learning requires the largest number of parameters, to the exclusion, however, of cognition and memory operation!

Attention should be drawn at this stage to some cogent elaborations of Guilford's model. Messick (1973) has argued that the model provides for a taxonomy of individual differences in information processing strategies. He suggests that the behavioural content dimension must include response dispositions involved in 'attitudes, needs, desires, moods, feelings, intentions . . .' in a social interaction context. These aspects of behaviour, previously called 'social intelligence' by Thorndike (1927), fit into the structure-of-intellect framework because of their demands for person perception, social sensitivity, and self-appraisal (Messick, 1973, p. 285). Messick just touches on the possibility that social intelligence requires social problem-solving, and that cognitive differentiation and articulation contribute to the style of information processing within the Guilford model. He is not able to suggest, however, how all the interactions between the Guilford parameters and his own are to be facilitated, or how anticipatory knowledge of problem-solving outcomes are conveyed to the person. Of considerable relevance to the first proposition I offered at the beginning of this chapter is the relationship between tests of field-dependence/independence as measures of personality individuation and differentiation, and conventional measures of intelligence. Results obtained by Vernon (e.g. 1972, 1973) from a large heterogeneous group of children indicated that a substantial proportion of dependence/independence variance could be accounted for by a traditional 'g' factor, and that correlations between these measures and, for example, conceptual maturity tend towards zero when 'g' is held constant.

If the Guilford parameters exclude processing variables which must play an important role in intellectual task performance, let us briefly examine the omissions. These are probably determined by the structure- and test-oriented approach, and as a result there are few specifications matching the requirements of cognitive, information processing theory. For example, the memory operation requires separation between the input parameters of orienting, iconic-image-holding capacity, focused and selective attention and rehearsal, as well as the storage-related processes of schematic assimilation and accommodation in which the integration of recent and new information involves a range of restructuring processes.

A notable difficulty of the structural approach to intelligence is the definition of the difficulty level of a given intelligence test question. This difficulty cannot be directly and systematically resolved by any combination of the Guilford parameters. The customary method of defining difficulty in terms of pass/fail rates of subjects in normalization studies is non-analytic and precludes a systematic approach to an item's information processing demands. I have already discussed one alternative, capacity-oriented approach in Chapter 5. Another way of defining difficulty involves paying regard to the number of stages of processing, or component processes, as suggested by Sternberg (1977). Sternberg studied analogical reasoning as required by the Miller Analogies Tests, and identified three components: attribute identification, attribute comparison, and a controller. These are served by six processes: encoding, inference, mapping, application, justification, and response preparation. Problem difficulty is additively defined by either the time requirement of each process, or by working memory capacity for operating on the information (presumably defined by errors of omission and commission). I would like to suggest that this analysis of problem-solving stages and processes in analogical reasoning resembles in its essential features those processes which I have identified in earlier chapters as being involved in generating preferred responses for the achievement of preferred goal-outcomes in a context of environmental constraints and facilitations.

Further difficulties for a structural model arise if one considers different types of attention. Whereas sustained attention as in vigilance tasks has near-zero correlation with a global intelligence measure, selective attention is reliably related to it (Jerrison, 1977). Another relevant parameter is speed. Two sets of experimental findings are important here: (i) more intelligent subjects are faster in acquiring new learning, as well as in recall (e.g. Gaudry and Spielberger, 1970); (ii) so-called impulsive subjects are worse at inductive reasoning, serial recall, and tachistostopic recognition than reflective subjects who generally make few errors (Kagan, 1966; Kagan et al., 1966). Conceptually relevant are Furneaux's (1960) mathematical separation between the speed and power factors of an intelligence test (which is one instance of the speed-error trade-off), and findings that difficult problems are more readily abandoned without solution than easy problems (White, 1973).

The faster processing speed of intelligent subjects must have important implications for all types of cognitive operations, and impulsiveness and non-persistence which are frequently associated with extraversion can be regarded a examples of behavioural characteristics which indicate a need for the reassessment of the relationship between intelligence and personality and motivation. It does not seem to be either coincidence or low arousal that accounts for the lower level of intellectual power in extreme (neurotic) extraverts compared with extreme introverts (e.g. Brierley, 1961). Even though extraverts are assumed to have generally low arousal levels in the

Eysenckian framework (H. J. Eysenck, 1973; M. W. Eysenck, 1977), it is difficult to accept a necessary corollary that extravert neurotic impulsiveness occurs in the presence of low arousal. The inverse relationship between extraversion and recall performance after long retention intervals (M. W. Eysenck, 1977) is probably not directly related to arousal as measured either physiologically or by individual introspection. It is much more likely that the higher level of sensation-seeking of extraverts (Zuckerman, 1978) affects their orienting and selective attention input so that new incoming information restricts the permanent integration of previously coded stimuli. This suggestion of proneness to informational interference is substantially supported by a study on the distracting effects of car-radio listening on the auditory reaction time of drivers (Fagerström and Lisper, 1977). Extraverts had reliably and progressively slower RTs, that is showing interference-proneness, despite a regular decrease in arousal (HR beats/min.). Quite inexplicable in this, or any other, context are the findings of McLaughlin and Eysenck (1967) that *stable* introverts perform worse on a difficult paired-associate task than unstable introverts and unstable extraverts even though long-term retention was not required. This result is particularly odd since there is substantial evidence (i) that unstable extraverts are consistently of lower test intelligence than unstable introverts (Payne, 1960), (ii) that there is a reliable positive correlation between introversion and verbal intelligence (Eysenck, 1967), and (iii) equally substantial evidence that introverts produce superior performances in secondary and tertiary education (e.g. Furneaux, 1962). As M. W. Eysenck (1977, p. 218) himself says, '. . . the precise nature of the link between introversion–extraversion and arousal has not been established. . .'. If that is so, it might have been better if any evidence of interactions had been related to more than one theoretical framework.

Two further deficiencies of the Guilford model need to be considered for the aims of this section. Firstly, none of the three categorical dimensions seems to be able to supply parameters which facilitate inferences from given data. Inference means going beyond the information given and, therefore, and in this model, requires interactions between cognitive, memory and evaluation operations, appropriate contents parameters, and several product parameters. It is a process of hypothesis-testing and, therefore, of problem-solving in a context of current set, of goals, and of available methods. Without modification, it cannot handle interactions with dominant personal dispositions whose data are parallel to those presented in objective and neutral intelligence test questions, and which may interfere with their solution. Secondly, Guilford's convergent and divergent production operations categories are overspecific as basic operators unless they are conceived as motivational parameters, a definition clearly inappropriate for a structural approach to intelligence, and inconsistent with Guilford's special interest in creativity. The statistical independence of creativity and intelligence tests has fewer implications for the prediction of academic and occupational performance than for general adaptive capacity. Except in those contexts where innovation for its own sake is a major performance criterion, performance requires relevant and appropriate associative thinking with convergent goals. That is, optimal convergence may require divergent sidesteps. Associative productivity and novelty in themselves are irrelevant unless they can conform to general criteria of utility, excellence, or economy. Behavioural flexibility, however, has internal as well as external criteria, and the capacity to interpret a demand situation in a way that satisfies both requires not only some of the Guilford parameters that have been discussed already, but patterns of goal-structures and goal-outcomes with their preferred strategies of achieving them.

So far I have discussed only those intelligence-related processes which facilitate cognitive capacity generally. Before applying these considerations to processes involved in characteristic and preferred goal-directed behaviour, let us briefly examine other evidence of the relationship between intelligence and personality and motivational variables. Reference has been made already to the consistently lower intelligence test scores of social extraverts. It is possible to argue that impulsivity, unstable selective attention, sensation-seeking, and suboptimal verbal ability contribute to this relationship. We may well need to ask, however, which came first: extraversion or intelligence, or whether a given set of cognitive characteristics jointly affects the development of both.

This comment may have considerable relevance for the development of delinquent and criminal behaviour. In the taxonomy of personality types these groups are extraverts and as groups of no better than average or below intelligence. These were Burt's (1925) original findings which have been replicated many times and in different societies and epochs (e.g. Glueck and Glueck, 1950, 1968; West, 1963; West and Farrington, 1973). Extraversion as well as low intelligence in these groups are repeatedly found in association with parental criminality, low socio-economic status, suboptimal parenting, large family size, and low levels of educational attainment in parents and offspring. Delinquents as well as adult criminals (particularly those convicted of theft, robbery, and acts of violence) commonly have a history of school truancy, and their verbal ability is generally lower than their non-verbal test scores. The latter, too, however, are generally lower than those of appropriate control groups so that less frequent exposure to the formal educational tasks of reading, verbal comprehension, and verbalized inference cannot provide a full answer to the low test scores. This must be correct even though non-verbal tests of deductive and analogical reasoning require cognitive-semantic operations on verbally coded concepts which are less well acquired through inadequate schooling (e.g. Trasler, 1970). Although we have here evidence of multivariate determinants producing a socially undesirable end result, the component shared by all or most of them is average to below test intelligence. This conclusion may be interpreted as politically reactionary. If it is a correct conclusion it follows that social engineering can only ameliorate the situation, not eradicate it.

Whatever the biological pre-determinants of orienting thresholds, of lability of mid-brain excitation, or the optimal capacity for deductive reasoning, the social and familial setting provides the context for their development and expression in actual behaviour. Cross-cultural differences in cognitive skills and strategies provide some of the evidence. These indicate that there is a reliable relationship between socialization strategies aiming to perpetuate patterns of cultural and social organization, and cognitive differentiation as defined by field-dependence/independence tests (e.g. Witkin, Price-Williams *et al.*, 1974; Witkin and Berry, 1975). The major mediators identified by these investigators were mechanisms for inducing conformity to existing social, familial, religious, and political norms. The design of the Witkin, Price-Williams *et al.* study was particularly interesting because their data were obtained from a comparison of two villages differing in social conformity in each of three different countries. Their results from children aged approximately 10 and 13 years showed without exception that the less conforming villages induced a greater degree of cognitive differentiation. In view of the contribution of general intelligence to field-dependence/independence performance, authoritative demands for conformity are likely to affect cognitive differentiation generally. A link for the negative relationship between conformity and cognitive differentiation is provided by small-group research which has repeatedly found negative correlations between test intelligence level and conformity (e.g. Divesta and Cox, 1960; Vaughan, 1964; Vaughan and White, 1966). This raises another question, however, as to whether the dominance of an authoritative, conformity-oriented socialization style in a society or social subgroup is in itself a reflection of somewhat limited intellectual group competence. In the case of the Witkin, Price-Williams *et al.* study, the conformity-cognitive differentiation linkage could have been affected by the departure from their villages of individuals seeking better opportunities for the expression of their own more flexible social cognitions of which they had become aware, and which were at variance with those of the parent community. This outcome has been observed in many communities in a number of countries which have become depopulated. It seems plausible to propose, therefore, that the more homogeneous the characteristics of the members of a society or its subgroups the greater the probability of behavioural and cognitive stereotypy (see also the discussion in Chapter 5).

This brings us to the relationship between intelligence and, respectively, the social attitude dimensions of authoritarianism, dogmatism, and prejudice. A recent review of the correlates of authoritarianism (Dillehay, 1978) reiterates and supports the results of the Berkeley studies. These have shown, as is well-known, significant negative relationships with intelligence. Critical appraisals of these studies (Christie and Jahoda, 1954) estimated the true size of the correlation to be approximately -0.50 when allowing for the restricted ranges of intelligence and of authoritarianism tapped. The size of obtained and estimated correlations is all the more surprising because the research samples tended to be of above average intelligence and well educated. Intelligence test performance is not correlated with dogmatism, and this poses an awkward question considering the most widely accepted definition of dogmatism (Rokeach, 1960). According to this, dogmatism is the consequence of closed cognitive structures which prevent the acceptance and integration of information that is at variance with an affect-dominated stereotyped belief system about objects, situations, and issues. These characteristics make it functionally similar to convergent thinking which, as indicated before, is not supposed to be related to standard intelligence test levels. If we accept, however, a process-oriented definition of intelligence, we must conclude that dogmatic belief structures are referent-attribute assemblies which store information that defines concepts, their inter-relationships, and their behavioural implications. When such a system is exposed to information-arousing incongruent inferences, which it must reject, we have a cognitive-social behaviour variable which is predominantly rigidly structured. Since standard intelligence tests possess considerable cultural and educational loading, these do not conflict with belief systems which are determined by the same factors. Discrepancies occur only when the information to be required is dissonant with and threatening to tightly controlled knowledge structures. These processes and strategies were demonstrated in the experiment cited before in which subjects with Marxist and non-Marxist political views learnt and remembered best new material which was consistent with their dominant beliefs (Levine and Murphy, 1943). The result was most strongly influenced by non-Marxists learning and remembering a non-Marxist prose passage better. Today, of course, we are more likely to cite the influence of cognitive-affective schemata in determining affect-related learning and memory as discussed by reference to the experiments by Bower (1981), and my own in Chapters 6 and 8.

We have already examined the favourable effect of achievement motivation on cognitive performance, and the slowly emerging trend to interpret some of its influences cognitively (e.g. Weiner, 1972). It seems reasonable, however, to try to take this development a step further by considering the possibility that achievement-orientation is a significant *component of all* cognitive processes and operations. What, for example, is actually involved – taking Guilford's scheme first – when in a task set units of input obtain class-defining labels, and when relationships between labelled events are transformed into conceptual implications? I would argue that where a task-appropriate response is made, the *act* of producing it is a component of a cognitive chain of events. Thus, operating with a response set, even though the response produced is slow and/or incorrect, and even though the nAch score is low, is evidence nevertheless of the operation of an end result-oriented response system. A similar proposition can be phrased in the context of Sternberg's analysis of analogical reasoning processes. Once a respondent has accepted a task, attribute identification, attribute comparison, and control components will operate with the processes required until a response is generated. Even the unhelpful intrusion of impulsivity, social stimulation-seeking and fluctuations of selective attention can be included then under the heading of autonomous, end result-seeking events. The necessary rider for these arguments, however, is that the responding system has accepted the requirement to make a response in the service of which the subsidiary processes operate.

I will now address myself directly to the proposition that the differentiation of personality and motivation cannot exceed the general conceptual differentiating capacity of the cognitive system. Because differentiated concepts are also subject to differential amounts of labelled elaboration, there are two corollaries to the proposition.

(1) The capacity for semantic or alternative symbolic labelling of the referent-attribute schemata of personality and motivation *cannot exceed the labelling capacity* available for the conceptualization of objects, events, situations, people, and issues generally.
(2) The elaboration of conceptual structures serving goal-definition, goal-hierarchies and preferred characteristic ways of obtaining preferred goal-outcomes *cannot exceed the conceptual elaborating capacity* generally of the cognitive system.

In other words I am proposing that less intelligent persons have less complex personalities and motives, and that the more intelligent possess, or have the potential for, greater behavioural complexity, and alternative goal-directed behavioural strategies. (The converse proposition is not necessarily plausible since, for example, we have schizophrenics of high test intelligence, but simultaneously with some oversimplified concept and response categories.)

These statements should not be a cause of social controversy because they do not imply either antecedent or prospective value judgements. They follow plausibly, and I would say logically, from the formal propositions presented in Chapter 6, Section 3. Let me recapitulate the relevant central statements of the model without going into detail. All behaviour is goal-directed and the combination of behaviour strategies and goal-achievement is evidence of problem-solving. Knowledge, or anticipation of behaviour outcome, is derived from conceptual operations matching a goal-achieving task-set in working memory with previously rewarded strategies retrieved from permanent memory. The greater the elaborations of referent-attribute structures and their schematic relationships in permanent memory, the greater the available range of response alternatives. The greater the capacity for fine-grained semantic labelling of stimulus attributes, the greater the capacity for fine-grained analysis of goal-directed behavioural constraints, facilitations, and alternatives. In other words, goals, goal-outcomes, and goal-directed behavioural strategies must possess conceptual representation in order to provide meaning of their implications for adaptation, to convey self-knowledge, to facilitate knowledge and evaluation of the behaviour of others, and to facilitate preparedness to respond to social stimulation. And optimal and economic representation of these conceptual structures is achieved by verbal labels, as it is for any other concepts.

These conceptualizations can be grossly summarized by an adaptation of Figure 5.1 above and its associated discussion. Utilizing Hebb's distinction between intelligence 'A' and 'B', we can distinguish between the capacities of contrasting cognitive systems to encode, store, integrate, elaborate, and functionally organize objects, situations, events, etc. as well as their attributes, implications, and analogical relationships. In other words they are systems which differ in the structural cognitive components of the Guilford model and the process-oriented Sternberg model of intelligence. And let us assume that these capacities are analogous to Hebb's intelligence 'B' because, as suggested before, they require instigation and use through experience. If it were then accepted that the very same structures and processes are those required for the development, diversification, and availability of characteristic preferred ways of achieving preferred goal-outcomes, the proposition concerning the relationship between intelligence and personality and motivation is logically supported. This deductive exercise can be continued by considering a quantitative information processing capacity definition of intelligence as implicit in the Sternberg approach. Figure 10.1 tries to illustrate two consequences for the differentiation of personality and motivation. The first of these refers to the cognitive potential of the four hypothetical processing systems 'W', 'X', 'Y', 'Z'. Of these 'Y' and 'Z' have greater potential than 'W' and 'X'. All four systems have acquired goal- and

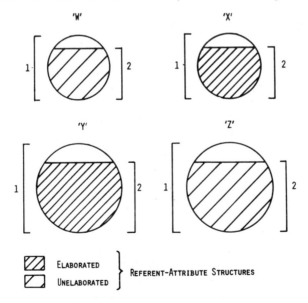

Figure 10.1 Hypothetical relationship between stimulus differentiating capacity and the elaboration of goal-directed behaviour

outcome-directed conceptual structures, including structures storing information about costs and rewards. Systems 'X' and 'Y' have achieved the greatest degree of conceptual elaboration as shown by heavy cross-hatching, while systems 'W' and 'Z' have remained relatively unelaborated. Because system 'Z' started off with greater cognitive processing potential, however, its overall adaptive capacity in terms of goal achievement (shown by dimension Z'_2) is greater than that of system 'W' (shown by dimension W'_2). The second consequence of this approach appears when comparing the two highly elaborated systems 'X' and 'Y'. Although the degree of concept elaboration is assumed to be at the same level, their cognitive processing potential was assumed to differ (see X'_1 vs. Y'_1). In that event it is reasonable to assume that the elaboration of goal-directed and goal-outcome preferences and the characteristic strategies of achieving them available to system 'X' will be confined to a smaller number of goals, and to an *overall smaller number* of outcome expectancies and alternative behavioural strategies. The processing potentials 'WXYZ', refer to Hebb's intelligence 'B', that is, that proportion of physiological and neurochemical intelligence 'A' that has been utilized by and has participated in environmental interactions.

The propositions sketched in Figure 10.1 are capable of further expansion. They can be extended, for example, by speculating about the effect of different symbolic notations, or of mixed notations, for the specification of referent-attribute assemblies. My own preference throughout has been in favour of the greater differentiating capacity of semantic labels. At the same time, however, there are no good reasons why semantically undifferentiated proprioceptive and affective feeling tones associated with events cannot contribute to a conceptual structure. The labels 'feeling good', 'feeling bad' contribute to concept structure, but by virtue of the gross class of attribute thus signified, differentiation between attributes must remain gross.

Two further points can be advanced in support of the proposition that the factors determining intelligent cognitive performance are the same as those which facilitate personality and motivational differentiation. The first of these arises from the influential developmental studies in New York by Birch, Chess, and Thomas (e.g. Thomas *et al.*, 1968; Chess *et al.*, 1968). The longitudinal study carried out by these investigators on the temperament of children concentrated on parameters which might serve as long-term predictors of subsequent behaviour development. Defining temperament as those stylistic response characteristics which are evident in early childhood, they examined activity level, biological rhythm, approach or withdrawal to novel stimuli, adaptability of responses, intensity of response, response thresholds, quality of mood, distractability, attention span, and persistence. Although Chess (1980) and Thomas and Chess (1977, 1980, 1982) argue that temperament style defines the 'how' of behaviour rather than the 'why', there can be little doubt that the 'how' taps a useful proportion of personality and motivational indices, and that a reasonable case can be made equally well that they are predictors of cognitive potential. Possible exceptions are biological rhythm and mood. In other respects the remaining eight parameters can be considered as contributors to Guilford's operations, contents and products of intelligence test performance, as well as to Sternberg's attribute-oriented processes. Whatever model of intelligence appeals most, type, range, and lability of responding in infancy and in the years of accelerating development are as relevant to intelligence as they are for the appearance of individuality in goal-directed behaviour.

My second and final point is consistent with the speculative direction of the rest of this section. It is made in answer to the hypothetical question as to whether the attempted analogy does not actually and finally fail when considering the affective components of characteristic and preferred goal-directed behaviour. Cross-reference to Chapter 6, Section 2 will remind us that a relatively strong case can be made for a cognitive conceptualization of affect even where the degree of attribute differentiation is likely to be gross, and even where 'words fail to express it'. Are there analogues for joy, anger, happiness, anxiety, satisfaction, contentment in intellectual cognitive activity? I am tempted to propose that there are, and that they are the components of affect categories generally. The simplest case is when joy, satisfaction, frustration, or anger are respectively associated with generating or failing to generate, logically acceptable answers to problems requiring solution. Equally plausible and only slightly more complex are the experiences of tension, of 'tip-of-the-tongue', or of puzzlement, while operating on the requirements of a conceptually difficult task, that is problem-solving, with its many parallels in adapting personal goals to the restrictions of social and physical barriers. In both cases feeling experiences may be difficult to communicate verbally. An intensely pleasant experience for any problem-solver, however, is the emergence of a missing link in a deductive or inductive reasoning process – the appearance of a logically satisfying inferential step. The relief from cognitive tension in an 'Aha!' experience has been likened to falling in love, even if the end result is meaningful and logical only to the person involved, and to no one else!

2 SOCIAL CONFLICT, AND THE REFERENT-ATTRIBUTE STRUCTURES OF GOAL-DIRECTED BEHAVIOUR

Let me clarify the second proposition advanced at the beginning of this chapter which basically defines social conflict in terms of inadequate coping strategies in the presence of stressor-strain vulnerability. By conflict I am referring to the original Miller categories involving approach and avoidance in single or double pair-wise opposition, but in a context extending beyond the single person. Although intra-individual conflict as previously discussed always involves the availability vs. non-availability of goals in a social setting, social conflict specifically assumes competition between individuals or groups of individuals for the same goal in the same social setting. The term 'same goal' needs elaboration, however, because appearances suggest that conflict between groups arises because they strive for different goals which are also incompatible.

Three examples will make the point. Envy and distrust between different levels of the socio-economic group hierarchy become focused in conflict when a lower income group demands higher wages without changes in working conditions, justifying the claim by reference to an increasing cost of living. The higher income group, that is management, is prepared to grant this only in return for improved productivity, or not at all. But increased productivity most commonly means higher unit production per man hour worked, achieved at the cost of speeding up industrial processes, usually with a reduction of rest pauses and by replacing people with computerized machine processes. Incompatibility resides in the opposition between no changes in working conditions, and changes demanded to finance workers' requests. A 'same goal' conflict is present when each side *insists on its own conditions*. In practice, position-taking in this type of conflict has become a formalized role-playing interaction in which negotiators know in advance that ultimately the 'same goal' will have to be 'shared', and that it will not be a question of who loses face but how well any loss of face by each side can be disguised. Turning to the vulnerability aspect of this type of conflict, we can observe on the one hand real anxiety about economic pressure on family security, about loss of financial and social status, about the effect of further advances in automated production, and last but not least, anxiety about loss of bargaining power. Vulnerability in the other side to the conflict also involves anxiety about employment security and status maintenance, but in addition anxiety about satisfying shareholders, creditors, and last but not least about customers waiting for products which are also available from another source. Inadequate coping strategies are observable whenever conflict is crystallized in *threats of action* which both sides to the conflict realize cannot be carried out to the full. Although these implications are now known in advance of the emergence of conflict in most societies with formalized labour relations, the game is played according to the conventions for two reasons. Both sides to the conflict are expected by their own group to obtain maximum gain, and negotiators are appointed to their posts for their ability to represent these expectations. The fundamental antitheses are not removed by compromise if group loyalty and self-interest prevent the emergence and utilization of cognitive processes and strategies by which incompatible goals are restructured into inter-related goals, and common cause to achieve them. In this example that means a sound economic and competitive position for the industry in order to meet better the wishes of its workers at *all* levels.

As a second example of social conflict let us consider the increasing evidence of the results of what is somewhat euphemistically termed 'inner-city-deprivation'. Ostensibly the conflict is between the maintenance of consensus 'law-and-order', and law-breaking; and between aggressive, violent, and destructive actions against members of a community and their property, and the legalized protectors of public and personal safety. These are different and incompatible goals disguising each side's *belief in the justification of its actions*. Vulnerability to stressor-strain is demonstrated by law-breakers, muggers, and rioters in their resort to violations and violence, and by police forces responding with excessive zeal, personal abuse, and with physical excesses to provocations added to law-breaking itself. The poverty of adaptive coping strategies and processes is shown by actions which cannot result in long-term effects experienced as satisfying and as meeting the needs of each of the social groups. Moreover, both sides are aware that environmental, physical, and social factors limit the amount of time and effort spent on violence in any given period.

There are many differences between these two types of social conflict. The obvious differences are that 'labour–management' conflicts are sanctioned within fairly wide limits, whereas crime and rioting are not; and that industrial disputes involve formally elected leaders sanctioned by rules and/or conventions, none of which applies to gang activity or mobs. Secondly, physical violence and law-breaking occur only infrequently in industrial conflict and are rejected as methods of goal-achievement by the leadership and the vast majority of their electorate. The achievement of compromise solutions permanently changes industrial relations which have the goal of better wages and/or conditions of work. Crime and violent rioting and attempts to control them, however, are only partially and, it can be argued, only minimally effective in the removal of social deprivation. The most important similarity between strike action and rioting is that their occurrence and maintenance depend on the activities and influence of a minority of individuals.

Rather more speculatively, it could be suggested that this feature applies to a large extent to the development of international conflicts through actions or threats of action by one *government* against another which then responds, or threatens to respond, reciprocally. Governments claim legitimacy of representation either by institutionalized free choice of the people, or through the absence of alternative representation as in single-party states established by force, or by the agreed absence of opposition parties during periods of 'national emergency'. Unless countries are geographically adjoining, the incompatibility of the goals sought by them is indirect rather than direct. In these circumstances the implications of conflict-inducing actions may be either long-term, or hypothetical and ideological where they are most likely to express principles and beliefs about forms of government, or international relationships and their management. (Obvious and depressing exceptions to this outcome occur when conflicting ideologies go to war by proxy in support of other nations that support them, or during wars of conquest initiated, disguised, and rationalized by reference to altruistic or self-protective motives.) 'Same goal' conflict is present, however, because the contestants insist on the justification and validity of *their own national need and its interpretation*.

Vulnerability to stressor-strain underlying international conflict may be inferred from the *degree of incompatibility* of both sides' actions, from the severity of position-taking, and from the suddenness and unexpectedness of action. Coping strategies and processes may be regarded as inadequately adaptive if the responses dictated by vulnerability substantially exclude the possibility of a compromise solution which can satisfy the need to reduce the stressor-strain of both sides to the conflict. Where this possibility is absent, an unresolved state of conflict can be maintained without war-like action provided the countries involved are not bordering on each other, and provided that indirect threats to the goals of one side do not become more direct. When this occurs and where the countries are adjoining and depend on a shared traffic system for the exchange of food and goods, incompatible goal-seeking must lead to war-like acts unless alternative cognitive structures of the conflict situation can be generated. Modifications of national need and its justification, however, must result in a reduction of experienced vulnerability. It is worth noting that the small group of individuals in positions of leadership and authority, even when freely elected, does not necessarily command the agreement and allegiance of the majority of the elective group. In international conflict, therefore, efforts are made by both sides to transform conflicts between governments, and between the abstraction of national interests, into conflicts sensitizing group loyalty by reference to threats to personal integrity and preferred national modes of living.

The question to which I would like to try to make a contribution is not whether social conflict is inevitable on any of the three scales sketched in the above examples. Instead let us briefly examine the characteristics of the leadership minority on whom the solubility or persistence of conflicts depends. These are the individuals in whom resides the power and responsibility for decision-making and generating problem-solving steps which determine the level of incompatibility of goal-seeking, the possibility of compromise or goal-sharing, and the implications of the difference between disagreement and conflict. I will focus on those behavioural parameters whose reanalysis has been the subject of the preceding chapters: the cognitive structures and processes representing individual goals and preferred characteristic ways of achieving preferred goal-outcomes; the bases and levels of vulnerability to threats to self-esteem and physical and social integrity; and the effect of these factors on the capacity to avoid and cope with conflicts by appropriate conceptual restructuring of the critical features of social reality. The discussion will follow the three examples given above because, like many other people, I consider them prototypical of the types of group conflict which are likely to become more frequent and more dangerous to the maintenance and survival of orderly social life, as the methods and tools to disrupt it become more powerful.

Industrial dissension and conflict has a long history. It runs largely parallel with social class conflict generally, with the development of large production units, overspecialized and repetitive work roles, improvements in educational standards, and with the spread of social and political information through the media of mass communication. Union legalization and sequences of employment- and health-protection legislation achieved new levels of self-esteem for workers in mass production industries, and a realization of the negotiating power of unified action. While these changes occured, ownership of factories and industries was transferred from individuals in direct contact with their workers, to Boards of Management, corporations, and international conglomerates. Hierarchies of managers with different skills, educational backgrounds, and social identifications were interposed between the ultimate decision-makers and the production workers. Not only did authority structures become impersonal where conditions and rewards for work were involved, but stressor-strain from role-playing and communication problems between levels of supervisory and management grades could now intrude into the workers' collective bargaining situation. Three additional factors appear to have contributed to what seem to be the increasing difficulties of preventing and settling industrial conflict. Least frequently mentioned are overt or underlying conflicts between groups of workers with overlapping skills and responsibilities belonging to different unions. Most clearly manifest and publicized is the intrusion of party-political and ideological beliefs held by many union negotiators into their position-taking on behalf of their group. This intrusion may not be overt, and may be unavoidable in any case, because committed individuals are likely to be strongly motivated to participate actively in any discussions with their working colleagues, and to attend all union meetings. They will be seen, therefore, as suitable representatives by less vocal and less confident members. Management may also be politically and ideologically motivated, or at least be all too ready to respond with hostility to its introduction by the other side. A third factor, also frequently ignored, arises from the verbal labels 'workers' and 'managers' assigned to the two sides of this conflict. Obvious implications are the common inferences that a manager does not work, that a worker possesses only limited skills of the manual type, and that management enjoys superior powers and security of employment.

These issues and others have been recognized as contributing to the social and productive climate of a factory or an industry, and my own highly condensed comments are no substitute for the large and cogently argued literature on the human factor in industrial peace and progress (e.g. Jaques, 1951, 1976; Argyris, 1962; Kahn and Boulding, 1965; Schein and Bennis, 1965; Sofer, 1972; Payne, 1979). This has presented substantial consensus on the psychological determinants of industrial conflict. Cited most frequently are between-group differences and intra-group similarities in social perception, beliefs, and attitudes related to role-playing and to levels of social status; and the ability and willingness, or otherwise, to communicate clearly each side's thoughts and feelings for objective consideration. These determinants, however, reside in the participants' or contestants' conceptual structures and in the content of the referent-attribute assemblies of the principal schemata involved in attempts to resolve conflict. The content of the cognitive structures varies not only along dimensions of envy, distrust, anger, hostility, or of co-operation, empathy, and patience, but along all those dimensions which identify individual goals, preferred goal-outcomes, methods of achieving them, and the cognitive capacity to reach the greatest number of goals with the greatest degree of satisfaction and the smallest amount of stressor-strain.

Figure 10.2 and 10.3 show two hypothetical sets of cognitive structures with which two different pairs of union and management negotiators might enter into wages negotiations. For reasons of space and clarity I have limited the display to a small number of referents and attributes, and to those schemata which store the cognitive core of subject matter involved in the solution of the conflict. Figure 10.2 assumes the presence of undogmatic, realistic, and insightful evaluations of the issues and of the negotiating situation by both sides to the conflict. Although this example describes a basis of mutual respect, understanding of each others' negotiating difficulties, and the critical anticipation that the 'same goal' may have to be shared, conflict of interest and method is clearly present. This is shown by the hypothetical union attitude to find the cash needed from a reduction in the number of 'middle management', whereas the company wants to insist on meeting the higher wages costs from improvements in methods of production. The hypothetical attribute structures assigned to the negotiators in this example have been chosen because they are empathic and free from exaggerated class conflict and its associated hostility, anger, and envy. As a result, it may be assumed that the conflict is soluble at what I have called 'minimal cost'. That is, the compromise solution of a 'shared goal' may involve some production changes, more direct production-oriented roles for some management staff with non-replacement of retiring personnel, and a wage settlement somewhat below the maximum 'local going rate', but associated with an improved sickness cover.

In contrast, Figure 10.3 presents sets of hypothetical conceptual structures which will exacerbate a wages conflict by confrontation between antithetical power orientations. There is mutual social and personal hostility and distrust between the negotiators which is unrelated to the objective requirements of negotiation concerning wages so that an industrial conflict assumes the character of personal, political, and social conflicts. Cognitive-developmental aspects of the origins of social attitudes and their capacity and resistance to change have been discussed in earlier chapters. In the present example these influences are assumed to have led to the presence of referent-attribute structures which negatively define the characteristics of other social groups, to anxiety and suspicion in relation to their numerical social and political power, and to individual anxiety over vulnerability to these assumed threats to personal integrity, and to self- and group-esteem. It is likely that a compromise, 'shared goal' solution will eventually be found since the families of the workforce and of management depend on the company remaining in business. By my assumptions this will be achieved only at 'counter-productive cost' since it is unlikely that the conflict will be settled without a walk-out, loss of production, damage to future orders, and a residual climate of anger, frustration, and opposition. One other factor contributes to this hypothetical case history which is minimal or absent from the case described in Figure 10.2. The intrusion of schemata and their referent-attribute structures which are not relevant to the issues to be resolved by the negotiators increases the information processing load, and thus the difficulty of the problem to be solved. Consequently, the negotiators displayed in Figure 10.3 will find it harder to restructure their issues so as to yield the best solution from short- *and* long-term points of view. Apart from a concurrent longer solution time, more problem-solving 'errors' will occur. These will include verbal and non-verbal signals which will in turn elicit cognitive-affective responses which do not help to solve the conflict.

Inner-city delinquency, crime, gang warfare, or rioting have been considered examples of social conflict involving each group's goal of having its own way. As suggested earlier, a cognitive analysis of leadership characteristics and their origins may contribute some answers to the solubility or otherwise of this type of conflict. For present purposes I will limit my examination to those groups which lack formal structure, organization, and well-defined goals. I will exclude, therefore, established gangs and organized criminal fraternities associated with the supply of drugs and prostitution, and with the organized disposal of stolen property. We are thus considering a different kind of leadership which is informal, often temporary and determined by the type of activity and goal, and frequently emerging spontaneously. These leaders obtain their position and influence, however, because at any given time they match adequately the goals and anticipated goal-outcomes of their followers. This is not the place to reiterate the large number of generally consistent social facts and sociological explanations of the emergence of inner-city crime and violence (e.g. Cohen, 1955; Rock and McIntosh, 1974; Morris, 1976; Ribes-Inesta and Bandura, 1976). These have to some extent oversimplified a causal analysis by focusing on environmental deprivations and on the role of political interests, attitudes, and priorities. One often feels that such explanations are themselves more politically motivated than logically defensible in their reference to the *effects* rather than the *causes* of unemployment, overcrowding, poverty, poor housing, poor health, educational deprivation, and feelings of psychological in addition to economic rejection. We are dealing here, of course, with descriptions of correlates rather than with explanations in terms of necessary antecedents. It can be argued further that even as descriptions they are incomplete as long as they ignore some other basic facts. For example, sociological analyses of delinquency, and anti-social behaviour generally, ignore the evidence from ostensibly egalitarian, classless societies which cannot and do not claim to have eradicated widespread law-breaking. Also unexplained is the fact that the persons and objects against which crime and rioting are directed are not those in whom resides the power to diminish deprivation. Most frequently they are directed against members of their own social class, and shops and

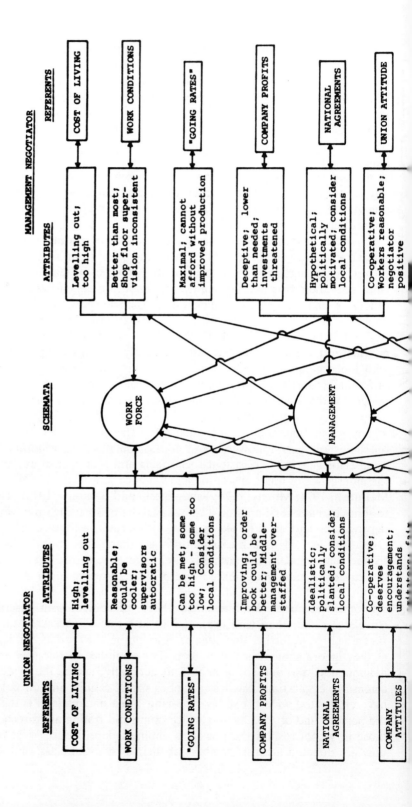

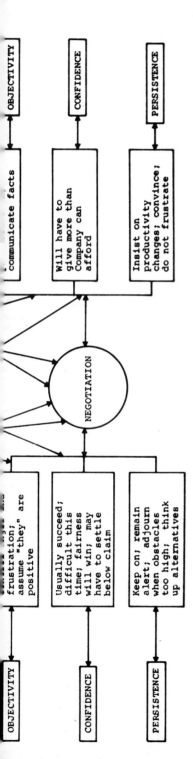

Figure 10.2 Cognitive structures of industrial conflict soluble at 'minimal cost'

298

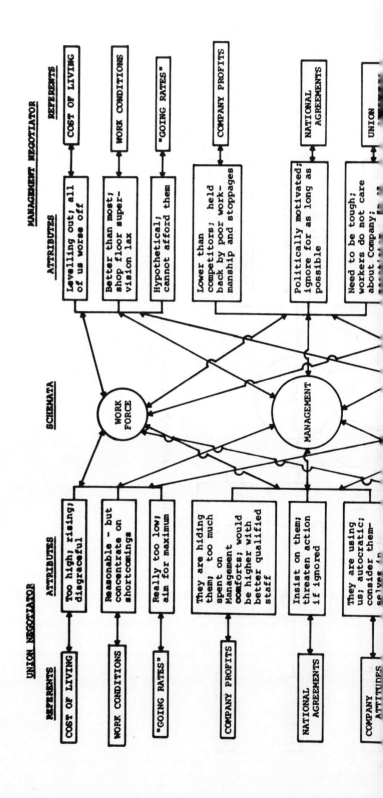

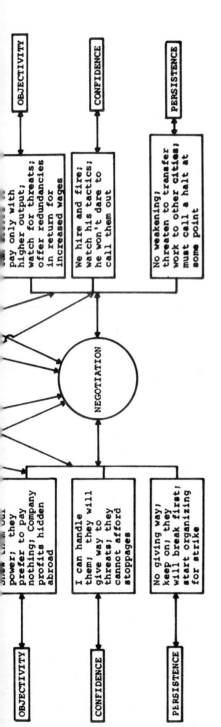

Figure 10.3 Cognitive structures of industrial conflict soluble at 'counter-productive cost'

facilities serving their own community. Most importantly, the sociological approch tends to ignore the presence of an overwhelming number of law-abiding individuals who are resident in socially deprived inner-city areas, and that social group conflict as shown by, for example, mugging or rioting is confined to a relatively and absolutely small number of individuals. Mini-mally, therefore, inner-city behaviour problems are the result of complex interactions. These involve social deprivations, constraints imposed by a consensus legal system, and individual characteristics developed in this con-text and as a result of differential capacities to handle vulnerability to stres-sors by adaptive and productive strategies. Destructive strategies cannot reduce the experience of deprivation without generating or exacerbating social conflict, and do not solve the basic depriving issues.

Law-abiding society can and often does contribute to this conflict in a number of ways. Examples are: tolerating extreme forms of deprivation without giving evidence of ameliorating action; condoning attitudes in schools and the media which implicitly denigrate members of social, ethnic, or reli-gious minority groups living in problem areas; policing in an unnecessarily aggressive and provocative manner by personnel with rigidly hostile and prejudiced concepts of the population characteristics of inner-city residents. Factors such as these will be assimilated to individuals' existing conceptual structures encoding the frustrative and controlling referent-attribute concepts of a hostile society. Those who engage in mugging and rioting do not know, or are not prepared to utilize, alternative methods of dealing with their problems. Their interaction with law-enforcement of the type described above, therefore, will have a similar incompatible decision-making and problem-solving structure as the second example of industrial conflict solution displayed in Figure 10.3, and the temporary solution of the suppression of rioting will have counter-productive costs. It is valid to recall that this level of social conflict has occurred in all societies at some point or other in their history, and that it can, but need not be, the ultimate response of a sorely tried subgroup to draw attention to its forgotten needs (see for example Caplan and Paige, 1968, and Berkowitz, 1970 for a discussion of ghetto riots in the USA).

The most deprived subgroups often have been those who migrated in search of personal and religious freedom, those seeking opportunities to work to maintain their families, or those who might otherwise have been subjugated as a result of territorial conquest. There appear to be no examples where such groups became biologically extinct as a result of even prolonged periods of social deprivation and suppression, or where all members of such groups inevitably succumbed to violent and anti-social action for lack of alternative adaptive strategies. Quite the contrary, even if the vast oppor-tunities for economic expansion in the USA at the turn of the century are discounted. A number of workers have suggested that what determine the overcoming of deprivation are value systems which characterize the non-deprived members of a society (e.g. Matza and Sykes, 1961; Young, 1974).

This is a non-prescriptive term for cognitive structures encoding goals and ways of achieving them.

In Table 10.1 I have drawn up a hypothetical and incomplete set of plausible referent-attribute assemblies which may characterize persons participating in street riots. It generalizes from mainly psychological studies on deviant behaviour (e.g. Glueck and Glueck, 1968) which are often considered as irrelevant by sociologists (e.g. Cohen, 1974).

Table 10.1 attempts to show the *differences between informal leaders* thrown up by what may have started as spontaneous and unpremeditated street violence, but which threatens community safety under this leadership, *and their followers*. Both subgroups show a rejection of the generally accepted evaluations of the community and its services, hostility to 'law-and-order' concepts, envy of those who supply needs, and depressive and denigrating concepts defining 'work'. The major and significant differences, as I see them, between the informal riot leaders and their followers are in terms of *intensity* of rejection, hostility, envy, and negativism, and in the degree of focused elaboration of anti-societal attribute structures. With re-

Table 10.1 Hypothetical Referent-attribute Structures of Inner-city Rioters

	REFERENTS					
	POLICE		'SOCIAL WORKERS'		SHOPKEEPERS	
	Leaders	Followers	Leaders	Followers	Leaders	Followers
ATTRIBUTES	'Pigs'	Make trouble	Hypocritical	Disinterested	Capitalists	Keep you
	Rough	Keep checking	Carry out	Do not try	Overcharge	waiting
	Provoke	Suspicious	Government	hard	Cheat	Overcharge
	Fascist	Interfere with	policy	Pretend	No sympathy	Suspicious
	Violent	friends	Bureaucratic	Criticize	Make false	Never help
	Keep you	Control	Prejudiced		accusations	
	down	Stop enjoy-	Hostile			
	Smash them	ment	Conceited			
	They are the					
	Government					

	REFERENTS					
	WORK		'RULES'		PARENTS	
	Leaders	Followers	Leaders	Followers	Leaders	Followers
ATTRIBUTES	Who wants it	There is none	To keep us	Don't like	'Dead loss'	Criticize
	Underpaid	No good at it	down	them	Brainwashed	Don't care
	Wage slaves	Get turned	For the ruling	Who cares!	Stupid	Do nothing
	Companies use	down	classes	Everyone	Work for	Watch TV
	workers	No qualifica-	Need to be	breaks them	peanuts	
	Autocratic	tions	changed		'Bow and	
	Uninteresting	Get ordered	Dictatorial		scrape'	
		about			Religious	
					maniacs	

spect to the referents of 'police' and 'work' I have indicated that political concepts may contribute to the intensity and elaboration factors. If this is accepted, then, taken in conjunction with greater conceptual elaboration, it suggests that this leadership like others is more intelligent than the followers. My hypothetical example has deliberately excluded concept attributes required for a peaceful, long-term productive development of improved social conditions. Table 10.1, therefore, structures an irreconcilable conflict, and shows an inadequate level of cognitive capacity to evaluate reality by the absence of any alternative interpretations of its built-in constraints *and* its opportunities. Such structures are plausible in any case, perhaps, with a history of actual deprivation, of contact with others similarly deprived, and because of a concomitant inability, or unwillingness, to profit from educational facilities.

To conclude this limited examination of inner-city conflict, attention is drawn to the referent-attribute structure of 'parents'. In my hypothetical case-study I propose that parents are seen by rioters as unsuitable authority figures, as weak, submissive, old-fashioned, and rejecting. In the light of my earlier discussion of the social factors in conceptual structuring, a generalized rejection of authority, discipline, and of achievement-oriented activity to standards set by authority figures, cannot really be surprising. The well-known study by McCord and McCord (1958) fully supports these conclusions. These investigators carried out a reassessment of subjects from a lower socio-economic group urban background who were first seen an average of 20 years before as part of the Cambridge–Somerville Youth Study which commenced in 1935. Since the social factors of inner-city deprivation were controlled, it was possible to examine the influence of parental factors on groups of subjects who subsequently had, or had not, engaged in delinquent or criminal activities. The investigators were able to demonstrate that various combinations, in respect of one or both parents, of rejection, maternal warmth, maternal deviance, paternal criminality, and particularly the consistent non-transmission of a rule-conforming value system, distinguished law-breakers from law-conformers.

Etzioni's (1968) monumental socio-political analysis of the processes required by an 'active society' struggling to control its technological powers could be regarded as putting the cart before the horse, or closing the stable door after the horse has bolted. A dynamic society, Etzioni proposes, must be capable of responding to changes in its membership and must engage in intensive and perpetual transformations. A cognitive-developmental view of human motivation and personality would argue, however, that the capacity to do so depends in the first instance on the capacity to comprehend, to evaluate, and to accept the role-playing demands of dynamic instability. These are not only complex cognitive demands, but the motivation to accept them and their implications depends on affection, respect, and admiration for the supportive family members who usually, often lovingly, and certainly initially, transmit them. It must also remain an unanswered conjecture that the 'active society' can still retain its sometimes unlimited opportunities for purely permissive, ideal-self-seeking, non-contributory activities.

No more than a cursory and necessarily subjective examination of the contribution of leadership characteristics to the solution, avoidance, or persistence of inter-nation conflict can be undertaken. In this exercise I will confine myself to governments which have been freely elected by an electorate which has been able to choose equally freely between the alternative programme platforms of different political parties, and between alternative individuals competing for the confidence assigned to a constituency representative. Excluded here, therefore, will be an analysis of the goal- and solution-structures of the leadership of single-party states, dictatorial or tyrannical leadership, and a consideration of the issue of whether the degree of psychopathological deviance of such leaderships, where it is considered present, is imposed on, or reflects already existing dispositions among their followers. We might just mention, however, some pertinent material in the literature. The clinical studies by Dicks (e.g. 1950, 1972), for example, of German savagery and sadism in the 1930s and 1940s indicate that the Nazi party had no difficulty in finding a substantial core of early followers whose perception of reality and methods of changing it matched those of the leadership. Psychopathological aspects of political leadership in other contexts have also been discussed in relation to the Stalinist system (e.g. Tucker, 1973). A collection of essays edited by Robins (1977) examines not only other dictatorships, but also the contribution of personality and motivational dispositions to political decision-making in the USA by reference to President Woodrow Wilson, Secretary of State Forrestal, and President Kennedy's handling of the 'Cuba Crisis'. What follows, therefore, is not so much an excursion into psychohistory as a very limited examination of hypothetical dispositions potentially distributed in individuals exercising democratic constitutional governmental power which may affect significantly the outcome of inter-nation conflict.

Governing politicians operating in the constitutional setting selected here must possess a number of shared dispositions towards goal-directed actions and a number of shared belief systems, that is conceptual structures, defining their potential responses and anticipated response outcomes. The shared belief systems include concepts of national characteristics, national history, and past and present status power defining the national stereotype and those of other national groups. These concepts are integrated into a party-political philosophy consisting of social and economic concepts of what is, or will be, acceptable to the largest number of individuals in the electorate, and certainly to those that voted them into power. In the prolonged phases of activity to achieve a position on a 'short list' of constituency candidates and of potential members of Government and Cabinet, the individuals concerned will have been able to exhibit a sufficient number of favourable dispositions acceptable to an electorate and to party leadership. These will have included charm, charisma, personal conviction on representative issues, unflappability, a capacity to work efficiently for excessive hours over long periods, while assimilating a large amount of social, political, and inter-personal information in a wide variety of contexts. Thus, they are clearly of more than average intelligence, though not so outstandingly intelligent that they will generate envy, anxiety, and unpopularity among their peers. This, it will be recalled, was one of the interesting findings of Bales' (1950) original experiments on social interactions in small groups.

In addition, they will bring to their candidature and to their office other sets of dispositions. These will include personal goal hierarchies, preferred methods of achieving them, concepts defining their role-playing expectations and needs in relation to the consensus goals which helped them to achieve positions of leadership, as well as dominant ways of perceiving, controlling, or modulating conflict, anxiety, anger, disappointment, and frustration. An aspect of being in a position of national leadership only infrequently considered is the personal economic and financial goals and rewards available to those in positions of power, and in possession of important items of information which are available as a rule for only a limited period of an active working life. While there may be a grain of truth in the saying that 'power corrupts, and absolute power corrupts absolutely', it is a common assumption that a national leadership acts unselfishly, at considerable cost to its health and economic security, without thought of personal gain, and entirely in the service of the community. Biographical and autobiographical evidence indicates, however, that politicians do not forget about their own and their families' goals and expectations, and that far from becoming a charge on social security services after completion of their terms of office, they have frequently acquired, even when representing an egalitarian ideology, possessions and goods in excess of what can usually be obtained by salary savings alone. It seems entirely plausible, therefore, that decision-making with far-reaching consequences for millions of others cannot exclude intrusion of conceptual structures and the goal-outcomes they serve which are of primary relevance only to the individual politician. Thus, *all* cognitive referent-attribute structures of personality and motivation represented in a political leadership play a role in the problem-solving decision-making processes of international conflict. It is equally plausible to propose, therefore, that the capacity to transform conflicts which threaten to become confrontations into the more benign variety of residual disagreement following a 'shared goal' conference interaction, depends on the inter-play of conceptual structures which are similar to those that facilitate industrial peace.

An epoch capable of resorting to ultimate destructive sanctions requires optimism to control the anxiety which would otherwise interfere with the optimal information processing demands of restructuring what appears to be an insoluble conflict. The hope that solutions can be achieved, depends not only on the interpretation of apparently irreconcilable differences between the countries in a state of conflict, but on the attributional elaboration of the conflict-relevant schemata of the negotiators who meet to resolve it. In a necessarily superficial illustration of two alternative teams of negotiators *of one* of the adversaries, I will try to illustrate shortly how the chances of 'minimal cost' conflict reduction may well depend to a greater extent than usually admitted on the general cognitive-affective dispositions of negotiators assigned to the negotiating role. I will adopt the role of an idealist and argue that it is possible to face directly the conflict between groups of nations who have armed forces stationed outside the frontiers of their own countries. The direct approach implies that one group will finally request that both groups should withdraw to within their own borders so that everyone should be relieved of the ever-present stressor-strain of a potential shooting conflict of catastrophic proportion. I am assuming, therefore, that concerns with arms race control and verbal declarations of 'the rights of man to be free' can be interpreted as displacement strategies which avoid the immediate source of conflict and anxiety: physical, face-to-face, confrontation of armies. It is a curious fact that the same contestants who find the disengagement and withdrawal of the instruments of war so difficult to achieve for themselves, often opt for it as a productive technique in other parts of the world.

There have been a number of attempts in recent years to apply general psychological principles to the analysis and reduction of international conflict. A model advanced by Osgood (1962) termed 'Graduated Reciprocation in Tension Reduction' (GRIT), validly assumed that mutual distrust between adversaries is a key issue, and that the behaviour of nations in many ways parallels the interaction of individuals. Etzioni (1967) correctly pointed to the chain of events by which mutually perceived hostility leads to an incremental process of increasing hostility. He also argued correctly that reality becomes progressively more distorted by rigid adherence to response strategies which may have fitted earlier international crises, but not the present ones. Osgood (1962) appropriately referred to stress-induced responses which exacerbate a state of conflict, such as denial of the consequences of actions, projection, and '. . . illogical pseudo-syllogistic reasoning where false conclusions result from faulty premises in the interest of cognitive consistency' (as quoted by Segall, 1976, p. 248). These various conceptions will be recognized to match quite closely the propositions advanced in my earlier chapters about the relationship between poorly differentiated cognitive-affective structures resulting from experiences of threats in individuals vulnerable to stressor-strain, and difficulties in generating alternative adaptive problem-solving processes and operations.

While the psychological appraisal of international conflict in the 1960s favoured an approach by 'unilateral initiative', there have been other suggestions for action with similar objectives and underlying conceptualizations. White (1970), for example, favoured 'enhanced communication of psychological principles' to policy-makers. He pointed out that national negotiators often did not seem to be aware of the need for empathy in conference interactions, the dangers of introducing self-fulfilling prophecies, and the fundamental cognitive disadvantages of thinking in rigidly classified, mutually exclusive alternatives. Group interaction techniques have actually been applied in attempting to resolve frontier disputes between Kenya, Somalia, and Ethiopia. So-called 'T' (training) group techniques were made available to the African negotiators, to help them to create conditions for conflict resolution. From this 'field experiment' in attitude change it became apparent that concepts of nationality and of European nineteenth-century concepts of sovereignty negatively affected the outcome of the discussion groups. More disappointing were the participants' own conclusions that the conflict under discussion appeared insoluble because no novel solutions were generated that could be accepted by all negotiators (Doob, 1970, 1971). The major obstacles, as recognized by Doob (1974), lay in the attributes of the negotiators and their concepts of tension reduction requirements. To achieve success these must include (I have called them 'shared goal' concepts): goal-achievement by one side to the conflict with minimum interference with the goals of the other side; the ability to interact constructively with other individuals; tolerant attitudes towards actual or potential adversaries; rejection of the concept of the use of force and war; a favourable concept of negotiation as a tool for conflict solution; and fullest knowledge of all information relevant to the issue (viz. Doob, 1974, pp. 325–6). We must assume, of course, that conflict reduction rather than its maintenance is the principal goal-outcome preferred by negotiators.

If these principles are valid, it follows that negotiators should be favoured by stressor-strain resisting concepts in which the representation of experiences and implications of 'loss' do not form the most significant components of schematic structures encoding anxiety, frustration, and low self-esteem. The reason for this proposition is that a 'shared goal' compromise solution involves giving-up the notion of total gain and undisputed superiority. It further follows that when not identifying the probability of a reduction of hypothetical national power and status with a personal vulnerability to personal security and self-esteem, the information processing capacities of the negotiators are higher than if such task-irrelevant intrusions are likely to occur. Figure 10.4 presents two hypothetical and subjectively exaggerated referent-attribute profiles, and their appropriate schemata, of two alternative 'Teams' of negotiators available in a country which freely elects its representatives in a setting of equally free speech. The availability of alternative negotiators is one expression of the relative freedom to express opposing views as long as these have substantial support from an electorate. It is quite clear that I have chosen deliberately antithetical negotiating attitudes and their antecedent individual goal-directed preferences to make a relatively simple point. It is equally clear that there are many alternative combinations of referent-attribute structures which could make the same point, but in the presence of some internal contradictions within any or all of the negotiators of each 'Team'. Moreover, the most important conflicts and their solution difficulties cannot really emerge unless the disposition structures of the other party to the conflict are added. If the referent-attribute structures of the

307

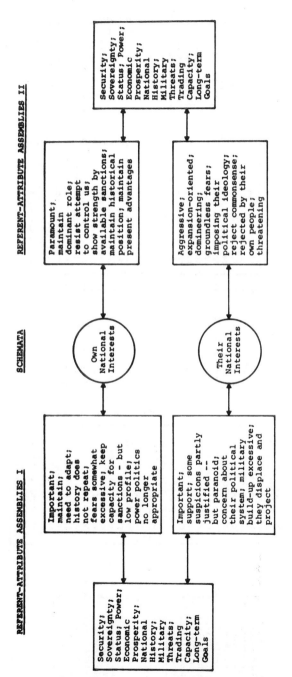

Figure 10.4 (*Continued over page*)

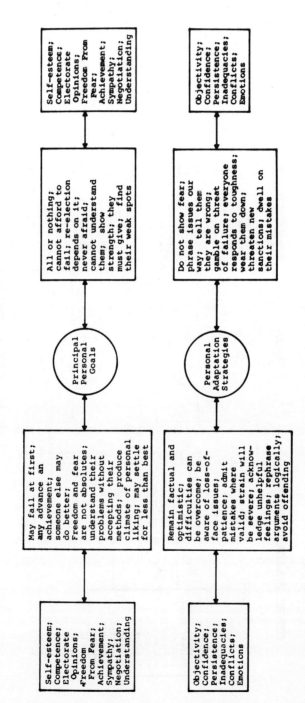

Figure 10.4 Hypothetical cognitive structures of alternative 'teams' negotiating international conflict reduction

negotiators fielded by the adversary should be similar to those of the hypothetical 'Team II' illustrated in Figure 10.4 their capacity to resolve or reduce international conflict will be as deficient as that of 'Team II'.

The difference between an optimistic and idealistic view and an omnipotent assessment of the threat of human conflict on a global extinction-threatening scale, is that the former reflects hope which the latter has surpassed with an unwarranted degree of certainty. We may also note that at least one influential theory has proposed that omnipotence is a reaction to the anxiety of experiencing weakness and vulnerability, and that optimistic idealism can reflect underlying inadequacies of reality awareness. There need be no objection in principle, however, to the aims of one branch of behavioural science in offering an available therapeutic method for the reduction of the ills of a conflict situation, even if, as in the case of pharmacological therapeutics, the effects cannot be observed unless the treatment is tried out. Self-evidently they cannot be worse than the outcome they are trying to prevent. It seems entirely illogical, however, to continue with conflict-solving techniques which are not experienced as tension-reducing. Such behavioural stereotypy and its stupendous denial processes in the face of frightening dangers can be validly interpreted as pathological, that is, consistent with all the criteria by which we define abnormality.

3 A LAST, BUT OBVIOUSLY NOT FINAL WORD

I have tried to derive a model of the person which I believe to be consistent with our present state of knowledge. This model regards the person as information-receptive, and as acting on the internalized, descriptive, and outcome-signifying meaning of information. The capacity to absorb, elaborate, and utilize information for the benefit of the individual's optimal and preferred state of existence has been regarded as an interactive function of cognitive processing capacity, of the informational characteristics of the social environment, and of the capacity to experience, modulate, encode, and store the dominant affective states to which interaction has given rise. I have proposed that the accumulation of information occurs in organized structures or schemata in which functionally related needs and strategies to achieve response outcomes are assembled. In addition I have proposed that the knowledge contained in informational data stores is semantically labelled in all societies and their subgroups, because language labels have a superior capacity for economically and succinctly conveying knowledge, its meaning, and its implications. I have regarded the distinction between concepts and theories of personality and motivation as misleading, unhelpful and, therefore, as redundant, because they represent functionally related components of the same event or action selectively determined by the outcome of decision-making processes towards the solution of a goal-seeking problem.

In deriving and stating the cognitive model of the structures and processes of personality and motivation, I have *tried* to avoid making or implying social and moral evaluations. Where such intentions are thought to be present, they should be regarded as inadvertent, or conceivably as projections on my part, or of those of the reader. The aim throughout has been to be objective in the selection of examples and their analysis, and to indicate that certain individual advantages or disadvantages are fortuitous and amenable to modification with different environmental conditions, and by rewarding individual powers of goal-seeking. These factors, however, define the willingness and competence to solve individual problems of sufficiency and self-realization with skills and capacities available to the person. Just as height, weight, and manual strength are confined by genetic factors to a range of upper limits, so it must be accepted that patterns of skills and problem-solving capacities have biological limitation. These limits are accepted by the vast majority of individuals because what is important to them is the achievement of the goals they set themselves – the goals which they anticipate achieving with the skills and methods available to them, rather than the differing goals of other individuals with different skills and goal-seeking methods.

The availability of goals in the environment is largely determined by the skills, aims, and efforts of our leaders. The examples of social conflict discussed in a rather oversimplifying manner in the last section, show that the partial autonomy presented to a leadership may be misguiding, misused, and become counter-productive where their personal goals and their preferred means of achieving them deviate from those of the majority of the led. The reasons for those deviations have been sought in profiles of idiosyncratic cognitive structures, which in some of the examples given verge on what can be termed psychopathological. Charm, charisma, personal conviction, and intellectual ability are some of the commonly accepted principal components of the selection criteria for leadership. But we have not yet utilized our new knowledge of the inadequacy, and even ultimate danger, of these gifts in the context of fundamentally vulnerable individuals. Here they can undermine the capacity to subordinate personal goals to group goals by not generating goal-achieving strategies which are to the long-term benefit of others as well as to themselves.

References

Abramson, L. Y., Seligman, M. E. P., and Teasdale, J. D. (1978). Learned help-lessness in humans: critique and reformulation. *Journal of Abnormal Psychology*, **87**, 49–74.

Ainsworth, M. D. S., Bell, S. M. V., and Stayton, D. J. (1972). Individual differences in the development of some attachment behaviors. *Merrill-Palmer Quarterly*, **18**, 123–43.

Allport, D. A. (1975). The state of cognitive psychology. *Quarterly Journal of Experimental Psychology*, **27**, 141–52.

Allport, D. A. (1980). Patterns and actions: cognitive mechanisms are content-specific. In G. Claxton (ed.), *Cognitive Psychology – New Directions*. London: Routledge and Kegan Paul.

Allport, D. A., Antonis, B., and Reynolds, P. (1972). On the division of attention: a disproof of the single channel hypothesis. *Quarterly Journal of Experimental Psychology*, **24**, 225–35.

Allport, G. W. (1937). *Personality: A Psychological Interpretation*. New York: Holt.

Allport, G. W. and Postman, L. (1948). *The Psychology of Rumor*. New York: Henry Holt.

Alston, W. P. (1976). Traits, consistency and conceptual alternatives for personality theory. In R. Harré (ed.), *Personality*. Oxford: Blackwell.

Amsel, A. (1962). Frustrative non-reward in partial reinforcement and discrimination learning: some recent history and a theoretical extension. *Psychological Review*, **69**, 306–28.

Anderson, J. R. (1976). *Language, Memory, and Thought*. Hillsdale, NJ: Lawrence Erlbaum.

Anderson, J. R. (1978). Arguments concerning representations for mental imagery. *Psychological Review*, **85**, 249–77.

Anderson, J. R. (1980). *Cognitive Psychology and its Implications*. San Francisco: Freeman.

Anderson, J. R. (1981). Concepts, propositions and schemata: what are the cognitive units? In H. E. Howe Jr. (ed.), *Nebraska Symposium on Motivation*, **28**, 121–62. Lincoln: University of Nebraska Press.

Anderson, J. R. and Bower, G. H. (1973). *Human Associative Memory*. Washington, DC: Winston.

Anscombe, G. E. (1957). *Intention*. Oxford: Blackwell.

Argyris, C. (1962). *Interpersonal Competence and Organizational Effectiveness*. London: Tavistock.

Arnold, M. B. (1969). Human emotion and action. In T. Mischel (ed.), *Human Action*. New York: Academic Press.

311

Arnold, M. B. (1970). *Feelings and Emotions: The Loyola Symposium*. New York: Academic Press.

Asch, S. (1952). *Social Psychology*. New York: Prentice-Hall.

Aserinsky, E. and Kleitman, N. (1953). Regularly occurring periods of eye motility, and concomitant phenomena, during sleep. *Science*, **118**, 273–4.

Ashby, W. R. (1952). *Design for a Brain*. London: Chapman Hall.

Atkinson, J. W. (1958). *Motives in Fantasy, Action, and Society*. Princeton, NJ: Van Nostrand.

Atkinson, J. W. (1977). Motivation for achievement. In T. Blass (ed.), *Personality Variables in Social Behavior*. Hillsdale, NJ: Lawrence Erlbaum.

Averbach, E. and Coriell, A. S. (1961). Short term memory in vision. *Bell Systems Technical Journal*, **40**, 309–28.

Averill, J. R. (1979). Anger. In H. E. Howe, Jr. (ed.), *Nebraska Symposium on Motivation*, **26**, 1–80. Lincoln: University of Nebraska Press.

Averill, J. R., DeWitt, G. W., and Zimmer, M. (1978). The self-attribution of emotion as a function of success and failure. *Journal of Personality*, **46**, 323–47.

Averill, J. R., O'Brien, L., and DeWitt, G. W. (1977). The influence of response effectiveness on the preference for warning and on psychophysiological stress reactions. *Journal of Personality*, **45**, 395–418.

Baddeley, A. D. (1976). *The Psychology of Memory*. New York: Harper & Row.

Baddeley, A. D. (1978). The trouble with levels: a re-examination of Craik and Lockhart's framework for memory research. *Psychological Review*, **85**, 139–52.

Bainbridge, L. (1979). Verbal reports as evidence of the process operator's knowledge. *International Journal of Man-Machine Studies*, **11**, 411–36.

Baldwin, A. L. (1969). A cognitive theory of socialization. In D. A. Goslin (ed.),, *Handbook of Socialization Theory and Research*. Chicago: Rand McNally.

Bales, R. F. (1950). *Interaction Process Analysis*. Cambridge, Mass.: Addison-Wesley.

Bandura, A. (1977). *Social Learning Theory*. Englewood Cliffs, NJ: Prentice-Hall.

Bandura, A., Blanchard, E. B., and Ritter, B. (1969). The relative efficacy of desensitization and modeling approaches for inducing behavioral, affective, and attitudinal changes. *Journal of Personality and Social Psychology*, **13**, 173–99.

Bandura, A. and Walters, R. (1963).*Social Learning and Personality Development*. New York: Holt, Rinehart and Winston.

Bannister, D. (1970) (ed.). *Perspectives in Personal Construct Theory*. London: Academic Press.

Bannister, D. (1977) (ed.). *New Perspectives in Personal Construct Theory*. London: Academic Press.

Bartlett, F. C. (1932). *Remembering*. Cambridge: Cambridge University Press.

Bates, E. (1979). *The Emergence of Symbols: Cognition and Communication in Infancy*. New York: Academic Press.

Bateson, G., Jackson, D. D., Haley, J., and Weakland, J. (1956). Toward a theory of schizophrenia. *Behavioral Science*, **1**, 251–64.

Baumrind, D. (1967). Child care practices anteceding three patterns of preschool behavior. *Genetic Psychological Monographs*, **75**, 43–88.

Baumrind, D. (1971). Current patterns of parental authority. *Developmental Psychology Monographs*, **41**, (1, Part 2).

Baumrind, D. (1972). Socialization and instrumental competence in young children. In W. W. Hartup (ed.), *The Young Child: Reviews of Research*, Vol. 2. Washington DC: National Association for the Education of Young Children.

Beck, A. T. (1976). *Cognitive Therapy and the Emotional Disorders*. New York: International Universities Press.

Beck, A. T., Laude, R., and Bohnert, M. (1974). Ideational components of anxiety neurosis. *Archives of General Psychiatry*, **31**, 319–25.

Beck, A. T. and Rush, A. J. (1975). A cognitive model of anxiety formation and anxiety resolution. In I. G. Sarason and C. D. Spielberger (eds), *Stress and Anxiety*, Vol. 2. Washington DC: Hemisphere.

Bell, S. M. (1970). The development of the concept of object as related to infant-mother attachment. *Child Development*, **41**, 291–311.

Bendefeldt, F., Miller, L. L., and Ludwig, A. M. (1976). Cognitive performance in conversion hysteria. *Archives of General Psychiatry*, **33**, 1250–4.

Berkowitz, L. (1970). Impulse, aggression, and the gun. In J. V. McConnell (ed.), *Readings in Social Psychology Today*. Del Mar, Cal.: CRM Books.

Berkowitz, L. (1978) (ed.). *Cognitive Theories in Social Psychology*. New York: Academic Press.

Berlyne, D. E. (1957). Conflict and information theory variables as determinants of human perceptual curiosity. *Journal of Experimental Psychology*, **53**, 399–404.

Berlyne, D. E. (1963). Complexity and incongruity variables as determinants of exploratory choice and evaluative ratings. *Canadian Journal of Psychology*, **17**, 274–90.

Berlyne, D. E. (1970). Novelty, complexity and hedonic value. *Perception and Psychophysics*, **8**, 279–86.

Berlyne, D. E. and McDonnell, P. (1965). Effect of stimulus complexity and incongruity on duration of EEG desynchronization. *Electroencephalography and Clinical Neurophysiology*, **18**, 156–61.

Bernstein, B. B. (1961). Social class and linguistic development: a theory of social learning. In A. H. Halsey (ed.), *Education, Economy and Society*. Glencoe, NY: Free Press.

Bernstein, B. B. (1971). *Class, Codes and Control*. London: Routledge and Kegan Paul.

Bexton, W. H., Heron, W., and Scott, T. H. (1954). Effects of decreased variation in the sensory environment. *Canadian Journal of Psychology*, **8**, 70–6.

Bieri, J. (1955). Cognitive complexity – simplicity and predictive behavior. *Journal of Abnormal and Social Psychology*, **51**, 263–8.

Bieri, J. (1966). Cognitive complexity and personality development. In O. J. Harvey (ed.), *Experience, Structure, and Adaptability*. New York: Springer.

Bindra, D. (1968). A unified interpretation of emotion and motivation. *Annals of the New York Academy of Science*, **159**, 1071–83.

Bing, E. (1963). Effect of child-rearing practices on development of differential cognitive abilities. *Child Development*, **34**, 631–48.

Blakemore, C., Carpenter, R. H. S., and Georgeson, M. A. (1970). Lateral inhibition between orientation detectors in the human visual system. *Nature*, **228**, 29–39.

Blank, H. R. (1958). Dreams of the blind. *Psychoanalytic Quarterly*, **27**, 158–74.

Blatt, S. J. and Wild, C. M. (1976). *Schizophrenia – A Developmental Analysis*. New York: Academic Press.

Block, J. (1977). Advancing the psychology of personality – paradigmatic shift, or improving the quality of research. In D. Magnusson and N. S. Endler (eds), *Personality at the Crossroads: Current Issues in Interactional Psychology*. Hillsdale, NJ: Lawrence Erlbaum.

Block, J. (1981). Some enduring and consequential structures of personality. In A. I. Rabin, J. Aronoff, A. M. Barclay, and R. A. Zucker (eds), *Further Explorations in Personality*. New York: Wiley.

Blumenthal, A. L. (1977). *The Process of Cognition*. Englewood Cliffs, NJ: Prentice-Hall.

Bobrow, D. G. and Norman, D. A. (1975). Some principles of memory schemata. In D. G. Bobrow and A. M. Collins (eds), *Representation and Understanding: Studies in Cognitive Science*. New York: Academic Press.

Bolles, R. C. (1972). Reinforcement, expectancy, and learning. *Psychological Review*, **79**, 394–409.

314

Bolles, R. C. (1974). Cognition and motivation: some historical trends. In B. Weiner (ed.), *Cognitive Views of Human Motivation*. New York: Academic Press.

Borkovec, T. D. (1976). Physiological and cognitive processes in the regulation of anxiety. In G. E. Schwartz and D. Shapiro (eds), *Consciousness and Self-Regulation*, Vol. 1. Chichester: Wiley.

Bousfield, W. A. (1953). The occurrence of clustering in the recall of randomly arranged associates. *Journal of General Psychology*, **49**, 229–40.

Bower, G. H. (1972). Mental imagery and associative learning. In L. W. Gregg (ed.), *Cognition in Learning and Memory*. New York: Wiley.

Bower, G. H. (1981). Mood and memory. *American Psychologist*, **36**, 129–48.

Bower, G. H., Black, J. B., and Turner, T. J. (1979). Scripts in memory for texts. *Cognitive Psychology*, **11**, 177–220.

Bower, G. H. and Gilligan, S. G. (1979). Remembering information related to one's self. *Journal of Research in Personality*, **13**, 420–32.

Bower, G. H., Karlin, M. B., and Dueck, A. (1975). Comprehension and memory for pictures. *Memory and Cognition*, **3**, 216–20.

Bower, G. H., Monteiro, K. P., and Gilligan, S. G. (1978). Emotional mood as a context of learning and recall. *Journal of Verbal Learning and Verbal Behavior*, **17**, 573–85.

Bowlby, J. (1951). *Maternal Care and Mental Health*. Geneva: WHO Monographs Series, No. 2.

Bowlby, J. (1971). *Attachment and Loss*, Vol. 1. Harmondsworth: Penguin.

Brachman, R. J. (1979). The epistemological status of semantic networks. In N. V. Findler (ed.), *Associative Networks: Representation and Use of Knowledge by Computers*. Englewood Cliffs, NJ: Prentice-Hall.

Breznitz, S. (1982). Denial-like behavior. In S. Breznitz (ed.), *The Denial of Stress*. New York: International Universities Press.

Bridges, K. M. B. (1932). *The Social and Emotional Development of the Pre-School Child*. London: Kegan Paul.

Brierley, H. (1961). The speed and accuracy characteristics of neurotics. *British Journal of Psychology*, **52**, 273–80.

Broadbent, D. E. (1958). *Perception and Communication*. London: Pergamon.

Broadbent, D. E. (1971). *Decision and Stress*. London: Academic Press.

Broadbent, D. E. (1977a). The hidden pre-attentive process. *American Psychologist*, **32**, 109–18.

Broadbent, D. E. (1977b). Levels, hierarchies, and locus of control. *Quarterly Journal of Experimental Psychology*, **29**, 181–201.

Broadbent, D. E. and Broadbent, M. H. P. (1976). General shape and local detail in word perception. In S. Dornic (ed.), *Attention and Performance VI*, Hillsdale, NJ: Lawrence Erlbaum.

Brody, S. and Axelrad, S. (1971). Maternal stimulation and social responsiveness in infants. In H. R. Schaffer (ed.), *The Origins of Human Social Relations*. London: Academic Press.

Brooks, L. R. (1968). Spatial and verbal components of the act of recall. *Canadian Journal of Psychology*, **22**, 349–68.

Brown, G. W. (1979). The social etiology of depression – London Studies. In R. A. Depue (ed.),, *The Psychobiology of the Depressive Disorders*. New York: Academic Press.

Brown, G. W., Harris, T. O., and Peto, J. (1973). Life events and psychiatric disorders. 2. Nature of causal link. *Psychological Medicine*, **3**, 159–76.

Brown, J. S. (1961). *The Motivation of Behavior*. New York: McGraw-Hill.

Bruner, J. S. (1951). Personality dynamics and the process of perceiving. In R. R. Blake and G. V. Ramsay (eds), *Perception – An Approach to Personality*. New York: Ronald Press.

Bruner, J. S. (1956). A cognitive theory of personality. Review of G. Kelly's *Psychology of Personal Constructs. Contemporary Psychology*, **1**, 355–8.

Bruner, J. S. (1974). *Beyond the Information Given: Studies in the Psychology of Knowing*. London: Allen & Unwin.

Bruner, J. S. (1977). Early social interaction and language acquisition. In H. R. Schaffer (ed.), *Studies in Mother–Infant Interaction*. London: Academic Press.

Bruner, J. S., Goodnow, J. J., and Austin, G. A. (1956). *A Study of Thinking*. New York: Wiley.

Bruner, J. S. and Postman, L. (1947). Emotional selectivity in perception and reaction. *Journal of Personality*, **16**, 69–77.

Bruner, J. S. and Tajfel, H. (1961). Cognitive risk and environmental change. *Journal of Abnormal and Social Psychology*, **62**, 231–41.

Buchsbaum, M. (1976). Self-regulation of stimulus intensity – augmenting, reducing and the average evoked response. In G. E. Schwartz and D. Shapiro (eds), *Consciousness and Self-Regulation – Advances in Research*. Vol. 1. London: Wiley.

Buck, R. (1976). *Human Motivation and Emotion*. New York: Wiley.

Burt, C. (1925). *The Young Delinquent*. London: University of London Press.

Butler, R. A. and Harlow, H. F. (1954). Persistence of visual exploration in monkeys. *Journal of Comparative and Physiological Psychology*, **47**, 258–63.

Cameron, N. (1947). *The Psychology of Behavior Disorders*. Boston: Houghton Mifflin.

Cameron, N. (1951). Perceptual organization and behavior pathology. In R. R. Blake and G. V. Ramsay (eds), *Perception: An Approach to Personality*. New York: Ronald Press.

Cameron, N. (1959). The paranoid pseudo-community revisited. *American Journal of Sociology*, **65**, 52–8.

Cantor, N. and Kihlstrom, J. (1981). *Personality, Cognition and Social Interaction*. Hillsdale; NJ: Lawrence Erlbaum.

Cantor, N. and Mischel, W. (1977). Traits as prototypes: effects on recognition memory. *Journal of Personality and Social Psychology*, **35**, 38–48.

Caplan, N. S. and Paige, J. M. (1968). A study of ghetto rioters. *Scientific American*, **219**, 15–21.

Carmichael, L., Hogan, H. P., and Walter, A. A. (1932). An experimental study of the effect of language on the reproduction of visually perceived form. *Journal of Experimental Psychology*, **15**, 73–86.

Cattell, R. B. (1950). *Personality*. New York: McGraw-Hill.

Cattell, R. B. (1957). *Personality and Motivation Structure and Measurement*. Yonkers: World Book.

Cattell, R. B. (1965). *The Scientific Analysis of Personality*. Chicago: Aldine.

Cattell, R. B. (1973). Key issues in motivation theory (with special reference to structured learning and the dynamic calculus). In J. R. Royce (ed.), *Multivariate Analysis and Psychological Theory*. London: Academic Press.

Cattell, R. B. and Dreger, R. M. (1977). *Handbook of Modern Personality Theory*. Washington, DC: Hemisphere.

Cattell, R. B. and Kline, P. (1977). *The Scientific Analysis of Personality and Motivation*. London: Academic Press.

Chapman, A. J. and Crompton, P. (1978). Humorous presentations of material, and presentations of humorous material: a review. In M. M. Gruneberg, P. E. Morris, and R. N. Sykes (eds), *Practical Aspects of Memory*. London: Academic Press.

Chess, S. (1980). Developmental theory revisited. In A. Thomas and S. Chess (eds), *Annual Progress in Child Psychiatry and Child Development*. New York: Brunner/Mazel.

Chess, S., Thomas, A., and Birch, H. G. (1968). Behavior problems revisited:

findings of an anteroceptive study. In S. Chess and A. Thomas (eds), *Annual Progress in Child Psychiatry and Child Development*. New York: Brunner/Mazel.

Christie, R. and Jahoda, M. (1954) (eds). *Studies in the Scope and Method of 'The Authoritarian Personality'*. Glencoe, Ill.: Free Press.

Clark, E. (1977). Strategies and the mapping problem in first language acquisition. In J. Macnamara (ed.), *Language, Learning and Thought*. New York: Academic Press.

Clark, H. H. and Clark, E. (1977). *Psychology and Language – An Introduction to Psycholinguistics*. New York: Harcourt Brace Jovanovich.

Clarke, A. M. and Clarke, A. D. B. (1974). *Mental Deficiency: The Changing Outlook*, 3rd ed. London: Methuen.

Clarke-Stewart, K. A. (1973). Interactions between mothers and their young children: characteristics and consequences. *Monographs of the Society for Research in Child Development*, **38**, No. 153.

Cofer, C. N. and Appley, M. H. (1964). *Motivation: Theory and Research*. New York: Wiley.

Cohen, A. K. (1955). *Delinquent Boys: The Culture of the Gang*. London: Collier-Macmillan.

Cohen L. B. and Salapatek, P. (1975) (eds). *Infant Perception: From Sensation to Cognition*. New York: Academic Press.

Cohen, S. (1974). Criminology and the sociology of deviance in Britain. In P. Rock and M. McIntosh (eds), *Deviance and Socail Control*. London: Tavistock.

Colby, K. M. (1975). *Artificial Paranoia*. New York: Pergamon.

Collins, A. M. and Loftus, E. F. A. (1975). A spreading activation theory of semantic processing. *Psychological Review*, **82**, 407–28.

Collins, A. M. and Quillian, M. R. (1969). Retrieval time from semantic memory. *Journal of Verbal Learning and Verbal Behavior*, **8**, 240–8.

Collins, A. M. and Quillian, M. R. (1972). Experiments on semantic memory and language comprehension. In L. W. Gregg (ed.), *Cognition in Learning and Memory*. New York: Wiley.

Coltheart, M. (1976). Contemporary models of the cognitive processes: I. iconic storage and visual masking. In V. Hamilton and M. D. Vernon (eds), *The Development of Cognitive Processes*. London: Academic Press.

Coltheart, M., Patterson, K. E., and Marshall, J. C. (1980) (eds). *Deep Dyslexia*. London: Routledge and Kegan Paul.

Constanzo, P. R. and Shaw, M. E. (1966). Conformity as a function of age level. *Child Development*, **37**, 967–75.

Cox, T. (1978). *Stress*. London: Macmillan.

Craik, F. I. M. and Jacoby, L. L. (1980). Elaboration and distinctiveness in episodic memory. In L.-G. Nilson (ed.), *Perspectives on Memory Research*. Hillsdale, NJ: Lawrence Erlbaum.

Craik, F. I. M. and Lockhart, R. S. (1972). Levels of processing: a framework for memory research. *Journal of Verbal Learning and Verbal Behavior*, **11**, 671–84.

Craik, F. I. M. and Tulving, E. (1975). Depth of processing and the retention of words in episodic memory. *Journal of Exoerimental Psychology*, **104**, 268–94.

Crockett, W. H. (1965). Cognitive complexity and impression formation. In B. A. Maher (ed.), *Progress in Experimental Personality Research*, Vol. 2. New York: Academic Press.

Croog, S. H., Shapiro, D. C., and Levine, S. (1971). Denial among male heart patients. *Psychosomatic Medicine*, **33**, 385–92.

Crossman, E. R. F. W. (1953). Entropy and choice time: the effect of frequency unbalance on choice response. *Quarterly Journal of Experimental Psychology*, **5**, 41–51.

Darwin, C. J., Turvey, M. T., and Crowder, R. G. (1972). An auditory analogue of the Sperling partial-report procedure: evidence for brief auditory storage. *Cognitive Psychology*, **3**, 255–67.

Davidson, R. J. and Erlichman, H. (1980). Lateralized cognitive processes and the electroencephalogram. *Science*, **207**, 1005–6.

Décarie, T. H. (1978). Affect development and cognition in a Piagetian context. In M. Lewis and L. A. Rosenblum (eds), *The Development of Affect*. New York: Plenum Press.

Dement, W. and Kleitman, N. (1957). Cyclic variations in EEG during sleep, and their relations to eye movements, bodily motility and dreaming. *Electroencephalographic Clinical Neurophysiology*, **9**, 673–90.

Denny, J. P. (1966). Effects of anxiety and intelligence on concept formation. *Journal of Experimental Psychology*, **72**, 596–602.

Dethier, V. G. (1964). Microscopic brains. *Science*, **143**, 1138–45.

Dicks, H. V. (1950). Personality traits and National Socialist ideology. *Human Relations*, **3**, 111–54.

Dicks, H. V. (1972). *Licensed Mass Murder: A Socio-Psychological Study of Some SS Killers*. London: Chatto-Heinemann.

Dillehay, R. C. (1978). Authoritarianism. In H. London and J. E. Exner, Jnr. (eds), *Dimensions of Personality*. New York: Wiley.

Divesta, F. J. and Cox, L. (1960). Some dispositional correlates of conformity behavior. *Journal of Social Psychology*, **52**, 259–68.

Dixon, N. F. (1958). The effect of subliminal stimulation upon autonomic and verbal behavior. *Journal of Abnormal and Social Psychology*, **57**, 29–36.

Dixon, N. F. (1971). *Subliminal Perception – The Nature of a Controversy*. London: McGraw-Hill.

Dixon, N. F. (1980). Humor: a cognitive alternative to stress. In I. G. Sarason and C. D. Spielberger (eds), *Stress and Anxiety*, Vol. 7. Washington, DC: Hemisphere.

Dixon, N. F. (1981). *Preconscious Processing*. Chichester: Wiley.

Dixon, N. F. and Haider, M. (1961). Changes in the visual threshold as a function of subception. *Quarterly Journal of Experimental Psychology*, **13**, 229–35.

Dodd, D. H. and White, R. M. Jr. (1980). *Cognition – Mental Structures and Processes*. Boston: Allyn and Bacon.

Dollard, J. and Miller, N. E. (1950). *Personality and Psychotherapy: An Analysis in Terms of Learning, Thinking and Culture*. New York: McGraw-Hill.

Doob, L. W. (1970) (ed.). *Resolving Conflict in Africa: The Fermeda Workshop*. New Haven: Yale University Press.

Doob, L. W. (1971). The impact of the Fermeda workshop on the conflicts in the Horn of Africa. *International Journal of Group Tensions*, **1**, 91–101.

Doob, L. W. (1974). The analysis and resolution of international disputes. *Journal of Psychology*, **86**, 313–26.

Douglas, J. W. (1964). *The Home and the School: A Study of Ability and Attainment in the Primary School*. London: MacGibbon & Kee.

Dunn, R. F. (1968). Anxiety and verbal concept learning. *Journal of Experimental Psychology*, **76**, 286–90.

Easterbrook, J. A. (1959). The effect of emotion on cue-utilization and the organization of behavior. *Psychological Review*, **66**, 183–201.

Edwards, A. C. (1953). *Edwards Personal Preference Schedule*. New York: Psychological Corporation.

Eibl-Eibesfeldt, I. (1979). Human ethology: concepts and implications for the sciences of man. *Behavioral and Brain Sciences*, **2**, 1–57.

Elkind, D. (1961). Children's discovery of the conservation of mass, weight and volume: Piaget replication study II. *Journal of Genetic Psychology*, **98**, 219–27.

Emler, M. P., Heather, N., and Winton, M. (1978). Delinquency and the development of moral reasoning. *British Journal of Social and Clinical Psychology*, **17**, 325–31.

Endler, N. S. (1981). Persons, situations, and their interactions. In A. I. Rabin, J. Aronoff, A. M. Barclay, and R. A. Zucker (eds), *Further Explorations in Personality*. New York: Wiley.

Endler, N. S. and Magnusson, D. (1976a). *Interactional Psychology and Personality*. New York: Wiley.

Endler, N. S. and Magnusson, D. (1976b). Toward an interactional psychology of personality. *Psychological Bulletin*, **83**, 956–74.

Epstein, S. (1976). Anxiety, arousal, and the self-concept. In I. G. Sarason and C. D. Spielberger (eds), *Stress and Anxiety*, Vol. 3. New York: Wiley.

Erdelyi, M. H. (1974). A new look at the new look: perceptual defense and vigilance. *Psychological Review*, **81**, 1–25.

Erdelyi, M. H. and Applebaum, G. A. (1973). Cognitive masking: the disruptive effect of an emotional stimulus upon the perception of contiguous neutral items. *Bulletin of the Psychonomic Society*, **1**, 59–61.

Erdelyi, M. H. and Blumenthal, D. G. (1973). Cognitive masking in rapid sequential processing: the effect of an emotional picture on preceding and succeeding pictures. *Memory and Cognition*, **1**, 201–4.

Escalona, S. K. (1968). *The Roots of Individuality: Normal Patterns of Development in Infancy*. Chicago: Aldine.

Estes, W. K. (1972). An associative basis for coding and organization in memory. In A. W. Melton and E. Martin (eds), *Coding Processes in Human Memory*. Washington, DC: Winston.

Estes, W. K. (1973). Memory and conditioning. In F. J. McGuigan and D. B. Lunsden (eds), *Contemporary Approaches to Conditioning and Learning*. New York: Wiley.

Estes, W. K. (1976a). Structural aspects for associative models for memory. In C. N. Cofer (ed.), *The Structure of Human Memory*. San Francisco: Freeman.

Estes, W. K. (1976b) (ed.). *Handbook of Learning and Cognitive Processes Vol. 4.: Attention and Memory*. Hillsdale, NJ: Lawrence Erlbaum.

Estes, W. K. (1978). On the organization and core concepts of learning theory and cognitive psychology. In W. K. Estes (ed.), *Handbook of Learning and Cognitive Processes*, Vol. 6. Hillsdale, NJ: Lawrence Erlbaum.

Etzioni, A. (1967). The Kennedy experiment. *Western Political Quarterly*, **20**, 361–80.

Etzioni, A. (1968). *The Active Society: A Theory of Societal and Political Processes*. New York: The Free Press.

Eysenck, H. J. (1950). Criterion analysis – an application of the hypothetico-deductive method of factor analysis. *Psychological Review*, **57**, 38–53.

Eysenck, H. J. (1952). *The Scientific Study of Personality*. London: Routledge & Kegan Paul.

Eysenck, H. J. (1957). *The Dynamics of Anxiety and Hysteria*. London: Routledge & Kegan Paul.

Eysenck, H. J. (1960). *The Structure of Human Personality*. London: Methuen.

Eysenck, H. J. (1967a). *The Biological Basis of Personality*. Springfield, Ill.: C. C. Thomas.

Eysenck, H. J. (1967b). Intelligence assessment: a theoretic and experimental approach. *British Journal of Educational Psychology*, **37**, 81–98.

Eysenck, H. J. (1968). A theory of the incubation of anxiety/fear responses. *Behaviour Research and Therapy*, **6**, 309–21.

Eysenck, H. J. (1970). *Crime and Personality*. 2nd ed. London: Routledge & Kegan Paul.

Eysenck, H. J. (1973). Personality, learning and 'anxiety'. In H. J. Eysenck (ed.), *Handbook of Abnormal Psychology*, 2nd ed. London: Pitman.

Eysenck, H. J. (1976a). The learning theory model of neurosis – a new approach. *Behaviour Research and Therapy*, **14**, 251–67.

Eysenck, H. J. (1976b). *Sex and Personality*. London: Open Books.

Eysenck, H. J. and Eysenck, S. B. G. (1969). *Personality Structure and Measurement*. London: Routledge & Kegan Paul.

Eysenck, H. J. and Wilson, G. D. (1973). *The Experimental Study of Freudian Theories*. London: Methuen.

Eysenck, M. W. (1977). *Human Memory: Theory, Research and Individual Differences*. Oxford: Pergamon.

Eysenck, M. W. and Eysenck, H. J. (1980). Mischel and the concept of personality. *British Journal of Psychology*, **71**, 191–204.

Fägerstrom, K. O. and Lisper, H. O. (1977). Effects of listening to car radio, experience, and personality of the driver on subsidiary reaction time and heart rate in a long-term driving task. In R. R. Mackie (ed.), *Vigilance: Theory, Operational Performance, and Physiological Correlates*. New York: Plenum Press.

Fantz, R. L. (1963). Pattern vision in newborn infants. *Science*, **140**, 296–7.

Farnham-Diggory, S. (1976). Development of logical operations and reasoning. In V. Hamilton and M. D. Vernon (eds), *The Development of Cognitive Processes*. London: Academic Press.

Faught, W. F., Colby, K. M., and Parkison, R. C. (1977). Inferences, effects and intentions in a model of paranoia. *Cognitive Psychology*, **9**, 153–87.

Feather, N. T. (1963). Mowrer's revised two-factor theory and the motive-expectancy-value model. *Psychological Review*, **70**, 500–15.

Feffer, M. (1970). Developmental analysis of interpersonal behavior. *Psychological Review*, **77**, 197–214.

Feld, S. C. and Lewis, J. (1969). The assessment of achievement anxieties in children. In C. P. Smith (ed.), *Achievement–Related Motives in Children*. New York: Russell Sage.

Fenz, W. D. (1964). Conflict and stress as related to physiological activation and sensory, perceptual and cognitive functioning. *Psychological Monographs: General and Applied*, **78**, No. 8., Whole No. 585.

Fenz, W. D. (1975). Strategies for coping with stress. In I. G. Sarason and C. D. Spielberger (eds), *Stress and Anxiety*, Vol. 2. Washington, DC: Hemisphere.

Ferguson, E. D. (1976). *Motivation – An Experimental Approach*. New York: Holt, Rinehart & Winston.

Fiedler, F. E. (1977). What triggers the person-situation interaction in leadership? In D. Magnusson and N. S. Endler (eds), *Personality at the Crossroads: Current Issues in Interactional Psychology*. Hillsdale, NJ: Lawrence Erlbaum.

Findler, N. V. (1979). A heuristic information retrieval system based on associative networks. In N. V. Findler (ed.), *Associative Networks: Representation and Use of Knowledge by Computers*. Englewood Cliffs, NJ: Prentice-Hall.

Fiske, D. W. (1974). The limits for the conventional science of personality. *Journal of Personality*, **42**, 1–11.

Folkman, S., Schaefer, C., and Lazarus, R. S. (1979). Cognitive processes as mediators of stress and coping. In V. Hamilton and D. M. Warburton (eds), *Human Stress and Cognition: An Information Processing Approach*. Chichester: Wiley.

Forgus, R. and Shulman, B. H. (1979). *Personality: A Cognitive View*. Englewood Cliffs, NJ: Prentice-Hall.

Foulds, G. A. (1952). Temperamental differences in Maze performance. *British Journal of Psychology*, **43**, 33–41.

Foulds, G. A. (1953). A method of scoring the TAT applied to psychoneurotics. *Journal of Mental Science*, **99**, 235–46.

320

Foulds, G. A. (1956). Distraction and affective disturbance. *Journal of Clinical Psychology*, **12**, 291–2.

Foulkes, D. (1978a). *A Grammar of Dreams*. New York: Basic Books.

Foulkes, D. (1978b). Dreaming as language and cognition. *Scientia*, **113**, 481–99.

Foulkes, D. (1981). *Children's Dreams: Longitudinal Studies*. New York: Wiley.

Frenkel-Brunswik, E. (1949). Intolerance of ambiguity as an emotional and perceptual personality variable. *Journal of Personality*, **18**, 108–43.

Frenkel-Brunswik, E. (1954). Psychoanalysis and the unity of science. *Proceedings of the American Academy of Arts and Sciences*, **80**, No. 4, 273–347.

Freud, A. (1945). *The Ego and the Mechanisms of Defence*. London: Hogarth Press.

Freud, S. (1917). Mourning and melancholia. In *Collected Papers*, **4**, 152–70. London: Hogarth Press (1950).

Furneaux, W. D. (1960). Intellectual ability and problem-solving behaviour. In H. J. Eysenck (ed.), *Handbook of Abnormal Psychology*, 1st ed. London: Pitman.

Furneaux, W. D. (1962). The psychologist and the University. *University Quarterly*, **17**, 33–47.

Furth, H. G. (1964). Research with the deaf: implications for language and cognition. *Psychological Bulletin*, **62**, 145–64.

Gagné, R. (1965). *The Conditions of Learning*. New York: Holt, Rinehart & Winston.

Gardner, R. W. (1953). Cognitive styles in categorizing behavior. *Journal of Personality*, **22**, 214–33.

Gardner, R. W., Holzman, P. S., Klein, G. S., Linton, H. B., and Spence, D. P. (1959). Cognitive control: a study of individual consistencies in cognitive behavior. *Psychological Issues*, **1**, Monograph 4.

Gaudry, E. and Spielberger, C. D. (1970). Anxiety and intelligence in paired-associate learning. *Journal of Educational Psychology*, **61**, 386–91.

Gevins, A. S., Doyle, J. C., Schaffer, R. E., Callaway, E., and Yeager, C. (1980). Lateralized cognitive processes and the electroencephalogram. *Science*, **207**, 1006–7.

Glass, D., Singer, J., and Pennebaker, J. (1977). Behavioral and physiological effects of uncontrollable environmental events. In D. Stokols (ed.), *Perspectives on Environment and Behavior*. New York: Plenum Press.

Glueck, S. and Glueck, E. T. (1950). *Unraveling Juvenile Delinquency*. Cambridge, Mass.: Harvard University Press.

Glueck, S. and Glueck, E. T. (1968). *Delinquents and Non-Delinquents in Perspective*. Cambridge, Mass.: Harvard University Press.

Goldschmid, M. L. (1968). The relation of conservation to emotional and environmental aspects of development. *Child Development*, **39**, 579–89.

Gray, J. A. (1971). *The Psychology of Fear and Stress*. New York: McGraw-Hill.

Gray, J. A. (1981). *The Neuropsychology of Anxiety: An Enquiry into the Functions of the Septo-Hippocampal System*. Oxford: Oxford University Press.

Grey-Walter, W. (1953). *The Living Brain*. London: Duckworth.

Guilford, J. P. (1967). *The Nature of Human Intelligence*. New York: McGraw-Hill.

Hackett, T. P. and Cassem, N. H. (1974). Development of a quantitative rating scale to assess denial. *Journal of Psychosomatic Research*, **18**, 93–100.

Hackett, T. P., Cassem, N. H., and Wishnie, H. A. (1968). The coronary care unit: an appraisal of its psychological hazards. *New England Journal of Medicine*, **279**, 1365.

Hall, C. S. and Lindzey, G. (1970). *Theories of Personality*, 2nd ed. New York: Wiley.

Hamilton, D. L. (1981) (ed.). Stereotyping and intergroup behavior: some thoughts on the cognitive approach. In D. L. Hamilton (ed.), *Cognitive Processes in Stereotyping and Intergroup Behavior*. Hillsdale, NJ: Lawrence Erlbaum.

Hamilton, V. (1957). Perceptual and personality dynamics in reactions to ambiguity. *British Journal of Psychology*, **48**, 200–15.

Hamilton, V. (1959). Eysenck's theory of anxiety and hysteria – a methodological critique. *British Journal of Psychology*, **50**, 48–63.

Hamilton, V. (1960). Imperception of Phi: some further determinants. *British Journal of Psychology*, **51**, 257–66.

Hamilton, V. (1963a). Size constancy and cue responsiveness in psychosis. *British Journal of Psychology*, **54**, 25–39.

Hamilton, V. (1963b). I.Q. changes in chronic schizophrenia. *British Journal of Psychiatry*, **109**, 642–8.

Hamilton, V. (1966). Deficits in primitive perceptual and thinking skills in schizophrenia. *Nature* (London), **211**, 389–92.

Hamilton, V. (1970). *Some effects of parent–child interaction on the child's cognitive development*. Final Report, Research Grant No. 67-0285, Canada Council.

Hamilton, V. (1972a). Maternal rejection and conservation: an analysis of suboptimal cognition. *Journal of Child Psychology and Psychiatry*, **13**, 147–66.

Hamilton, V. (1972b). The size constancy problem in schizophrenia: a cognitive skill analysis. *British Journal of Psychology*, **63**, 73–84.

Hamilton, V. (1973). *The effect of maternal attitude on the development of children's thinking*. Final Report, Research Grant No. HR 1556/1/2, Social Science Research Council.

Hamilton, V. (1975). Socialization and information processing: a capacity model of anxiety-induced performance deficits. In I. G. Sarason and C. D. Spielberger (eds), *Stress and Anxiety*. Vol. 2. Washington, DC: Hemisphere.

Hamilton, V. (1976a). Motivation and personality in cognitive development. In V. Hamilton and M. D. Vernon (eds), *The Development of Cognitive Processes*. London: Academic Press.

Hamilton, V. (1976b). Cognitive development in the neuroses and schizophrenias. In V. Hamilton and M. D. Vernon (eds), *The Development of Cognitive Processes*. London: Academic Press.

Hamilton, V. (1976c). Introversion–extraversion. In S. Krauss (ed.), *Encyclopaedic Handbook of Medical Psychology*. London: Butterworth.

Hamilton, V. (1979a). 'Personality' and stress. In V. Hamilton and D. M. Warburton (eds), *Human Stress and Cognition: An Information Processing Approach*. Chichester: Wiley.

Hamilton, V. (1979b). Information processing aspects of neurotic anxiety and the schizophrenias. In V. Hamilton and D. M. Warburton (eds), *Human Stress and Cognition: An Information Processing Approach*. Chichester: Wiley.

Hamilton, V. (1980). An information processing analysis of environmental stress and life crises. In I. G. Sarason and C. D. Spielberger (eds), *Stress and Anxiety*, Vol. 7. Washington, DC: Hemisphere.

Hamilton, V. (1982a). A cognitive model of anxiety: implications for theories of personality and motivation. In C. D. Spielberger, I. G. Sarason, and P. B. Defares (eds), *Stress and Anxiety*, Vol. 9. New York: Hemisphere/McGraw-Hill.

Hamilton, V. (1982b). Information processing aspects of denial. In S. Breznitz (ed.), *The Denial of Stress*. New York: International Universities Press.

Hamilton, V. (1982c). Towards an information processing analysis of human depression. *Behavioral and Brain Sciences*, *5*, 105–6.

Hamilton, V. and Launay, G. (1976). The role of information processing capacity in the conserving operation. *British Journal of Psychology*, **67**, 191–201.

Hamilton, V. and Moss, M. (1974). A method of scaling conservation of quantity problems by information content. *Child Development*, **45**, 737–45.

Hamilton, V. and Vernon, M. D. (1976) (eds). *The Development of Cognitive Processes*. London: Academic Press.

Hamilton, V. and Warburton, D. M. (1979) (eds). *Human Stress and Cognition: An Information Processing Approach*. Chichester: Wiley.

322

Hampson, S. E. (1982). Person memory: a semantic category model of personality traits. *British Journal of Psychology*, **73**, 1–11.

Harvey, O. J. and Felknor, C. (1970). Parent–child relations as an antecedent to conceptual functioning. In R. A. Hoppe, G. A. Milton, and E. C. Simmel (eds), *Early Experiences and the Processes of Socialization*. New York: Academic Press.

Harvey, O. J., Hunt, D. E., and Schroder, H. M. (1961). *Conceptual Systems and Personality Organization*. New York: Wiley.

Hayes-Roth, B. (1977a). The prominence of lexical information in memory representation of meaning. *Journal of Verbal Learning and Verbal Behavior*, **16**, 119–36.

Hayes-Roth, B. (1977b). Evolution of cognitive structures and processes. *Psychological Review*, **84**, 260–78.

Hayes-Roth, B. and Hayes-Roth, F. (1977). Concept learning and the recognition and classification of exemplars. *Journal of Verbal Learning and Verbal Behavior*, **16**, 321–38.

Hebb, D. O. (1949). *The Organization of Behavior*. New York: Wiley.

Hebb, D. O. (1955). Drives and the C.N.S. (conceptual nervous system). *Psychological Review*, **62**, 243–54.

Hebb, D. O. (1974). What psychology is about. *American Psychologist*, **29**, 71–99.

Hebb, D. O. (1980). *Essay on Mind*. Hillsdale, NJ: Lawrence Erlbaum.

Heckhausen, H. (1967). *The Anatomy of Achievement Motivation*. New York: Academic Press.

Hess, R. D. and Shipman, V. C. (1965). Early experience and the socialization of cognitive modes in children. *Child Development*, **36**, 869–86.

Hess, R. D. and Shipman, V. C. (1967). Cognitive elements in maternal behavior. In J. P. Hill (ed.), *Minnesota Symposia on Child Psychology*, Vol. 1.

Hilgard, E. R. (1949). Human motivation and the concept of the self. *American Psychologist*, **4**, 374–82. Revised in R. S. Lazarus and E. M. Opton, Jr. (eds), *Personality: Selected Readings*. Harmondsworth: Penguin (1967).

Hill, K. T. (1972). Anxiety in the evaluative context. In W. W. Hartup (ed.), *The Young Child: Reviews of Research*, **2**. Washington, DC: National Association for the Education of Young Children.

Hill, K. T. and Sarason, S. B. (1966). The relationship of test anxiety and defensiveness to test and school performance over the elementary school years: a further longitudinal study. *Monographs of the Society for Research in Child Development*, **31**, No. 104.

Hindley, C. B. (1965). Stability and change in abilities up to five years: group trends. *Journal of Child Psychology and Psychiatry*, **6**, 85–99.

Hobson, J. A. and McCarley, R. W. (1977). The brain as a dream state generator: an activation-synthesis hypothesis of the dream process. *American Journal of Psychiatry*, **134**, 1335–48.

Hockey, G. R. J. (1979). Stress and the cognitive components of skilled performance. In V. Hamilton and D. M. Warburton (eds), *Human Stress and Cognition: An Information Processing Approach*. Chichester: Wiley.

Hodges, W. F. and Spielberger, C. D. (1969). Digit span: an indicant of trait or state anxiety? *Journal of Consulting and Clinical Psychology*, **33**, 430–4.

Hollingshead, A. B. and Redlich, F. C. (1958). *Social Class and Mental Illness*. New York: Wiley.

Holmes, D. S. (1978). Projection as a defense mechanism. *Psychological Bulletin*, **85**, 677–88.

Holzman, P. S. and Klein, G. S. (1954). Cognitive system principles of leveling and sharpening: individual differences in assimilation effects in visual time-error. *Journal of Personality*, **37**, 105–22.

Honzik, M. P. (1967). Environmental correlates of mental growth: predictions from the family setting at 21 months. *Child Development*, **38**, 337–64.

Horowitz, M. J. (1975). Intensive and repetitive thoughts after experimental stress: a summary. *Archives of General Psychiatry*, **32**, 1457–63.

Horowitz, M. J. (1976). *Stress Response Syndromes*. New York: Aronson.

Horowitz, M. J. (1979). Psychological response to serious life events. In V. Hamilton and D. M. Warburton (eds), *Human Stress and Cognition: An Information Processing Approach*. Chichester: Wiley.

Huang, M.-S. (1981). Category width and differentiation in semantic categories. *British Journal of Psychology*, **72**, 339–52.

Hubel, D. H. and Wiesel, T. N. (1962). Receptive fields, binocular interaction, and functional architecture in the cat's visual cortex. *Journal of Physiology*, **166**, 106–54.

Hubel, D. H. and Wiesel, T. N. (1965). Receptive fields and functional architecture in two nonstriate visual areas (18 and 19) of the cat. *Journal of Neurophysiology*, **28**, 229–89.

Hull, C. L. (1943). *Principles of Behavior*. New York: Appleton-Century.

Humphrey, G. (1951). *Thinking*. London: Methuen.

Hurley, J. R. (1965). Parental acceptance–rejection and children's intelligence. *Merrill-Palmer Quarterly*, **11**, 19–31.

Husén, T. (1951). The influence of schooling on I.Q. *Theoria*, **17**, 61–88.

Hyde, T. S. and Jenkins, J. J. (1973). Recall for words as a function of semantic, graphic, and syntactic orienting tasks. *Journal of Verbal Learning and Verbal Behavior*, **12**, 471–80.

Ickes, W. J., Wicklund, R. A., and Ferris, C. B. (1973). Objective self-awareness and self-esteem. *Journal of Experimental Social Psychology*, **9**, 209–19.

Iscoe, I., Williams, M., and Harvey, J. (1963). Modification of children's judgements by simulated group techniques. *Child Development*, **34**, 963–78.

Isen, A. M., Clark, M., Shalker, T. E., and Karp, L. (1978). Affect, accessibility of material in memory, and behavior: a cognitive loop? *Journal of Personality and Social Psychology*, **36**, 1–12.

Izard, C. E. (1977). *Human Emotions*. New York: Plenum Press.

Janis, I. L. (1982). Stress inoculation as a means for preventing pathogenic denial. In S. Breznitz (ed.), *The Denial of Stress*. New York: International Universities Press.

Janis, I. L. and Mann, L. (1977). *Decision-Making: A Psychological Analysis of Conflict, Choice, and Commitment*. New York: Free Press.

Jaques, E. (1951). *The Changing Culture of a Factory*. London: Tavistock.

Jaques, E. (1976). *A General Theory of Bureaucracy*. London: Halstead-Heinemann.

Jerrison, H. J. (1977). Vigilance: biology, psychology, theory and practice. In R. R. Mackie (ed.), *Vigilance: Theory, Operational Performance, and Physiological Correlates*. New York: Plenum Press.

Johnson, J. H. and Sarason, I. G. (1979). Recent developments in research on life stress. In V. Hamilton and D. M. Warburton (eds), *Human Stress and Cognition: An Information Processing Approach*. Chichester: Wiley.

Jones, A. (1966). Information deprivation in humans. In B. A. Maher (ed.), *Progress in Experimental Personality Research*, **3**, 241–307.

Jusczyk, P. W. and Earhard, B. (1980). The lingua mentis and its role in thought. In P. W. Jusczyk and R. M. Klein (eds), *The Nature of Thought: Essays in Honor of D. O. Hebb*. Hillsdale, NJ: Lawrence Erlbaum.

Jusczyk, P. W. and Klein, R. M. (1980). *The Nature of Thought: Essays in Honor of D. O. Hebb*. Hillsdale, NJ: Lawrence Erlbaum.

Kagan, J. (1966). Reflection–impulsivity: the generality and dynamics of conceptual tempo. *Journal of Abnormal Psychology*, **71**, 17–24.

324

Kagan, J. (1972). Motives and development. *Journal of Personality and Social Psychology*, **22,** 51–66.

Kagan, J. (1978). On emotion and its development: a working paper. In M. Lewis and L. A. Rosenblum (eds), *The Development of Affect*. New York: Plenum Press.

Kagan, J., Kearsley, R. B., and Zelaso, P. R. (1978). *Infancy: Its Place in Human Development*. Cambridge, Mass.: Harvard University Press.

Kagan, J. and Moss, H. A. (1962). *Birth to Maturity: A Study in Psychological Development*. New York: Wiley.

Kagan, J., Pearson L., and Welch, L. (1966). Conceptual impulsivity and inductive reasoning. *Child Development*, **37,** 583–94

Kahn, R. L. and Boulding, D. (1965) (eds). *Power and Conflict in Organizations*. London: Tavistock.

Kahneman, D. (1973). *Attention and Effort*. Englewood Cliffs, NJ: Prentice-Hall.

Kail, R. V., Jr. and Hagen, J. W. (1977). *Perspectives on the Development of Memory and Cognition*. Hillsdale, NJ: Lawrence Erlbaum.

Kamin, L. J. (1974). *The Science and Politics of I.Q.* Potomac, Md.: Lawrence Erlbaum.

Kanouse, D. E. and Hanson, L. R. (1972). Negativity in evaluations. In E. E. Jones, D. E. Kanouse, H. H. Kelley, R. E. Nisbett, S. Valins, and B. Weiner (eds), *Attribution: Perceiving the Causes of Behavior*. Morristown, NJ: General Learning Press.

Kearsley, R. B. (1973). The newborn's response to auditory stimulation. *Child Development*, **44,** 582–90.

Kelley, H. H. (1967). Attribution theory in social psychology. In D. Levine (ed.), *Nebraska Symposium on Motivation*. Lincoln: University of Nebraska Press.

Kelly, G. A. (1955). *The Psychology of Personal Constructs*. New York: Norton.

Kimura, D. (1967). Functional asymmetry of the brain in dichotic listening. *Cortex*, **3,** 163–78.

Kimura, D. (1981). Neuromotor mechanisms in communication in man. Paper presented to The Royal Society of London for a Symposium on *The Neuropsychology of Cognitive Function*.

Klatzky, R. L. (1980). *Human Memory: Structure and Processes* (2nd ed.). San Francisco: Freeman.

Klein, G. S. (1951). The personal world through perception. In R. R. Blake and G. V. Ramsay (eds), *Perception – An Approach to Personality*. New York: Ronald Press.

Klein, G. S. (1954). Need and regulation. In M. R. Jones (ed.), *Nebraska Symposium on Motivation*. Lincoln: University of Nebraska Press.

Klein, G. S. (1976). *Psychoanalytic Theory – An Exploration of Essentials*. New York: International Universities Press.

Klein, G. S. and Holzman, P. S. (1950). The schematizing process: personality qualities and perceptual attitudes in sensitivity to change. *American Psychologist*, **5,** 312.

Klein, G. S. and Schlesinger, H. (1951). Perceptual attitudes towards instability: I. Prediction of apparent movement experiences from Rorschach responses. *Journal of Personality*, **19,** 289–302.

Klein, G. S. and Smith, G. J. W. (1953). Cognitive controls in serial behavior patterns. *Journal of Personality*, **22,** 188–213.

Kline, P. (1972). *Fact and Fantasy in Freudian Theory*. London: Methuen.

Koffka, K. (1935). *Principles of Gestalt Psychology*. New York: Harcourt, Brace.

Kogan, N. and Wallach, M. A. (1964). *Risk Taking: A Study in Cognition and Personality*. New York: Holt, Rinehart & Winston.

Kohlberg, L. (1969). *Stages in the Development of Moral Thought*. New York: Holt, Rinehart & Winston.

Kohn, M. and Rosman, B. L. (1973). Cognitive functioning in 5-year-old boys as related to social-emotional and background-demographic variables. *Developmental Psychology*, **8**, 277–94.

Kohn, M. L. (1976). The interaction of social class and other factors in the etiology of schizophrenia. *American Journal of Psychiatry*, **133**, 177–80.

Koriat, A., Melkman, R., Averill, J. R., and Lazarus, R. S. (1972). The self-control of emotional reactions to a stressful film. *Journal of Personality*, **40**, 601–19.

Krech, D. and Crutchfield, R. (1948). *Theory and Problems of Social Psychology*. New York: McGraw-Hill.

Krohne, H. W. (1978). Individual differences in coping with stress and anxiety. In C. D. Spielberger and I. G. Sarason (eds), *Stress and Anxiety*, Vol. 5. Washington, DC: Hemisphere.

Krohne, H. W. (1980). Parental child-rearing behavior and the development of anxiety and coping strategies in children. In I. G. Sarason and C. D. Spielberger (eds), *Stress and Anxiety*, Vol. 7. Washington, DC: Hemisphere.

Kuhn, A. (1974). *The Logic of Social Systems*. San Francisco: Jossey-Bass.

Lacey, J. I. (1967). Somatic response patterning and stress: some revisions of activation theory. In M. H. Appley and R. Trumbull (eds), *Psychological Stress: Issues in Research*. New York: Appleton-Century-Crofts.

Lacey, J. I. and Lacey, B. C. (1958). Verification and extension of the principle of autonomic response stereotypy. *American Journal of Psychology*, **71**, 50–73.

Landsbaum, J. and Willis, R. (1971). Conformity in early and late adolescence. *Developmental Psychology*, **4**, 344–7.

Langford, P. E. and George, S. (1971). Intellectual and moral development in adolescence. *British Journal of Educational Psychology*, **45**, 330–2.

Lashley, K. S. (1950). In search of the engram. *Symposium of the Society of Experimental Biology*, No. 4. New York: Cambridge University Press.

Lassen, N. A., Ingvar, D. H., and Skinhøy, E. (1978). Brain function and blood flow. *American Psychologist*, **239**, 50–9.

Laurendeau, M. and Pinard, A. (1963). *Causal Thinking of the Child*. New York: International Universities Press.

Lawick-Goodall, J. (1971). Some aspects of mother–infant relationships in a group of wild chimpanzees. In R. H. Schaffer (ed.), *The Origins of Human Social Relations*. London: Academic Press.

Lazarus, R. S. (1966). *Psychological Stress and the Coping Process*. New York: McGraw-Hill.

Lazarus, R. S. (1968). Emotions and adaptation: conceptual and empirical relations. In W. J. Arnold (ed.), *Nebraska Symposium on Motivation*. Lincoln: University of Nebraska Press.

Lazarus, R. S. (1974). Cognitive and coping processes in emotion. In B. Weiner (ed.), *Cognitive Views of Human Motivation*. New York: Academic Press.

Lazarus, R. S. (1976). *Patterns of Adjustment*. New York: McGraw-Hill.

Lazarus, R. S. and Launier, R. (1980). Stress-related transactions between person and environment. In L. A. Pervin and M. Lewis (eds), *Perspectives in Interactional Psychology*.New York: Plenum.

Leeper, R. W. (1970). Feelings and emotions. In M. D. Arnold (ed.), *Feelings and Emotions: The Loyola Symposium*. New York: Academic Press.

Levine, J. M. and Murphy, G. (1943). The learning and forgetting of controversial material. *Journal of Abnormal and Social Psychology*, **38**, 507–17.

Levine, S. (1957). Infantile experience and resistance to physiological stress. *Science*, **126**, 405.

Levine, S. (1962). Psychophysiological effects of infantile stimulation. In E. L. Bliss (ed.), *Roots of Behavior*. New York: Hoeber.

Levinger, G. and Clark, J. (1961). Emotional factors in the forgetting of word associations. *Journal of Abnormal and Social Psychology*, **62**, 99–105.

Levy, D. M. (1943). *Maternal Overprotection*. New York: Columbia University Press.

Lewin, K., Dembo, T., Festinger, L., and Sears, P. S. (1944). Level of aspiration. In J. McV. Hunt (ed.), *Personality and the Behaviour Disorders*. New York: Ronald Press.

Livesley, W. J. and Bromley, D. B. (1973). *Person Perception in Childhood and Adolescence*. London: Wiley.

London, H. (1978) (ed.). *Personality: A New Look at Metatheories*. New York: Wiley.

London, H. and Exner, J. E. Jnr. (1978) (eds). *Dimensions of Personality*. New York: Wiley.

Lovell, K. and Ogilvie, E. (1960). A study of conservation of substance of the junior school child. *British Journal of Educational Psychology*, **30**, 109–18.

Lykken, D. T. and Venables, P. H. (1971). Direct measurement of skin conductance: a proposal for standardization. *Psychophysiology*, **8**, 656–72.

Macfarlane, J. W. (1938). Studies in child guidance. I. Methodology of data collection and organization. *Monographs of the Society for Research in Child Development*, **3**, No. 6, 1–254.

Mackintosh, N. J. (1974). *The Psychology of Animal Learning*. New York: Academic Press.

Macnamara, J. (1972). Cognitive basis of language learning in infants. *Psychological Review*, **79**, 1–13.

Macnamara, J. (1977) (ed.). *Language, Learning and Thought*. New York: Academic Press.

Madsen, K. B. (1974). *Modern Theories of Motivation: A Comparative Metascientific Study*. Copenhagen: Munksgaard.

Magnusson, D. and Endler, N. R. (1977). *Personality at the Crossroads: Current Issues in Interactional Psychology*. Hillsdale, NJ: Lawrence Erlbaum.

Maier, N. R. F. (1956). Frustration theory: restatement and extension. *Psychological Review*, **63**, 370–88.

Maier, S. F. and Seligman, M. E. P. (1976). Learned helplessness: theory and evidence. *Journal of Experimental Psychology: General*, **105**, 3–46.

Malmo, R. B. (1975). Motivation and affective arousal. In A. M. Freedman, H. I. Kaplan, and B. J. Sadock (eds), *Comprehensive Textbook of Psychiatry*, Vol. 2. Baltimore: Williams & Wilkins.

Mandler, G. (1975). *Mind and Emotion*. New York: Wiley.

Mandler, G. (1979). Thought processes, consciousness and stress. In V. Hamilton and D. M. Warburton (eds), *Human Stress and Cognition: An Information Processing Approach*. Chichester: Wiley.

Mandler, G. and Sarason, S. B. (1951). A study of anxiety and learning. *Journal of Abnormal and Social Psychology*, **47**, 166–73.

Mandler, G., Worden, P. E., and Graesser, A. C. (1974). Subjective disorganization: search for the locus of list organization. *Journal of Verbal Learning and Verbal Behavior*, **13**, 220–35.

Mandler, J. M. and Ritchey, G. H. (1977). Long-term memory for pictures. *Journal of Experimental Psychology: Human Learning and Memory*, **3**, 386–96.

Marmo, G. and Vitale, B. (1980). Quality, form and globality: an assessment of catastrophe theory. *Fundamenta Scientiae*, **1**, 35–54.

Maslow, A. H. (1954). *Motivation and Personality*. New York: Harper & Bros.

Matza, D. and Sykes, G. (1961). Juvenile delinquency and subterranean values. *American Sociological Review*, **26**, 712–19.

McClelland, D. C. (1976). *The Achieving Society*. Princeton, NJ: Van Nostrand.

McClelland, D. C. (1978). Is personality consistent? In A. I. Rabin, J. Aronoff, A.

M. Barclay, and R. A. Zucker (eds), *Further Explorations in Personality*. New York: Wiley.

McClelland, D. C., Atkinson, J. W., Clark, R. A., and Lowell, E. L. (1953). *The Achievement Motive*. New York: Appleton-Century-Crofts.

McCord, J. and McCord, W. (1958). The effects of parental role model on criminality. *Journal of Social Issues*, **14**, 66–75.

McDougall, W. (1923). *An Outline of Psychology*. London: Methuen.

McGeorge, C. (1974). Situational variation in levels of moral judgement. *British Journal of Educational Psychology*, **44**, 116–22.

McGuigan, F. J. (1978). *Cognitive Psychophysiology: Principles of Covert Behavior*. Englewood Cliffs, NJ: Prentice-Hall.

McKinnon, J. A. (1979). Two semantic forms: neuropsychological and psychoanalytic descriptions. *Psychoanalysis and Contemporary Thought*, **2**, 25–76.

McLaughlin, R. J. and Eysenck, H. J. (1967). Extraversion, neuroticism and paired-associate learning. *Journal of Experimental Research in Personality*, **2**, 128–32.

McReynolds, P. (1976). Assimilation and anxiety. In M. Zuckerman and C. D. Spielberger (eds), *Emotion and Anxiety: New Concepts, Methods and Applications*. Hillsdale, NJ: Lawrence Erlbaum.

Mechanic, D. (1962). *Students Under Stress*. New York: Free Press.

Mednick, S. A., Schulsinger, F., and Garfinkel, R. (1975). Children at high risk for schizophrenia: predisposing factors and intervention. In M. Kietzman, S. Sutton, and J. Zubin (eds), *Experimental Approaches to Psychopathology*. New York: Academic Press.

Meichenbaum, D. (1977). *Cognitive-Behavior Modification: An Integrative Approach*. New York: Plenum.

Melzack, R. (1973). *The Puzzle of Pain*. Harmondsworth: Penguin Books.

Merrifield, P. R. (1966). An analysis of concepts from the point of view of the structure of intellect. In H. J. Klausmeier and C. W. Harris (eds), *Analyses of Concept Learning*. New York: Academic Press.

Messick, S. (1973). Multivariate models of cognition and personality: the need for both process and structure in psychological theory and measurement. In J. R. Royce (ed.), *Multivariate Analysis and Psychological Theory*. London: Academic Press.

Miller, G. A. (1956). The magical number seven, plus or minus two: some limits on our capacity for processing information. *Psychological Review*, **63**, 81–97.

Miller, G. A. (1978). The acquisition of word meaning. *Child Development*, **49**, 999–1004.

Miller, G. A., Galanter, E., and Pribram, K. H. (1960). *Plans and the Structure of Behavior*. New York: Holt, Rinehart & Winston.

Miller, J. G. (1960). Information input overload and psychopathology. *American Journal of Psychiatry*, **116**, 321–32.

Miller, N. E. (1944). Experimental studies of conflict. In J. McV. Hunt (ed.), *Personality and the Behavior Disorders*, Vol. 1. New York: Ronald Press.

Miller, N. E. (1948). Theory and experiment relating psychoanalytic displacement to stimulus-response generalization. *Journal of Abnormal and Social Psychology*, **43**, 155–78.

Miller, N. E. (1959). Liberalization of basic S-R concepts: extensions to conflict behavior, motivation and social learning. In S. Koch (ed.), *Psychology: A Study of a Science*. New York: McGraw-Hill.

Miller, W. R., Rosellini, R. A., and Seligman, M. E. P. (1977). Learned helplessness and depression. In J. D. Maser and M. E. P. Seligman (eds), *Psychopathology: Experimental Models*. San Francisco: Freeman.

Miller, W. R. and Seligman, M. E. P. (1975). Depression and learned helplessness in man. *Journal of Abnormal and Social Psychology*, **84**, 228–38.

Milner, B. (1981). Cognition effects of frontal-lobe lesions in man. Paper presented to The Royal Society of London for a symposium on *The Neuropsychology of Cognitive Function*.

Mischel, W. (1968). *Personality and Assessment*. New York: Wiley.

Mischel, W. (1973). Toward a cognitive social learning reconceptualization of personality. *Psychological Review*, **80**, 252–83.

Mischel, W. (1977). The interaction of person and situation. In D. Magnusson and N. S. Endler (eds), *Personality at the Crossroads: Current Issues in Interactional Psychology*. Hillsdale, NJ: Lawrence Erlbaum.

Mischel, W. (1978). Personality research: a look at the future. In H. London (ed.), *Personality: A New Look at Metatheories*. New York: Wiley.

Mischel, W. (1979). On the interface of cognition and personality. *American Psychologist*, **34**, 740–54.

Modgil, S. and Lunzer, E. A. (1971). The patterning of educational performance in relation to parental attitudes. *Bulletin of the British Psychological Society*, **24**, (No. 84), 232 (Abstract).

Montgomery, K. C. (1953). Exploratory behavior as a function of 'similarity' of stimulus situations. *Journal of Comparative and Physiological Psychology*, **46**, 129–33.

Moore, T. (1968). Language and intelligence: a longitudinal study of the first eight years. Part II: environmental correlates of mental growth. *Human Development*, **11**, 1–24.

Morris, T. (1976). *Deviance and Control: The Secular Heresy*. London: Hutchinson.

Morton, J. (1969). Interaction of information in word recognition. *Psychological Review*, **76**, 165–78.

Morton, J. (1970). A functional model for memory. In D. A. Norman (ed.), *Models of Human Memory*. New York: Academic Press.

Morton, J. (1979). Word recognition. In J. Morton and J. C. Marshall (eds), *Structures and processes, Psycholinguistics Series 2*. London: Paul Elek.

Moscovitch, M. and Craik, F. I. M. (1976). Depth of processing, retrieval cues, and uniqueness of encoding as factors in recall. *Journal of Verbal Learning and Verbal Behavior*, **15**, 447–58.

Moulden, B. (1980). After-effects and the integration of patterns of neural activity within a channel. *Philosophical Transactions of the Royal Society of London*, **290**, 39–55.

Mueller, J. H. (1976). Anxiety and cue-utilization in human learning and memory. In M. Zuckerman and C. D. Spielberger (eds), *Emotions and Anxiety: New Concepts, Methods and Applications*. Hillsdale, NJ: Lawrence Erlbaum.

Murphy, L. B. and Moriarty, A. E. (1976). *Vulnerability, Coping and Growth*. New Haven: Yale University Press.

Murray, H. A. (1938). *Explorations in Personality*. New York: Oxford University Press.

Nassefat, M. (1963). *Étude quantitative sur l'évolution des opérations intellectuelles*. Neuchatel: Delachaux and Niestle.

Neisser, U. (1967). *Cognitive Psychology*. New York: Appleton-Century-Crofts.

Neisser, U. (1976). *Cognition and Reality*. San Francisco: Freeman.

Nelson, K. (1977). The conceptual basis for naming. In J. Macnamara (ed.), *Language, Learning and Thought*. New York: Academic Press.

Newell, A. and Simon, H. A. (1972). *Human Problem Solving*. Englewood Cliffs, NJ: Prentice-Hall.

Nielsen, S. L. and Sarason, I. G. (1980). Personality and selective attention. Technical Report, SCS–LS–010, Office of Naval Research, Arlington.

Norman, D. A. (1966). Acquisition and retention in short-term memory. *Journal of Experimental Psychology*, **72,** 369–81.

Norman, D. A. (1976). *Memory and Attention: An Introduction to Human Information Processing*, 2nd ed. New York: Wiley.

Norman, D. A. (1980). Perception, memory and mental processes. In L.-G. Nilsson (ed.), *Perspectives on Memory Research*. Hillsdale, NJ: Lawrence Erlbaum.

Norman, D. A. and Bobrow, D. G. (1975). On data-limited and resource-limited processes. *Cognitive Psychology*, **7,** 44–64.

Norman, D. A. and Bobrow, D. G. (1976). On the role of active memory processes in perception and cognition. In C. N. Cofer (ed.), *The Structure of Human Memory*. San Francisco: Freeman.

Norman, D. A. and Rummelhart, D. E. (1975). *Explorations in Cognition*. San Francisco: Freeman.

Novaco, R. W. (1979). The cognitive regulation of anger and stress. In P. C. Kendall and S. D. Hollon (eds), *Cognitive-Behavioral Interventions – Theory, Research and Procedures*. New York: Academic Press.

Ogden, C. K. and Richards, I. A. (1923). *The Meaning of Meaning*. New York: Harcourt, Brace & World.

O'Keefe, J. and Nadel, L. (1978). *The Hippocampus as a Cognitive Map*. Oxford: Clarendon Press.

Olsen, D. R. (1970). Language and thought: aspects of a cognitive theory of semantics. *Psychological Review*, **77,** 257–73.

Osgood, C. E. (1962). *An Alternative to War or Surrender*. Urbana: University of Illinois Press.

Osgood, C. E., Suci, G. J., and Tannenbaum, P. H. (1957). *The Measurement of Meaning*. Urbana: University of Illinois Press.

Osler, S. F. and Kofsky, E. (1965). Stimulus uncertainty as a variable in the development of conceptual ability. *Journal of Experimental Child Psychology*, **2,** 264–79.

Paivio, A. (1975). Perceptual comparisons through the mind's eye. *Memory and Cognition*, **3,** 635–47.

Paivio, A. (1978). Mental comparisons involving abstract attributes. *Memory and Cognition*, **6,** 199–208.

Pascual-Leone, J. (1970). A mathematical model for the transition rule in Piaget's developmental stages. *Acta Psychologica*, **32,** 301–45.

Payne, R. L. (1979). Stress and cognition in organization. In V. Hamilton and D. M. Warburton (eds), *Human Stress and Cognition: An Information Processing Approach*. Chichester: Wiley.

Payne, R. W. (1960). Cognitive abnormalities. In H. J. Eysenck (ed.), *Handbook of Abnormal Psychology*, 1st ed. London: Pitman.

Payne, R. W. (1973). Cognitive abnormalities. In H. J. Eysenck (ed.), *Handbook of Abnormal Psychology*, 2nd ed. London: Pitman.

Pervin, L. A. (1978). *Current Controversies and Issues in Personality*. New York: Wiley.

Peterfreund, E. (1971). Information systems and psychoanalysis: an evolutionary biological approach to psychoanalytic theory. *Psychological Issues*, **7,** Monographs No. 25–26.

Peterfreund, E. and Franceschini, E. (1973). On information, motivation, and meaning. In B. B. Rubinstein (ed.), *Psychoanalysis and Contemporary Science*, Vol. 2. New York: Macmillan.

Peters, R. S. (1958). *The Concepts of Motivation*. London: Routledge & Kegan Paul.

Pettigrew, T. F. (1958). The measurement and correlates of category width as a cognitive variable. *Journal of Personality*, **26,** 532–44.

Piaget, J. (1932). *The Moral Judgement of the Child*. London: Routledge & Kegan Paul.

Piaget, J. (1952). *The Child's Conception of Number*. London: Routledge & Kegan Paul.

Piaget, J. and Inhelder, B. (1969). *The Psychology of the Child*. London: Routledge & Kegan Paul.

Piaget, A. and Inhelder, B. (1973). *Memory and Intelligence*. London: Routledge & Kegan Paul.

Pinard, A. and Laurendeau, M. (1969). 'Stage' in Piaget's cognitive-developmental theory: exegis of a concept. In D. Elkind and J. H. Flavell (eds), *Studies in Cognitive Development: Essays in Honor of Jean Piaget*. New York: Oxford University Press.

Plutchik, R. A. (1980). *Emotion: A Psychoevolutionary Synthesis*. New York: Harper & Row.

Popper, K. R. (1959). *The Logic of Scientific Discovery*. London: Hutchinson.

Pribram, K. (1971). *Languages of the Brain*. Englewood Cliffs, NJ: Prentice-Hall.

Pribram, K. H. and McGuiness, D. (1975). Arousal, activation and effort in the control of attention. *Psychological Review*, **77**, 568–73.

Proshansky, H. M., Ittelson, W. H., and Rivlin, L. G. (1976). *Environmental Psychology: People and their Physical Settings*. 2nd ed. New York: Holt, Rinehart & Winston.

Pylyshyn, Z. W. (1977). What does it take to bootstrap a language? In J. Macnamara (ed.), *Language, Learning and Thought*. New York: Academic Press.

Rabbitt, P. M. A. (1979). Current paradigms and models in human information processing. In V. Hamilton and D. M. Warburton (eds), *Human Stress and Cognition: An Information Processing Approach*. Chichester: Wiley.

Rabkin, J. G. and Struening, E. L. (1976). Life events, stress and illness. *Science*, **194**, 1013–20.

Rachman, S. J. (1978). *Fear and Courage*. San Francisco: Freeman.

Rahe, R. H. (1968). Life-change measurement as a predictor of illness. *Proceedings of the Royal Society of Medicine*, **61**, 1124–6.

Rahe, R. H. (1978). Life change and illness studies: past history and future directions. *Journal of Human Stress*, **4**, 3–14.

Rapaport, D. (1953). On the psychoanalytic theory of affects. *International Journal of Psychoanalysis*, **34**, 177–98.

Reed, S. K. (1972). Pattern recognition and categorization. *Cognitive Psychology*, **3**, 382–407.

Ribes-Inesta, E. and Bandura, A. (1976) (eds). *Analysis of Delinquency and Aggression*. Hillsdale, NJ: Lawrence Erlbaum.

Robins, R. S. (1977) (ed.). *Psychopathology and Political Leadership*. New Orleans: Tulane University Press.

Rock, P. and McIntosh, M. (1974). *Deviance and Social Control*. London: Tavistock.

Rohmert, W. and Luczak, H. (1979). Stress, work and productivity. In V. Hamilton and D. M. Warburton (eds), *Human and Stress and Cognition: An Information Processing Approach*. Chichester: Wiley.

Rokeach, M. (1951). Prejudice, concreteness of thinking and reification of thinking. *Journal of Abnormal and Social Psychology*, **46**, 85–91.

Rokeach, M. (1960). *The Open and the Closed Mind*. New York: Basic Books.

Rollins, H. A. Jr. and Hendricks, R. (1980). Processing of words presented simultaneously to eye and ear. *Journal of Experimental Psychology: Human Perception and Performance*, **6**, 99–109.

Rommetveit, R. and Blakar, R. M. (1979). *Studies of Language, Thought and Verbal Communication*. London: Academic Press.

Rosch, E. (1973). Natural categories. *Cognitive Psychology*, **4**, 328–50.

Rosch, E. (1975). Cognitive representations of semantic categories. *Journal of Experimental Psychology: General*, **104**, 192–233.

Rosch, E. and Mervis, C. B. (1975). Family resemblances: studies in the internal structure of categories. *Cognitive Psychology*, **7**, 573–605.

Rosch, E., Mervis, C. B., Gray, W. D., Johnson, D. M., and Boyes-Braem, P. (1976). Basic objects in natural categories. *Cognitive Psychology*, **8**, 382–439.

Rosenberg, S., Nelson, C. and Vivekanauthan (1968). A multidimensional approach to the structure of personality impressions. *Journal of Personality and Social Psychology*, **9**, 293–4.

Rosenman, R., Brand, R. J., Jenkins, C. D., Friedman, M., Strauss, R., and Wurm, M. (1975). Coronary heart disease in the Western Collaborative Group Study: final follow-up experience of 8.5 years. *Journal of the American Medical Association*, **233**, 872–7.

Rosenthal, T. L. and Zimmerman, B. J. (1978). *Social Learning and Cognition*. New York: Academic Press.

Roskies, E. and Lazarus, R. S. (1980). Coping theory and the teaching of coping skills. In P. Davidson (ed.), *Behavioral Medicine: Changing Health Life Styles*. New York: Brunner/Mazel.

Rothbart, M. (1981). Memory processes and social beliefs. In D. L. Hamilton (ed.), *Cognitive Processes in Stereotyping and Intergroup Behavior*. Hillsdale, NJ: Lawrence Erlbaum.

Rotter, J. B. (1966). Generalized expectancies for internal versus external control of reinforcement. *Psychological Monographs*, **80** (Whole No. 609).

Rotter, J. B., Chance, J., and Phares, E. (1972). *Applications of a Social Learning Theory of Personality*. New York: Holt, Rinehart & Winston.

Russell, D. G. and Sarason, I. G. (1965). Test anxiety, sex and experimental conditions in relation to anagram solution. *Journal of Personality and Social Psychology*, **1**, 493–6.

Rutter, M. L. and Quinton, D. (1976). Psychiatric disorders: ecological factors and concepts of causation. In H. McGurk (ed.), *Ecological Factors in Human Development*. Amsterdam: North Holland.

Rutter, M. L., Quinton, D., and Yule, B. A. (1976). *Family Pathology and Disorders in Children*. Chichester: Wiley.

Rutter, M. L., Tizard, J., and Whitmore, K. (1970) (eds). *Education, Health and Behaviour*. London: Longman.

Ryle, G. (1949). *The Concept of Mind*. London: Hutchinson.

Saltz, E. (1970). Manifest anxiety: have we misread the data? *Psychological Review*, **77**, 568–73.

Sanford, N. (1970). *Issues in Personality Theory*. San Francisco: Jossey-Bass.

Sarason, I. G. (1972a). *Personality: An Objective Approach*, 2nd ed. New York: Wiley.

Sarason, I. G. (1972b). Experimental approaches to test anxiety: attention and the uses of information. In C. D. Spielberger (ed.), *Anxiety – Current Trends in Theory and Research*. New York: Academic Press.

Sarason, I. G. (1975). Anxiety and self-preoccupation. In I. G. Sarason and C. D. Spielberger (eds), *Stress and Anxiety*, Vol. 2. New York: Hemisphere.

Sarason, I. G. and Spielberger, C. D. (1980) (eds). *Stress and Anxiety*. Vol. 7. Washington, DC: Hemisphere.

Sarason, S. B., Davidson, K. S., Lighthall, F. F., Waite, R. R., and Ruebush, B. K. (1960). *Anxiety in Elementary Schoolchildren: A Report of Research*. New York: Wiley.

Sarason, S. B., Hill, K. T., and Zimbardo, P. G. (1964). A longitudinal study of the relation of test anxiety to performance on intelligence and achievement tests. *Monographs of the Society for Research in Child Development*, **29**, No. 98.

Schachter, S. (1964). The interaction of cognitive and physiological determinants of emotional state. In L. Berkowitz (ed.), *Advances in Experimental Social Psychology*, **1,** 49–80.

Schachter, S. and Singer, J. (1962). Cognitive, social and physiological determinants of emotional state. *Psychological Review*, **69,** 379–99.

Schaefer, E. S. (1965). A configurational analysis of children's reports of parent behavior. *Journal of Consulting Psychology*, **29,** 552–7.

Schaffer, H. R. (1971). *The Origins of Human Social Relations*. London: Academic Press.

Schaffer, H. R., Collis, G. M., and Parsons, G. (1977). Vocal interchange and visual regard in verbal and pre-verbal children. In H. R. Schaffer (ed.), *Studies in Mother–Infant Interaction*. London: Academic Press.

Schaffer, H. R. and Crook, C. K. (1978). The role of the mother in early social development. In H. McGurk (ed.), *Issues in Childhood Social Development*. London: Methuen.

Schank, R. C. (1975). *Conceptual Information Processing*. Amsterdam: North-Holland.

Schank, R. and Abelson, R. (1977). *Scripts, Plans, Goals and Understanding*. Hillsdale, NJ: Lawrence Erlbaum.

Schein, E. H. and Bennis, W. G. (1965) (eds). *Personal and Organizational Change through Group Methods: The Laboratory Approach*. New York: Wiley.

Schmale, A. and Iker, H. (1966]. The affect of hopelessness and the development of cancer. *Psychosomatic Medicine*, **28,** 714–21.

Schneirla, T. C. (1959). An evolutionary and developmental theory of biphasic processes underlying approach and withdrawal. In M. R. Jones (ed.), *Nebraska Symposium of Motivation*. Lincoln: University of Nebraska Press.

Schroder, H. M., Driver, M. J., and Streufert, S. (1967). *Human Information Processing*. New York: Holt, Rinehart and Winston.

Schuham, A. I. (1967). The double-bind hypothesis a decade later. *Psychological Bulletin*, **68,** 409–16.

Schwartz, G. E., Davidson, R. J., and Maer, F. (1975). Right hemisphere lateralization for emotion in the human brain: interactions with cognition. *Science*, **190,** 286–8.

Schwartz, G. E. and Shapiro, D. (1976). *Consciousness and Self-Regulation: Advances in Research*, Vol. 1. London: Wiley.

Schwartz, S. and Kirsner, K. (1982). Laterality effects in visual information processing: hemispheric specialization or the orienting of attention. *Quarterly Journal of Experimental Psychology – A. Human Experimental Psychology*, **34A,** 61–77.

Schweder, R. A. (1975). How relevant is an individual difference theory of personality. *Journal of Personality*, **43,** 455–84.

Sears, R. R., Maccobi, E. E., and Levin, H. (1957). *Patterns of Child Rearing*. Evanson: Row, Peterson.

Segall, M. H. (1976). *Human Behavior and Public Policy: A Political Psychology*. New York: Pergamon.

Sekuler, R. and Levinson, E. (1974). Mechanisms of motion perception. *Psychologia*, **17,** 38–49.

Selfridge, O. G. (1959). Pandemonium: A paradigm for learning. In D. V. Blake and A. M. Vittey (eds), *The Mechanisation of Thought Processes*. London: HM Stationery Office.

Seligman, M. E. P. (1968). Chronic fear produced by unpredictable shock. *Journal of Comparative and Physiological Psychology*, **66,** 402–11.

Seligman, M. E. P. (1975). *Helplessness*. San Francisco: Freeman.

Selye, H. (1976). *The Stress of Life*. 2nd ed. New York: McGraw-Hill.

Selye, H. (1979). The stress concept and some of its implications. In V. Hamilton and D. M. Warburton (eds), *Human Stress and Cognition: An Information Processing Approach*. Chichester: Wiley.

Seymour, P. H. K. (1976). Contemporary models of the cognitive processes: II. Retrieval and comparison operations in permanent memory. In V. Hamilton and M. D. Vernon (eds), *The Development of Cognitive Processes*. London: Academic Press.

Shalit, B. (1977). Structural ambiguity and the limits of coping. *Journal of Human Stress*, **3**, 32–45.

Shallice, T. (1972). Dual functions of consciousness. *Psychological Review*, **79**, 383–93.

Shannon, C. E. and Weaver, W. (1949). *The Mathematical Theory of Communication*. Urbana: University of Illinois Press.

Simon, H. A. (1980a). Address to XXII International Congress of Psychology, Leipzig, GDR.

Simon, H. A. (1980b). Information-processing explanations of understanding. In P. W. Jusczyk and R. K. Klein (eds), *The Nature of Thought: Essays in Honor of D. O. Hebb*. Hillsdale, NJ: Lawrence Erlbaum.

Simon, H. A. and Reed, S. K. (1976). Modeling strategy shifts in a problem-solving task. *Cognitive Psychology*, **8**, 86–97.

Sjöberg, H. (1977). Interaction of task difficulty, activation and work load. *Journal of Human Stress*, **3**, 33–8.

Skinner, B. F. (1969). *Contingencies of Reinforcement: A Theoretical Analysis*. New York: Appleton-Century-Crofts.

Smith, E. E. (1978). Theories of semantic memory. In W. K. Estes (ed.), *Handbook of Learning and Cognitive Processes*, Vol. 6. Hillsdale, NJ: Lawrence Erlbaum.

Sofer, C. (1972). *Organizations in Theory and Practice*. London: Heinemann.

Sokolov, E. W. (1963). *Perception and the Conditioned Reflex*. New York: Macmillan.

Solomon, R. L. and Wynne, L. C. (1953). Traumatic avoidance learning: the principles of anxiety conservation and partial irreversibility. *Psychological Review*, **61**, 353–85.

Spence, D. P. (1982). The paradox of denial. In S. Breznitz (ed.), *The Denial of Stress*. New York: International Universities Press.

Spence, J. T. and Spence, K. W. (1966). The motivational components of manifest anxiety: drive and drive stimuli. In C. D. Spielberger (ed.), *Anxiety and Behavior*. London: Academic Press.

Sperling, G. A. (1960). The information available in brief visual presentations. *Psychological Monographs*, **7**, No. 11, Whole No. 498.

Sperling, G. A. (1967). Successive approximations to a model for short-term memory. *Acta Psychologica*, **27**, 285–92.

Spielberger, C. D. (1980). *Preliminary Manual for the State-Trait Personality Inventory*. Tampa: University of Southern Florida.

Spielberger, C. D. and Smith, L. H. (1966). Anxiety (drive) stress and serial position effects in serial-verbal learning. *Journal of Experimental Psychology*, **72**, 589–95.

Staats, A. W. (1971). *Child Learning, Intelligence, and Personality*. New York: Harper & Row.

Staats, A. W. (1975). *Social Behaviorism*. Homewood, Ill.: Dorsey Press.

Staats, A. W. (1977). Social behaviorism: unified theory in learning and personality. In R. B. Cattell and R. M. Dreger (eds), *Handbook of Modern Personality Theory*. Washington, DC: Hemisphere.

Stayton, D. J., Hogan, R., and Ainsworth, M. D. S. (1971). Infant obedience and maternal behavior: the origins of socialization reconsidered. *Child Development*, **42**, 1057–69.

334

Sternberg, R. J. (1977). *Intelligence, Information Processing, and Analogical Reasoning: The Componential Analysis of Human Abilities*. Hillsdale, NJ: Lawrence Erlbaum.

Sternberg, S. (1966). High-speed scanning in human memory. *Science*, **153**, 652–4.

Stokols, D. (1978). Environmental psychology. *Annual Review of Psychology*, **29**, 253–95.

Stokols, D. (1979). A congruence analysis of human stress. In I. G. Sarason and C. S. Spielberger, (eds), *Stress and Anxiety*, Vol. 6. Washington, DC: Hemisphere.

Strongman, K. T. (1978). *The Psychology of Emotion* (2nd ed.). Chichester: Wiley.

Sullivan, H. S. (1953). *The Interpersonal Theory of Psychiatry*. New York: Norton.

Tajfel, H. (1957). Value and the perceptual judgement of magnitude. *Psychological Review*, **64**, 192–204.

Tajfel, H. (1969). Cognitive aspects of prejudice. *Journal of Biosocial Science*, Supplement 1, 173–91.

Terman, L. M. and Oden, M. (1959). *The Gifted Group in Mid-Life*. Stanford, Cal.: Stanford University Press.

Thom, R. (1972). *Structural Stability and Morphogenesis: An Outline of a General Theory of Models*. Reading, Mass.: Benjamin (1975).

Thomas, A. and Chess, S. (1977). *Temperament and Development*. New York: Brunner/Mazel.

Thomas, A. and Chess, S. (1980). *The Dynamics of Psychological Development*. New York: Brunner/Mazel.

Thomas, A. and Chess, S. (1982). Temperament and follow-up to adulthood. In *Temperamental Differences in Infants and Young Children. Ciba Symposium 89*. London: Pitman.

Thomas, A., Chess, S., and Birch, H. G. (1968). *Temperament and Behavior Disorders in Children*. New York: New York University Press.

Thorndike, E. L. (1927). *The Measurement of Intelligence*. New York: Teachers College.

Thurstone, L. L. (1944). *A Factorial Study of Perception*. Chicago: University of Chicago Press.

Tomlinson-Keasey, C. and Keasey, C. B. (1974). The mediating role of cognitive development in moral judgement. *Child Development*, **45**, 291–8.

Trasler, G. B. (1970). Delinquency. In H. J. Butcher and H. B. Pont (eds), *Educational Research in Britain, 2*. London: University of London Press.

Treisman, A. M. (1969). Strategies and models of selective attention. *Psychological Review*, **76**, 282–99.

Tucker, R. C. (1973). Stalin as Revolutionary 1879–1929: *A Study in History and Personality*. New York: Norton.

Tulving, E. (1964). Intratrial and intertrial retention: notes towards a theory of free recall verbal learning. *Psychological Review*, **71**, 219–37.

Tulving, E. (1972). Episode and semantic memory. In E. Tulving and W. Donaldson (eds), *Organization and Memory*. London: Academic Press.

Tyler, S. (1981). The relationship between anxiety and left versus right hemisphere cognitive performance. Paper presented to IXth Annual Meeting, International Neuropsychological Society, Atlanta, Georgia.

Tyrer, P. (1976). *Role of Bodily Feelings in Anxiety. Maudsley Monograph*, No. 23. Oxford: Oxford University Press.

Underwood, G. (1979). Memory systems and conscious processes. In G. Underwood and R. Stevens (eds), *Aspects of Consciousness: Vol. 1, Psychological Issues*. London: Academic Press.

Underwood, G. and Stevens, R. (1979). *Aspects of Consciousness Vol. 1. Psychological Issues*. London: Academic Press.

Underwood, G. and Stevens, R. (1981). *Aspects of Consciousness Vol. 2. Structural Issues*. London: Academic Press.

Ursin, H., Baade, E., and Levine, S. (1978) (eds). *Psychology of Stress: A Study of Coping Men*. New York: Academic Press.

Vaughan, G. M. (1964). The trans-situational aspect of conforming behavior. *Journal of Personality*, **32**, 335–54.

Vaughan, G. M. and White, K. D. (1966). Conformity and authoritarianism re-examined. *Journal of Personality and Social Psychology*, **3**, 363–6.

Venables, P. H., Mednick, S. A., Schulsinger, F., Raman, A. C., Bell, B., Dalais, J. C., and Fletcher, R. P. (1978). Screening for risk of mental illness. In G. Serban (ed.), *Cognitive Defects in the Development of Mental Illness*. New York: Brunner/Mazel.

Vernon, McCay (1967). Relation of language to thinking process. *Archives of General Psychiatry*, **16**, 325–33.

Vernon, M. D. (1969). *Human Motivation*. Cambridge: Cambridge University Press.

Vernon, M. D. (1970). *Perception Through Experience*. London: Methuen.

Vernon, M. D. (1976). Development of perception of form. In V. Hamilton and M. D. Vernon (eds), *The Development of Cognitive Processes*. London: Academic Press.

Vernon, P. E. (1972). The distinctiveness of field dependence. *Journal of Personality*, **40**, 366–91.

Vernon, P. E. (1973). Multivariate approaches to the study of cognitive styles. In J. R. Royce (ed.), *Multivariate Analysis and Psychological Theory*. London: Academic Press.

Vernon, P. E. (1976). Development of intelligence. In V. Hamilton and M. D. Vernon (eds), *The Development of Cognitive Processes*. London: Academic Press.

Vernon, P. E. (1979). *Intelligence – Heredity and Environment*. San Francisco: Freeman.

Vogel, G. W. (1975). A review of REM sleep deprivation. *Archives of General Psychiatry*, **32**, 749–61.

Vogel, G. W., Thurmond, A., Gibbons, P., Sloan, K., Boyd, M., and Walker, M. (1975). REM sleep reduction effects on depressive syndromes. *Archives of General Psychiatry*, **32**, 765–77.

Vogel, G. W., Vogel, F., McAbee, R. S., and Thurmond, A. (1980). Improvement of depression by REM sleep deprivation. *American Journal of Psychiatry*, **37**, 247–53.

Vurpillot, E. (1976). Development of identification of objects. In V. Hamilton and M. D. Vernon (eds), *The Development of Cognitive Processes*. London: Academic Press.

Wachs, T. D., Uzgiris, I. C., and Hunt, J. McV. (1971). Cognitive development in infants of different age levels and from different environmental backgrounds: an explanatory investigation. *Merrill-Palmer Quarterly*, **17**, 283–317.

Wachtel, P. L. (1968). Conceptions of broad and narrow attention. *Psychological Bulletin*, **68**, 417–29.

Wagner, A. R. (1976). Priming in STM: an information-processing mechanism for self-generated or retrieval-generated depression in performance. In T. H. Tighe and R. N. Leaton (eds), *Habituation: Perspectives from Child Development, Animal Behavior, and Neurophysiology*. Hillsdale, NJ: Lawrence Erlbaum.

Walker, E. L. (1958). Action decrement and its relation to learning. *Psychological Review*, **65**, 129–42.

Walker, E. L. (1967). Arousal and the memory trace. In D. P. Kimble (ed.), *The Organization of Recall*. New York: Academic Sciences.

Walley, R. E. and Weiden, T. D. (1973). Lateral inhibition and cognitive masking: a neuropsychological theory of attention. *Psychological Review*, **80**, 284–302.

Warburton, D. M. (1977). Stimulus selection and behavioural inhibition. In L. L. Iverson, S. D. Iverson, and S. Snyder (eds). *Handbook of Psychopharmacology,* Vol. 6. New York: Plenum.

Warburton, D. M. (1979). Physiological aspects of information processing and stress. In V. Hamilton and D. M. Warburton (eds), *Human Stress and Cognition: An Information Processing Approach.* Chichester: Wiley.

Warburton, D. M. (1981). Neurochemistry of behaviour. *British Medical Bulletin,* **37,** 121–5.

Warburton, D. M. and Wesnes, K. (1978). Individual differences in smoking and attentional performance. In R. E. Thornton (ed.), *Smoking Behaviour: Physiological and Psychological Influences.* London: Churchill-Livingstone.

Warburton, D. M., Wesnes, K., and Revell, A. (1982). Personality factors in self-medication by smoking. In W. Janke (ed.), *Response Variability to Psychotropic Drugs.* London: Pergamon.

Waterman, D. A. and Hayes-Roth, F. (1978). An overview of pattern-directed inference systems. In D. A. Waterman and F. Hayes-Roth (eds), *Pattern-Directed Inference Systems.* New York: Academic Press.

Watson, J. B. (1930). *Behaviorism.* New York: Norton.

Wegner, D. M. and Vallacher, R. R. (1977). *Implicit Psychology.* New York: Oxford University Press.

Weiner, B. (1972). *Theories of Motivation: From Mechanisms to Cognition.* Chicago: Markham Publishing.

Weiner, B. (1978). Achievement strivings. In H. London and J. E. Exner, Jr. (eds), , *Dimensions of Personality.* New York: Wiley.

Weiss, R. L. and Silverman, J. (1966). Anxiety and response stereotyping: an experimental critique. *Perceptual and Motor Skills,* **22,** 95–104.

West, D. J. (1963). *The Habitual Prisoner.* London: Macmillan.

West, D. J. and Farrington, D. P. (1973). *Who Becomes Delinquent?* London: Heinemann.

White, P. O. (1973). Individual differences in speed, accuracy and persistence: a mathematical model for problem solving. In H. J. Eysenck (ed.), *The Measurement of Intelligence.* Lancaster: Medical and Technical Publishing.

White, R. K. (1970). Three not-so-obvious contributions of psychology to peace. In F. Korten, S. W. Cook, and J. I. Lacy (eds), *Psychology and the Problems of Society.* Washington, DC: American Psychological Association.

Whitehurst, G. J. (1979). Meaning and semantics. In G. J. Whitehurst and B. J. Zimmerman (eds), *The Functions of Language and Cognition.* New York: Academic Press.

Whorf, B. L. (1956). *Language, Thought, and Reality.* Cambridge, Mass.: MIT Press.

Wiener, N. (1948). *Cybernetics.* New York: Wiley.

Wiggins, J. S., Renner, K. E., Clore, G. L., and Rose, R. J. (1976). *Principles of Personality.* Reading, Mass: Addison-Wesley.

Wilson, G. (1977). Introversion-extraversion. In T. Blass (ed.), *Personality Variables in Social Behavior.* Hillsdale, NJ: Lawrence Erlbaum.

Wine, J. (1971). Test anxiety and direction of attention. *Psychological Bulletin,* **76,** 92–104.

Winter, D. G. (1978). *Navy Leadership and Management Competencies: Convergence Among Tests, Interviews and Performance Ratings.* Boston: McBer.

Witkin, H. A. and Berry, J. W. (1975). Psychological differentiation in cross-cultural perspective. *Journal of Cross-Cultural Psychology,* **6,** 4–87.

Witkin, H. A., Dyk, R. B., Faterson, H. F., Goodenough, D. R., and Karp, S. A. (1962). *Psychological Differentiation: Studies of Development.* New York: Wiley.

Witkin, H. A., Lewis, H. B., Hertzman, M., Machover, K., Meissner, P. B., and Wapner, S. (1954). *Personality Through Perception.* New York: Harper.

Witkin, H. A., Price-Williams, D. R., Bertini, M., Christiensen, B., Oltman, P. K., Ramirez, M., and Van Meel, J. (1974). Social conformity and psychological differentiation. *International Journal of Psychology*, **9**, 11–29.

Wohlwill, J. F. (1960). A study of the development of the number concept by scalogram analysis. *Journal of Genetic Psychology*, **97**, 345–77.

Wong, R. (1976). *Motivation: A Biobehavioral Analysis of Consummatory Activities*. New York: Macmillan.

Woodward, M. (1959). The behaviour of idiots interpreted by Piaget's theory of sensori-motor development. *British Journal of Educational Psychology*, **29**, 60–71.

Yarrow, L. J., Goodwin, M. S., Mannheimer, H., and Milowe, I. D. (1974). Infant experiences and cognitive and personality development at ten years. In L. J. Stone, H. T. Smith, and L. B. Murphy (eds), *The Competent Infant*. London: Tavistock.

Young, J. (1974). Mass media, drugs and deviance. In P. Rock and M. McIntosh (eds), *Deviance and Social Control*. London: Tavistock.

Young, P. T. (1961). *Motivation and Emotion*. New York: Wiley.

Youniss, J. (1978). The nature of social development: a conceptual discussion of cognition. In H. McGurk (ed.), *Issues in Childhood Social Development*. London: Methuen.

Zajonc, R. B. (1980). Feeling and thinking: preferences need no inferences. *American Psychologist*, **35**, 151–75.

Zaphorozhets, A. V. (1965). The development of perception in the preschool child. In P. H. Mussen (ed.),, European research in cognitive development. *Monographs of the Society for Research in Child Development*, **30**, (Whole No. 100), 82–101.

Zeeman, E. C. (1976). Catastrophe theory. *Scientific American*, **234**, 65–83.

Zeeman, E. C. (1977). *Catastrophe Theory: Selected Papers 1962–1977*. New York: Addison Wesley.

Zimbardo, P. G. (1969). *The Cognitive Control of Motivation*. Glenview, Ill.: Scott, Foresman.

Zimmerman, B. J. (1979). Concepts and classification. In G. J. Whitehurst and B. J. Zimmerman (eds), *The Functions of Language and Cognition*. New York: Academic Press.

Zubin, J., Eron, L. D., and Schumer, F. (1965). *An Experimental Approach to Projective Techniques*. New York: Wiley.

Zubin, J. and Spring, B. (1977). Vulnerability – a new view of schizophrenia. *Journal of Abnormal Psychology*, **86**, 103–26.

Zuckerman, M. (1978). Sensation seeking. In H. London and J. E. Exner Jr. (eds), *Dimensions of Personality*. New York: Wiley.

Author Index

338

Subject Index